INSTRUCTOR'S MANUAL TO ACCOMPANY

AN INTRODUCTION TO POETRY

INSTRUCTOR'S MANUAL TO ACCOMPANY

AN INTRODUCTION TO POETRY

TWELFTH EDITION

X. J. Kennedy

Dorothy M. Kennedy

Dana Gioia

New York Boston San Francisco
London Toronto Sydney Tokyo Singapore Madrid
Mexico City Munich Paris Cape Town Hong Kong Montreal

Vice President and Editor-in-Chief: Joseph P. Terry
Executive Marketing Manager: Ann Stypuloski
Senior Supplements Editor: Donna Campion
Electronic Page Makeup: Grapevine Publishing Services, Inc.

This work is protected by United States copyright laws and is provided solely for the use of instructors in teaching their courses and assessing student learning. Dissemination or sale of any part of this work (including on the World Wide Web) will destroy the integrity of the work and is not permitted. The work and materials from it should never be made available to students except by instructors using the accompanying text in their classes. All recipients of this work are expected to abide by these restrictions and to honor the intended pedagogical purposes and the needs of other instructors who rely on these materials.

Instructor's Manual to accompany *An Introduction to Poetry*, Twelfth Edition.

Copyright © 2007 by X. J. Kennedy, Dorothy M. Kennedy, and Dana Gioia

All rights reserved. No part of this book may be reproduced in any manner whatsoever without permission, except in the case of brief quotations embodied in critical articles and reviews. Printed in the United States.

ISBN: 0-321-47945-9

2 3 4 5 6 7 8 9 10—OPM—09 08 07

Contents

POETRY

WRITING

Preface

We've always found, before teaching a knotty piece of literature, no preparation is more helpful than to sit down and discuss it with a colleague or two. If this manual supplies you with such a colleague at inconvenient hours, such as 2:00 A.M., when there's no one in the faculty coffee room, it will be doing its job.

This manual tries to provide exactly that sort of collegial conversation—spirited but specific, informal but informed. We offer you a sheaf of diverse notes to supply—if you want them—classroom strategies, critical comments, biographical information, historical context, and a few homemade opinions. These last may be wrong, but we set them down to give you something clear-cut with which to agree or disagree. Candor, we think, helps to enliven any conversation.

The manual includes:

- Commentary on almost every poem presented in the text, except for a few brief poems quoted in the text as illustrations
- Additional classroom questions and discussion strategies
- A listing of poems arranged by subject and theme (page 3)
- A list of poems in "Poems for Further Reading," arranged by elements (page 21)
- A list of poems students like most (page 29)

Plan of the Book

There is one, but you are under no obligation to follow it. Chapters may be taken up in any sequence. Many instructors find that a surefire chapter to begin with is "Imagery." If, because you skip around in the book, students meet a term unknown to them, let them look it up in the Index of Terms. They will be directed to the page where the term first occurs and is defined and illustrated.

So that parts of the book may be taught in any order, the sections called "For Review and Further Study" do not review the whole book up to that moment; they review only the main points of the chapter. These sections provide extra material for the instructor who wants to go further into a certain element of poetry. Most contain poems a little more difficult than those in the main body of the chapter.

The assumption behind the book is that an appreciation of poetry cannot be created but may be increased. Without trying to usurp the right of instructors to teach poetry in ways after their own hearts, the book offers short discussions of the elements of poetry, which students may read for themselves, freeing class time for the study of poems.

Features of this Edition

The twelfth edition of *An Introduction to Poetry* incorporates many changes. We have revised this edition with the simple aim of bringing in useful new features and selections without losing the best-liked material. We have been guided in this effort by scores of instructors and students who use the book in their classrooms. Teaching is a kind of conversation—between instructor and student, between reader and text. Revising *Poetry*, we try to help keep this conversation fresh by mixing the classic with the new, the familiar with the surprising.

Casebooks on Major Authors and a Literary Masterpiece

We continue to include a substantial special chapter on Emily Dickinson and Langston Hughes, and we now supplement those author studies with a fascinating new casebook on T. S. Eliot's immensely popular but challenging poem "The Love Song of J. Alfred Prufrock." These special chapters present a variety of material: biographies, photographs, critical commentaries, and statements by the authors. The "Prufrock" casebook also includes some interesting early reviews of the poem which demonstrate to students the slowness and difficulty of building literary reputations. Our aim has been to provide everything a student might need to begin an in-depth study of each author or poem.

Latin American Poetry Chapter

The unique bilingual chapter on Latin American poetry introduced in the last edition proved very popular. Using excellent Spanish-language poems, this chapter provides students with the opportunity to experience poetry in another language (with English translation) and to see how literature represents and illuminates a different cultural experience. We have revised the chapter slightly to give greater emphasis to Mexican poetry. Students are also introduced to the role of surrealism in Latin American poetry with an image from Frida Kahlo and words from César Vallejo and Olga Orozco. This important chapter will not only broaden most students' knowledge of world poetry, it will also recognize the richness of Spanish-language poetry in the literature of the Americas—a very relevant subject to today's multicultural classrooms. The bilingual selections may also give your Spanish-speaking students additional chances to shine in class.

New Poems

An Introduction to Poetry provides the most extensive selection of poems found in any comparable book in the field—over 500 poems in the new edition. We have added 58 new poems to the book—to freshen the selections, update our coverage of contemporary work, and update our ambitious Latin American poetry chapter.

While streamlining our bilingual chapter on Latin American poetry, with the added focus on contemporary Mexican poetry, we continue to offer the masterworks of Sor Juana, Pablo Neruda, Jorge Luis Borges, and Octavio Paz.

We have freshened the casebooks on Emily Dickinson and Langston Hughes with new poems, and we have added a provocative new selection by Aimee Mann in the chapter on "Song." Many other fine new poems have been added, by Gwendolyn Brooks, Andrea Hollander Budy, E. E. Cummings, Marisa de los Santos, Rita Dove, Paul Laurence Dunbar, Alice Fulton, Jane Hirschfield, Suji Kwock Kim, Ted Kooser, David Lehman, Shirley Geok-lin Lim, April Lindner, Heather McHugh, Ogden Nash, Lorine Niedecker, Jacqueline Osherow, Kenneth Rexroth, Charles Simic, Larissa Szporluk, Amy Uyematsu, Gina Valdés, William Carlos Williams, Christian Wiman, Bernice Zamora, and many others. We also continue to include comic poems amid the classics. Why? Students love them, and a little lightness helps make poetry less intimidating.

New Writing Material

All of the writing material in the twelfth edition of *An Introduction to Poetry* is either new or radically revised. Writing instruction has always been an important focus of this book. Because today's students need a more concise, visual, and schematic approach than did the previous generation, we have streamlined every aspect of our extensive coverage so that students can easily find useful and accessible information—in outline form wherever possible.

Every thematic chapter includes a new WRITING EFFECTIVELY section that has four elements: WRITERS ON WRITING, which personalizes the composition process; WRITING ABOUT ——, which discusses the specific topic of the chapter; a WRITING CHECKLIST, which provides a step-by-step approach to composition and critical thinking; and a WRITING ASSIGNMENT and MORE TOPICS FOR WRITING, which provide a rich source of ideas for writing a paper. These features are designed to make the writing process easier, clearer, and less intimidating.

We now have four full writing chapters at the end of *Poetry* to provide comprehensive coverage of the composition and research process. All the chapters have been substantially revised for clarity and accessibility. We strove to simplify the text but not dumb it down. Clarity and concision are never out of place in a textbook, but condescension is fatal. One of our chief aims has been to make the information and structure of the writing chapters more visual for today's Internet-oriented students. Instructors will note how information that appeared in prose paragraphs in earlier editions now appears in outline or checklist form.

We have reprinted and annotated 7 complete student papers to provide models for critical writing. Each paper focuses on a poem in the book and often provides a close reading that emphasizes specific elements of its structure and meaning.

We also now show many samples of student work-in-progress as a way of illustrating the writing process. We include, for example, a step-by-step presentation of how students can develop topics, generate ideas, and formulate a strong thesis, and we show how an early draft is revised into a more precise final version. We include sample brainstorming notes and other pre-writing techniques, to provide students with a more helpful and systematic account of the writing process. We have also integrated the concept of developing a cogent literary argument (with attention to thesis, purpose, audience, support, and organization) throughout the writing chapters.

Critical Approaches to Literature

Chapter 26, "Critical Approaches to Literature," has proven to be a popular feature of the last few editions of *Poetry*. There are two selections for every major critical school—twenty selections in all. The critical excerpts have been carefully chosen both to illustrate the major theoretical approaches and to be accessible to beginning students. The critical selections focus on literary works found in the present edition. Be sure to note the interesting new piece by Camille Paglia on William Blake in the section on Cultural Studies. Taken together with the many commentaries in the casebooks and WRITERS ON WRITING feature, *Poetry* now includes a total of 64 critical excerpts. This expanded coverage gives *Poetry* more depth and greater flexibility for instructors who prefer to incorporate literary theory and criticism into their introductory courses.

Glossary of Literary Terms

The comprehensive Glossary of Literary Terms at the back of the book has been retained by popular demand. It includes every term highlighted in boldface throughout the text as well as other important terms—over 200 entries in all—providing a clear and accurate definition, usually with cross references to related terms. The purpose of the glossary is to provide students with a single accessible reference for all key literary terms.

STATISTICS ON POETRY

The twelfth edition of *An Introduction to Poetry* includes more than 500 complete poems. In case you wish to teach a poet's work in greater depth than a single poem affords, these 25 poets are most heavily represented (listed by number of poems):

Emily Dickinson	21
Langston Hughes	17
Robert Frost	13
William Shakespeare	8
William Carlos Williams	8
W. B. Yeats	8
Alfred, Lord Tennyson	7
Walt Whitman	7
W. H. Auden	6
William Blake	6

E. E. Cummings	6
Thomas Hardy	6
John Keats	6
John Donne	5
Gerard Manley Hopkins	5
Elizabeth Bishop	4
Gwendolyn Brooks	4
T. S. Eliot	4
George Herbert	4
A. E. Housman	4
Edna St. Vincent Millay	4
Edwin Arlington Robinson	4
William Stafford	4
Wallace Stevens	4
William Wordsworth	4

Also, there are three poems each by Buson, Billy Collins, Wendy Cope, Robert Graves, Robert Herrick, Ben Jonson, Omar Khayyam, Philip Larkin, Sylvia Plath, Alexander Pope, Ezra Pound, Alastair Reid, Adrienne Rich, Theodore Roethke, and John Updike. Many other poets are represented twice.

Texts and Editorial Policy

Spelling has been modernized and rendered American, unless to do so would change the sound of a word. Untitled poems are identified by their first lines, except for those that have titles assigned by custom ("The Twa Corbies"). The poems of Emily Dickinson are presented as edited by Thomas H. Johnson.

It would have been simpler to gloss no word a student could find in a desk dictionary, on the grounds that rummaging through dictionaries is good moral discipline; but it seemed best not to require the student to exchange text for dictionary as many as thirty times in reading a poem. Glosses have been provided, therefore, for whatever seemed likely to get in the way of pleasure and understanding.

The spelling *rime* is used instead of *rhyme* on the theory that rime is easier to tell apart from *rhythm*.

Additional Teaching Resource

Ask your Longman representative for our *Teaching Composition with Literature: 101 Writing Assignments from College Instructors*, a collection of proven writing exercises based on selections from the book contributed by dozens of teachers from across North America.

A Note on Live Readings

Many find that, for drumming up zeal for poetry, there is no substitute for a good live poetry reading by a poet whose work students have read before. Anyone who wants to order a live poet is advised to visit the Web site of Poets and Writers <www.pw.org> and use their online directory of writers to get information about inviting a poet to visit your college or university. Not all poets give stirring performances, of course, so ask your colleagues on other campuses for suggestions, lest you get stuck with some mumbling prima donna.

If you want the poet to visit classes or confer with student writers, be sure to specify your expectations ahead of time. Some poets, especially media figures whose affairs are managed by agents, will charge for extra services; less-known visitors grateful for a reading are often pathetically happy to oblige (they may even walk your dog). All poets, if they are to do their best for you, need an occasional hour of solitude to recharge their batteries.

With a Little Help from Our Friends

If we have described this manual as a 24-hour teacher's lounge, we are pleased to report how many interesting colleagues have stopped in to chat. We receive a steady stream of letters on *Poetry* from instructors throughout North America and abroad. Sometimes they disagree with our comments. More often they add new information or perspective. Frequently they pass on stories about what works or does not work in their classrooms. Much of this information is simply too good not to share. We have, therefore, supplemented our own comments with hundreds of comments from instructors (always properly credited to their authors).

Thanks

Two fine writers helped prepare the material used in the new edition. April Lindner of Saint Joseph's University in Philadelphia, Pennsylvania, served as associate editor for the writing section. Using her extensive teaching experience in both literature and composition, she not only developed materials with the editors for this book but also tested them in her classroom. Meanwhile, Michael Palma scrupulously examined and updated every chapter from the previous edition. His deep knowledge of literature and crisp sense of style kept the new edition fresh, informed, and accessible. Ongoing thanks also go to Diane Thiel of the University of New Mexico, who originally helped develop the Latin American poetry chapter in the previous edition, and to Susan Balée, who contributed to the chapter on writing a research paper.

Many instructors, most of whose names appear in this manual, generously wrote us with their suggestions and teaching experiences. Other instructors are noted in the introductory remarks to the textbook itself. We thank them all for their pragmatic and informed help. We are grateful to Donna Campion at Pearson Longman and to Dianne Hall for their formidable effort and good will in managing the design and production of the manual. Finally, we would like to thank Mary Gioia, whose remarkable planning and editorial skills kept this manual in running order despite its erratic drivers.

On Teaching Literature

We'll close with a poem. It is by Billy Collins, from his collection *The Apple That Astonished Paris* (University of Arkansas Press, 1988), and it sets forth an experience that may be familiar to you.

INTRODUCTION TO POETRY

I ask them to take a poem
and hold it up to the light
like a color slide
or press an ear against its hive.

I say drop a mouse into a poem
and watch him probe his way out,
or walk inside the poem's room
and feel the walls for a light switch.

I want them to waterski
across the surface of a poem
waving at the author's name on the shore.
But all they want to do
is tie the poem to a chair with rope
and torture a confession out of it.

They begin beating it with a hose
to find out what it really means.

As you might expect, Billy Collins, a past U.S. Poet Laureate, is himself a professor of English—at Lehman College of the City University of New York.

May this manual help you find ways to persuade your students to set aside rope and hose, and instead turn on a few lights.

XJK, DMK, and DG

Guide to

myliteraturelab™

Where literature comes to life!

http://www.myliteraturelab.com

Introduction

Welcome, instructors, to *MyLiteratureLab*, a specially configured interactive Web site for users of Kennedy/Gioia's *Literature* series. If you choose to bundle *An Introduction to Poetry*, Twelfth Edition, with *MyLiteratureLab*, your students will gain access to *MyLiteratureLab* at no additional cost. For help in using *MyLiteratureLab* in your course, the following pages include listings of the available resources by author, on a chapter-by-chapter basis, and in the relevant entries on each selection.

If you have used *The Craft of Literature* CD-ROM that accompanied previous editions of *Literature*, please note that all the resources on the CD (and more) are now available at *MyLiteratureLab*.

Features

This brief guide highlights the main benefits and features of *MyLiteratureLab*. You may refer to the Instructor Resource section of *MyLiteratureLab* for a more extensive Faculty Teaching Guide.

- *Video clips of the authors*—X. J. Kennedy and Dana Gioia—introduce most chapters with suggestions for approaching the chapter's content.

- *Film and audio clips* of stories, poems, and plays.

- *Longman Lectures*—Longman's award-wining authors, including X. J. Kennedy, discuss popular literary works in ten-minute illustrated lectures designed to help students find a way "in" to a literary selection and then write about it.

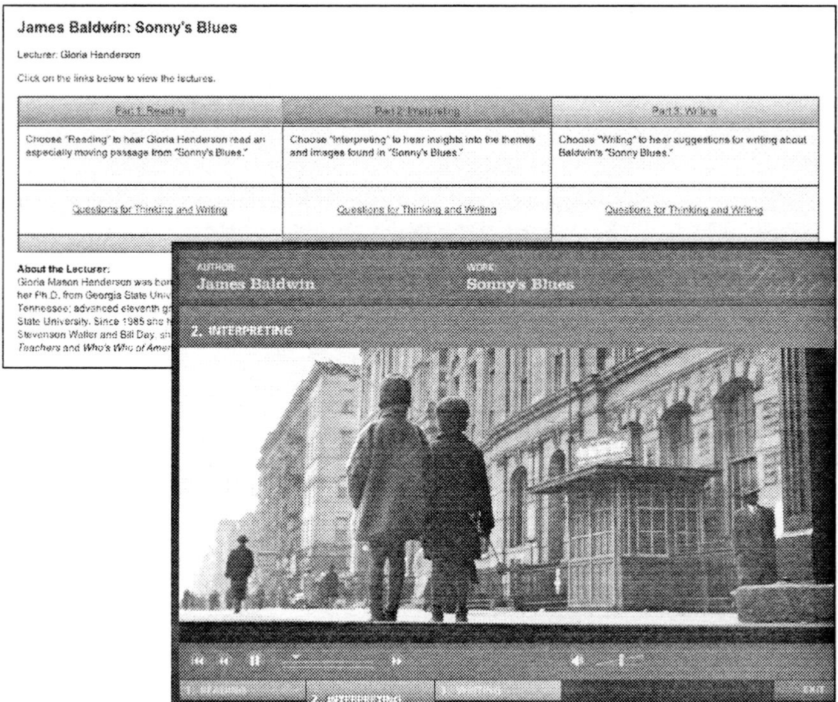

- *Interactive Readings*—with hyperlinked text, give insight into the work's craft elements and provide study questions to illuminate the meaning.

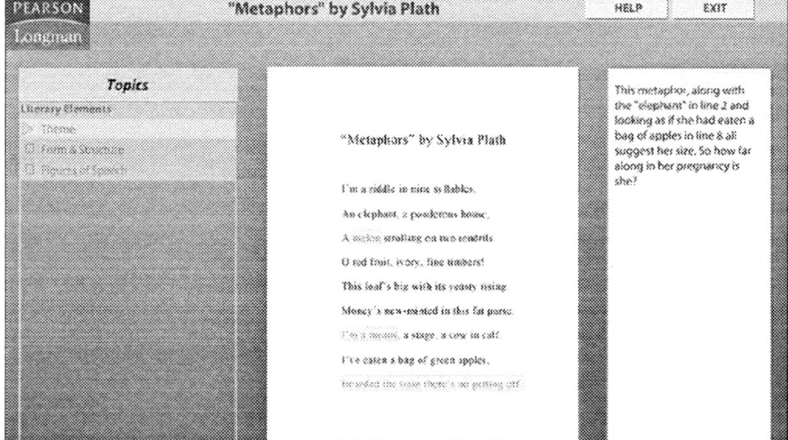

- *Interactive Writing Guidance*—step-by-step explanations and student exercises that support writing a paper, from generating ideas to developing a thesis to organizing a literary argument.

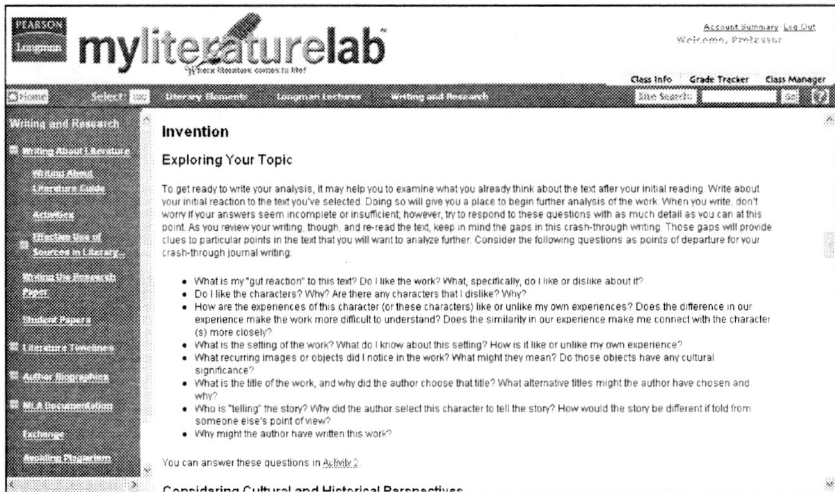

- *Interactive Guidance on Acknowledging Sources*—helpful tutorials and exercises for students to learn how to acknowledge sources and to understand and avoid plagiarism.

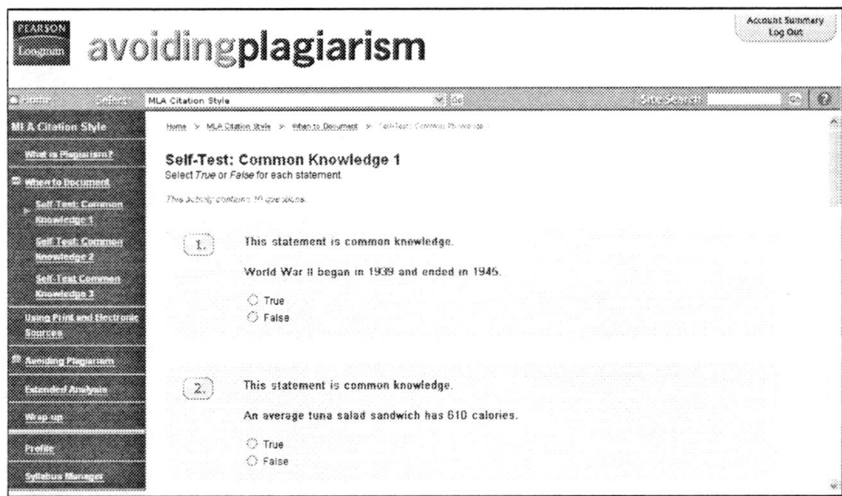

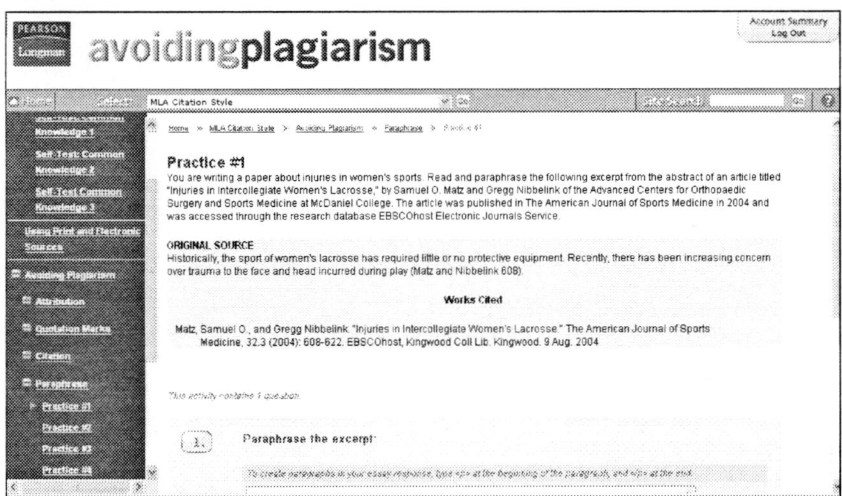

- *MLA Documentation*—explanations, examples, helpful links for students to learn about and use MLA documentation.

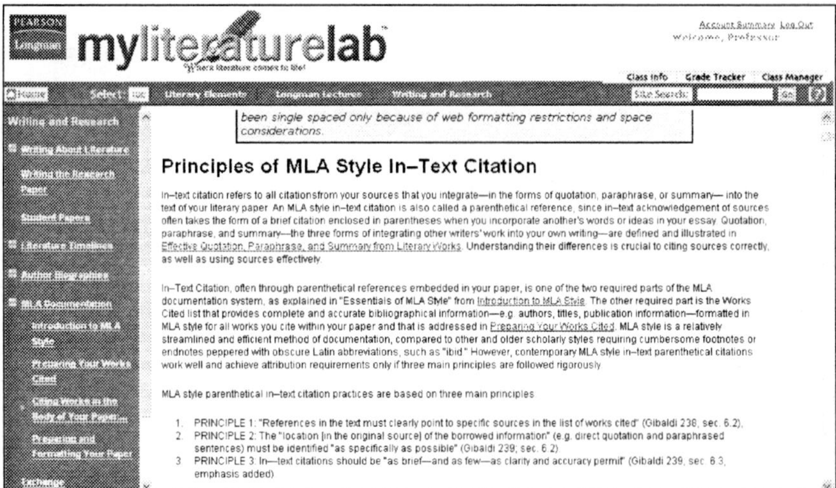

- *Research Navigator*—extensive help on the research process and access to four reliable, useful databases (**EBSCO** Academic Journal and Abstract Database, ***New York Times*** Search by Subject Archive, **"Best of the Web"** Link Library, and ***Financial Times*** Article Archive).

- *Sample Student Papers*—papers on selections found in the book.

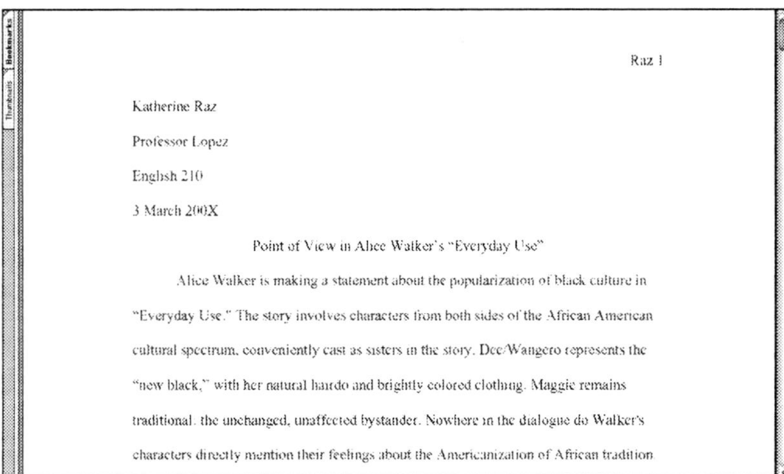

Raz 1

Katherine Raz

Professor Lopez

English 210

3 March 200X

Point of View in Alice Walker's "Everyday Use"

Alice Walker is making a statement about the popularization of black culture in "Everyday Use." The story involves characters from both sides of the African American cultural spectrum, conveniently cast as sisters in the story. Dee/Wangero represents the "new black," with her natural hairdo and brightly colored clothing. Maggie remains traditional, the unchanged, unaffected bystander. Nowhere in the dialogue do Walker's characters directly mention their feelings about the Americanization of African tradition

Using MyLiteratureLab *in Your Course*

You can use *MyLiteratureLab* to help build student interest.

- *MyLiteratureLab* helps make literature come alive. Audio and video clips and Longman Lectures encourage student interest—not only from hearing a poem read expertly or seeing a professional production of a story or play, but also by opening the door to the ways literature can be interpreted.

- *MyLiteratureLab* helps create a theatrical experience. Approximately half of today's college freshmen have never seen a live professional play, and the clips shown here give them the flavor of live performance.

- *MyLiteratureLab* gives background material and critical essays that allow students an opportunity to study an author, selection, or critical theory in depth.

- *MyLiteratureLab* offers X. J. Kennedy's and Dana Gioia's informal comments on how literature can enrich a student's life (see "Why Literature Matters" on the opening screen), as well as video clips of them reading their own poetry.

MyLiteratureLab helps students read and interpret.

- *Chapter Introductions* offer reinforcement of the discussions given in the book. The video and text introductions by X. J. Kennedy and Dana Gioia succinctly cover the related chapter in the book's content.

- *Interactive Readings* give practice in understanding the craft topic in the text's chapter. It takes students line by line through a story, poem, or scene from a play, giving them guidance about what is "happening" in the selections as well as asking them questions about the craft.

- *Longman Lectures* include words and images to contextualize and enrich the content of each lecture. Each lecture is organized into three parts: reading, interpreting, and writing, all supported with writing prompts. The three-part structure encourages students to read and interpret the work more thoughtfully and spark ideas for research and writing.

- *Student Papers* can be used as models. Students are also asked to read the papers critically and answer questions about them, helping to sharpen their own rhetorical skills.

You can use *MyLiteratureLab* to supplement and enrich your assignments.

- Every major section of *MyLiteratureLab* is supported with pedagogy. Students don't just watch a video clip and then turn to something else. Critical thinking questions accompany every element.

You can incorporate *MyLiteratureLab* into your course in a number of ways.

- *As homework*—to reinforce the content covered in class and in the anthology.

- *In class*—to promote discussion and provide alternative ways of covering the syllabus.

- *For research assignments*—to get students started on researching an author or a work via the Background and Critical Essays sections and with the very useful Researcher Navigator tool.

- *For independent study.*

You can access *MyLiteratureLab* to best suit your needs.

- A special section on the site just for Kennedy/Gioia users lets you access the resources of *MyLiteratureLab* via the Kennedy/Gioia table of contents.

- You can also use the content on *MyLiteratureLab* through its "regular" access. Entering the site in this way gives you immediate access to Diagnostics, Interactive Readings, Longman Lectures, and Writing and Research content including Research Navigator.

- Available in Course Compass, Web CT, and Blackboard course management systems.

Author Index

 *MyLiteratureLab* Resources

T. S. Eliot	*The Love Song of J. Alfred Prufrock*: Student Paper ▪ Biography, Critical Archive, Bibliography
Carolyn Forché	*The Colonel*: Student Paper
Robert Frost	*Acquainted with the Night*: Longman Lecture ▪ *Birches*: Audio ▪ *Mending Wall*: Longman Lecture "*Out, Out—*": Interactive Reading, Critical Essay ▪ *The Road Not Taken*: Critical Essay Biography, Critical Archive, Bibliography
Dana Gioia	*California Hills in August*: Video ▪ *Money*: Video ▪ *Summer Storm*: Video ▪ *Unsaid*: Video
Thomas Hardy	*Neutral Tones*: Critical Essay ▪ *The Ruined Maid*: Critical Essay ▪ Biography, Critical Archive, Bibliography
Robert Hayden	Biography, Critical Archive, Bibliography
Seamus Heaney	*Digging*: Longman Lecture
George Herbert	*Easter Wings*: Critical Essay
Gerard Manley Hopkins	*Pied Beauty*: Audio, Critical Essay ▪ Biography/Photos
A. E. Housman	Biography, Critical Archives, Bibliography
Langston Hughes	*The Weary Blues*: Longman Lecture ▪ *Dream Boogie*: Critical Essay ▪ Biography, Critical Archive, Bibliography
John Keats	*Bright star*: Longman Lecture ▪ *Ode on a Grecian Urn*: Audio, Student Paper ▪ Biography/Photos, Critical Archive, Bibliography
X. J. Kennedy	*For Allen Ginsberg*: Video ▪ *In a Prominent Bar in Secaucus One Day*: Video ▪ *Nude Descending a Staircase*: Video ▪ *Snowflake Souffle*: Video
Edna St. Vincent Millay	*What lips my lips have kissed, and where, and why*: Video, Student Paper ▪ Biography/Photos
Wilfred Owen	*Dulce et Decorum Est*: Longman Lecture, Interactive Reading, Critical Essay
Dorothy Parker	*Résumé*: Video ▪ Biography/Photos
Sylvia Plath	*Lady Lazarus*: Longman Lecture ▪ *Metaphors*: Critical Essay, Interactive Reading

Edgar Allan Poe	*To Helen*: Audio ▪ Biography/Photos, Critical Archive, Bibliography
Adrienne Rich	Biography, Critical Archive, Bibliography
Edwin Arlington Robinson	*Luke Havergal*: Critical Essay ▪ *Richard Cory*: Longman Lecture, Critical Essay
Theodore Roethke	*Root Cellar*: Interactive Reading, Critical Essay
Mary Jo Salter	*Welcome to Hiroshima*: Longman Lecture
William Shakespeare	*Let me not to the marriage of true minds*: Critical Essay ▪ *Shall I compare thee to a summer's day?*: Audio, Student Paper, Critical Essay (2) Biography/Photos, Critical Archive, Bibliography
Percy Bysshe Shelley	*Ozymandias*: Audio
Wallace Stevens	*Anecdote of the Jar*: Interactive Reading ▪ Biography, Critical Archive, Bibliography
Alfred, Lord Tennyson	*The splendor falls on castle walls*: Audio Biography/Photos, Critical Archive, Bibliography
Dylan Thomas	*Do not go gentle into that good night*: Interactive Reading, Critical Essay
John Updike	*Recital*: Student Paper ▪ Biography/Photos, Critical Archive, Bibliography
Walt Whitman	*Cavalry Crossing a Ford*: Interactive Reading, Critical Essay ▪ Biography, Critical Archive, Bibliography
Richard Wilbur	*Cold War Poetry*: Critical Essay ▪ *Love Calls Us to the Things of This World*: Interactive Reading
William Carlos Williams	Biography, Critical Archive, Bibliography
William Wordsworth	*A Slumber Did My Spirit Seal*: Critical Essay ▪ *Composed upon Westminster Bridge*: Audio Biography, Critical Archive, Bibliography
William Butler Yeats	*The Lake Isle of Innisfree*: Longman Lecture, Critical Essay ▪ *Leda and the Swan*: Critical Essay ▪ *Who Goes with Fergus?*: Interactive Reading ▪ Biography, Critical Archive, Bibliography

Chapter Guide

 *MyLiteratureLab* Resources

Poetry

Reading a Poem

Chapter Introduction to Reading a Poem
Video Introduction to Reading a Poem
X. J. Kennedy
Background
Robert Browning
Adrienne Rich
Audio Clip
My Last Duchess
Longman Lecture
My Last Duchess
Interactive Reading
"*Out, Out—*," by Robert Frost
Critical Essays
Frost's " 'Out, Out—,'" by Gloriana Locklear
Structure and Meaning in Browning's "My Last Duchess," by Joshua Adler
Yeats's "The Lake Isle of Innisfree": Images of Dark Desires, by Scott C. Holstad
Student Essay
A Feminist Reading of Browning's "My Last Duchess," by Artavia Lineszy-Overton

Listening to a Voice

Chapter Introduction to Listening to a Voice
Video Introduction to Listening to a Voice
Dana Gioia
Background
William Blake
Audio Clip
The Chimney Sweeper
Longman Lectures
Wilfred Owen, *Dulce et Decorum Est*
William Butler Yeats, *The Lake Isle of Innisfree*
Interactive Reading
Wilfred Owen, *Dulce et Decorum Est*

Critical Essays
Fact and Symbol in "The Chimney Sweeper" of Blake's "Songs of Innocence," by Martin K. Nurmi
"Dulce Et Decorum Est"—A Dramatist's Point of View, by Troy M. Hughes
Robinson's "Luke Havergal," by Ronald E. McFarland

Words

Chapter Introduction to Words
Video Introduction to Words
X. J. Kennedy
Background
Billy Collins
E. E. Cummings
John Donne
Audio Clip
anyone lived in a pretty how town
Longman Lectures
Billy Collins, *The Names*
John Donne, *Batter my heart, three-personed God, for You*
Lewis Carroll, *Jabberwocky*
Interactive Reading
Lewis Carroll, *Jabberwocky*
Critical Essays
Thomas Hardy's "The Ruined Maid," Elsa Lanchester's Music-Hall, and the Fall into Fashion, by Keith Wilson
Carroll's "Jabberwocky," by Karen Alkalay-Gut
Anyone's Any: A View of Language and Poetry Through an Analysis of "anyone lived in a pretty how town," by James Paul Gee

Saying and Suggesting

Chapter Introduction to Saying and Suggesting
Video Introduction to Saying and Suggesting
Dana Gioia
Interactive Reading
Richard Wilbur, *Love Calls Us to the Things of This World*
Critical Essays
"Kubla Khan": The Poet in the Poem, by Geoffrey Little
From Cold War Poetry, by Edward Brunner
Student Essay
Symbolic Language in Coleridge's "Kubla Khan," by Patrick Mooney

Imagery

Chapter Introduction to Imagery
Video Introduction to Imagery
X. J. Kennedy

Background
Gerard Manley Hopkins
Video Clip
Gerard Manley Hopkins, *Pied Beauty*
Longman Lecture
John Keats, *Bright star! would I were steadfast as thou art*
Interactive Reading
Theodore Roethke, *Root Cellar*
Critical Essays
Seeing "Pied Beauty": A Key to Theme and Structure, by Amy Lowenstein
Some Observations on Elizabeth Bishop's "The Fish," by Ronald E. McFarland
Roethke's "Root Cellar," by George Wolff

Figures of Speech

Chapter Introduction to Figures of Speech
Video Introduction to Figures of Speech
Dana Gioia
Background
Sylvia Plath
William Shakespeare
Audio Clip
William Shakespeare, *Shall I compare thee to a summer's day?*
Longman Lecture
Robert Burns, *Oh, my love is like a red, red rose*
Interactive Reading
Sylvia Plath, *Metaphors*
Critical Essays
Shakespeare's "Sonnet 18" ["Shall I compare thee to a summer's day?"], by Robert H. Ray
Shakespeare's "Sonnet 18" ["Shall I compare thee to a summer's day?"], by Mark Howell
"Metaphors," by Karen Alkalay-Gut
Atwood's "You fit into me," by Jes Simmons
Student Essay
Shakespeare's Eternal Summer, by Laura Todd

Song and Sound

Chapter Introduction to Sound
Video Introduction to Sound
X. J. Kennedy
Background
Alfred, Lord Tennyson
Audio Clip
The splendor falls on castle walls

Longman Lecture
Edward Arlington Robinson, *Richard Cory*
Interactive Reading
William Butler Yeats, *Who Goes with Fergus?*
Critical Essays
A Re-examination of "Richard Cory," by Charles A. Sweet, Jr.
Cosmic Irony in Wordsworth's "A Slumber Did My Spirit Seal," by Warren Stevenson
Rhetorical Figures in Yeats's "Leda and the Swan," by Barbara Edwards-Aldrich
Student Essay
Playing upon Words [On Updike's "Recital"], by Bryan C. Smith

Rhythm

Chapter Introduction to Rhythm
Video Introduction to Rhythm
Dana Gioia
Background
Dorothy Parker
Gwendolyn Brooks
Video Clip
Jack Lemmon reads *Résumé*
Interactive Reading
Gwendolyn Brooks, *We Real Cool*
Critical Essays
Creating the Blues ("Dream Boogie"), by Steven C. Tracy
On "We Real Cool," by James D. Sullivan
Student Essay
The Tides of "We Real Cool," by Juli Grace

Closed Form

Chapter Introduction to Closed Form
Video Introduction to Closed Form
X. J. Kennedy
Background
Robert Frost
Edna St. Vincent Millay
Video Clip
Edna St. Vincent Millay, *What lips my lips have kissed, and where, and why*
Longman Lectures
Robert Frost, *Acquainted with the Night*
The Theme of Love in Shakespeare's Sonnets
Interactive Reading
Dylan Thomas, *Do not go gentle into that good night*

Critical Essays
The Making of a Poem: Dylan Thomas's "Do not go gentle into that good night," by Oliver Evans
Clerihews, by Israel Shenker
Student Essay
Analysis of Edna St. Vincent Millay's "What lips my lips have kissed, and where, and why," by Stephanie Willson

Open Form

Chapter Introduction to Open Form
Video Introduction to Open Form
Dana Gioia
Background
E. E. Cummings
Audio Clip
Buffalo Bill 's
Interactive Reading
Walt Whitman, *Cavalry Crossing a Ford*
Critical Essays
Cummings's "Buffalo Bill 's," by Thomas Dilworth
Whitman's Theme in "Cavalry Crossing a Ford," by Dale Doepke
"Easter Wings," by Joan Klingel Ray
Student Essay
The Emotional Response of Forché's "The Colonel," by Michelle Brown

Symbol

Chapter Introduction to Symbol
Video Introduction to Symbol
X. J. Kennedy
Interactive Reading
Wallace Stevens, *Anecdote of the Jar*
Critical Essays
Frost's "The Road Not Taken": A 1925 Letter Comes to Light, by Larry Finger
Stevens's "Anecdote of the Jar": Art as Entrapment, by A. R. Coulthard
The God-Curst Sun: Love in "Neutral Tones," by James Hazen

Poetry and Personal Identity

Longman Lecture
Sylvia Plath, *Lady Lazarus*

Recognizing Excellence

Longman Lecture
Elizabeth Bishop, *One Art*

Casebooks: Emily Dickinson and Langston Hughes

Background
Emily Dickinson
Langston Hughes
Longman Lectures
Emily Dickinson, *Because I could not stop for Death*
Langston Hughes, *The Weary Blues*

Casebook: T. S. Eliot's "The Love Song of J. Alfred Prufrock"

Student Paper
The Existential Anguish of J. Alfred Prufrock, by Patrick Mooney

Poems for Further Reading

GWENDOLYN BROOKS'S "THE MOTHER"
Background
Gwendolyn Brooks
Longman Lecture
Gwendolyn Brooks, *The Mother*

SAMUEL TAYLOR COLERIDGE'S "KUBLA KHAN"
Background
Samuel Taylor Coleridge
Audio Clip
Kubla Khan
Critical Essay
"Kubla Khan": The Poet in the Poem, by Geoffrey Little

ROBERT FROST'S "MENDING WALL"
Background
Robert Frost
Longman Lecture
Mending Wall

SEAMUS HEANEY'S "DIGGING"
Longman Lecture
Digging

JOHN KEATS'S "ODE ON A GRECIAN URN"
Background
John Keats
Audio Clip
Ode on a Grecian Urn
Student Essay
John Keats's "Ode on a Grecian Urn": Dissolving into the Moment, by Michelle Brown

MARY JO SALTER'S "WELCOME TO HIROSHIMA"
Longman Lecture
Welcome to Hiroshima

WILLIAM SHAKESPEARE'S "THAT TIME OF YEAR THOU MAYST IN ME BEHOLD"
Longman Lecture
That time of year thou mayst in me behold [Sonnet 73]

X. J. Kennedy and Dana Gioia Read Their Poems

X. J. Kennedy

For Allen Ginsberg
Snowflake Soufflé
Nude Descending a Staircase
In a Prominent Bar in Secaucus One Day

Dana Gioia

California Hills in August
Summer Storm
Unsaid
Money

POETRY

Poems Arranged by Subject and Theme

This list sorts out and classifies most of the poems in the textbook. Besides subjects or themes, it includes some genres (i.e., elegies, poems of spring and other seasons).

How to Use This Information. Browse through this list and you will find many poems worth teaching side by side. This list will be particularly helpful to the instructor who wishes to organize a poetry course differently from the way the book is structured: to teach poetry not by the elements of poems, but by themes. However you prefer to organize your course, you will find this list a ready source of possible writing assignments.

For Writing Topics. You might have students read three or four poems in a group (say, those in the category "Apocalypse," or a few of your choice from "Coming of Age"), then ask them to reply, in a page or two, to the question, "What do these poems have in common?" Or, "How do these poets differ in their expressions of a similar theme?"

What follows is thorough but not exhaustive. We have left out some categories that sounded unpromising. Would you have cared that the book has four locomotive poems (by Dickinson, Stillman, Whitman, and William Carlos Williams) or three (by Yeats, Hollander, and Anonymous) about swans? Not all these themes and subjects are central to their poems, but all will be fairly evident.

ANGELS, DEVILS, GHOSTS, WITCHES, AND ASSORTED MONSTERS

Anonymous	The Cruel Mother
Anonymous	The Three Ravens
Atwood	Siren Song
Bogan	Medusa
Budy	Snow White
Keats	La Belle Dame sans Merci
Martin	Taken Up
Orr	Two Lines from the Brothers Grimm
Poe	Annabel Lee
Robinson	Luke Havergal
Sexton	Her Kind
Simic	Fork
Yeats	The Second Coming

ANIMALS (BEAST AND BIRD)

Blake	The Tyger
Chesterton	The Donkey
Clare	Mouse's Nest

Collins	Care and Feeding
Frost	Design
Hall	Names of Horses
Hardy	The Darkling Thrush
Hollander	Swan and Shadow
Hopkins	The Windhover
T. Hughes	Hawk Roosting
Layton	The Bull Calf
Levin	Brief Bio
Lowell	Skunk Hour
Nash	The Panther
Ryan	Turtle
Smart	For I will consider my Cat Jeoffry
Tennyson	The Eagle
Wiman	Poštolka

APOCALYPSE

Dylan	The Times They Are a-Changin'
Frost	Fire and Ice
L. Hughes	Harlem [Dream Deferred]
L. Hughes	End
Levine	They Feed They Lion
Salter	Welcome to Hiroshima
Yeats	The Second Coming

ART

Auden	Musée des Beaux Arts
Blake	The Tyger
Cherry	Advice to a Friend Who Paints
Keats	Ode on a Grecian Urn
Morgan	The Master
Pastan	Ethics
Stevens	Anecdote of the Jar
W. C. Williams	The Dance

ASIAN EXPERIENCE / ASIAN POETRY

Basho	Heat-lightning streak
Basho	In the old stone pool
Buson	On the one-ton temple bell
Buson	The piercing chill I feel
Issa	Cricket
Issa	Only one guy and
Jin	Missed Time
Khayyam	Rubaiyat
Kim	Monologue for an Onion
Lim	Learning to love America
Lim	Riding into California
Li Po	Drinking Alone by Moonlight
Matsushita	Rain shower from mountain
Morgan	The Master

Moritake	The falling flower
Ozawa	War forced us from California
Salter	Welcome to Hiroshima
Satyamurti	I Shall Paint My Nails Red
Song	Stamp Collecting
Uyematsu	Deliberate
Wada	Even the croaking of frogs

BELONGING TO A MINORITY (*see also* BLACK EXPERIENCE, NATIVE AMERICAN LIFE)

Abeyta	thirteen ways of looking at a tortilla
Alarcón	The X in My Name
Cofer	*Quinceañera*
Dunbar	We Wear the Mask
Espaillat	Bilingual / Bilingüe
L. Hughes	Harlem [Dream Deferred]
L. Hughes	Ku Klux
L. Hughes	Theme for English B
Lim	Learning to love America
Lim	Riding into California
Olds	The One Girl at the Boys' Party
Osherow	Song for the Music in the Warsaw Ghetto
Reid	Speaking a Foreign Language
Trethewey	White Lies
Uyematsu	Deliberate
Valdés	English con Salsa

BLACK EXPERIENCE (*see also* BELONGING TO A MINORITY)

Brooks	Southeast Corner
Brooks	We Real Cool
Cullen	For a Lady I Know
Dunbar	We Wear the Mask
Hayden	Those Winter Sundays
Hayden	The Whipping
L. Hughes	As Befits a Man
L. Hughes	Dream Boogie
L. Hughes	Dream Deferred [Harlem]
L. Hughes	I, Too
L. Hughes	Ku Klux
L. Hughes	The Negro Speaks of Rivers
L. Hughes	Song for a Dark Girl
L. Hughes	Subway Rush Hour
L. Hughes	Theme for English B
Nelson	A Strange Beautiful Woman
Randall	A Different Image
Randall	Ballad of Birmingham
B. Smith	Jailhouse Blues
Stillman	In Memoriam John Coltrane
Trethewey	White Lies
Walcott	The Virgins

CARPE DIEM

Herrick	To the Virgins, to Make Much of Time
Horace	*Carpe Diem* Ode
Housman	Loveliest of trees, the cherry now
Marvell	To His Coy Mistress
Millay	Second Fig
Milton	How soon hath time
Shakespeare	O mistress mine
Waller	Go, Lovely Rose

CHILDHOOD (*see also* FATHERS AND CHILDREN, MOTHERS AND CHILDREN)

Bishop	Sestina
Blake	The Chimney Sweeper
Cleghorn	The Golf Links
Cummings	in Just–
Espaillat	Bilingual / Bilingüe
Frost	Birches
Grosholz	Listening
Hayden	The Whipping
Justice	On the Death of Friends in Childhood
Lawrence	Piano
Olds	The One Girl at the Boys' Party
Orr	Two Lines from the Brothers Grimm
Roethke	My Papa's Waltz
Simic	The Magic Study of Happiness
Stroud	Missing
Thiel	*Memento Mori* in Middle School
Thomas	Fern Hill
Trethewey	White Lies

CITY LIFE

Blake	London
Brooks	Southeast Corner
Brooks	We Real Cool
Dove	Silos
Eliot	The *Boston Evening Transcript*
Eliot	The Love Song of J. Alfred Prufrock
Eliot	The winter evening settles down
Ginsberg	A Supermarket in California
Hardy	The Ruined Maid
L. Hughes	Ballad of the Landlord
L. Hughes	Prayer ("Gather up")
Millay	Recuerdo
Swift	A Description of the Morning
Whitman	I Hear America Singing
Wilbur	Love Calls Us to the Things of This World
C. K. Williams	Elms
W. C. Williams	The Term
Wordsworth	Composed upon Westminster Bridge

COMING OF AGE

Cofer	Quinceañera
de los Santos	Perfect Dress
Espaillat	Bilingual / Bilingüe
Housman	When I was one-and-twenty
Milton	How soon hath time
Uyematsu	Deliberate

DEATH (*see also* ELEGIES)

Anonymous	Lord Randall
Anonymous	The Three Ravens
Anonymous	The Twa Corbies
Ashbery	At North Farm
Auden	Funeral Blues
Bensley	Last Haiku
Brooks	The Mother
Brooks	Southeast Corner
Ciardi	A Box Comes Home
Collins	The Names
Dickinson	Because I could not stop for Death
Dickinson	I heard a Fly buzz – when I died
Donne	Death be not proud
Dryden	To the Memory of Mr. Oldham
Frost	Birches
Frost	"Out, Out—"
Gunn	The Man with Night Sweats
Housman	To an Athlete Dying Young
Hudgins	Elegy for My Father, Who Is Not Dead
L. Hughes	As Befits a Man
Jonson	On My First Son
Justice	On the Death of Friends in Childhood
Keats	This living hand, now warm and capable
Keats	When I have fears that I may cease to be
Kooser	Carrie
Larkin	Aubade
Lennon/McCartney	Eleanor Rigby
Merwin	For the Anniversary of my Death
Owen	Anthem for Doomed Youth
Pastan	Ethics
Pinsky	ABC
Plath	Lady Lazarus
Poe	Annabel Lee
Ransom	Piazza Piece
Robinson	Luke Havergal
Roethke	Elegy for Jane
Rossetti	Uphill
W. J. Smith	American Primitive
Stevens	The Emperor of Ice-Cream
Stillman	In Memoriam John Coltrane
Tennyson	Break, Break, Break

Tennyson	Dark house, by which once more I stand
Tennyson	Tears, Idle Tears
Whitman	O Captain! My Captain!
Wordsworth	A Slumber Did My Spirit Seal

ELEGIES (*see also* DEATH)

Collins	The Names
Dryden	To the Memory of Mr. Oldham
Housman	To an Athlete Dying Young
Hudgins	Elegy for My Father, Who Is Not Dead
Jonson	On My First Son
Merwin	Elegy (*quoted in Scholes, "How Do We Make a Poem?"*)
Osherow	Song for the Music in the Warsaw Ghetto
Poe	Annabel Lee
Roethke	Elegy for Jane
Stillman	In Memoriam John Coltrane
Whitman	O Captain! My Captain!

FAITH, DOUBT, AND RELIGIOUS VISION

Arnold	Dover Beach
Bible	The Parable of the Good Seed
Brooks	the preacher: ruminates behind the sermon
Brutschy	Born Again
Dickinson	Because I could not stop for Death
Dickinson	Some keep the Sabbath going to Church
Donne	Batter my heart, three-personed God, for You
Donne	Death be not proud
Eliot	Journey of the Magi
Hardy	Hap
Herbert	Easter Wings
Herbert	Love
Herbert	The World
Hopkins	God's Grandeur
Hopkins	No worst, there is none
Hopkins	Pied Beauty
Hopkins	The Windhover
Hudgins	Elegy for My Father, Who Is Not Dead
Jarman	Unholy Sonnet: Hands Folded
Larkin	Aubade
Martin	Taken Up
Menashe	The Shrine Whose Shape I Am
Milton	How soon hath time
Milton	When I consider how my light is spent
Rossetti	Uphill
Sáenz	To the Desert
Wilbur	Love Calls Us to the Things of This World
Wordsworth	The World Is Too Much with Us
Yeats	The Magi
Yeats	The Second Coming
Zamora	Penitents

FAME

Dickinson	I'm Nobody! Who are you?
Dickinson	Victory comes late
Guiterman	The Vanity of Earthly Greatness
Keats	When I have fears that I may cease to be
Lehman	Rejection Slip
Shelley	Ozymandias

FAMILIES / PARENTS AND CHILDREN

Anonymous	The Cruel Mother
Bishop	Filling Station
Brooks	The Mother
H. Crane	My Grandmother's Love Letters
Espaillat	Bilingual / Bilingüe
Foley	Haiku ("Learning to Shave")
Grosholz	Listening
Gurga	Visitor's Room
Hayden	Those Winter Sundays
Heaney	Digging
Hecht	Adam
Hudgins	Elegy for My Father, Who Is Not Dead
Kees	For My Daughter
Kooser	Abandoned Farmhouse
Larkin	Home is so Sad
Lawrence	Piano
Olds	Rites of Passage
Orr	Two Lines from the Brothers Grimm
Phillips	Running on Empty
Pound	Salutation
Plath	Daddy
Roethke	My Papa's Waltz
W. J. Smith	American Primitive
Stroud	Missing
Uyematsu	Deliberate
Wilbur	The Writer
Wright	Autumn Begins in Martins Ferry, Ohio

FARM AND COUNTRY

Frost	Birches
Frost	"Out, Out—"
Frost	Stopping by Woods on a Snowy Evening
Hall	Names of Horses
Hardy	The Ruined Maid
Kooser	Abandoned Farmhouse
Layton	The Bull Calf
Stafford	The Farm on the Great Plains
Toomer	Reapers

FATE

Anonymous	The Three Ravens

Anonymous	The Twa Corbies
Atwood	Siren Song
Fulton	Failure
Hardy	The Convergence of the Twain
Hardy	Hap
Horace	*Carpe Diem* Ode
Milton	How soon hath time
Slavitt	Titanic

FATHERS AND CHILDREN

Foley	Haiku ("Learning to Shave")
Hayden	Those Winter Sundays
Heaney	Digging
Hecht	Adam
Hudgins	Elegy for My Father, Who Is Not Dead
Jonson	On My First Son
Kees	For My Daughter
Phillips	Running on Empty
Plath	Daddy
Roethke	My Papa's Waltz
W. J. Smith	American Primitive
Stallings	Sine Qua Non
Thomas	Do not go gentle into that good night
Uyematsu	Deliberate
Wilbur	The Writer
Wright	Autumn Begins in Martins Ferry, Ohio

FRIENDSHIP

Dryden	To the Memory of Mr. Oldham
Justice	On the Death of Friends in Childhood
Markham	Outwitted
Reid	Speaking a Foreign Language
Whitman	Song of the Open Road

GLORY BE TO GOD / RELIGIOUS EXPERIENCE

Brooks	the preacher: ruminates behind the sermon
Chesterton	The Donkey
Donne	Batter my heart, three-personed God
Herbert	Easter Wings
Herbert	Love
Hopkins	God's Grandeur
Hopkins	Pied Beauty
Hopkins	The Windhover
Sáenz	To the Desert
Zamora	Penitents

GRIEF (*see also* ELEGIES)

Collins	The Names
Dickinson	After great pain, a formal feeling comes
Dickinson	The Bustle in a House

Dickinson	Success is counted sweetest
Hopkins	No worst, there is none
L. Hughes	As Befits a Man
Jonson	Slow, slow, fresh fount, keep time with my salt tears
Osherow	Song for the Music in the Warsaw Ghetto
Poe	Annabel Lee
Tennyson	Break, Break, Break
Tennyson	Dark house, by which once more I stand

HAPPINESS

Anonymous	Carnation Milk
Cummings	somewhere i have never traveled
Dickinson	I taste a liquor never brewed
Hix	I Love the World As Does Any Dancer
Kenyon	The Suitor
Lehman	Rejection Slip
Millay	Recuerdo
Pound	Salutation
Reeser	Winter-proof
Simic	The Magic Study of Happiness
Whitman	I Hear America Singing
Wright	A Blessing
Yeats	The Lake Isle of Innisfree

HATRED AND INVECTIVE

Atwood	You fit into me
Betjeman	In Westminster Abbey
R. Browning	Soliloquy of the Spanish Cloister
Frost	Fire and Ice
H. D.	Helen
Kim	Monologue for an Onion
Lehman	Rejection Slip
Markham	Outwitted
S. Smith	This Englishwoman
Steele	Epitaph
Stephens	A Glass of Beer

HEROES

Anonymous	Sir Patrick Spence
Carroll	Jabberwocky
Ciardi	A Box Comes Home
Cummings	Buffalo Bill 's
Cummings	next to of course god america i
Nemerov	The War in the Air
Tennyson	Ulysses
Whitman	O Captain! My Captain!
W. C. Williams	El Hombre

INNOCENCE AND EXPERIENCE

Behn	When maidens are young

Blake	The Chimney Sweeper
Hopkins	Spring and Fall
Kees	For My Daughter
Pastan	Ethics

LANGUAGE (*see also* WRITING)

Carroll	Jabberwocky
Espaillat	Bilingual / Bilingüe
Gioia	Money
Li Po	Drinking Alone by Moonlight
McHugh	Language Lesson, 1976
Raine	A Martian Sends a Postcard Home
Reid	Speaking a Foreign Language
Valdés	English con Salsa
Wiman	Poštolka

LEAVE-TAKING

Anonymous	Lord Randall
Donne	A Valediction: Forbidding Mourning
Drayton	Since there's no help, come let us kiss and part
Larkin	Poetry of Departures
Lovelace	To Lucasta
Mann	Deathly
Reeves	Rough Weather

LONELINESS AND ALIENATION

Bogan	Medusa
Brooks	the preacher: ruminates behind the sermon
Collins	Embrace
Dickinson	After great pain, a formal feeling comes
Dickinson	I felt a Funeral, in my Brain
Dickinson	I'm Nobody! Who are you?
Dickinson	The Soul selects her own Society
Dickinson	Success is counted sweetest
Eliot	The Love Song of J. Alfred Prufrock
Eliot	The winter evening settles down
Fairchild	A Starlit Night
Frost	Acquainted with the Night
Frost	Desert Places
Ginsberg	A Supermarket in California
Jonson	Slow, slow, fresh fount
Joyce	All day I hear
Kooser	Abandoned Farmhouse
Lehman	Rejection Slip
Lennon/McCartney	Eleanor Rigby
Levertov	The Ache of Marriage
Lim	Learning to love America
Lim	Riding into Califonia
Li Po	Drinking Alone by Moonlight
Lowell	Skunk Hour

Poe	Annabel Lee
Pound	The River Merchant's Wife: A Letter
Reeves	Rough Weather
Rexroth	Vitamins and Roughage
Rich	Living in Sin
Sexton	Cinderella
Shakespeare	My mistress' eyes are nothing like the sun
Shakespeare	O mistress mine
Shakespeare	Shall I compare thee to a summer's day?
Stevenson	Sous-Entendu
Waller	Go, Lovely Rose
Wyatt	They flee from me
Wyatt	With serving still
Yeats	Crazy Jane Talks with the Bishop
Yeats	When You Are Old

MAGIC AND VISION

Anonymous	The Cruel Mother
Anonymous	The Three Ravens
Anonymous	The Twa Corbies
Atwood	Siren Song
Bogan	Medusa
Coleridge	Kubla Khan
Cummings	somewhere i have never traveled
Keats	La Belle Dame sans Merci
Mason	Song of the Powers
Menashe	The Shrine Whose Shape I Am
Sexton	Cinderella
Sexton	Her Kind
Simic	The Magic Study of Happiness
Wiman	Poštolka
Yeats	The Second Coming
Yeats	Who Goes with Fergus?

MARRIAGE AND DIVORCE

R. Browning	My Last Duchess
Donne	A Valediction: Forbidding Mourning
Fairchild	A Starlit Night
Hardy	The Workbox
Kooser	Abandoned Farmhouse
Levertov	The Ache of Marriage
Pound	The River Merchant's Wife: a Letter
Rich	Living in Sin
Shakespeare	Let me not to the marriage of true minds

MEDICINE

Frost	"Out, Out—"
W. C. Williams	Spring and All ("By the road to the contagious hospital")

MOTHERS AND CHILDREN

Anonymous	The Cruel Mother
Bradstreet	The Author to Her Book
Grosholz	Listening
Lawrence	Piano
Lim	Learning to love America
Olds	The One Girl at the Boys' Party
Olds	Rites of Passage
Plath	Metaphors
Randall	Ballad of Birmingham
Stevenson	The Victory
Trethewey	White Lies

MUSIC

Atwood	Siren Song
Campion	Rose-cheeked Laura, come
L. Hughes	Song for a Dark Girl
L. Hughes	The Weary Blues
Osherow	Song for the Music in the Warsaw Ghetto
Stillman	In Memoriam John Coltrane
Whitman	I Hear America Singing

MYTH AND LEGEND (*other than poems in Chapter on "Myth and Narrative"*; *see also* SCRIPTURE AND APOCRYPHA)

Atwood	Siren Song
Keats	La Belle Dame sans Merci
Tennyson	Ulysses
Thiel	*Memento Mori* in Middle School
Yeats	Leda and the Swan
Yeats	Sailing to Byzantium
Yeats	Who Goes with Fergus?

NATIVE AMERICAN LIFE

Anonymous	Last Words of the Prophet ("Navajo Mountain Chant")
Erdrich	Indian Boarding School: The Runaways
Jeffers	Hands
Momaday	Simile

NATURE (*see also* ANIMALS, THE SEASONS)

Bishop	The Fish
Blake	To see a world in a grain of sand
Blake	The Tyger
Chesterton	The Donkey
Clare	Mouse's Nest
Dickinson	I taste a liquor never brewed
Dickinson	The Lightning is a yellow Fork
Dickinson	A Route of Evanescence
Frost	Desert Places
Hall	Names of Horses

Hardy	The Darkling Thrush
Hirshfield	Tree
Hollander	Swan and Shadow
Hopkins	Pied Beauty
Hopkins	Spring and Fall
Hopkins	The Windhover
Housman	Loveliest of trees, the cherry now
T. Hughes	Hawk Roosting
Joyce	All day I hear
Keats	To Autumn
Kim	Monologue for an Onion
Layton	The Bull Calf
Levin	Brief Bio
Lindner	Low Tide
Nash	The Panther
Reeser	Winter-proof
Roethke	Root Cellar
Rossini	Final Love Note
Ryan	Blandeur
Ryan	Turtle
Smart	For I will consider my Cat Jeoffry
Stafford	Traveling Through the Dark
Steele	Summer
Stephens	The Wind
Stevens	Anecdote of the Jar
Stevens	Thirteen Ways of Looking at a Blackbird
Teasdale	The Flight
Tennyson	The Eagle
Tennyson	Flower in the Crannied Wall
W. C. Williams	El Hombre
W. C. Williams	Smell
W. C. Williams	Spring and All
Wiman	Poštolka
Wordsworth	I Wandered Lonely as a Cloud
Wright	A Blessing
Yeats	The Lake Isle of Innisfree

OLD AGE (AND AGING)

Collins	Care and Feeding
Hardy	The Darkling Thrush
Larkin	Aubade
Shakespeare	That time of year thou mayst in me behold
Tennyson	Ulysses
W. C. Williams	To Waken an Old Lady
Yeats	Sailing to Byzantium
Yeats	When You Are Old

POVERTY

Alarcón	The X in My Name
Blake	The Chimney Sweeper

Cleghorn	The Golf Links
L. Hughes	Prayer ("Gather up")
Niedecker	Popcorn-can Cover

PRAISE AND EXALTATION

Blake	To see a world in a grain of sand
Burns	Oh, my love is like a red, red rose
Dickinson	I taste a liquor never brewed
Hopkins	God's Grandeur
Hopkins	Pied Beauty
Shakespeare	Shall I compare thee to a summer's day?
Tennyson	The splendor falls on castle walls
Whitman	I Hear America Singing
Whitman	Song of the Open Road
Wilbur	Love Calls Us to the Things of This World

PROTEST POEMS

Alarcón	The X in My Name
Auden	September 1, 1939
Blake	London
Ciardi	A Box Comes Home
Cleghorn	The Golf Links
Cullen	For a Lady I Know
Cummings	next to of course god america i
Dunbar	We Wear the Mask
Dylan	The Times They Are a-Changin'
L. Hughes	Dream Deferred
L. Hughes	I, Too
L. Hughes	Ku Klux
Levine	They Feed They Lion
Lim	Riding into California
McKay	America
Owen	Dulce et Decorum Est
Randall	Ballad of Birmingham
Rich	Aunt Jennifer's Tigers
Wordsworth	The World Is Too Much with Us

SCIENCE AND TECHNOLOGY

Eberhart	The Fury of Aerial Bombardment
Frost	Design
Martin	Taken Up
Reed	Naming of Parts

SCRIPTURE AND APOCRYPHA

Bible	Parable of the Good Seed
Chesterton	The Donkey
Hecht	Adam

THE SEASONS

Spring

Frost	Nothing Gold Can Stay

Housman	Loveliest of trees, the cherry now
W. C. Williams	Smell
W. C. Williams	Spring and All
Summer	
Steele	Summer
Toomer	Reapers
Autumn	
Hopkins	Spring and Fall
Keats	To Autumn
Longfellow	Aftermath
Robinson	Luke Havergal
Stephens	The Wind
Wright	Autumn Begins in Martins Ferry, Ohio
Winter	
Bly	Driving to Town Late to Mail a Letter
Frost	Stopping by Woods on a Snowy Evening
Haines	Winter News
Hardy	The Darkling Thrush
Hayden	Those Winter Sundays
Niedecker	Popcorn-can cover
Reeser	Winter-proof
SPORTS	
Fehler	If Richard Lovelace Became a Free Agent
Housman	To an Athlete Dying Young
Rexroth	Vitamins and Roughage
Stroud	Missing
Updike	Ex-Basketball Player
Whitman	The Runner
Wright	Autumn Begins in Martins Ferry, Ohio
TIME, THE PASSAGE OF (*see also* CARPE DIEM, OLD AGE)	
Auden	As I Walked Out One Evening
Cummings	anyone lived in a pretty how town
Eliot	The Love Song of J. Alfred Prufrock
Hirshfield	Tree
Horace	*Carpe Diem* Ode
Housman	Loveliest of trees, the cherry now
Jeffers	To the Stone-cutters
Levertov	Ancient Stairway
Milton	How soon hath time
Pastan	Ethics
Shakespeare	Not marble nor the gilded monuments
Shakespeare	That time of year thou mayst in me behold
Shelley	Ozymandias
Stafford	The Farm on the Great Plains
Stroud	Missing
Yeats	Sailing to Byzantium

VIOLENCE

Eberhart	The Fury of Aerial Bombardment
Hayden	The Whipping
L. Hughes	Ku Klux
L. Hughes	Song for a Dark Girl
Orr	Two Lines from the Brothers Grimm
Owen	Dulce et Decorum Est
Randall	Ballad of Birmingham

WAR

Arnold	Dover Beach
Auden	September 1, 1939
Betjeman	In Westminster Abbey
Ciardi	A Box Comes Home
Cummings	next to of course god america i
Eberhart	The Fury of Aerial Bombardment
Jarrell	The Death of the Ball Turret Gunner
Kees	For My Daughter
Komunyakaa	Facing It
Lovelace	To Lucasta
Nemerov	The War in the Air
Osherow	Song for the Music in the Warsaw Ghetto
Owen	Anthem for Doomed Youth
Owen	Dulce et Decorum Est
Reed	Naming of Parts
Salter	Welcome to Hiroshima
Whitman	Beat! Beat! Drums!
Whitman	Cavalry Crossing a Ford

A WOMAN'S IDENTITY (*see also* MOTHERS AND CHILDREN)

Boland	Anorexic
Brooks	The Mother
Brooks	Southeast Corner
Clifton	Homage to my hips
Cofer	*Quinceañera*
de los Santos	Perfect Dress
Nelson	A Strange Beautiful Woman
Olds	The One Girl at the Boys' Party
Plath	Daddy
Rich	Aunt Jennifer's Tigers
Rich	Women
Sexton	Cinderella
Sexton	Her Kind
Uyematsu	Deliberate

WORK

Alarcón	The X in my Name
Blake	The Chimney Sweeper
Cleghorn	The Golf Links
Kooser	Abandoned Farmhouse

Kooser	Carrie
Larkin	Poetry of Departures
Niedecker	Poet's Work
Pound	Salutation
Robinson	Miniver Cheevy
Whitman	I Hear America Singing

WRITING

Belloc	Fatigue
Blake	Her whole life is an epigram
Collins	Care and Feeding
Cope	*from* Strugnell's Rubaiyat
Dickinson	After great pain, a formal feeling comes
Dickinson	I Dwell in Possibility
Dickinson	Tell all the Truth but tell it slant
Gwynn	Shakespearean Sonnet
Heaney	Digging
L. Hughes	Theme for English B
Jeffers	To the Stone-cutters
Lehman	Rejection Slip
MacLeish	*Ars Poetica*
Milton	How soon hath time
Moore	Poetry
Morgan	The Master
Niedecker	Poet's Work
Pope	True Ease in Writing comes from Art, not Chance
Shakespeare	My mistress' eyes are nothing like the sun
Shakespeare	Not marble nor the gilded monuments
Simpson	American Poetry
Wilbur	The Writer

Poems for Further Reading, Arranged by Elements

Many instructors tell us that they use the poems in Chapter 21, "Poems for Further Reading," as an extra reservoir or second fuel tank of illustrations. Others, to be sure, think the book already offers too many examples; if that is your feeling, don't bother with this section.

If, however, you would like a few more poems (or some different poems) to illustrate matters taken up in the body of the book, then the following list can help you put your finger on them. It classifies only poems in the "Poems for Further Reading" section, and it works through the book chapter by chapter.

For Writing Topics. After your students have studied a chapter of the book, you can direct them to certain poems in the "Poems for Further Reading." Assign a poem or two and a short paper that springs from their reading. (An essay of two or three paragraphs might be enough: at this stage, overlong papers on topics such as figures of speech, rime and meter, stanza form, etc., might be debilitating.) Topics will occur: The Character of the Soliloquist in Browning's "Spanish Cloister" (after studying *The Person in the Poem*); The Attitude of the Daughter in Plath's "Daddy" *(Tone)*, and more.

For suggesting that this manual could use such a classification of the "Poems for Further Reading," our thanks to Professor Harvey Birenbaum of San Jose State University.

Chapter 2: Listening to a Voice

TONE

Poems in which the poet's attitude is especially clear:

Jonson	On My First Son
Owen	Anthem for Doomed Youth
Plath	Daddy
Shakespeare	My mistress' eyes are nothing like the sun
Tennyson	Dark house, by which once more I stand
Whitman	I Hear America Singing
C. K. Williams	Elms
Wordsworth	Composed upon Westminster Bridge

Poems that express, as Auden says, "a clear expression of mixed feelings":

Bishop	Filling Station
Hardy	The Darkling Thrush
Larkin	Poetry of Departures
Lowell	Skunk Hour
Nelson	A Strange Beautiful Woman
Nemerov	The War in the Air

THE PERSON IN THE POEM

Poems in which the identity of the speaker is interestingly different from the poet's "I":

Boland	Anorexic
R. Browning	Soliloquy of the Spanish Cloister
Chesterton	The Donkey
Gunn	The Man with Night Sweats
Pound	The River Merchant's Wife: A Letter

IRONY

Other kinds besides ironic point of view, as in the poems just listed:

Hardy	The Convergence of the Twain (*irony of fate*)
Reed	Naming of Parts (*a discrepancy between the study of a gun and the study of nature, between the voice of the instructor and the view of the soldier; verbal irony in the pun "easing the spring"*)

Chapter 3: Words

LITERAL MEANING: WHAT A POEM SAYS FIRST

Poems that can be taken at face value, without looking for symbols, endless suggestions, huge significance (not that they won't repay thought and close reading):

Clifton	Homage to my hips
Hall	Names of Horses
Larkin	Poetry of Departures
Millay	Recuerdo
Poe	A Dream within a Dream
Slavitt	Titanic
Updike	Ex-Basketball Player
Whitman	Song of the Open Road
C. K. Williams	Elms

THE VALUE OF A DICTIONARY

Poems containing two or more brief allusions:

Dryden	To the Memory of Mr. Oldham
Hecht	Adam
Nemerov	The War in the Air

Poems with central allusions:

Atwood	Siren Song
Auden	Musée des Beaux Arts
Chesterton	The Donkey
Eliot	Journey of the Magi
Milton	When I consider how my light is spent
Tennyson	Ulysses
Yeats	The Magi

WORD CHOICE AND WORD ORDER

Poems in dialect:

Anonymous	The Twa Corbies

Poems in Middle English:

Chaucer	Merciless Beauty

Poems whose diction and syntax depart from those of speech:

Blake	The Tyger
Coleridge	Kubla Khan
Cummings	somewhere i have never travelled
Hardy	The Convergence of the Twain
Hopkins	No worst, there is none
Hopkins	Spring and Fall
Hopkins	The Windhover
Keats	To Autumn
Levine	They Feed They Lion
Moore	Poetry
Thomas	Fern Hill

Poems containing technical words:

Reed	Naming of Parts

Poems in colloquial diction:

Frost	Birches
Frost	Stopping by Woods on a Snowy Evening
Olds	The One Girl at the Boys' Party
Updike	Ex-Basketball Player

Poems containing an interesting mix of formal and colloquial diction:

Bishop	Filling Station
Ginsberg	A Supermarket in California
Larkin	Poetry of Departures
Levine	They Feed They Lion
Simpson	American Poetry

Chapter 4: Saying and Suggesting

Poems especially full of words rich in connotations:

Anonymous	The Three Ravens
Anonymous	The Twa Corbies
Coleridge	Kubla Khan
Cummings	somewhere i have never travelled
Keats	To Autumn
Ransom	Piazza Piece
Thomas	Fern Hill

Chapter 5: Imagery

Bishop	Filling Station
Erdrich	Indian Boarding School: The Runaways
Fairchild	A Starlit Night
Keats	To Autumn
Kooser	Abandoned Farmhouse
Randall	A Different Image
Ransom	Piazza Piece
Swift	A Description of the Morning

Tennyson	Dark house, by which once more I stand
Thomas	Fern Hill
W. C. Williams	Spring and All
W. C. Williams	To Waken an Old Lady

Chapter 6: Figures of Speech

METAPHOR AND SIMILE

Poems with central metaphors:

Hopkins	The Windhover
Phillips	Running on Empty
Song	Stamp Collecting
W. C. Williams	To Waken an Old Lady
Wordsworth	Composed upon Westminster Bridge
Wroth	In this strange labyrinth

Other poems with prominent metaphors:

Shakespeare	That time of year thou mayst in me behold
Wilbur	The Writer
Wright	A Blessing

Poem with a prominent simile:

Teasdale	The Flight

OTHER FIGURES OF SPEECH

Blake	The Sick Rose (*apostrophe*)
Donne	A Valediction: Forbidding Mourning (*paradox*)
Frost	Birches (*understatement*)
Keats	To Autumn (*apostrophe, personification*)
Marvell	To His Coy Mistress (*hyperbole*)
Plath	Daddy (*hyperbole*)
Reed	Naming of Parts (*pun*)
Waller	Go, Lovely Rose (*apostrophe, personification*)
W. C. Williams	Spring and All (*personification*)

Chapter 7: Song

BALLADS

Anonymous	Lord Randall
Anonymous	The Three Ravens
Anonymous	The Twa Corbies

A balladlike poem:

Auden	As I Walked Out One Evening

Chapter 8: Sound

ALLITERATION AND ASSONANCE

Blake	The Tyger
Coleridge	Kubla Khan
Hopkins	No worst, there is none

Hopkins	Spring and Fall
Hopkins	The Windhover
Thomas	Fern Hill
Waller	Go, Lovely Rose

RIME

Poems whose rimes may well repay study:

Blake	The Sick Rose
Lowell	Skunk Hour
Owen	Anthem For Doomed Youth
Plath	Daddy

Chapter 9: Rhythm

STRESSES AND PAUSES

In any good metrical poem, rhythms matter, of course, and can't be disentangled from meanings. Here are some poems in open or syllabic forms in which rhythms play strong parts:

Hall	Names of Horses
Levine	They Feed They Lion
Reed	Naming of Parts
Smart	For I will consider my Cat Jeoffry
Thomas	Fern Hill
Whitman	I Hear America Singing

METER

Wyatt	They flee from me that sometime did me sekë
Yeats	The Magi (*worth scanning: irregularities battle with regularity for supremacy*)

Chapter 10: Closed Form

FORMAL PATTERNS, SONNETS, OTHER FORMS

Poems in blank verse:

Frost	Birches
Justice	On the Death of Friends in Childhood
Tennyson	Ulysses
Updike	Ex-Basketball Player

Poems in closed (heroic) couplets:

Dryden	To the Memory of Mr. Oldham
Jonson	On My First Son
Swift	A Description of the Morning

Poems in tercets:

Hardy	The Convergence of the Twain

Poems in tightly structured riming stanzas:

Donne	The Flea
Frost	Stopping by Woods on a Snowy Evening

Gunn	The Man with Night Sweats
Hardy	The Darkling Thrush
Hecht	Adam
Herbert	Love
Keats	To Autumn

Poems in syllabic stanzas:

Moore	Poetry
Noguchi	Hokku
Thomas	Fern Hill

Sonnets:

E. B. Browning	How Do I Love Thee?
Hopkins	No worst, there is none
Hopkins	The Windhover
Keats	When I have fears that I may cease to be
Milton	How soon hath time
Milton	When I consider how my light is spent
Owen	Anthem for Doomed Youth
Shakespeare	My mistress' eyes are nothing like the sun
Shakespeare	That time of year thou mayst in me behold
Shakespeare	When, in disgrace with Fortune and men's eyes
Wordsworth	Composed upon Westminster Bridge
Wroth	In this strange labyrinth

Villanelles:

Bishop	One Art

Chapter 11: Open Form

Classics of open form poetry:

Cummings	somewhere i have never travelled
Eliot	Journey of the Magi
Ginsberg	A Supermarket in California
Pound	The River Merchant's Wife: A Letter
Roethke	Elegy for Jane
W. C. Williams	Spring and All
W. C. Williams	To Waken an Old Lady
Wright	A Blessing

Chapter 12: Symbol

Ashbery	At North Farm
Blake	The Sick Rose
Lowell	Skunk Hour
Randall	A Different Image

Chapter 13: Myth and Narrative

Atwood	Siren Song
Eliot	Journey of the Magi
Hecht	Adam
Ransom	Piazza Piece
Yeats	The Magi

Chapter 14: Poetry and Personal Identity

Boland	Anorexic
Brooks	The Mother
Browning	How Do I Love Thee?
Clifton	Homage to my hips
de los Santos	Perfect Dress
Gunn	The Man with Night Sweats (*gay identity*)
Hayden	Those Winter Sundays (*being a son*)
Heaney	Digging
Hecht	Adam (*fatherhood as an identity*)
Jonson	On My First Son
Larkin	Poetry of Departures
Lowell	Skunk Hour
Milton	When I consider how my light is spent (*Milton on his disability*)
Nelson	A Strange Beautiful Woman
Owen	Anthem for Doomed Youth (*war poem written by a soldier*)
Phillips	Running on Empty
Plath	Daddy
Tennyson	Dark house, by which once more I stand
Thomas	Fern Hill

Poems Students Like Most

At the end of the book is a short student questionnaire that solicits each student's opinion about his or her reactions to the book. The editors read and save each completed questionnaire they receive. These candid student responses often help improve the anthology from edition to edition.

One of the most interesting insights afforded by these questionnaires is a good sense of the poems students like most. (Their favorites often differ from the poems instructors rate most highly, though there is also much overlap.) Significantly, both students and instructors lean heavily toward twentieth-century poems and poets. Instructors might enjoy learning what poems and poets are most frequently chosen by students. Some choices may be surprising.

Students often identify their favorite poets rather than a specific poem. The five poets most frequently named by students are (in order):

FAVORITE POETS

1. William Carlos Williams
2. Robert Frost
3. E. E. Cummings
4. Emily Dickinson
5. Langston Hughes

The individual poems most frequently praised by students are listed below. Some are familiar favorites; others are pleasant surprises. There may be poems high on this list that some instructors do not teach. It might be worthwhile to consider adding them to your reading list.

FAVORITE POEMS *(Student Choices in Rank Order)*

1. Robert Frost, "Fire and Ice"
2. Stevie Smith, "Not Waving but Drowning"
3. Walt Whitman, "O Captain! My Captain!"
4. Margaret Atwood, "You fit into me"
5. Robert Frost, "'Out, Out—'"
6. Elizabeth Bishop, "The Fish"
7. Robert Browning, "My Last Duchess"
8. Robert Frost, "The Road Not Taken"

9. Sylvia Plath, "Metaphors"
10. James Stephens, "A Glass of Beer"
11. W. H. Auden, "The Unknown Citizen"
12. William Blake, "The Tyger"
13. E. E. Cummings, "anyone lived in a pretty how town"
14. Emily Dickinson, "Because I could not stop for Death"
15. Stephen Crane, "The Heart"
16. A. E. Housman, "To an Athlete Dying Young"
17. Robert Frost, "The Secret Sits"
18. Theodore Roethke, "My Papa's Waltz"
19. Lewis Carroll, "Jabberwocky"
20. William Shakespeare, "Shall I compare thee to a summer's day?"

This list of student favorites is not statistically reliable, and it changes slightly with each new batch of responses, but the results are nonetheless interesting to ponder. A purist might blanch at the particular Whitman poem chosen from the many in the book, but if the list indicates anything, it is that the students responding have pretty good taste in poetry. No matter how discouraging some days in the classroom may occasionally feel, you can take heart that you are making a strong impression on many students.

1
Reading a Poem

William Butler Yeats, THE LAKE ISLE OF INNISFREE, page 5

As a young man in London in 1887–1891, Yeats found himself hating the city and yearning for the west of Ireland. He recalled: "I was going along the Strand, and passing a shop window where there was a little ball kept dancing by a jet of water, I remembered waters about Sligo and was moved to a sudden emotion that shaped itself into 'The Lake Isle of Innisfree'" (*Memoirs* [New York: Macmillan, 1972] 31). In London (he recalled in his *Autobiography*), he sometimes imagined himself "living in imitation of Thoreau on Innisfree, a little island in Lough Gill." The nine bean rows of the poem were evidently inspired by Thoreau's bean patch.

Yeats's lines provide rich rows of sound for the student to hoe: assonance (from *I . . . arise* in the first stanza through the o-sounds in the closing stanza), onomatopoeia (*lapping*), initial alliteration, internal alliteration (*arise, Innisfree; hear, heart's core*). Sound images of bees, cricket, linnet, and lake water are predominate. Whatever noises come from roadway or pavement, however, are left unspecified.

Perhaps, in London, Yeats thought himself one of Ireland's prodigal sons. At least, A. Norman Jeffares has noticed in the first line an echo from the parable of the prodigal son (Luke 15:18): "I will arise and go to my father" (*A Commentary on the Collected Poems of W. B. Yeats* [Stanford: Stanford UP, 1968] 35).

In later years, according to John Unterecker, Yeats was shocked that "The Lake Isle" had become his most popular poem. He had taken a dislike to its "Biblical opening lines." But audiences always demanded it of him, and his sonorous reading of the poem is available on a recording (Spoken Arts, 753).

MyLiteratureLab Resources. Biography, critical overview, and bibliography for Yeats. Longman Lecture and critical essay on "The Lake Isle of Innisfree."

LYRIC POETRY

D. H. Lawrence, PIANO, page 8

About the first question: it's really a quick writing assignment. Ten minutes of class time might be enough to let students write their paraphrases. To be sure, you could let them wing it and paraphrase the poem out loud, but the results may not be so thoughtful or accurate. A few of the students might then be asked to read their efforts aloud, for others to agree or disagree with.

Reader response theory, if crudely applied, might claim that every paraphrase is valid. But we think it greatly helps a class discussion to assume that it is possible to find an interpretation of a poem that all or most will agree comes closest to it.

"Piano" isn't a flawless poem. Lawrence was seldom at ease in rime, and the strained juxtaposition of *clamor* and *glamor* indicates his discomfort. Still, *glamor* is an accurate word in its context: the mature man knows that the child's eyes endowed the past with an illusory beauty. The quality of Lawrence's poem may be seen in the specificity of its detail: "the boom of the tingling strings," "the small, poised feet." Lawrence enters into the child's perspective, while able to criticize it from outside. The speaker is resisting his urge to cry, as the connotations of his words indicate (the song is *insidious*, it *betrays*). But at last he is unable to hold back his tears and, sensibly, yields to them.

How does Lawrence's poem escape bathos? Robert Pinsky has offered an explanation in "Poetry and Pleasure," in *Threepenny Review* (Fall 1983). The subject of "Piano," Pinsky finds, is a stock source for poems, "as mothers-in-law or airplanes with ethnically various passengers are stock sources for jokes." Yet the poem strikes us with "something fresh, not stock." Its language is vivid, unconventional; its words *insidious* and *betrays* add a "steely spring"; it sets up an energetic tension between present and past.

Adrienne Rich, AUNT JENNIFER'S TIGERS, page 8

Rich's own comments on "Aunt Jennifer's Tigers" (found in this chapter's "Writers on Writing") provide an interesting view of the poem. Rich explains how an artist can put many things into a poem which he or she is not fully conscious of until much later. Today Rich is universally recognized as the chief poet of American feminism, but that was neither her public image nor her private identity in 1951. Yet Rich's feminist perspective had already begun to emerge intuitively in her early poems such as "Aunt Jennifer's Tigers."

It is apparent in the poem that the poet perceived something wrong with the passive role assigned to women. The pride, confidence, and fearlessness ("masculine" virtues, whatever the sex of the tigers) of Aunt Jennifer's imaginary creations contrast sharply with Aunt Jennifer herself—a frail lady with fluttering fingers, *terrified hands*. Worth comment is the poet's use of the word *ringed*—suggesting "encircled"—to refer both to the wedding ring that "sits heavily upon Aunt Jennifer's hand" and to "ordeals she was mastered by," specifically marriage and being expected to conform. Although she goes down in defeat, her tigers triumph.

Possible questions for discussion include:

1. In literal terms, what are Aunt Jennifer's tigers? What sort of "panels" does she appear to be making?

2. The speaker depicts Aunt Jennifer mainly through her hands. What specific details characterize these hands?

3. Why are Aunt Jennifer's hands "terrified"?

4. What attributes characterize the tigers?

5. What does Aunt Jennifer express in the panel she weaves that she does not so easily express in her daily life?

Compare Aunt Jennifer with the dead woman who once embroidered fantails in Wallace Stevens's "The Emperor of Ice-Cream." For another contrast between a dull world of reality and the colorful life of the imagination, see Stevens's "Disillusionment of Ten O'Clock," in which:

Only, here and there, an old sailor,
Drunk and asleep in his boots,
Catches tigers
In red weather.

For an interesting classroom discussion, ask students why this poem is lyric rather than narrative. There is certainly a story implied in the images that describe Aunt Jennifer and her surroundings, and Rich surely intends us to ponder the significance of these images. The poem remains essentially lyric, however, in its brevity, musicality, and evocative emotionality. A lyric poem characteristically focuses on a particular instant in time and explores—usually in subjective and imagistic terms—the emotional, intellectual, and imaginative implications of that instant. (A narrative poem, by contrast, must move from one significant point in time to another.) A good lyric poem, however, will often contain secondary narrative elements, just as a strong narrative poem will incorporate lyric effects to heighten its impact.

Mary Slowik discusses "Aunt Jennifer's Tigers" and other early poems of Rich in "The Friction of the Mind," *Massachusetts Review* (Spring 1984): 142–60.

MyLiteratureLab Resources. Biography, critical overview, and bibliography for Rich.

Narrative Poetry

Anonymous, Sir Patrick Spence, page 9

On the questions in the book: We really don't think the king's motive can be known for sure from this bare portrait of him; we ask this question mainly to prompt students to pay attention to what they find on the page and to be wary of deep extrapolations. As far as we see him in the poem, the king sits around drinking wine, leading a life of ease, and (with a deliberate official gesture) sends his best sea-captain and a loyal contingent of naval officers to their doom. Although the poet takes a sour view of the comfortable life at court, he feels for the Scots nobles, and we too are moved by his spare sketch of the bereaved ladies, futilely waiting for their men, who will never return. The great stanza about the new and old moons, apparently an ill omen, serves further to heighten the tension of the story and foreshadow its conclusion.

Here are two more questions:

1. Comment on Sir Patrick's character. What do you make of his abrupt transition from laughter to tears (lines 13–16)? (He is not only brave and loyal to obey the king's order; he is a passionate man with quick, open, unconcealed feelings.)

2. In what lines do you notice a wry comment on the soft life that the nobles led at court? What does this attitude suggest about this anonymous poet? (lines 29–30: The nobles are loath to get their fine shoes wet. Probably the poet wasn't a noble, but a sarcastic commoner.)

In the famous image of the slim new moon, W. D. Snodgrass finds visual reminders of the king's golden crown and of the gold combs in the ladies' hair. For him, withering scorn for the Scottish lords afraid to dampen their fancy French pumps comes naturally to the singer, who probably went barefoot for much of his life. And he concludes: "This ballad, at least partly because of its scorn for the ignorant court, seems superbly successful in recognizing a more genuine nobility. Not that I need agree with its values: personally, I'd prefer (though not expect to find) a captain with more loyalty to his men than to king and office. Yet while the song lasts, I partake of the Scottish singer's world, and am broadened by entrance to another's experience, another's values." See "Shapes Merging and Emerging," *Shenandoah* (Winter 1991): 58–83.

Robert Frost, "Out, Out—," page 11

Like Sir Patrick Spence's, the boy's initial reaction to his terrible realization is to laugh; then, almost at once, dismay sets in. And like the folk ballad, "'Out, Out—'" tells a story of sudden, meaningless death, and does so with spare economy.

Perhaps the "they"—the doctor and the hospital staff—who turn to their own affairs are not merciless. The "watcher at his pulse" grows frightened when the pulse fails; no one wants to believe the boy will die. Radcliffe Squires finds no one to blame for the "faceless accident." In his view, "Simultaneously, one sees the human watchers touched by normal griefs and fears. And yet life must turn to a more important task finally, that of continuing. . . . Only the grand composer could hold together in one poem the two severe and mutually accusing ideas that one must be moved to pity and compassion and that one must coldly and sternly pursue the duty of endurance and survival" (*The Major Themes of Robert Frost* [U of Michigan P, 1963] 46). Frost's poem offers no comfort, but it seems a realistic view of what happens in an emergency ward. Any student interested in a career in medicine might be asked for a response to this poem.

Frost's allusion to *Macbeth* is part of the meaning of the poem, and students may be asked to think about it. Perhaps Frost suggests that the snarling buzz-saw full of sound and fury, reaching out its friendly handshake, just doesn't make sense. This, as Stanley Burnshaw has noticed, is one among several of Frost's poems that seem to question the existence of a benevolent order in the universe. Others include "A Servant to Servants," "The Housekeeper," "Home Burial," and (we would add) "Design" (*Robert Frost Himself* [New York: Braziller, 1986] 298).

Frost based his poem on an actual incident: an accident that had happened in 1910 to a sixteen-year-old boy he knew in Bethlehem, New Hampshire; five years went by before the poem took form (in 1915–1916). See Lawrance Thompson, *Robert Frost: The Early Years* (New York: Holt, 1966) 566–67.

In the article just cited in the previous entry, W. D. Snodgrass contrasts "Sir Patrick Spence" with "'Out, Out—.'" The first poem is about a man who looks unflinchingly at the world's horror ("the buzz-saw of the world"); the second, about a boy who tries to avoid beholding it.

Of Frost's poem, he remarks: "The one thing you must never do while working with machinery is to lift your eyes. The boy does just that—not to count ranges, but perhaps to count time 'saved from work' by his sister's call. A horrifying salvation is granted him: not just a half hour, but a lifetime, saved from work." Why the vision of five mountain ranges on the horizon (lines 4–6)? "To lift one's view from saw to horizon, reveals a terrifying similarity. We are given one glimpse, ironically lovely, of the edged and jagged teeth of a world only too ready to take us for its 'Supper.'" If the poem had a superscription, it ought to come from the old hymn: "Work, for the night is coming when man (or boy) works no more."

Jean Tobin, who teaches at the University of Wisconsin Center in Sheboygan County, reports the powerful effect Frost's poem usually has on students.

> Your discussions of narrative, lyric, and dramatic poetry work well for the kinds of students I have. I read Frost's "'Out, Out—'" and was pleased by absolute silence at the end followed by one student's under-the-breath "Damn." As the discussion roared along, even that first hour, one student remarked how strange it was that the boy's first reaction was to laugh. "Oh, no," said a girl, holding up a hand and keeping it raised until we all saw it had no fingers, "that's exactly what you do." After that I didn't have to convince anybody about the relevance of poetry to daily life.

MyLiteratureLab Resources. Biography, critical overview, critical articles, and bibliography for Frost. Interactive reading and critical essay on "'Out, Out—.'"

Dramatic Poetry

Robert Browning, My Last Duchess, page 12

We include this famous dramatic monologue in the book because of instructor demand; we received more requests to reinstate the poem after dropping it from a revised edition than any other selection. Students generally find it fascinating, and instructors consider it an invaluable means of teaching the idea of a persona poem.

Some teachers may want to assign this poem in conjunction with Browning's "Soliloquy of the Spanish Cloister," which is in the "Poems for Further Reading" chapter. These two dramatic poems, both uttered by speakers we find unsympathetic, may be taken together as memorable works of character-drawing. In each poem, Browning places us in the midst of a society remote from our own in time and thoroughly undemocratic. Of the two, only "My Last Duchess" is a typical dramatic monologue. "Soliloquy," as its title indicates, addresses no listener.

"My Last Duchess" may be familiar to students from high school literature courses; if a show of hands indicates that they have met it before, we would spend less time with it. Whether or not it is familiar, it makes a useful companion to "Soliloquy." Students may be asked to define their feelings toward the Duke, to point to lines in the poem that helped define those feelings. Browning stresses the Duke's arrogance ("I choose / Never to stoop"; "I gave commands; / Then all smiles stopped together") and engages our sympathies for the poor

Duchess in lines 21–31, despite the Duke's contempt for her facility to be gladdened. We know one instructor who in teaching this classic takes the tack, "Shouldn't we feel sorry for the Duke, with all his marital troubles?" (Students of both sexes are usually provoked to rise and trounce him.) Another question: to what extent is the Duke's attitude toward women presumably typical of his society? That the Count, the visitor's master, would offer a daughter to a man who had just disposed of his wife, suggests that the Duke is not alone in regarding women as chattel. Still, even for a Renaissance duke he seems cold-hearted: wives and works of art seem identified as objects to collect.

What were the Duke's commands that stopped the Duchess's smiles? "That she should be put to death, or he might have had her shut up in a convent," Browning once explained. But lines 2 ("Looking as if she were alive") and 46–47 ("There she stands / As if alive") seem to hint that she was executed. Hypocrisy is still another aspect of the Duke's character: compare his protest that he lacks skill in speech (lines 35–36) with his artful flattery of the Count (49–53).

Instructors should note that this book includes Robert Langbaum's insightful commentary on "My Last Duchess" in the "Critical Approaches to Literature" chapter.

MyLiteratureLab Resources. Photographs and biographical information for Browning. Longman Lecture, audio clip, student paper, and critical essay on "My Last Duchess."

Writing Effectively

William Stafford, Ask Me, page 16
William Stafford, A Paraphrase of "Ask Me," page 16

The author himself so skillfully paraphrases this poem in the prose excerpt that follows it, that an editor offers further analysis at his own risk. A few comments, however, may provide a departure point for classroom discussions. Notice how the speaker asks several questions in the poem that are never specifically answered. *What* mistakes has the speaker made? *What* difference has love or hate made in his life? *Is* what he has done his life? The speaker answers the questions only with the final enigmatic and imagistic line. Stafford clearly trusts the reader's intuition to understand the ending.

Stafford's paraphrase is a bit freer and more interpretive than we might want from a student, but he proceeds through the poem line by line, image by image. Notice how Stafford spends more time on the final image than on earlier ones. He knows it requires more commentary—and a small imaginative leap—to explain. Stafford's deft paraphrase of "Ask Me" should demonstrate to students that close reading and critical discussion are not antithetical to the spirit of poetry.

2
Listening to a Voice

TONE

Theodore Roethke, MY PAPA'S WALTZ, page 18

Theodore Roethke's poem is one of the most widely taught selections in the book, and it usually proves a provocative topic for classroom discussion. We revised the critical discussion of the poem in earlier editions to reflect the broad range of opinion on this powerful poem. We have also included a student essay focused directly on the main issues that usually emerge from classroom discussions.

Many instructors have shared their reactions with us. Steven Hind of Hutchinson Community College disagreed with a previous edition's comments on this poem—"It seems to me that the poem is richer than Professor Kennedy's discussion would allow"—and finds its view of Papa ambivalent. "Kennedy hears a 'playfulness' in the slant rhyme *dizzy* and *easy*. Would it be possible to hear that as a slight dissonance? The only other double rhyme in the poem is *knuckle* and *buckle*, which has a hard edge to it, to my ear, [Mother] doesn't seem to be having such a good time. The involuntary response suggests that this isn't a novel experience. She will be the one who picks up the pans, one supposes. *Scraped* is a harsh verb. The ear is a sensitive organ. Certainly the boy loves his father and relishes the recollection of the dear brute's drunken revelry that included him, but these verbs present an unavoidable tension, it seems to me. The father may, as Professor Kennedy says, be 'happily using his son's head for a drum,' but that doesn't mean the drum is entirely comfortable with the impact."

Hind adds a sobering anecdote:

> Last year in composition class I taught the recovering alcoholic son of an alcoholic father. He wrote papers about the loving and terrible bond he felt with his father, and some of his experiences reminded me of this poem. I saw Rick in the hall two weeks ago and asked how his summer had gone. "It would have been better if I hadn't learned that my father has been molesting his daughter the past four years and I didn't know about it," he said. They are in therapy. "My mother's countenance / Could not unfrown itself."

Ann Barnard of Blackburn College, in a provocative article, also thinks the poem's dark side worth emphasis. She and a colleague had expressed chagrin that half their students had read "My Papa's Waltz" as a poem about child abuse, reducing it to a social tract. But their mutual rediscovery of the poem "included the idea of covert *emotional* abuse." Papa, whose waltz gives the child both pleasure and pain, is a figure of ambivalence. See "'My Papa's Waltz' as a Problem in Pedagogy," *Teaching English in the Two-Year College* 18 (Feb. 1991): 43–47.

Fred Roux of Shippensburg University of Pennsylvania reports that his students' interpretations of "My Papa's Waltz" have differed according to sex. Young men almost unanimously respond to the poem as a happy childhood memory of a loving father's exuberant horseplay. A few young women react negatively. For them, "I hung on like death" and "You beat time on my head," as well as "battered" and "scraped," suggest that the speaker's recollection is unhappy. They also assume that a man with whiskey on his breath must be drunk. None has perceived an ironic parallel between their responses and that of the speaker's frowning mother. "From this," adds Professor Roux, "it would appear that student response to 'My Papa's Waltz' is, to a degree, the result of a difference in socializing experiences during early childhood." Haven't any young women had boisterous fathers? We'd like to hear about other classroom experiences.

As Alan Seager discerns in his biography of Roethke, *The Glass House* (New York: McGraw, 1968) 23, the mature Roethke seems to have felt a certain guilty resentment against his father, a sense of how (as an awkward, chubby, bookish, and sensitive child) the young poet had failed to make the old man proud of him.

"My Papa's Waltz" may have had its genesis in a wish-fulfilling dream. After his father's death Roethke wrote a memoir (calling himself "John"): "Sometimes he dreamed about Papa. Once it seemed Papa came in and danced around with him. John put his feet on top of Papa's and they'd waltz. Hei-dee-dei-dei. Rump-tee-tump. Only babies expected dreams to come true" (qtd. in Seager, 24).

Countee Cullen, FOR A LADY I KNOW, page 19

From Cullen's first book, *Color* (1925), this is one of a series of twenty-nine epitaphs. Compare it with another brief poem that makes a biting social comment: Sarah N. Cleghorn's "The Golf Links." Cleghorn's poem seems angrier; the tone of Cullen's poem seems to be one of wry amusement at stupidity.

Cullen's early biography is sparsely documented. Raised by his grandmother until he was eleven, he was then adopted by the Reverend Frederick A. Cullen, pastor of a Methodist church in Harlem, who gave the future poet not only a name but a new life of books and conversation. Famed as the leading poet of the Harlem Renaissance, Cullen suffered a decline in reputation when militant black critics of the 1960s reevaluated his work and found it wanting in anger and social consciousness. But his wit can bite, as it does in "For a Lady I Know"; and Houston A. Baker has rightly called much of his work an "ironical protest . . . against economic oppression" in his short study of Cullen, *A Many-Colored Coat of Dreams* (Detroit: Broadside, 1974).

Anne Bradstreet, THE AUTHOR TO HER BOOK, page 20

The "rags" (line 5) worn by this bastard brat of a book may have been the first edition's abundance of typographical errors. Although Bradstreet patiently revised her work, she did not live to see her "brat" appear in better dress. This poem prefaced the Boston edition published in 1678, six years after the author's death.

Robert Hutchinson, in the introduction to his edition of *Poems of Anne Bradstreet* (New York: Dover, 1969), gives a concise account of the book's publication. Evidently the author's family, proud of her poetry, felt that it deserved more notice than New England could then give. The Reverend John Woodbridge, Bradstreet's brother-in-law, took with him to England the manuscript of the collection. London at the time had sixty printers; New England, one—and so it must have been difficult, even then, to print poetry in America. "The fact," notes Hutchinson, "that Herrick's *Hesperides* had just appeared in England while the latest venture of Samuel Green, the Cambridge, Massachusetts, printer, was a revision of *The Bay Psalm Book* to rid it of its crudities, gives an indication of the intellectual distance between the two countries."

Walt Whitman, TO A LOCOMOTIVE IN WINTER, page 21
Emily Dickinson, I LIKE TO SEE IT LAP THE MILES, page 22

Though both of these great nineteenth-century Americans take almost the same subject, in tone and in form the two poems differ as sharply as opera differs from chamber music. (Some students might argue that the mutual subject isn't a moving locomotive but the poet's praise of it. While seeing a real similarity, they would be missing the distinction between subject and tone.) Whitman addresses his machine in awe and exultation. In lines 14–19 he practically prays to it (almost like Henry Adams on bended knees before the dynamo in *Education*). Dickinson is evidently more playful in her affectionate view of the locomotive as a great beast. It is horselike in that it neighs and has a stable, but it isn't quite a horse: it crawls and hoots. Both poets, incidentally, see not only a locomotive, but a whole train. Dickinson's seeing it "chase itself" suggests cars trying to catch their locomotive as they roll downhill. Dickinson's allusion to Boanerges means no more, we think, than that the locomotive is a servant and is thunderous.

Whitman's poem is full of diction from music: *recitative*, *beat*, *ringing bell*, *notes*, *chant*, *harp*, *piano*, *trills*. The locomotive embodies poetry, too, in its *metrical* pant and roar, and in its ability to serve the Muse. The word *recitative* indicates the form the poem will be cast in. In Italian opera, to which Whitman was devoted, Rossini had introduced the use of the full orchestra to accompany the recitative, the passage of half-sung, half-spoken declamation; and it may be that, as Robert D. Faner has argued, such recitative was a basic model for Whitman's poetry. "The recitative, highly rhythmic and emotional, punctuated by instrumental accompaniment with thrilling effect, and in its chanted delivery giving the impression of the rhythms of speech, he found well adapted to the bulk of his work, which he thought of as a sort of bardic chant" (*Walt Whitman and Opera* [Carbondale: Southern Illinois UP, 1951] 234).

MyLiteratureLab Resources. Biography, critical overview, and bibliography for Whitman and Dickinson.

Benjamin Alire Sáenz, TO THE DESERT, page 23

Benjamin Alire Sáenz's passionate "To the Desert" is an unrhymed sonnet—fourteen lines of blank verse. (There is also a conscious pattern of assonance at the line ends to suggest rhyme—*night/sky*, *your/thirst*, *dios/me*—as well as one slant rhyme, *bend/brand*.) Sáenz's language is both erotic and religious, which is not an unusual situation for Catholic religious poetry, especially in the Spanish tradition. (Sáenz once studied for the priesthood, and the poem's bilingual diction and religious language announce its Latin Catholic heritage.)

"I came to you one rainless August night," the poem begins as it sets up thirst as its central metaphor. In the poem thirst becomes both physical and spiritual, emotional and topographic. Students should be asked to consider how Sáenz's title helps us understand the meaning of the poem. A reader can learn much not only from understanding the speaker of a poem but also from its stated listener. In religious writing, the desert is the place of spiritual self-knowledge, trial, and purification. Sáenz's poem uses that archetype to build a compressed drama of spiritual discovery.

Weldon Kees, For My Daughter, page 23

Weldon Kees, who was born in Beatrice, Nebraska, in 1914, was one of the most talented artists of his generation. In his short life he managed to do distinguished work in poetry, fiction, painting, film, criticism, and music. In 1955, shortly after the breakup of his marriage, Kees disappeared. Most evidence suggests that he killed himself by jumping off the Golden Gate Bridge, but some of his friends believed that Kees faked a suicide so that he could go off to Mexico and start a new life. In either event, Kees was never seen again.

"For My Daughter" usually creates a lively classroom discussion, but the conversation often veers in two different directions—one literary, the other ethical. On the literary side, students are often divided on the question of whether the poet should mislead the reader for thirteen lines and then reveal the truth (that he has no daughter) only in the final line. Some beginning students may feel that the author isn't playing fair with his readers, that he is exploiting their emotions. This discussion can be important for students because it dramatizes the fact that literature isn't necessarily considerate of our emotions—it has more important goals than leaving us at ease. Kees was a particularly savage poet in respect to pointing out the cruel and unjust parts of life that most people *want* to overlook. The important point is that the speaker comes clean in the last line, and that admission changes the meaning of everything said before. The first thirteen lines, therefore, can be read in two different ways—once coming up to the end (a father's worst fears for his daughter) and again retrospectively from the end (a man's reasons for not wanting children, especially on the brink of a world war).

The other discussion of "For My Daughter" concerns the ethical responsibilities faced by any parent bringing children into the world. (It may be worth noting here that Kees is not striking a hollow pose in this poem. He and his wife decided not to have children.)

One small technical note is worth mentioning: "For My Daughter" is a Shakespearean sonnet.

The Person in the Poem

Natasha Trethewey, White Lies, page 24

This poem is discussed at some length in the prose paragraph following the text. Once given the biographical information contained in the paragraph, some students may complain that the poem cannot be properly understood—or, worse, cannot be understood at all—without a knowledge of the author's background. It might be better to have the class read and interpret the poem on its own before introducing the biographical material. In this way, you may be better able to emphasize the distinction between a satisfactory engagement with the text itself and a deeper reading based on outside facts, a reading that enhances, but is not necessary to, a full understanding of the poem.

Edwin Arlington Robinson, LUKE HAVERGAL, page 26

Teaching this poem consistently produces some of the most interesting classes that I (DG) have ever conducted. I read the poem aloud in class, then I ask students to answer three questions:

1. Who is the speaker of the poem?
2. What does the speaker ask Luke Havergal to do?
3. Should Luke Havergal follow the speaker's advice?

Students immediately agree that these are sensible questions to ask. In order to answer them, however, they have to learn how to interpret the poem. Have them list on the blackboard everything they know about the speaker (there isn't much to know) in one column. Then have them list in another column essential information they wish they knew but are not told. They will soon discover that the voice speaking claims to be from beyond the grave.

It helps to ask students how many characters are in the poem. There are only three, and each of them—this discovery will show students how much grammar reinforces meaning—is associated with a specific personal pronoun. There is the *I* (the speaker), the *you* (Luke Havergal), and the *she* (Havergal's lost love). Have students collectively put on the blackboard what they can find out about each character.

To figure out what the speaker asks Luke Havergal to do, students must interpret "the western gate." It will help to notice all the imagery of time and seasons in the poem. The *West* in most poetry is often associated with death because the sun sets in the west. (For an illuminating comparison, notice how the aged Ulysses in Tennyson's poem sails west "beyond the sunset, and the baths / Of all the western stars until I die.") Let students spend the time necessary to figure "the western gate" out by themselves. At that point, it will be easy for them to discuss whether Havergal should follow this questionable advisor and his deadly suggestion.

MyLiteratureLab Resources. Critical essay on "Luke Havergal."

Ted Hughes, HAWK ROOSTING, page 27

Hughes's beautifully unnerving "Hawk Roosting" provides an excellent basis for any classroom discussion of poetic voice and persona. The poem is a dramatic monologue spoken by a non-human voice—a powerful antidote to any student who believes all poems are direct autobiographical statements from the author's life. A lesser poet might have settled merely for the basic situation of the poem—the world seen from the hawk's perspective. Hughes explores the deeper implications of his subject. Using human language, he tries to articulate how alien the hawk's worldview is to our own. The effect is quietly astonishing.

When writers treat animals as their subjects, they often become sentimental. They project human emotions and values—often childish ones—on the animals and overly dramatize these situations, especially the vulnerability of creatures in nature. The resulting stories—from *Bambi* and *The Wind in the Willows* to *Watership Down*—are often compelling stories, but they tell us more about the author than the animals because they completely humanize their subjects. Hughes instead emphasizes how differently a hawk might view existence. "Hawk Roosting" reveals a predator's perspective—merciless, efficient, and utterly self-assured. The hawk sits "in the top of the wood" both literally and metaphorically. It rests on the top of the food chain. ("I kill where I please because it is all mine.") Perfectly adapted to its ecological niche, it also sees the world finely suited to its own needs. ("The convenience of the high trees!")

The poem disturbs us not only for its celebration of predation but also because it suggests how many of our own assumptions about the world depend upon our being members of our own species, *homo sapiens*.

Suji Kwock Kim, MONOLOGUE FOR AN ONION, page 28

Archibald MacLeish famously states that "A poem should not mean / But be" ("Ars Poetica"). We might half-seriously state the theme of this poem as "An onion does not mean; it is." Though the onion moves us to tears, it remains cool and detached, and even as it is being chopped to bits, the speaker unsparingly slices through what it sees as the pretension, sentimentality, and self-delusion of the human heart in its quest for "meaning." The onion prides itself on its integrity, the purity of its "union / Of outside and in, surface and secret core," in contrast to the human being "divided at the heart" both physically and emotionally (just as our hearts will "beat [us] to death" both physically and emotionally). From its heartless depths, it sneers at the wreckage that we inflict on ourselves and on everything around us. While it protests humanity's waste and squalor, its disdain for our emotional wallowing is at the furthest remove from "Be gentle with me because I am just like you." We can no doubt take a lesson from the onion's rebuke of some of our worst excesses, but it is difficult to imagine that the author wholly endorses its viewpoint. It is our egg-breaking, omelet-making quest for meaning that makes us most human in the best sense of the term; like the figures depicted on Keats's Grecian urn, the onion, while spared from our worst excesses, is also cut off from our glories and fulfillments.

William Wordsworth, I WANDERED LONELY AS A CLOUD, page 29
Dorothy Wordsworth, JOURNAL ENTRY, page 30

To point out the distance between art and reporting, it may be helpful to read Wordsworth's poem aloud—at least part of it. In their rhythm, lines such as "Fluttering and dancing in the breeze" and "Tossing their heads in sprightly dance" make the motion of the daffodils come alive. By comparison, Dorothy Wordsworth's record of the incident ("the rest tossed and reeled and danced") seems merely excellent prose.

Wordsworth's sister was a distinguished poet in her own right, as Hyman Eigerman demonstrates in *The Poetry of Dorothy Wordsworth* (New York: Columbia UP, 1940), an anthology of passages from her journals arranged into formally open verse.

MLL *MyLiteratureLab Resources*. Biography, critical overview, and bibliography for Wordsworth.

James Stephens, A GLASS OF BEER, page 30

The high regard of the Irish for the magical powers of speech has given them a long and glorious tradition of poetic cursing. In the ancient tales of the Ulster saga, we read of kings who wouldn't go to battle without an accompanying druid: a poet-priest charged with pronouncing magnificent metrical curses upon the enemy. Who knows?—in the pubs of Stephens's native Dublin, curses like the one in "A Glass of Beer" may well have seemed ordinary, even mild.

Although the speaker—some frustrated drinker hard up for cash—is in a towering rage at the barmaid who denied him, the tone of the poem is not anger but high amusement. There is irony, too, in the obvious contrast between the speaker's stupendous hyperboles and the puny occasion for them. Save this poem, if you like, for teaching figures of speech.

There is hardly a better modern poem, however, for reminding students that the feelings expressed in poetry aren't always positive. A poem may be written in rage or chagrin, as well as in love or joy. This seems an essential truth and one that XJK has tried to demonstrate at some length in *Tygers of Wrath: Poems of Hate, Anger, and Invective* (Athens: U of Georgia P, 1981), an annotated anthology showing the tradition of dark emotion in British, Irish, and American poetry from the Middle Ages to the present. Naturally, in this tradition, "A Glass of Beer" holds an honored place.

"A Glass of Beer" is a free translation from the Irish of Daíbhí Ó Bruadair (c. 1625–1698). The original with a translation by Thomas Kinsella ("A Shrewish, Barren, Bony, Nosey Servant") is given by Seán Ó Tuama and Kinsella in *An Duanaire: An Irish Anthology* (Philadelphia: U of Pennsylvania P, 1981) 116–17.

Anne Sexton, HER KIND, page 31

This poem was one of Sexton's favorites, and she usually recited it as the opening of her public readings. (She even named a rock performance group with which she was briefly involved "Anne Sexton and Her Kind.") Published in her first collection, *To Bedlam and Part Way Back* (1960), it became her signature poem.

Who is the speaker? It may help to know that, according to Diane Middlebrook's fascinating *Anne Sexton: A Biography* (Boston: Houghton, 1991), the first draft was titled "Night Voice on a Broomstick" and a later draft labeled "Witch." But there really do seem to be two voices in the poem—one a witch, the other a housewife (see lines 9–11 with their "skillets, carvings, shelves, / closets, silks, innumerable goods; / fixed suppers for worms and elves"). Middlebrook calls this technique "the double 'I,'" and she points out how at the end of each stanza, the speaker "steps through the frame of 'like that' to witness, interpret, and affirm her alter ego . . . ."

William Carlos Williams, The Red Wheelbarrow, page 32

Evidently many readers have found it easy to admire this poem without feeling a need to know the circumstances in which it was written. For an interesting appreciation, see Louis Untermeyer, *The Pursuit of Poetry* (New York: Simon, 1969) 25. Untermeyer views the poem as a kind of haiku that makes us aware of glories in commonplaces. A more sharply critical estimate is that of Roy Harvey Pearce in his fine essay "Williams and the 'New Mode'" in *The Continuity of American Poetry* (Princeton: Princeton UP, 1961) 335–48. Pearce charges the poem with sentimentality: "At its worst this is togetherness in a chickenyard." However, in Pearce's view, the poem also has a better aspect: what "depends" is the poet's vocation as a poet. He needs common objects in order to write poems, and the objects in turn need him to imagine them into poetry.

Direct your students to the first writing topic on page 49 that provides some biographical information on the "inspiration" for this poem. If the librarian is right about the situation in which the poem was written, "The Red Wheelbarrow" seems a better poem than we had realized: a kind of prayer, a work of compassion. However, that the poem fails to give us an intimation of the reasons for the poet's feelings (and of why we ought to share them) does expose it to Pearce's accusation that it is sentimental. Whatever the instructor's opinion, students may be invited to debate the merits and demerits of the poem.

MyLiteratureLab Resources. Biography, critical overview, and bibliography for Williams.

Irony

Robert Creeley, Oh No, page 32

"What interests me about 'Oh No' is its tone," Cynthia Edelberg remarks in an interview with the poet. "How would you describe it?" Creeley replies that he sees it as wry irony, the poem being "self-parody," a comment on his feelings at the time. "As Joel Oppenheimer said, that would qualify me to be a Jew. He really liked that poem. It's that kind of humor" (Edelberg's *Robert Creeley's Poetry: A Critical Introduction* [Albuquerque: U of New Mexico P, 1978] 168).

"Oh No" seems to be another poem about where you arrive when you die. Creeley, we suspect, kids a conventional notion of heaven: he makes it a smug, artificial place where the saved sit around smirking at one another.

W. H. Auden, The Unknown Citizen, page 34

For making students better aware of irony, Auden's familiar satire remains as dependable as any poem we know. Little seems to have dated in it, other than the praise of the citizen for adding five children to the population. Students are usually good at seeing that, unlike the unknown soldier, the citizen is all too thoroughly identified; and that, nevertheless, his true nature and inmost wants remain unknown. Meaty questions for discussion naturally arise: What are the premises of such a society? It seems dedicated to the proposition that to conform to a norm is the highest virtue—any individual traits, of course, being an annoyance to statisticians. What is a "Modern Man?" One with animal needs, but no aspirations. The epitaph, often overlooked, is worth dwelling on: it tells us at once that the unknown citizen is only a number, and that bureaucrats keep track of him—and, incidentally, like the rest of the poem, the epitaph is in rime.

"The Unknown Citizen" is one of six poems in this chapter in which we hear a voice obviously not the poet's. (The others are the ones by Robinson, Hughes, Betjeman, Stephens, and Blake.)

MyLiteratureLab Resources. Biography, critical overview, and bibliography for Auden.

Sharon Olds, RITES OF PASSAGE, page 35

This poem will not require much explanation. Anyone familiar with six- and seven-year-old boys will understand the situation. The interesting exercise in class is to search out the ironic metaphors and language in the poem ("short men," "small bankers," "celebrating my son's life") and then discuss their effect on our reading of the poem. If some students complain that the poem overstates its case and makes too much of the boys' penchant for mock violence, it will provide a good opportunity to ask if a poem (and one might even classify this short descriptive work as "lyric," since it explores a moment's perception) needs to provide a balanced view of life or if it is acceptable to create the sudden, overwhelming, and perhaps unbalanced emotions we feel in a particular moment or situation.

John Betjeman, IN WESTMINSTER ABBEY, page 36

Cadogan Square was an especially fashionable London address around the turn of the century, and the fact that the reader owns stocks (line 30) also indicates her style of life. Her mind, however, is ordinary: her ideals seem bounded by drugstore novels and by plumbing that works properly.

Students usually have a fine time picking out the easy contradictions in the lady's beliefs: that the Lord may allow bombs to hit German women but not English women; that He protects whites more dutifully than blacks; that it is all very well for the "gallant blacks" to die, but let the Empire remain united; that democracy and class distinction go hand in hand.

The speaker's attitude seems to be: "Let God wait upon my convenience." To call His word a "treat" reduces Scripture to the importance of candy. That Betjeman first printed this ironic blast at smug, hate-mongering chauvinism in the midst of World War II strikes us as a brave and large-minded plea for genuine Christian charity.

Sarah N. Cleghorn, THE GOLF LINKS, page 37

What a great epigram!—no verbal irony in it, just matter-of-fact notation of a social condition that seems ironic in the extreme. As Robert Frost said in his introduction to Cleghorn's autobiography, *Threescore* (1936), "There is more high explosive for righteousness in the least little line of Sarah Cleghorn's poem about the children working in the mill . . . than in all the prose of our radical-bound-boys pressed together under a weight of several atmospheres of revolution." (The conservative Frost didn't like Marxists, but he called Cleghorn "a saint and a reformer" anyway.) For a more recent tribute, see Irving Dilliard, "Four Short Lines," *The Nation* 222 (10 Apr. 1976): 444–45.

Stanley Kunitz and Howard Hayward's *Twentieth Century Authors* (New York: Wilson, 1942), in an article on Cleghorn that she apparently helped write, explains the twenty-year hiatus between her early books and her later ones: "This was caused by the fact that her socialism and pacifism made editors and publishers reluctant to use her later writing, and partly by the fact that in middle age she became a teacher." Among her other works is a novel, *The Spinster* (1916), and a last collection, *Poems of Peace and Freedom* (1945).

Edna St. Vincent Millay, SECOND FIG, page 37

This couplet is the second poem in Millay's volume *A Few Figs from Thistles*, whose title may remind you of A. E. Housman's lines "Out of a stem that scored the hand / I wrung it in a weary land." Like the "First Fig," the universally known quatrain that begins "My candle burns at both ends," this poem celebrates the brief and beautiful in contrast to the substantial and dull. It is of course ironic that the speaker should disdain what is "safe" and "solid" in favor of that which is built upon the sand, but "ugly" in the first line and "shining" in the second should leave us in no doubt regarding the author's intentions.

 *MyLiteratureLab Resources*. Biography and photos for Millay.

Joseph Stroud, MISSING, page 38

1. *Is the first line of this poem sarcastic? Why or why not?* Rather than being "conspicuously bitter, heavy-handed, and mocking" (the attributes of sarcasm discussed in the textbook), the tone of the opening line of this poem is gentle and somewhat wistful. The speaker is not mocking anyone, not even himself; he is expressing his feeling of being more and more out of touch with the world and the family he knew (and may have loved—he doesn't really say) when he was nine or ten years old.

2. *What do you make of the poem's last word?* The speaker is now out of touch with that little boy, with whom, as the poem's last word suggests, he no longer seems to identify, perceiving the boy instead as someone completely separate from the man he has become.

Thomas Hardy, THE WORKBOX, page 38

Dramatic irony is present in the discrepancy between the carpenter's limited knowledge and the reader's growing conviction that the wife knew John much better than she cares to admit. Her phrase "mere accidental things" contains verbal irony, and in general the whole speech in lines 25–28 is a verbal irony.

Cosmic irony may be operating too (and one is sure that it is, knowing Hardy) in the Fate or chance that caused the carpenter to select a piece of poor John's coffin out of all pieces of wood in the world.

To us, the situation in the poem had seemed like that in James Joyce's "The Dead": the wife, by remembering a young man who died of love for her, has a bleak realization that she might have known a joyous life had she married him instead. However, Albert Furtwangler and his students at Mount Allison University found other possible levels of irony, as he kindly wrote to report. For Professor Furtwangler, "The Workbox" is marred by an excess of irony that runs too deep: "it remains fascinating in the long run more as a puzzle than as a clear disclosure of character." Among other readings he considered the two following, which he thinks overingenious and yet consistent with the poem.

The husband, aware of his wife's past, has contrived his present as a cunning torture for her. "He seems to offer it in love, but takes pleasure in drawing out his wife's confused replies . . . thus trapping her in her own hypocrisy."

The husband knows his wife's history; and she knows that he knows it. "But they coexist uneasily with each other by exercising an elaborate fiction of ignorance."

What will you and your students decide?

J. O. Bailey sees in this poem the "ballad-like theme of the lover who died of grief when his beloved married another." Like traditional English and Scottish ballads, the poem has a question-and-answer structure and ends in a surprise. (See *The Poetry of Thomas Hardy* [Chapel Hill: U of North Carolina P, 1970].) Compare "The Workbox" in these respects with "Bonny Barbara Allan."

MyLiteratureLab Resources. Biography, critical overview, and bibliography for Hardy.

For Review and Further Study

William Blake, The Chimney Sweeper, page 39

Set next to Cleghorn's "Golf Links," Blake's song will seem larger and more strange; yet the two poets seem comparable in their hatred of adults who enslave children. Though Blake is not a child, he obviously shares Tom Dacre's wish that the chimney sweepers be freed from their coffinlike chimneys, washed clean, and restored to childhood joys. The punning cry "'weep! 'weep! 'weep! 'weep!" is the street cry of the sweepers, sent through London to advertise their services. Compare the tone of this poem to that of Blake's "London"; the anger is similar, but in "The Chimney Sweeper," a poem also touching and compassionate, anger is not stated outright, but only implied.

Tom Dacre's dream has a basis in reality: in Blake's time, sweeps were often sent up chimneys naked, the better to climb through narrow spaces (and thus saving the expense of protective clothing). Martin K. Nurmi points out this fact in his essay "Fact and Symbol in 'The Chimney Sweeper' of Blake's *Songs of Innocence*" (*Bulletin of the New York Public Library* 68 [April 1964] 249–56). "Naked immersion in soot, therefore, is Tom's normal state now, and naked white cleanliness is its natural opposite."

Refer your students to the interesting commentary on "The Chimney Sweeper" by Camille Paglia in the chapter "Critical Approaches to Literature."

Music to "The Chimney Sweeper" has been supplied by Allen Ginsberg, who sings on *Songs of Innocence and Experience* (MGM recording FTS 3083), assisted by Peter Orlovsky.

MyLiteratureLab Resources. Photographs and biographical information for Blake. Audio clip and critical essay on "The Chimney Sweeper."

David Lehman, REJECTION SLIP, page 40

The humor here is obvious, as the first four stanzas carry their speaker through increasingly absurd exaggerations on the theme of sour grapes. The final stanza enlarges the frame of reference, and with it enlarges our perspective on what is happening in the poem. For those who know the statement, it is almost impossible to read "Rejection Slip" without being reminded of John Berryman's notorious comment in his *Paris Review* interview, published in 1972 (the year of his suicide, provoked largely by the chaos his alcoholism had made of his life): "The artist is extremely lucky who is presented with the worst possible ordeal which will not actually kill him. At that point, he's in business. . . . I hope to nearly be crucified." Lehman deftly skewers the image, nurtured by the so-called Confessional poets, of the poet as a wounded and self-destructive soul who fashions great art out of extreme states of misery and self-pity; the final stanza indicts as well the audience whose responsiveness encourages such themes and such behavior. Lehman's own attitude would seem to be much more in line with the corrective offered by Lewis Hyde: "In the future it would be nice if it were a little harder for the poet to come to town drunk and have everyone think that it's great fun."

William Stafford, AT THE UN-NATIONAL MONUMENT ALONG THE CANADIAN BORDER, page 41

This is a wonderful poem that celebrates an even more wonderful event—that two neighboring countries have lived in peace for nearly two hundred years. (It may be worthwhile in class to ask the obvious *factual* question about what this poem celebrates.)

Stafford's poem uses language memorably in at least two unusual ways. First, the poem characterizes the scene mainly by what did *not* happen there—no battles, no deaths, no monument, no memorable historical events of any kind. Second, Stafford consciously invokes the central non-event by borrowing the diction of patriotic oratory: heroic, soldier, battle, monument, ground, hallowed, people, celebrate. (One wonders if Lincoln's "Gettysburg Address" was in the back of Stafford's mind.) But Stafford uses these words in exactly the opposite way from an old-fashioned commemorative oration.

H. L. Hix, I LOVE THE WORLD, AS DOES ANY DANCER, page 41

H. L. Hix's exuberant short love poem is actually an individual section of his long, lyrical, and meditative sequence "Orders of Magnitude," which appeared in his second collection, *Rational Numbers* (2000). One remarkable aspect of this richly realized poem is how imaginatively it employs tactile imagery to communicate its effects. The dancer (and the speaker) love the world with the tips of their toes. The twenty digits of his hands and feet "tenders" the many textures of the world. The sensations that naked feet feel are listed: lush wet grass, piles of rose petals, hot summer sidewalks, sand, dirt, and finally the body of the beloved. The poem asserts the delectable continuity of all those phenomena for the speaker, for whom marital love is an extension of his physical joy in the world. Surely the human toes have never been more joyously acknowledged in verse.

Richard Lovelace, To Lucasta, page 42

"To Lucasta" may refer to an actual parting. During the Puritan Revolution of 1642–1645, Lovelace fought in the service of Charles I. Students will readily see the poet's theme that Honor (duty to God and King) takes priority over duty to Lucasta; the tone of the poem may give them greater difficulty. The closing line makes a serious affirmation: Honor for Lovelace is not an "old Lie," but a creed. Neither grim nor smug, the poem has wit and loving tenderness. The witty second stanza seems almost comic in its figures of speech: having renounced Lucasta's nunlike chastity and calm, the speaker will now go and whet his sword upon the body of someone wilder.

Wilfred Owen, Dulce et Decorum Est, page 42

Owen's theme is apparent: death in battle is hideous, no matter what certain ignorant poets say about it. For us, there seems irony in the fact that Owen himself was to be killed in action in France. Although in a wartime letter he called himself "a conscientious objector with a very seared conscience," Owen in this poem does not question that to die for one's country may be necessary. His attitude is overpowering disgust—with the butchery of war, with those who idealize it.

MyLiteratureLab Resources. Longman Lecture, interactive reading, and critical essay on "Dulce et Decorum Est."

Writers on Writing

Wilfred Owen, War Poetry, pages 43–44

Owen's fragmentary notes toward a preface to his still unpublished book are tremendously eloquent. It is interesting to find that Owen's heightened prose often reads like poetry.

A good classroom question is what Owen sees as the purpose of poetry. He does not see the contemporary poet as having direct political power, although there was a strong political element in the poems he wrote during the Great War. Instead, Owen sees the poet's role as telling the truth. By speaking the truth about difficult and, in this case, tragic events, the poet *warns*. Owen's sense of truth-telling predicts the current concept of poetry as witnessing.

3
Words

LITERAL MEANING: WHAT A POEM SAYS FIRST

Why a whole section on literal meaning? The need first occurred to XJK in a conversation with Robert Reiter and David Anderson of Boston College. Professor Reiter, who had been using the book in a previous edition, pointed out that, while it was well to encourage students to read poetry for its suggestions, his students tended to go too far in that direction and sometimes needed to have their attention bolted down to the denotations of words on a page. Early in a poetry course, the problem seemed especially large—"I try not to let them look for any symbols until after Thanksgiving!" Mr. Anderson had felt the same difficulty. In teaching Donne's "Batter my heart" sonnet, he had had to argue with students who couldn't see how, in a poem of spiritual aspiration, Donne could possibly be referring to anything so grossly physical as rape. They needed to see the plain, literal basis of Donne's tremendous metaphor, that they might then go on to understand the poet's conception of sanctifying grace.

With these comments in mind, the publishers sent a questionnaire to more than one hundred instructors who had used the book, asking them (among other questions) whether they felt the need for more emphasis on denotation. All who replied said that they would welcome such an emphasis (in addition to the emphasis on connotation)—all, that is, except for one instructor (God help him) who reported that he couldn't persuade his students to rise *above* the level of the literal, if indeed he could get them to rise that far.

Most instructors like to discuss imagery fairly early. They will find nothing to hinder them from taking the chapter on imagery ahead of this one. Another procedure would be to defer "Imagery" until after having discussed both denotation and connotation—taking in sequence the present chapter, "Words," and the following chapter, "Saying and Suggesting."

William Carlos Williams, THIS IS JUST TO SAY, page 51

Williams once recalled that this poem was an actual note he had written to his wife—"and she replied very beautifully. Unfortunately, I've lost it. I think what she wrote was quite as good as this" (conversation with John W. Gerber and Emily M. Wallace in *Interviews with William Carlos Williams*, ed. Linda Welshimer Wagner [New York: New Directions, 1976]).

For parodies of this famous poem, see Kenneth Koch's "Variations on a Theme by William Carlos Williams" in *Contemporary American Poetry*, ed. A. Poulin (Boston: Houghton, 1980), and other anthologies.

 *MyLiteratureLab Resources*. Biography, critical overview, and bibliography for Williams.

Marianne Moore, SILENCE, page 52

This poem appears autobiographical on the surface, but the notes that Marianne Moore scrupulously appended to her poems make it clear that it is a composite, imaginary portrait of a father. (Moore barely knew her father, who had suffered a nervous breakdown shortly after her birth; perhaps, for that reason, imaginary fathers were all the more important to her.) The first five lines were adapted from a "Miss A. M. Homans," according to Moore. "Make my house your inn" is a quotation from Edmund Burke, to which Moore added her telling last line. The father in the poem presumably lived in Cambridge, Massachusetts (from references to Longfellow's grave and Harvard), a town in which Moore never resided. We belabor these facts and sources only to demonstrate that poems are often not so autobiographical as they might seem.

A central theme of "Silence" is the eloquence of understatement and restraint. The poet Donald Hall praises this poem in his study *Marianne Moore: The Cage and the Animal* (New York: Pegasus, 1970), saying that by "eschewing the easy words for the ambiguous emotion," Moore displays "a species of honesty and not evidence of lack of depth." Precision is another key term. Notice how important the speaker considers distinctions between related words and situations (*silence/restraint, inn/residence*).

Robert Graves, DOWN, WANTON, DOWN!, page 53

This poem can be an astonisher, especially if students haven't read it in advance. One freshman group XJK sprang it on provided a beautiful gamut of reactions from stunned surprise to hilarity. At first, most didn't know quite what to make of the poem, but they soon saw that its puns and metaphors point to details of male and female anatomy; in catching these, they found themselves looking to literal meanings. After further discussion, they decided that the poem, however witty, makes a serious point about the blindness of lust. To get at this point, students may be asked to sum up the contrast Graves is drawing between Love and Beauty and the wanton's approach to them.

The title (and opening line) echo a phrase from Shakespeare in a passage about eels being rolled into a pie (*King Lear*, II, iv, 118–123):

> LEAR: O me, my heart, my rising heart! But down!
>
> FOOL: Cry to it, nuncle, as the cockney did to the eels when she put 'em i' th' paste alive. She knapped 'em o' th' coxcombs with a stick and cried, "Down, wantons, down!" 'Twas her brother that, in pure kindness to his horse, buttered his hay.

One instructor at a community college in New Jersey has reported an embarrassing experience. One morning, not having had time to prepare for class, he introduced this poem without having read it first. "What's it about?" he queried, and someone in the class replied, "An erection." "WHAT?" he exploded. "Come on, now, let's look at it *closely*. . . ." But as he stared at the poem before him, a chill stole over him. Luckily, he was saved by the bell.

John Donne, BATTER MY HEART, THREE-PERSONED GOD, FOR YOU, page 53

On Donne's last line: the literature of mysticism is full of accounts of spiritual experience seen in physical terms; any students who wish to pursue the matter might be directed, for instance, to the poems of St. John of the Cross (which have been splendidly translated by John Frederick Nims).

John E. Parish has shown that Donne's poem incorporates two metaphors, both worn and familiar: the traditional Christian comparison of the soul to a maiden and Christ to a bridegroom, and the Petrarchan conceit of the reluctant woman as a castle and her lover as an invading army. Donne brilliantly combines the two into a new whole. In lines 1 to 4, the sinner's heart is like a walled town fallen to Satan, the enemy. Now God the rightful King approaches and knocks for entrance. But merely to knock won't do—the King must break open the gates with a battering ram. The verbs in these lines all suggest the act of storming a citadel, "and even *blowe* may be intended to suggest the use of gunpowder to blow up the fortress" ("No. 14 of Donne's *Holy Sonnets*," *College English* 24 [January 1963]: 299–302).

"The paradox of death and rebirth, the central paradox of Christianity" is (according to A. L. Clements in another commentary) the organizing principle of the poem. To illustrate the paradox of destroying in order to revive, Donne employs two sorts of figurative language: one, military and destructive; the other, marital and uniting ("Donne's 'Holy Sonnet XIV,'" *Modern Language Notes* 76 [June 1961]: 484–89).

Both the Clements and the Parish articles are reprinted, together with four other discussions of the poem, in *John Donne's Poetry*, edited by Clements (New York: Norton, 1966).

It is hard to talk for long about rhythm in poetry without citing the opening lines of "Batter my heart." Both in meter and in meaning, they must be among the most powerful lines in English poetry.

MyLiteratureLab Resources. Biography, critical overview, and bibliography for Donne.

THE VALUE OF A DICTIONARY

Henry Wadsworth Longfellow, AFTERMATH, page 55

Like many seemingly abstract words, *aftermath* was originally a concrete descriptive term that referred to the usually meager second growth of crop in a field that had already been mowed that season: *after* + *math* (an obsolete word for *mowing*). Once you read Longfellow's quietly moving poem, you'll never forget the etymology. "Aftermath" shows how poets usually employ words with careful consideration of their histories.

"Aftermath" provides a literal description of mowing the second growth in a winter field, but the treatment suggests a hidden symbolic meaning. Longfellow is careful not to specify exactly what the subtext is and leaves every reader free to project his or her own private meaning into the poem. The structure of Longfellow's insight, however, is painfully clear: to revisit a scene of the past can be devastating.

Fledged means "having feathers" and refers to young birds who are now old enough to have grown feathers and flown from their nests. *Rowen* is a synonym for *aftermath*, a season's second crop, usually of hay.

John Clare, MOUSE'S NEST, page 56

The connection between the final couplet and the rest of the poem is one of metaphor. Small trickles of water that "scarce could run" are newborn mice; "broad old cesspools," their mother.

Milton Klonsky has praised the poem in his anthology of graphic and pictorial poetry, *Speaking Pictures* (New York: Harmony, 1975). He admires "the cinematic flow of Clare's imagery, with each picture flashing by to be replaced by the next before its own afterimage has completely faded." This comment might be discussed—do students agree that Clare's poem seems cinematic and contemporary?

A few facts of Clare's heartbreaking life might interest students. Born into grinding poverty, the son of a field laborer in Northamptonshire, Clare enjoyed brief fame for his *Poems Descriptive of Rural Life* (1820). Lionized by Coleridge and other London literati as an untutored genius, he was then forgotten. The latter half of his life was spent in lunatic asylums, where he wrote some remarkable lyrics and (under the delusion that he was Lord Byron) a continuation of *Don Juan*. Theodore Roethke, whose work shows a similar delight in close-up views of living creatures, has paid tribute (in his poem "Heard in a Violent Ward") to "that sweet man, John Clare."

J. V. Cunningham, FRIEND, ON THIS SCAFFOLD THOMAS MORE LIES DEAD, page 57

Cunningham's epigram states a metaphor: it likens two famous separations decreed by Henry VIII. Separation of the Body (the Church of England) from the Head (the Pope) is like the decapitation of More, who had opposed it. A possible original for Cunningham's epigram, a Latin epigram by John Owen (1606), has been discovered by Charles Clay Doyle:

> Abscindi passus caput est a corpore Morus;
>   Abscindi corpus noluit a capite.

In 1659 Thomas Pecke rendered it into English:

> What though Head was from Body severed!
>   *More* would not let Body be cut from Head.

Doyle remarks that in fact More played down the role of the Pope as "head" of the Church, preferring the allegorical view (derived from Paul) of Christ as head upon the Church's body ("The Hair and Beard of Thomas More," *Moreana* 18, 71–72 [Nov. 1981]: 5–14).

Kelly Cherry, ADVICE TO A FRIEND WHO PAINTS, page 58

The seemingly incongruous images of this poem are all common subjects in the paintings of Cezanne. The first question to ask the class is "Who is Cezanne?" Then ask how catching that allusion helps us understand the poem. It will also heighten the immediacy of the poem if one brings a book of his paintings into class. Almost any book on the artist will illustrate most if not all of the images in the poem.

Once the role of allusion is understood in the poem, it is interesting to ask students what the final line implies about the speaker's attitude toward the painter-friend in the title. What message does the poem subtly give the "tearing, tugging" painter-friend?

Carl Sandburg, GRASS, page 58

Carl Sandburg's poem, which was written while World War I was still raging, incorporates five place names into its brief length. All five proper nouns are the names of famously bloody battlegrounds. Austerlitz and Waterloo were scenes of major battles in the Napoleonic Wars. Gettysburg refers, of course, to the decisive Civil War battle in Pennsylvania. Ypres and Verdun were the sites of the battles in World War I that still rank among the deadliest military engagements in human history. Since the allusions are all used in parallel ways, a reader should be able to understand the role of any battle he or she does not know from the context as long as he or she recognizes some of the names.

It might be worth asking the class who is speaking in the poem. The speaker is the grass itself, a symbol of the natural world's enduring ability to reassert its power over human history. This aspect of Nature is often viewed in harsh terms, but Sandburg's poem displays it in a gentle, consolatory way. In historical terms, one might consider Sandburg's poem a vision of peace in the final days of World War I.

WORD CHOICE AND WORD ORDER

An exercise to make a class more aware of *le mot juste* is suggested by W. Jackson Bate and David Perkins in *British and American Poets* (San Diego: Harcourt, 1986). Print out several lines of a poem, with an admirably chosen word or words left out. Let students suggest ways to fill in the blank and debate their choices. Then the instructor whips out a trump card: the way the poet filled in the blank—if you're lucky, to "a collective sigh of appreciation."

Robert Herrick, UPON JULIA'S CLOTHES, page 60

This short classic is included in the book by popular demand. The poem deserves inclusion for beauty's sake alone, but it is also mighty useful in the classroom to illustrate the power of diction. *Liquefaction* is an unforgettable word in Herrick's poem—a strong metaphor clothed in suave music. Note that the poem contains only two Latinate words (one in each stanza)—*liquefaction* and *vibration*. Both of them are employed and positioned for their special resonance. Students will also learn something about the history of English by looking up *brave* in a dictionary. Herrick uses it here in a now slightly archaic sense to mean "finely dressed" or "splendidly turned out," though by Shakespeare's time the adjective was also employed, according to the *OED*, as "a general epithet of admiration." Remember Miranda's famous exclamation in *The Tempest*: "O brave new world / That has such people in't."

Kay Ryan, BLANDEUR, page 62

Kay Ryan's witty poem demonstrates that on certain occasions writers can invent the words they need. (Ryan actually coins two related words in her poem—the noun *blandeur* and the verb *blanden*.) Although the poem is in one sense a joke, it also seemingly reflects a sincere desire for the comfortable average rather than the sublime extremes of human experience. The poem states its preference for the undramatic "mean" and not for grand and terrible excess.

Ryan's poem is written in short free verse lines wonderfully interwoven with many irregular rimes. Many rimes occur at the ends of lines—*happen/flatten/blanden/Canyon*, *fissures/your*, and *hearts/parts*—but others appear elsewhere in the line like *rondure/fissures*, *hand/remand*, *calving/halving*. The effect of this intricate and unexpected riming is to slow down our reading and hear the many interconnections of sound and sense.

Thomas Hardy, THE RUINED MAID, page 63

In a London street, an innocent girl from Dorset encounters a friend who has run away from life on the farm. Now a well-paid prostitute, 'Melia calls herself *ruined* with cheerful irony. That this maid has been made, it would seem, has been the making of her. Hardy, of course, is probably less stricken with awe before 'Melia's glamorous clothes than is the first speaker. As the *ain't* in the last line indicates, 'Melia's citified polish doesn't go deep.

For a sequel to "The Ruined Maid," see "A Daughter Returns" in Hardy's last collection of poetry, *Winter Words*. With "Dainty-cut raiment" and "earrings of pearl," a runaway daughter returns to her country home only to be spurned by her father for having lost her innocence.

MyLiteratureLab Resources. Biography, critical overview, and bibliography for Hardy. Critical essay on "The Ruined Maid."

Richard Eberhart, THE FURY OF AERIAL BOMBARDMENT, page 64

Dr. Johnson said that technical language is inadmissible to poetry, but in the case of Eberhart's poem it is hard to agree. We do not need to know the referents of "belt feed lever" and "belt holding pawl" in order to catch the poet's meaning. Indeed, he evidently chooses these terms as specimens of a jargon barely comprehensible to the unlucky gunnery students who failed to master it. At a reading of his poems in public, Eberhart once remarked that he had added the last stanza as an afterthought. The tone (it seems to us) remains troubled and sorrowful but shifts from loftiness and grandeur to matter-of-fact. This shift takes place in diction as well: from the generality of "infinite spaces," "multitudinous will," "eternal truth," and "the Beast" in man's soul down to "Names on a list," "lever," and "pawl." The poem is a wonderful instance of a poet's writing himself into a fix—getting snarled in unanswerable questions—and then triumphantly saving the day (and his poem) by suddenly returning with a bump to the ordinary, particular world.

Wendy Cope, LONELY HEARTS, page 65

Wendy Cope's bittersweet villanelle demonstrates that old forms can easily accommodate new content, as long as the poet has enough imagination and skill.

Students never seem to have trouble understanding this poem. It is a fun exercise to have students write an additional personal ad in the same rime scheme, but, if you use this idea, be prepared for some odd results.

You might suggest that students read the biographical note on Cope in the "Lives of the Poets" section. Her late-blooming career and personal problems may add a personal dimension to this poem. If she is making gentle fun of the authors of personal ads, she also understands their emotional needs.

FOR REVIEW AND FURTHER STUDY

E. E. Cummings, ANYONE LIVED IN A PRETTY HOW TOWN, page 66

Trained in the classical languages, Cummings borrows from Latin the freedom to place a word in practically any location within a sentence. The first two lines are easy to unscramble: "How pretty a town anyone lived in, with so many bells floating up [and] down." The scrambling is artful, and pedestrian words call attention to themselves by being seen in an unusual order.

The hero and heroine of the poem are anyone and noone, whose names recall the pronoun-designated principals in Cummings's play "Him"—hero Him and heroine Me. Are they Everyman and Everywoman? Not at all: they're different; they're strong, loving individuals whom the poet contrasts with those drab women and men of line 5, "both little and small," who dully sow isn't (negation) and reap same (conformity). Unlike the wise noone and anyone, the everyones of line 17 apparently think they're really somebody.

In tracing the history of anyone and noone from childhood through their mature love to their death and burial, Cummings, we think, gives a brief tour through life in much the way that Thornton Wilder does in *Our Town*. But not all readers will agree. R. C. Walsh thinks that, in the last two stanzas, anyone and noone do not literally die but grow into loveless and lifeless adults, whose only hope of rejuvenation is to have children (*Explicator* 22 [May 1964]: item 72). But it seems unlike Cummings to make turncoats of his individualists. Bounded by the passage of the seasons, the rain, and the heavens, the mortal lives of anyone and noone seem concluded in their burial. But in the next-to-last stanza they go on sleeping in love and faith, dreaming of their resurrection.

 *MyLiteratureLab Resources.* Photographs and biographical information for Cummings. Audio clip and critical essay on "anyone lived in a pretty how town."

Billy Collins, THE NAMES, page 67

As Robert Francis observed in *The Satirical Rogue on Poetry* (1968): "Now the chief trouble with writing for and about an occasion is that you become so impressed with the importance of the occasion that you are likely to become impressed with the importance of your writing about it. Something big, obviously, is called for." By contrast, in "The Names" Billy Collins never directly mentions the horrific events of September 11, 2001, or the World Trade Center, or even the name of "this city" (line 22), nor does the speaker call attention to (and implicitly expect to be admired for) his own sensitivity. Instead, Collins achieves a great emotional effect through the quiet presentation of an alphabet of representative names of victims, embedding them in the details of the natural world both to show that our awareness of this event, with its immense human loss, has become permanently intertwined with our perceptions of the world about us, and to remind us that human life, like the natural world, is both fleeting and enduring. The effect is underscored by the simplicity and dignity of the poem's style, which is wholly appropriate to the subject and so restrained that, although every line is heavy with the emotions of pain and loss, there is no overt emotional reference at all until the very last line, which is made all the more powerful by the very modesty of its statement.

MyLiteratureLab Resources. Biography, critical overview, and bibliography for Collins. Longman Lecture on "The Names."

EXERCISE: *Different Kinds of English*, page 68

Anonymous, CARNATION MILK, page 68
Kenneth Rexroth, VITAMINS AND ROUGHAGE, page 69
Gina Valdés, ENGLISH CON SALSA, page 69

Students won't need much help to see that "Carnation Milk" is unschooled speech; that Rexroth alternates between straightforward diction and more "educated" phrasing; and that Valdés flavors her English with a strong seasoning of Spanish expressions, just as her title suggests.

Rexroth's "Vitamins and Roughage" turns on the conflict that is stated and resolved in line 6, "That nature is still stronger than man." There are two levels of diction employed, reflecting the two sides of the issue. "Reluctant humanists"—reluctant to acknowledge the primacy of instinct over intellect—and their values are characterized by the polysyllabic intellectual diction that predominates in the poem, but that diction is significantly undercut by the more direct and vivid phrasing of lines 1, 4, and 10. There is also meaningful use of straightforward phrasing in line 12, where intellectual systems are called "games"—flimsy artificial constructs that collapse when assaulted by earthy realities.

Like Rhina P. Espaillat's "Bilingual/Bilingüe," Gina Valdés's "English con Salsa" mixes—or, better, flavors—English diction with Spanish to reinforce its thematic preoccupation with the interaction between cultures. This larger point is quite clearly stated and illustrated throughout the text, but a careful reading will reveal some underlying subtleties: the allusion to the Mixtec language and civilization in the last line is a reminder that other cultures long predate both the English and the Spanish on this continent; the place names in line 27 underscore the fact that the interplay between English and Spanish has existed for centuries; and, despite these facts, lines 6–9 ironically point up the limits of the opportunities that await the new Americans in this ESL class.

Lewis Carroll, JABBERWOCKY, page 70

WRITERS ON WRITING

Lewis Carroll, HUMPTY DUMPTY EXPLICATES "JABBERWOCKY," page 71

"Jabberwocky" has to be heard aloud: you might ask a student to read it, alerting him or her in advance to prepare it, and offering tips on pronunciation. ("The *i* in *slithy* is like the *i* in *slime*; the *a* in *wabe*, like the *a* in *wave*.")

Although Carroll added *chortled* to the dictionary, not all his odd words are invented. *Gyre* of course means "to spin or twist about"—it is used as a noun in Yeats's "Sailing to Byzantium" and "The Second Coming." *Slithy* (sleazy or slovenly), *rath* (an earthen wall), *whiffling* (blowing or puffing), and *callooh* (an arctic duck that winters in Scotland, so named for its call) are legitimate words, too, but Carroll uses them in different senses. *Frabjous* probably owes something to *frab*, a dialect word meaning "to scold, harass, or nag," as Myra Cohn Livingston points out in her anthology *O Frabjous Day!* (New York: Atheneum, 1977).

Writing in 1877 to a child who had inquired what the strange words meant, Carroll replied:

> I am afraid I can't explain "vorpal blade" for you—nor yet "tulgey wood"; but I did make an explanation once for "uffish thought"—it seems to suggest a state of mind when the voice is gruffish, the manner roughish, and the temper huffish. Then again, as to "burble" if you take the three verbs "bleat," "murmur" and "warble," and select the bits I have underlined, it certainly makes "burble": though I am afraid I can't distinctly remember having made it that way.

Students can have fun unpacking other portmanteau words: *gimble (nimble, gambol)*; *frumious* (which Carroll said is *fuming* plus *furious)*; *vorpal (voracious, purple)*, *galumphing (galloping in triumph)*, and so on. *(Uffish* suggests *oafish* too.) Some of these suggestions come from Martin Gardner, who supplies copious notes on the poem (as well as translations of it into French and German) in *The Annotated Alice* (New York: Bramhall, 1960).

All other critics, however, must yield precedence to the estimable Humpty Dumpty, whose definite comments appear in "Writers on Writing" following the poem.

MyLiteratureLab Resources. Longman Lecture, interactive reading, and critical essay on "Jabberwocky."

4
Saying and Suggesting

John Masefield, CARGOES, page 76

Much of the effect of Masefield's contrast depends on rhythms and word-sounds, not just on connotations. In stanza 2, the poet strews his lines with dactyls, producing ripples in his rhythm: *diamonds, emeralds, amethysts, cinnamon.* In the third stanza, paired monosyllables *(salt-caked, smoke stack, Tyne coal, roadrails, pig-lead, firewood)* make for a hard-hitting series of spondees. Internal alliteration helps the contrast, too: all those *m*-sounds in the dactyls; and in the harsher lines "Dirty British coaster with a salt-caked smoke stack, / Butting," all the sounds of the *r*, the *t*, and the staccato *k*.

"Cargoes" abounds with lively, meaningful music, yet Masefield is generally dismissed nowadays as a mere balladeer—a jog-trot chronicler of the lives of the poor and unfortunate. In naming him poet laureate, George V (it is said) mistakenly thought him a hero of the working class; unluckily for his later fame, Masefield, like Wordsworth, enjoyed a long senility.

William Blake, LONDON, page 77

Blake's "London" broadens the themes explored in his "The Chimney Sweeper." The personal pathos of "The Chimney Sweeper" becomes a general indictment of a society in which such exploitation is possible. In "London," we see Blake as a prophetic poet—not prophesying the future like a tabloid seer, but speaking as a prophet who declares the moral necessity of just change in a time of evil.

In his essay "On Blake and His Critics" (1934), G. K. Chesterton singled out the third stanza of "London" for special praise. He called the images "two lightning-flashes revealing two separate Visions of Judgment." It is important to remember that Blake was a Londoner born and bred who spent most of his life within the city limits. He is not a country poet describing urban squalor; he is a native morally dissecting his own home town. He knows every image from the inside out.

If Blake were to walk the streets of an American city today, would he find any conditions similar to those he finds in "London"? Is this poem merely an occasional poem, with a protest valid only for its time, or does it have enduring applications?

MLL *MyLiteratureLab Resources.* Photographs and biographical information for Blake.

Wallace Stevens, DISILLUSIONMENT OF TEN O'CLOCK, page 79

Stevens slings colors with the verve of a Matisse. In this early poem, he paints a suggestive contrast between the pale and colorless homeowners, ghostlike and punctually going to bed at ten, and, on the other hand, the dreams they wouldn't dream of dreaming; and the bizarre and exotic scene inside the drunken head of our disreputable hero, the old seafarer. Who in the world would wear a beaded sash or *ceinture?* (A Barbary pirate? An Arabian harem dancer?) Ronald Sukenick has made a terse statement of the poem's theme: "the vividness of the imagination in the dullness of a pallid reality" (*Wallace Stevens: Musing the Obscure* [New York: New York UP, 1967]). Another critic, Edward Kessler, has offered a good paraphrase: "Only the drunkard, the irrational man ('Poetry must be irrational' [*Opus Posthumous* 162]), who is in touch with the unconscious—represented here, and often elsewhere, by the sea—can awake his own passionate nature until his blood is mirrored in the very weather" (*Images of Wallace Stevens* [New Brunswick: Rutgers UP, 1972]).

While they will need to see the contrast between pallor and color, students might be cautioned against lending every color a particular meaning, as if the poem were an allegory.

Stevens expressed further disappointment with monotonous neighbors in a later poem, "Loneliness in Jersey City," which seems a companion piece to this. In Jersey City, "the steeples are empty and so are the people," who can't tell a dachshund from a deer. Both poems probably owe some of their imagery to Stevens's days as a struggling young lawyer living in rooming houses in East Orange, New Jersey, and Fordham Heights, in New York City.

MyLiteratureLab Resources. Biography, critical overview, and bibliography for Stevens.

Gwendolyn Brooks, SOUTHEAST CORNER, page 79

This short poem first appeared in Brooks's debut volume, *A Street in Bronzeville* (1945). The book centered on a group of interrelated poems, including this one, set in Bronzeville, a fictional African American neighborhood in Chicago. In her autobiography *Report from Part One* (Detroit: Broadside P, 1972), Brooks praised Langston Hughes, whom she met during the time she was composing the poems in *A Street in Bronzeville*:

> Mightily did he use the street. He found its multiple heart, its tastes, smells, alarms, formulas, flowers, garbage, and convulsions. He brought them to his table-top. He crushed them to a writing paste. He himself became the pen . . .

In that passage, Brooks seems to be describing her own method in these early poems. Perhaps the key word in the poem is "tan" in line 11. As in others of her early poems, Brooks is concerned here with issues of intraracial prejudice. The Madam (the term inevitably suggests the mistress of a bordello) had engaged in a kind of prostitution, enriching herself by selling skin-lightening and hair-straightening products to African American girls who had been bred to reject themselves and to aspire to Caucasian standards of beauty. Even in death she is contented and impassive, and her gaudy coffin and monument show the same preoccupation with superficial appearances that was the basis of her fortune. Yet Brooks does not criticize the woman, probably born poor, for posthumously displaying her material success. The poet seems to revel in the tomb's ironic opulence.

MyLiteratureLab Resources. Biography, critical overview, and bibliography for Brooks.

Timothy Steele, EPITAPH, page 80

"Silence is golden"—but Sir Tact is obviously a coward, afraid to speak his mind. This epigram is included in Steele's first collection of poems, *Uncertainties and Rest* (Baton Rouge: Louisiana State UP, 1979).

E. E. Cummings, NEXT TO OF COURSE GOD AMERICA I, page 80

Even if the last line and the quotation marks around the rest of the text were omitted, it would be hard to miss the satiric intent of this sonnet. From the bland, empty affirmation of religious belief in the first line, through the piling up of stock patriotic phrases rendered meaningless by being pulled out of context (and syntactical wholeness), culminating in the string of idiotic interjections in lines 7 and 8, Cummings's sense of the ridiculousness of the rhetoric and the meritriciousness of the orator is all but palpable. In lines 9–12, the speechmaker plays a particularly nasty kind of moral trump card, manipulating the sacrifices of the war dead to close off debate, followed by the reflexive and hypocritical lip service to liberty in line 13. He is saying, in effect: We honor our heroes for their defense of our freedoms, but anyone who exercises those freedoms to dissent from my views is unpatriotic or worse. And then the entire speech is neatly deflated by the poem's final line.

You can hear Cummings read "next to of course god america i" and three others of his poems online at *Salon* (search "E. E. Cummings" at <www.salon.com>).

MyLiteratureLab Resources. Photographs and biographical information for Cummings.

Robert Frost, FIRE AND ICE, page 81

In his first line, Frost probably refers to those who accept the Biblical prophecy of a final holocaust; and in his second line, to those who accept scientists' forecasts of the cooling of the earth. We admire that final *suffice;* a magnificent understatement, it further shows the power of a rime to close a poem (as Yeats said) with a click like a closing box.

When we polled students about their favorite poems in the anthology, their number one choice was Frost's "Fire and Ice." This unforgettably incisive lyric clearly illustrates how the poet's mind works with contradiction. Point out how the poem wonderfully argues its way to an inconclusive but nonetheless apocalyptic finale. And note the darkness of the poet's vision: both of the alternatives he offers are terrifying. No wonder college students love it. How many nine-line poems manage to destroy the world not once but twice?

MyLiteratureLab Resources. Biography, critical overview, critical articles, and bibliography for Frost.

Clare Rossini, FINAL LOVE NOTE, page 81

Clare Rossini's "Final Love Note" employs the language of love poetry to suggest a profound depth of emotion regarding an elm dying in her yard. Although we are first led to believe that the speaker is addressing a human lover, we find later that "Final Love Note" is a nature poem. We are unaware of the lover's identity through the opening stanza, while the tone becomes erotic at times—"clothes strewn on the floor," "moaned over me at night, never tiring." Not until the second stanza, when the speaker addresses the "you" as elm, do we learn that the object of her affection is a dying tree. Even with that truth revealed, the speaker's diction does not stray from that of love poetry. For her, the tree is greater than a human lover. She attributes her past comfort to the beauty and shade the tree has provided, and her present restlessness and sense of "abandonment" is blamed on the imminent destruction of the elm.

The penultimate stanza shifts time to the present tense, the morning in which she is writing, while in her yard she can "hear the chain saw cry out ecstatically." The personification of the elm is completed in the last stanza: "Your many arms are falling." Rossini closes "Final Love Note" with a stroke of irony—the conventionally romantic image of an open sky is now inappropriate and disquieting in the elm's absence: "garish blue stretch / Or drafty ceiling harshly lit by stars." Even in the tree's absence, the speaker views the elm in terms of domestic space and erotic desire. The open sky now visible becomes the mourning lover's bedroom ceiling.

Jennifer Reeser, WINTER-PROOF, page 82

In the first stanza of this poem (the title piece and first poem in her second collection) the author is clearly *saying* she values the calendula (perhaps so named because it blooms in most months—that is, throughout the calendar—in warm climates, such as Reeser's Louisiana) and the other winter-proof blossoms for their resistance to the ravages of time and adversity. In the second stanza there is more *suggesting*: the flowers named there are traditionally associated with brevity and mortality—think of the tubercular courtesan in Alexandre Dumas's *The Lady of the Camellias* and reread Herrick's "To the Virgins, to Make Much of Time" and Waller's "Go, Lovely Rose." In calling that part of the garden where these fragile flowers are decomposing "the graveyard," Reeser draws the obvious parallel to human existence. She is indebted to the winter-proof blossoms because they help her focus on life and its joys, rather than obsessing over its inevitable end.

Alfred, Lord Tennyson, TEARS, IDLE TEARS, page 82

Tennyson's brooding lyric is a classic example of poetic suggestion. The poem opens with a paradox. The speaker unexpectedly finds himself weeping when "looking on the happy autumn-fields." The tears are declared *idle*, which is to say they seemingly lack any real basis. But are they really mysterious in their origin? The "Writing Assignment" at the end of the chapter asks students to explain why the speaker is weeping.

Tennyson loads the poem with suggestive imagery and situations to answer this question. It might help students to begin by noticing *when* the poem takes place. It is autumn—the time of harvest and completion. The speaker seemingly cannot help but reflect in this season on "the days that are no more." *Where* the poem takes place also reinforces the sense that the speaker is painfully cut off from the past. The speaker weeps while "looking on the happy autumn-fields." Seeing them and remembering the past triggers a series of revealing reveries about "the days that are no more."

The first image associated with the past is light on a sail. First, the sail seems "fresh" and dawn-like—bringing "our friends up from the underworld." The last word of that line, *underworld,* explicitly brings death into the poem. Any reassuring image of the dead returning to us, however, is quickly reversed as the ship sinks "with all we love below the verge." The death imagery becomes more explicit in stanza 3 when the dawn song of the birds falls on "dying ears," and the sun rises to "dying eyes." In the final stanza, the intensity of the speaker's mood heightens appreciably. He speaks explicitly of love—lost love—and the pain of remembering the beloved. By the end of the poem the reader recognizes (at least intuitively) that the speaker weeps from the memory of a dead or lost beloved (*both* circumstances are stated) and the pain of being unable to recapture the past.

The late Cleanth Brooks wrote a penetrating analysis of Tennyson's poem, "The Motivation of Tennyson's Weeper," which is found in his influential critical collection *The Well Wrought Urn* (New York: Harcourt, 1947). Brooks's analysis perfectly illustrates the power of close textual reading. Dean of the New Critics, however, Brooks does not discuss the biographical background of Tennyson's lyric. Although not necessary to understand the poem, the facts of its origin are interesting in themselves. Tennyson wrote the poem in the autumn of 1834 after the death of his closest friend, Arthur Hallam. It was composed—an interesting bit of literary trivia—in the ruins of Tintern Abbey, nearly within sight of Hallam's grave and on the same spot that William Wordsworth had conceived his great ode in 1798.

MLL *MyLiteratureLab Resources*. Biography, photographs, critical overview, and bibliography for Tennyson.

Richard Wilbur, LOVE CALLS US TO THE THINGS OF THIS WORLD, page 83

WRITERS ON WRITING

Richard Wilbur, CONCERNING "LOVE CALLS US TO THE THINGS OF THIS WORLD," page 84

Wilbur suavely explains this richly detailed poem in the "Writers on Writing" that follows "Love Calls Us to the Things of This World" in the book. The poem may seem a bit difficult to students until they catch the extended metaphor in the first twenty lines (laundry on the line as angels). The poem depends on a series of oppositions (laundry and angels, earth and heaven, soul and body, sleep and waking). Even the poetic language mixes the vulgar and the exalted ("the punctual rape of every blessèd day"). Have students find as many oppositions as possible, and you will watch them grasp the larger themes of the poem in the process. (You won't believe how many elegant oppositions blissfully coexist in this quietly visionary poem.)

MyLiteratureLab Resources. Interactive reading of "Love Calls Us to the Things of This World." Critical essay by Wilbur, "Cold War Poetry."

5
Imagery

Ezra Pound, In a Station of the Metro, page 87

Pound recalled that at first this poem had come to him "not in speech, but in little splotches of color." His account is reprinted by K. K. Ruthven in *A Guide to Ezra Pound's* Personae, *1926* (Berkeley: U of California P, 1969). Students might like to compare this "hokku-like sentence" (as Pound called the poem) with the more suggestive Japanese haiku freely translated later in this chapter.

For a computer-assisted tribute to this famous poem, see the curious work of James Laughlin and Hugh Kenner, reported in "The Mixpoem Program," *Paris Review* 94 (Winter 1984): 193–98. Following Laughlin's suggestion that the five nouns of "In a Station of the Metro" might interestingly be shuffled, Kenner wrote "A Little Program in Basic" that enabled a computer to grind out 120 scrambled versions of the poem, including these:

> The apparitions of these boughs in the face;
> Crowds on a wet, black petal
>
> The crowd of these apparitions in the petal;
> Faces on a wet, black bough.

Kenner then wrote a program in Pascal that would shuffle eight words and produce 40,320 different versions. We don't know what it all demonstrates, except that Pound's original version still seems the best possible.

Kenner's historical account of the London literary scene and its influences on the composition of this poem is found in the "Critical Approaches to Literature" section of this book.

Taniguchi Buson, The piercing chill I feel, page 87

Harold G. Henderson, who translated this haiku, wrote a good terse primer in *An Introduction to Haiku* (Garden City: Anchor, 1958). Most of Henderson's English versions of haiku rime like this one; still, the sense of the originals (as far as the reader ignorant of Japanese can tell from Henderson's glosses) does not seem greatly distorted.

T. S. Eliot, The winter evening settles down, page 89

This is the first of the series of four poems called "Preludes," originally published in the July 1915 issue of Wyndham Lewis's *Blast.* It was written during Eliot's days at Harvard. The "Preludes," writes Grover Smith in *T. S. Eliot's Poetry and Plays* (Chicago: U of Chicago P, 1965), belong to the era of "Prufrock." Of "The winter evening settles down," Smith says:

> The first "Prelude" begins with winter nightfall in an urban back street; from indoor gloom and the confined odor of cooking it moves outside into the smoky twilight where gusts of wind whip up leaves and soiled papers, and a shower spatters the housetops. Such adjectives as "burnt out," "smoky," "grimy," "withered," "vacant," "broken," and "lonely" carry the tone.

Some students may point out, though, that the lighting of the lamps seems to end the poem on a note of tranquillity.

MyLiteratureLab Resources. Biography, critical overview, and bibliography for Eliot.

Theodore Roethke, ROOT CELLAR, page 89

Probably there is little point in spending much time dividing imagery into touches and tastes and smells; perhaps it will be enough to point out that Roethke's knowledgeable poem isn't all picture-imagery. There's that wonderful "congress of stinks," and the "slippery planks" are both tactile and visual. Most of the language in the poem is figurative, most of the vegetation is rendered animal: bulbs like small rodents, shoots like penises, roots like a forgotten can of fishing worms. Roethke doesn't call the roots lovely, but obviously he admires their tough, persistent life.

MyLiteratureLab Resources. Interactive reading and critical essay on "Root Cellar."

Elizabeth Bishop, THE FISH, page 90

This poem is made almost entirely of concrete imagery. Except for *wisdom* (line 63) and *victory* (66), there is no very abstract diction in it.

Obviously the speaker admires this stout old fighter. The image "medals with their ribbons" (line 61) suggests that he is an old soldier, and the "five-haired beard of wisdom" (line 63) suggests that he is a venerable patriarch, of whom one might seek advice.

The poor, battered boat has become magnificent for having the fish in it. The feeling in these lines is joy: bilge, rust, and cracked thwarts are suddenly revealed to be beautiful. In a way, the attitude seems close to that in Yeats's "Sailing to Byzantium," in which the triumphant soul is one that claps its hands and louder sings for every tatter in its mortal dress. The note of final triumph is sounded in "rainbow, rainbow, rainbow!" (line 75). The connotations of *rainbow* in this poem are not very different from the connotations often given the word by misty-eyed romantic poets such as Rod McKuen, but we believe Bishop because of her absolutely hard-eyed and specific view of the physical world. (She even sees the fish with X-ray imagination in lines 27–33.)

Anne Stevenson says in *Elizabeth Bishop* (New York: Twayne, 1966):

> It is a testimony to Miss Bishop's strength and sensitivity that the end, the revelation or "moment of truth," is described with the same attention to detail as the rest of the poem. The temptation might have been to float off into an airy apotheosis, but Miss Bishop stays right in the boat with the engine and the bailer. Because she does so, she is able to use words like "victory" and "rainbow" without fear of triteness.

Because the fish has provided her with an enormous understanding, the speaker's letting it go at the end seems an act of homage and gratitude.

Compare "The Fish" with the same poet's richly imaged "Filling Station."

The poet reads this poem on a recording, *The Spoken Arts Treasury of 100 Modern American Poets*, vol. 10, SA 1049.

MyLiteratureLab Resources. Biography, critical overview, and bibliography for Bishop. Critical essay on "The Fish."

Anne Stevenson, The Victory, page 92

This powerful short poem rejects all of the sentimental versions of childbirth and motherhood. It focuses on the violent physical details and emotional shock of giving birth.

One of the chief strategies of Confessional and Feminist poetry has been to admit personal feelings that conventional "good manners" would consider inappropriate or even shameful. In "The Victory," Stevenson presents a new mother's pain and horror at her newborn son. By admitting these feelings, she implicitly confesses that she is a bad mother in conventional terms. But Stevenson's speaker is unconcerned with keeping up appearances; she is obsessed with getting at the difficult truth of the moment. She is trying to sort through her own unexpected feelings.

It may be worthwhile to stress that as a *lyric* poem, "The Victory" tries to capture the intensity of insight from a particular moment. Stevenson's poem does not imply that the speaker will feel this shocked aversion to her child in the future. In fact, the last two lines of the poem imply that she will—despite her initial reaction—grow to love him.

Charles Simic, Fork, page 92

Simic's surreal, short poem introduces an object familiar to us, a fork, and presents it as strange and threatening. The central image is plainly stated: the fork "resembles a bird's foot." An evil, indeed violent, world begins to take shape as one looks more closely at Simic's word choice. The fork, we are told at the start of the poem, is evidently visiting from hell. An eerie turn comes in the second stanza when the speaker addresses a "you" who may be the reader, another person in the poem, or the speaker himself. In any case, we are pulled into a dark landscape of cannibals, hell, stabbings, and naked bird heads—a scene right out of Hieronymus Bosch. We are perhaps pulled in against our will, through our familiarity with the object. Each of us has held a fork, so it is impossible to avoid identifying with the images. That is the real achievement of "Fork"—its surefire inclusion of the reader.

You might begin class discussion by having students point out the words that equip the fork with evil characteristics. A possible writing exercise is to have students come up with their own poems in which a familiar object is treated as foreign and unknown.

Emily Dickinson, A Route of Evanescence, page 93

"A Route of Evanescence" will probably inspire a heated guessing contest. Contestants will need to pay attention to Dickinson's exact words.

Enclosing this poem in a letter to Thomas W. Higginson, Dickinson gave it the title "A Humming-Bird."

The poet's report of the hummingbird's arrival from Tunis is fanciful: the creature could hardly fly 4,000 miles nonstop in one morning. And New England hummingbirds don't need to cross the Atlantic; to find a warmer climate, they migrate south. If it was a ruby-throated hummingbird that the poet saw, though, it might indeed have come a long distance from a winter in Mexico or Central America.

The poet's ornithology may be slightly cockeyed, but her imagery is accurate. Hummingbird wings appear to rotate, but they aren't seated in ball joints; they merely flap fast.

MyLiteratureLab Resources. Biography, critical overview, and bibliography for Dickinson.

Jean Toomer, Reapers, page 93

This ominous poem, with its contrasts between sound and silence, possibly contains a metaphor. The black field hands are being destroyed by something indifferent and relentless, much as the trapped rat is slain under the blade. (Or, as in "Scottsboro," as a cat stalks a "nohole mouse"?)

A grandson of P. B. S. Pinchback, the black who served for a short time during Reconstruction as acting governor of Louisiana, Toomer had only a brief public career as a writer. His one book, *Cane* (1923), which experimentally combined passages of fiction with poetry, helped to spearhead the Harlem Renaissance. "Reapers" is taken from it.

That Toomer was a man divided between his profound understanding of blacks and his own desire to pass for white emerges in a recent biography, *The Lives of Jean Toomer: A Hunger for Wholeness*, by Cynthia Earl Kerman and Richard Eldridge (Baton Rouge: Louisiana State UP, 1987). *The Collected Poems of Jean Toomer* (Chapel Hill: U of North Carolina P, 1988) is a slim volume of 55 poems, the best of them from *Cane*.

Gerard Manley Hopkins, Pied Beauty, page 94

Sumptuously rich in music (rime, alliteration, assonance), this brief poem demands to be read aloud.

Some students might agree with Robert Frost's objection that the poem "disappoints . . . by not keeping, short as it is, wholly to pied things" (1934 letter to his daughter Lesley, in *Family Letters of Robert and Elinor Frost* [Albany: State U of New York P, 1972] 162). But, as question 4 tries to get at, Hopkins had more in mind than dappled surfaces. Rough paraphrase of the poem: God is to be praised not only for having created variegation, but for creating and sustaining contrasts and opposites. In lines 5–6, tradesmen's tools and gear, like the plow that pierces and cuts the soil, strike through the surfaces of raw materials to reveal inner beauty and order that had lain concealed.

For a convincing argument that Hopkins in "Pied Beauty," like Dickens in *Hard Times*, complains about a drab, mechanical, industrial-age uniformity in Victorian England, see Norman H. MacKenzie, *A Reader's Guide to Gerard Manley Hopkins* (Ithaca: Cornell UP, 1981) 85–86. Few students will crave to fathom the poet's notions of *instress* and *inscape*, but if you do, see John Pick's unsurpassed *Gerard Manley Hopkins, Priest and Poet*, 2nd ed. (London: Oxford UP, 1966) 53–56.

The point of question 5 is that if the images of the poem were subtracted, its statement of theme would also disappear.

Hopkins discovered the form of "Pied Beauty" and called it the *curtal sonnet* (*curtal*, riming with *turtle:* "crop-tailed"). But, remarks MacKenzie, such sonnets are like a small breed of horse: "compressed, not merely cut short." Instead of two quatrains, the form calls for two tercets; then, instead of a sestet, four lines and one brief line more. (Other curtal sonnets by Hopkins: "Peace" and, even more closely cropped, "Ashboughs.")

MyLiteratureLab Resources. Photographs and biographical information for Hopkins. Audio clip and critical essay on "Pied Beauty."

About Haiku

We expanded the haiku section in an earlier edition, refreshing the contemporary section with a couple of new selections and adding a group of haiku by Japanese Americans who were confined to internment camps during World War II, in one of the more shameful episodes of modern American history. These poems provide a quietly devastating commentary on the ironies and the injustice of the situation in which these innocent people were placed.

There is also a selection of hokku by Yone Noguchi in "Poems for Further Reading." Please take a look at these early twentieth-century poems; Noguchi was the first Asian American poet, and he was in many ways the person who first helped bring the haiku tradition over into English. He has been neglected by literary historians, and we are proud to give his pioneering work additional attention.

A biographical/critical note on Noguchi is found in this manual (in the commentary on "Poems for Further Reading"). Biographies of the "Three Masters" of classical Japanese haiku (Basho, Buson, and Issa) are found in the anthology in the chapter "Lives of the Poets."

The response to the enlarged haiku coverage has been excellent; the section now allows instructors enough material to make a separate unit on the subject. Lee Gurga, associate editor of *Modern Haiku* and a master of the form in his own right, has praised our coverage of Basho, Buson, and Issa, but he wishes that we had also included work by Shiki (1876–1902), the fourth "Master" of the haiku, who was the originator of the modern haiku in Japan. Shiki was responsible for renaming the form from *hokku* (opening verse) to *haiku* (playful verse). We will take Gurga's suggestion under consideration for future editions, but meanwhile we include one of his own astute examples of the haiku form in our selection of contemporary haiku.

Basho's frogjump poem, "In the old stone pool," may well be the most highly prized gem in Japanese literature: in Japanese there exists a three-volume commentary on it.

For an excellent discussion of the problems of teaching haiku, and of trying to write English ones, see Myra Cohn Livingston's *When You Are Alone / It Keeps You Capone: An Approach to Creative Writing with Children* (New York: Atheneum, 1973) 152–62. Livingston finds it useful to tell students a famous anecdote. Kikaku, a pupil of Basho, once presented his master with this specimen:

> Red dragonflies—
> Tear off their wings
> And you have pepper pods.

As a haiku, said Basho, that's no good. Make it instead:

> Red pepper pods—
> Add wings
> And you have dragonflies.

A moment of triumph, such as all teachers of poetry hope for but seldom realize, has been reported in a letter to XJK from Maurice F. Brown of Oakland University, Rochester, Michigan:

> Last year, teaching W. C. Williams in an "invitational" course for a week, I began with "Red Wheelbarrow" . . . and a student hand went up (class of 100): "That's not a poem! That's junk. What if I say, 'Here I sit looking at a blackboard while the sun is shining outside.' Is that a poem?" It was one of those great teaching moments . . . and I did a quick count and wrote it on the board:
>
> Here I sit looking
>   At a blackboard while the sun
> is shining outside.
>
> Not only a poem . . . a perfect haiku.

A thorough guide to this rocky acre of poetry, by William J. Higginson with Penny Harter, is *The Haiku Handbook: How to Write, Share, and Teach Haiku* (New York: McGraw, 1985).

Several small journals focus on haiku and tanka. If you or your students want to pursue studying (and perhaps even publishing) haiku, you will want to look at some of these magazines. *Modern Haiku* has been in existence for over thirty years. And the Haiku Society of America publishes *Frogpond*. For information, go to <www.modernhaiku.org> and <www.hsa-haiku.org>.

Those interested in the "Three Masters" of the Japanese haiku tradition will want to consult Robert Hass's *The Essential Haiku: Versions of Basho, Buson, and*

Issa (Hopewell, NJ: Ecco, 1994). Hass provides both generous selections from the poets and an informed introductory essay for each writer.

Looking over the eight contemporary haiku, the reader will see that not every poet adheres to the traditional seventeen-syllable pattern. The skillful and illuminating combination of two images or ideas, however, remains central to the haiku's identity in English. The poems are too short to require much commentary, but the title of one poem invites a few remarks.

Why is John Ridland's "The Lazy Man's Haiku" the work of a slothful soul? Because, according to the poet (in a letter), "he's too lazy to write the proper number of syllables in any line—or to get rid of that occidental end-rhyme à la Harold Henderson's ever-unconvincing translations in that old Anchor book." Henderson, in *An Introduction to Haiku* (New York: Anchor, 1956), forced all the haiku to rime like his version from Buson given at the beginning of this chapter. (Reading it as a poem in English, we find it profoundly convincing, and suspect it took work.)

For Review and Further Study

John Keats, Bright star! would I were steadfast as thou art, page 98

Unlike Petrarchan poets, Keats isn't making the star into an abstraction (Love); he takes it for a visible celestial body, even though he sees it in terms of other things. His comparisons are so richly laden with suggestions (star as staring eye, waters as priestlike), that sometimes students don't notice his insistent negations. The hermit's all-night vigil is *not* what Keats desires. He wants the comfort of that ripening pillow, and (perhaps aware of his impending death) envies the cold star only its imperishability—oh, for unendurable ecstasy, indefinitely prolonged! Compare this to Keats's "To Autumn" in which the poet finds virtue in change.

Many readers find the last five words of the poem bothersome. Students might be asked, Does Keats lose your sympathy by this ending? If so, why? If not, how would you defend it? We can't defend it; it seems bathetic, almost as self-indulgent as Shelley's lines in "Indian Serenade":

> Oh, lift me from the grass!
>   I die! I faint! I fail!
> Let thy love in kisses rain
>   On my lips and eyelids pale.

Thomas Mauch, of Colorado College, intelligently disagrees, and suggests how "or else swoon to death" may be defended. The *or,* he thinks, is what grammarians call an inclusive *or,* not an exclusive.

> I believe that the speaker is saying, not that if he can't be forever in the close company of the beloved he would rather be dead—sort of like what Patrick Henry said about liberty—but rather that, given the closeness to the woman, dying in that condition would be just as good as experiencing it forever, since in either case he would not undergo a separation from her (and

still retain his consciousness of it). I think it is the same point he makes in the "Ode to a Nightingale":

Now more than ever seems it rich to die,
  To cease upon the midnight with no pain,
    While thou art pouring forth thy soul abroad
      In such an ecstasy!

The poem, Mr. Mauch concludes, illustrates the kind of closure that Keats admired when he affirmed that a poem should "die grandly."

MyLiteratureLab Resources. Photographs, biographical information, critical overview, and bibliography for Keats. Longman Lecture on "Bright star!"

EXPERIMENT: *Writing with Images*, page 98

To write a poem full of images, in any form, is probably easier for most students than to write a decent haiku. (On the difficulties of teaching haiku writing, see Myra Cohn Livingston, cited under "About Haiku.") Surprisingly, there is usually at least one student in every class who can't seem to criticize a poem to save his neck, yet who, if invited to be a poet, will bloom or at least bud.

Walt Whitman, THE RUNNER, page 98

Try reading "The Runner" without the adverbs *lightly* and *partially*. Does the poem even exist without those two delicate modifiers?

T. E. Hulme, IMAGE, page 98

Hulme's poems seem always to have been brief. In his own collection *Personae*, Ezra Pound took two pages to include "The Complete Poetical Works of T. E. Hulme" (in which "Image" does not appear). Pound remarked, "In publishing his *Complete Poetical Works* at thirty, Mr. Hulme has set an enviable example to many of his contemporaries who have had less to say."

William Carlos Williams, EL HOMBRE, page 99

This famous little poem engages one of Williams's principal themes, the primacy of the image, and the consequent need to look clearly at things in terms of themselves rather than obscure them with irrelevant comparisons. This concept is also treated in other Williams poems written in the same period, such as "Tract" and "To a Solitary Disciple," and it surfaces again twenty years later in "The Term." Nonetheless, it is almost impossible not to derive from these early poems some sense of Williams's feelings of isolation in the literary landscape of his time. As the critic Steven Gould Axelrod has observed, "Williams troped on his situation in 'El Hombre.'"

In 1918, the year after "El Hombre" appeared in book form, Wallace Stevens published in the *Little Review* a poem called "Nuances of a Theme by

Williams," in which he quotes Williams's text in its entirety and improvises on the phrases "shine alone" and "lend no part." Recalling this tribute many years later, Williams said, "I was deeply touched."

 *MyLiteratureLab Resources*. Biography, critical overview, and bibliography for Williams.

Chana Bloch, Tired Sex, page 99

Chana Bloch's brief poem tells its entire story through images (a very discreet thing to do considering the subject). The first image—the damp matchbook—is particularly clever since the poet develops it to represent both male (the match) and female (the matchbook) sexuality. Bloch also carefully avoids depicting the speaker's inner thoughts and focuses instead on the external images (watching "that sparrow the cat / keeps batting around") that suggest a great deal about what is happening both in bed and in the speaker's mind. The final image of joylessly paging through a supposedly great book provides a touch of wit to this ingenious poem.

Robert Bly, Driving to Town Late to Mail a Letter, page 99

No doubt the situation in this poem is real: Bly, who lives in frequently snow-bound Minnesota, emits hundreds of letters. Compare this simple poem to Frost's "Stopping by Woods on a Snowy Evening," which also has a speaker who, instead of going home, prefers to ogle snowscapes.

Note that this poem is examined in the "Writing Critically" section at the end of this chapter in the main book.

Rita Dove, Silos, page 99

"Silos" is a poem not only *of* images but *about* them as well, and it is particularly about what the silos suggest to those who perceive them. It is interesting to note that the most pleasing and fanciful suggestion is attributed to "a stranger." Those who live with the silos looming over them in their everyday lives, whether adults or children, have more mundane and at best ambiguous interpretations of them.

It is also interesting to note that the postmodern world has apparently transcended its ribs. The poem's silos are those of the Quaker Oats Company, whose factory once dominated the downtown section of Akron, Ohio, the poet's native city (see the prose poem "Quaker Oats" in the first section of Dove's largely autobiographical collection *Grace Notes*, which also contains "Silos"). The factory is now a mall, and its silos have been converted into suites of hotel rooms.

Louise Glück, Mock Orange, page 100

The sensory imagery of Glück's poem is nearly all-encompassing. In the course of the poem the speaker invokes the senses of sight, touch, hearing, and smell. The persistent image of the mock orange becomes associated with sex early in the poem—an association the speaker finds not merely unpleasant but terrifying. She associates sex with suffocation, paralysis, and humiliation. The title image also eventually becomes a pun on *mock* ("Do you see? / We were made fools of.")

Billy Collins, EMBRACE, page 100

Billy Collins has an extraordinary gift for ingenious imagery, and "Embrace" is no exception. Here Collins creates an image and then invites the reader to examine it from two sides. The extended image, which begins so playfully and even romantically, soon proves not only devastatingly lonely but foreboding. This poem contains a lesson every cinematographer knows—the same physical image can elicit a radically different effect depending on the angle from which it is depicted.

A CD of Billy Collins reading his poems, *The Best Cigarette*, has been released by Eric Antonow's small good productions (800-829-7552).

MyLiteratureLab Resources. Biography, critical overview, and bibliography for Collins.

John Haines, WINTER NEWS, page 101

We are struck by "the stiffening dogs" in this poem. It is possible both to picture such stiffening and to feel it in one's muscles and bones. Haines appeals mostly to the senses of sight ("clouds of steaming breath," "the white- / haired children") and sound ("Oil tins bang," "the voice of the snowman"). Clearly the children's hair, far from manifesting premature aging, is merely covered with snow. Is that snowman a surreal monster, or is his voice another name for the wind?

In 1947 John Haines went to Alaska as a homesteader and began to write poetry there. This is the title poem from his first collection, *Winter News* (Middletown, CT: Wesleyan UP, 1966).

Stevie Smith, NOT WAVING BUT DROWNING, page 101

Stevie Smith reportedly got the initial inspiration for this poem from a newspaper item that described a man who drowned in full view of his friends; they mistook his signals for help as playful waving. Smith pursued the fatal irony of this freak accident and found a chilling universal message in it. Students have no trouble understanding how a person's desperate signals for help can be misunderstood or ignored by others.

If you share the story of the poem's genesis with students, you might also point out how the poem's title reads like a tabloid headline.

It never hurts to belabor the obvious with students. You might suggest they read the short biographical note on Smith and discover that the poet is a woman. Any student particularly interested in Smith should be directed to the superb 1978 film *Stevie* starring Glenda Jackson, which contains an especially powerful rendition of this poem.

WRITERS ON WRITING

Ezra Pound, THE IMAGE, page 102

Pound's brief paragraphs on the image may be the most influential critical passage about modern poetry. This excerpt from his 1913 essay "A Few Don'ts by an Imagiste" (later retitled and incorporated into "A Retrospect") provided a list of issues and opinions that have helped shape the poetic practice of the last nine decades.

Pound's criticism itself unfolds most effectively in short imagistic bursts. Ask students to share the sentence or pair of sentences that most interest them. Are there any ideas with which they fervently agree or disagree?

One word in Pound's passage may need explanation: as its capitalization indicates, *Mosaic* refers to Moses (and his Ten Commandments).

6
Figures of Speech

Why Speak Figuratively?

Alfred, Lord Tennyson, The Eagle, page 111

For a hostile criticism of this poem, see Robert Graves, "Technique in Poetry," *On Poetry: Collected Talks and Essays* (New York: Doubleday, 1969) 402–405. Graves finds Tennyson's fragment unable to meet the minimal requirement that a poem should make good prose sense. He complains that if the eagle stands on its hands then its wings must be feet, and he ends up by rewriting the poem the way he thinks it ought to be. Though his remarks are fascinating, Graves reads the poem too literally.

Another critic has suggested that this poem is a product of Tennyson's hopeless nearsightedness. Celebrating the eagle's 20–20 zoom-lens vision and ability to see a fish from high up, Tennyson yearns for a goal he could not attain: "optical inclusiveness." (See Gerhard Joseph, "Tennyson's Optics: The Eagle's Gaze," *PMLA* 92 [May 1977]: 420–27.)

MyLiteratureLab Resources. Biography, photographs, critical overview, and bibliography for Tennyson.

William Shakespeare, Shall I compare thee to a summer's day?, page 111
Howard Moss, Shall I Compare Thee to a Summer's Day?, page 112

Shakespeare's original—rich in metaphor, personification, and hyperbole—means more, of course, than Moss's tongue-in-cheek desecration. The only figure of speech in Moss's rewrite is the simile in line 1, and even that is denigrated ("Who says?"). Moss manages to condense 115 great words to 78, a sonnet to a mere thirteen lines. It took a poet skilled in handling rimes to find such dull ones.

Shakespeare's nautical metaphor in line 8 may need explaining: a beautiful young person is a ship in full sail; accident or age can untrim the vessel. Compare this metaphor to "bare ruined choirs where late the sweet birds sang" ("That time of year").

MyLiteratureLab Resources. Photographs, biographical information, and bibliography for Shakespeare. Audio clip, student essay, and critical essays on "Shall I compare thee to a summer's day?"

METAPHOR AND SIMILE

Emily Dickinson, MY LIFE HAD STOOD – A LOADED GUN, page 114

This astonishing metaphysical poem (another hymnlike work in common meter) can be an excellent provoker of class debate. Before trying to fathom it, students might well examine its diction. *Sovreign Woods* ("sovereign" would be the more usual spelling) suggests an estate owned by a king. How do the Mountains *reply?* By echoing the gun's report. Apparently the *smile* is the flash from the gun's muzzle; and the *Vesuvian face*, a glimpse of the flaming crater of the volcano. The Eider-Duck, a sea duck, has particularly soft and silky down which is used in pillows and quilts. The gun's *Yellow Eye* seems, again, its flash, and the emphatic *Thumb* is presumably the impact of the bullet that flattens its victim. (Some will say the thumb is a trigger finger, but you don't pull a trigger with your thumb.)

Argument over the meaning of the poem will probably divide the class into two camps. One will see the poem, like "Because I could not stop for Death," as an account of resurrection, with the Owner being God or Christ, who carries away the speaker, life and all, to the Happy Hunting Grounds of Paradise. We incline toward the other camp, the view that the Owner seems a mere mortal, perhaps a lover. The last stanza reveals that he can die. So taken, the last two lines make more sense. Not having the power to die, the speaker feels something lacking in herself. She doesn't wish to outlive her huntsman and be a lonely killer.

Philip Larkin admits the possibility of both views: "This is a romantic love in a nutshell, but who is its object? A religious poet—and Emily was this sometimes—might even have meant God" (*Required Writing* [New York: Farrar, 1984] 193).

A third camp has appeared, proclaiming a feminist interpretation. The poem, as summed up by Adalaide Morris, "tells about a life packed with a potential that the self was not empowered to activate." From this point of view, the poem is overtly political and exhilarating to teach because it recognizes long suppressed animosities ("Dick, Jane, and American Literature Fighting with Canons," *College English* 47 [1985]: 477).

But the poem remains tantalizingly ambiguous. You won't know until you go into class what a discussion may reveal.

MyLiteratureLab Resources. Biography, critical overview, and bibliography for Dickinson.

Alfred, Lord Tennyson, FLOWER IN THE CRANNIED WALL, page 115

Why does Tennyson say "what God and man is" instead of "what God and man *are*"? Apparently, this isn't faulty grammar but higher pantheism. God and man are one.

MyLiteratureLab Resources. Biography, critical overview, and bibliography for Tennyson.

William Blake, TO SEE A WORLD IN A GRAIN OF SAND, page 115

This famous short poem begins Blake's "Auguries of Innocence." Written around 1803 in a notebook and then carefully transcribed by Blake into another notebook made from discarded sheets from his engraving business, this poem was not published until 1863, 35 years after the poet's death.

MyLiteratureLab Resources. Photographs and biographical information for Blake.

Sylvia Plath, METAPHORS, page 115

Students usually are prompt to see that the central fact of the poem is the speaker's pregnancy. The speaker feels herself to be a walking riddle, posing a question that awaits solution: What person is she carrying? The "nine syllables" are like the nine months of gestation. All the metaphors refer to herself or to her pregnancy, except those in lines 4–5, which refer to the unborn baby: growing round and full like an apple or plum, seeming precious as ivory (and with ivory skin?), fine-timbered in sinew and bone like a well-built house.

The tone of the poem is clear, if complicated. Humor and self-mockery are evident in the images of elephant and strolling melon. In the last line, there is a note of wonder at the inexorability of gestation and birth: "The train there's no getting off."

A lively class might be asked to point out any possible connection between what the poem is saying about the arbitrary, fixed cycle of pregnancy and its own form—the nine nine-syllable lines.

As Plath records in her Boston journal for 20 March 1959, the pregnancy she had hoped for ended in a miscarriage. Grieving and depressed, she went ahead and finished this poem, then explicitly called "Metaphors for a Pregnant Woman" (*Journals*, New York: Ballantine, 1983) 298–99.

MyLiteratureLab Resources. Interactive reading and critical essay on "Metaphors."

N. Scott Momaday, SIMILE, page 116

Momaday is best known as a novelist and prose writer; his *House Made of Dawn* won the 1969 Pulitzer Prize in fiction. But Momaday is also an accomplished poet whose work often combines a compressed formal style with the natural imagery of his native Southwest. The Oklahoma-born author of Kiowa ancestry also often incorporates tribal legends into his verse.

"Simile," true to its title, gives us a single, extended simile, but it withholds the emotional motivation for the choice of this particular image. The reader is forced to interpret the behavior of the metaphorical deer in order to answer the *what* of the opening line. Those familiar with T. S. Eliot's concept of "an objective correlative" ("a set of objects; a situation, a chain of events which shall be the formula" that unleashes a particular emotion in a reader) will recognize Momaday's "Simile" as a classic example of that technique. Momaday lets his image work on the reader's unconscious rather than specify its emotional meaning.

Emily Dickinson, It dropped so low – in my Regard, page 116

The whole poem sets forth the metaphor that someone or something the speaker had valued too highly proved to be like a silver-plated item (a chafing dish? a cream pitcher?) that she had mistaken for solid silver. Its smash revealed that it was made of cheap stuff.

In another version, lines 5–6 read: "Yet blamed the Fate that fractured—*less* / Than I reviled myself." Students may be asked which version they prefer, and why they prefer it. (We much prefer *reviled* to *denounced* because of its resonance—the sound of the *i*—and its alliteration, the *l* in *reviled* and *self*. Besides, *fractured* seems a more valuable word than *flung:* it gets across the notion of something cracked or shattered, and its *r* sets up an alliterative echo with the words *entertaining*, *Wares*, and *Silver.)*

Craig Raine, A Martian Sends a Postcard Home, page 117

When this poem won a 1978 magazine award in England, the judge James Fenton hailed the new "Martian School" of poetry. The name stuck because it referred to a tendency among several young British poets to use strange metaphors and outrageous similes to describe everyday objects.

In Raine's poem a Martian visitor tries to describe objects and activities on Earth. Seen from this alien perspective, everything appears quite strange. Half of what the Martian says is bizarrely wrong, but the other half is often weirdly insightful.

In a 1990 interview on BBC Radio, the poet Clive Wilmer elicited an interesting comment from Raine about the form of the poem:

> [T]he form of "A Martian Sends a Postcard Home" is the form of a postcard. We're all familiar with sonnets and couplets and odes and irregular odes, but it's possible to write a poem in a form that hasn't been used before, in this case the form of a postcard. Everybody writes a postcard saying: "Uncle Willy fell in the sea. Weather's been terrible for days. Lodgings not bad. See you next week. Wish you were here." In other words, it's an excuse for very, very heterogeneous subject-matter.

Exercise: *What Is Similar?*, page 118

We'd suggest that this exercise be run through rapidly. We wouldn't give students much time to ponder but would briskly call on people, and if anyone hesitated for long, we would skip to someone else. Give them time to cogitate about these items, and they are likely to dredge up all sorts of brilliant, reached-for similarities in each pair of things—possibly logical, but having nothing to do with the lines. Immediate flashes of understanding are the goal of this exercise, not ponderous explication. Do this one for fun, and so it might be; do it slowly and seriously, and it could be deadly.

Other Figures of Speech

On the subject of puns, students familiar with *Hamlet* and other classics of the Bard may be asked to recall other puns of Shakespeare (besides the celebrated lines about golden lads and girls). If such a discussion prospers, Dr. Johnson's well-known observation in his preface to Shakespeare's works may provide an assertion to argue with:

> A quibble is to Shakespeare what luminous vapors are to the traveler: he follows it at all adventures; it is sure to lead him out of his way, and sure to engulf him in the mire. . . . A quibble is the golden apple for which he will always turn aside from his career or stoop from his elevation. A quibble, poor and barren as it is, gave him such delight that he was content to purchase it by the sacrifice of reason, propriety, and truth. A quibble was to him the fatal Cleopatra for which he lost the world, and was content to lose it.

James Stephens, THE WIND, page 119

As a birthday present to Stephens, James Joyce once translated this poem into five other languages (French, German, Italian, Latin, and Norwegian). These versions are reprinted in *Letters of James Joyce*, ed. Stuart Gilbert (New York: Viking, 1957) 318–19.

Margaret Atwood, YOU FIT INTO ME, page 122

The first two lines state a simile. In the second couplet, *hook* and *eye* turn out (to our surprise) to be puns.

MyLiteratureLab Resources. Critical essay on "You fit into me."

John Ashbery, THE CATHEDRAL IS, page 122

Ashbery's unexpected pun on *slated* inspired student Steven B. Stanley of Metropolitan State University to coin "a more contemporary example of a pun" in a one-line poem of his own, "The Spelling Bee Champion":

> Studied a spell.

His instructor, Cathy Lewis, took a vote in class: Was Stanley better than Ashbery? Not surprisingly, Stanley triumphed. He adds: "I also came up with: 'The library is booked for demolition.' However, that sounded a little too like Ashbery." Perhaps your students might like to try writing one-liners in this vein, and so realize (as Ashbery does) that it is possible to have fun with poetry.

George Herbert, THE PULLEY, page 122

The title may need clarification. Man's need for rest is the pulley by which eventually he is drawn to rest everlasting. The pulley Herbert has in mind is probably not horizontal (like the one with a clothesline) but the vertical kind rigged to hoist a heavy weight. Despite the puns, the tone of the poem is of course devoutly serious, Herbert's concern in it being (in the view of Douglas Bush) "to subdue the wilful or kindle the apathetic self."

Lines 2–10, on the "glass of blessings" and its contents, set forth a different metaphor. As Herbert's editor, F. E. Hutchinson (*Works* [Oxford: Oxford UP, 1941]), and others have remarked, "The Pulley" seems a Christian version of the story of Pandora. At her creation Pandora received gifts from all the gods, mostly virtues and graces—though Hermes gave her perfidy. In some tellings of the myth, Pandora's gift (or vase) held not plagues but further blessings. When she became curious and opened it, they slipped away, all except the one that lay at the bottom—hope.

Herbert's poem, in its fondness for the extended metaphysical conceit, invites comparison with Donne's simile of the compasses in "A Valediction: Forbidding Mourning." If the instructor cares to discuss metaphysical poetry, "The Pulley" may be taken together with Herbert's "Love." ("Easter Wings" raises distracting contradictions and may be left for a discussion of concrete or graphic poetry.) Other poems of Donne and of Dickinson can also be mentioned.

Students might be encouraged to see that poets of the seventeenth century had certain habits of thought strikingly different from our own, but that some of these habits—like the fondness for startling comparisons of physical and spiritual things—haven't become extinct. Perhaps the closest modern equivalent to the conceits of Herbert and Donne may be found in fundamentalist hymns. Two earlier twentieth-century illustrations:

> If you want to watch old Satan run
> Just fire off that Gospel gun!

and

> My soul is like a rusty lock.
> Oh, oil it with thy grace!
> And rub it, rub it, rub it, Lord,
> Until I see thy face!

(The first example is attributed to a black Baptist hymn writer; the second, to the Salvation Army, according to Max Eastman in *Enjoyment of Laughter* [New York: Simon, 1936].) Another illustration, probably influenced by fundamentalist hymns, is a country and western song recorded in 1976 by Bobby Bare, "Dropkick Me, Jesus" ("through the goalposts of life").

Dana Gioia, MONEY, page 123

With a little effort, you should be able to find examples of the following figures of speech in this compendium of common references to our common currency: metaphor, epithet, personification, hyperbole, metonymy, synecdoche, and pun. *Note*: you will find no occurrences of simile or apostrophe.

MyLiteratureLab Resources. Video clip of Dana Gioia reciting "Money."

Charles Simic, My Shoes, page 123

While the descriptions in the poem seem fanciful or surrealistic throughout, many are expressed in straightforward language that does not employ figures of speech. Among those that do, we would cite metaphors in lines 1 and 2 (and by extension in line 10 and lines 15–16) and personification in line 14 and lines 17–19. In addition, the entire poem is an instance of apostrophe.

For Review and Further Study

Robert Frost, The Silken Tent, page 124

Although the word *as* in the opening line might lead us to expect a simile, "The Silken Tent" is clearly an immense metaphor, comparing woman and tent in a multitude of ways. What are the ropes or cords? Not merely commitments (or promises to keep) to friends and family, but generous sympathies, "ties of love and thought," on the part of a woman who cares about everything in the world.

While paying loving tribute to a remarkable woman, the poem is also a shameless bit of showing off by a poet cocksure of his technical mastery. Managing syntax with such grace that the poem hardly seems contrived, Frost has sustained a single sentence into an entire sonnet. "The whole poem is a performance," says Richard Poirier, "a display for the beloved while also being an exemplification of what it is like for a poem, as well as a tent or a person, to exist within the constrictions of space ('a field') and time ('at midday') wherein the greatest possible freedom is consistent with the intricacies of form and inseparable from them" (*Robert Frost: The Work of Knowing* [New York: Oxford UP, 1977] xiv–xv). Poirier points out, too, that the diction of the poem seems Biblical, perhaps echoing "The Song of Songs" (in which the bride is comely "as the tents of Kedar") and Psalm 92 (in which the godly "grow like a cedar in Lebanon"). Not only does the "central cedar pole" signify the woman's spiritual rectitude, it points toward heaven.

In teaching this poem, one can quote Frost's remark to Louis Untermeyer, "I prefer the synecdoche in poetry, that figure of speech in which we use a part for a whole." In 1931 Frost recalled that he had called himself a Synecdochist back when other poets were calling themselves Imagists: "Always, always a larger significance. A little thing touches a larger thing" (qtd. in Elizabeth Shepley Sergeant, *Robert Frost: The Trial by Existence* [New York: Holt, 1960] 325).

MyLiteratureLab Resources. Biography, critical overview, critical articles, and bibliography for Frost.

April Lindner, Low Tide, page 125

There is personification in the opening sentence (lines 1–4), with its suggestion that as the tide goes out, the ocean performs a sort of mild striptease; the figure is extended with "What's left veiled" in line 11. The simile occurs in the explicit comparison in lines 6–7. The descriptions are never overtly sensual, but throughout the poem the surf is invested with a sensuousness that stimulates and finds its response in the poem's human characters: "Our hands itch / for all they might gather." The very end of the poem, with its reference to silk, likewise intertwines the sensuousness of the natural world with the human.

Jane Kenyon, THE SUITOR, page 125

This economical poem moves from simile to simile: (1) "like the chest of someone sleeping" (steadily rising and falling); (2) "like a school of fish" (flashing their pale bellies), and (3) "like a timid suitor" (hesitant, drawing back, reluctant to arrive).

Until her untimely death from leukemia in 1995, Kenyon lived in Danbury, New Hampshire, with her husband, the poet Donald Hall. *Otherwise: New and Selected Poems* (Graywolf Press) was published posthumously in 1996.

Robert Frost, THE SECRET SITS, page 126

Besides its personification of the sitting Secret, Frost's poem contains an implied metaphor. To dance round in a ring is to make futile efforts to penetrate a secret—merely going around in circles.

A. R. Ammons, COWARD, page 126

Ammons's figure of speech is, of course, a pun, but it is also a pun that underlines the original metaphor of *run* in the expression "runs in my family."

Kay Ryan, TURTLE, page 126

Kay Ryan is one of the most interesting poets of recent years. Born in California in 1945, she was raised in the San Joaquin Valley and the Mojave Desert, but those dry landscapes do not suggest the densely written and lushly detailed imaginative terrain of her poetry. Ryan has a particular gift for evocative compression. Her characteristic poem is short but not small—full of wry observation, weirdly original images, interwoven figures of speech, and magically unpredictable musicality. The first time one reads a Ryan poem is almost always a pleasure, and one soon discovers that her poems not only allow and reward rereading, they insist on it.

Ryan's "Turtle" is so densely packed with image and metaphor that each rereading uncovers interesting details and correspondences. And yet the tone of the poem is wonderfully matter-of-fact as the speaker produces one extravagant metaphor after another. This strange combination of tone and figurative language gives the poem an arresting quality rather reminiscent of certain poems by Marianne Moore or Elizabeth Bishop, though Ryan's style is distinctly her own. Notice how many rimes the poem contains. Few are end-rimes. Many are off-rimes. Most occur mid-line: *graceless/case/places*; *slope/hopes*; *skirts/convert*; *ditch/which*; and so forth. The effect of the intricate wordplay and hidden rimes is to slow readers down and invite them to savor every detail.

Ryan has published six volumes of poetry: *Dragon Acts to Dragon Friends* (Taylor Street Press, 1983), *Strangely Marked Metal* (Copper Beech, 1985), *Flamingo Watching* (Copper Beech, 1994), *Elephant Rocks* (Grove, 1996), *Say Uncle* (Grove, 2000), and *The Niagara River* (Grove, 2005).

Kay Ryan has provided these comments on "Turtle":

> "Turtle" came out of an extended time of the most terrible and absolute frustration. That's why it's so giddy. Everything in it is compressed, image and rhymes jammed too tight, threatening to explode. But it can't explode, because all the pieces are twisted together, and twisted again.
>
> "Turtle" was written in a single morning, as almost all of my poems are. I began with the first line, "Who would be a turtle who could help it?" It's mysterious how a poem develops out of its beginnings; right now I am thinking that it is like lighting a fuse that came into existence by its own burning, creating the dynamite that it explodes. But now I'm thinking, maybe the dynamite doesn't explode; maybe it just forever threatens. That's even better.
>
> Rhyme tells me where to go in a poem. It is a big bully, really, and hard to control. A sound listens for companions out in the distance beyond what has been said; it strains the poem forward, calling it into existence. Rhyme is an engine of yearning. It makes me write what I couldn't imagine.
>
> The internal rhymes in this poem have a range of ridiculousness that I love. I doubt I'll ever do better than rhyming "a four-ore" with "afford." Or on a grander scale, may I point out the achievement of "Her track is graceless . . . / a packing-case places"? I love these dismantled and remantled rhymes, but I also love every other sort of rhyme. I see rhyme as a binding energy in the finished poem, something that generates integrity, making the poem loyal to itself. I could compare rhyme to the glueyness that holds molecules together.
>
> It was the most exquisite pleasure to write this poem. And it did nothing whatsoever to dissipate my frustration. The truth of that strikes me as funny.

Heather McHugh, LANGUAGE LESSON, 1976, page 126

Throughout her poetic career, Heather McHugh has taken a particular delight in the vagaries and peculiarities of the English language (in which the word *cleave*, for instance, is its own antonym). This poem, set in Philadelphia on the two-hundredth anniversary of that city's becoming the "cradle of liberty," sets its keynote by showing how, in the "American" language, that revered term is also suggestive of presumption and transgression. The poet revels in the drollery of the twin games of tennis and language, "in which love can mean nothing" and in which the rich, who are accustomed to being waited on by others, "prepare to serve." The seventh couplet is particularly ingenious, with its visual and verbal parallelism reinforcing the emphasis on "doubletalk" and setting up the surprisingly affecting conclusion, in which what sounds like its opposite turns out to be a tender declaration of dependence.

Robinson Jeffers, HANDS, page 127

This poem can be profitably read with Jeffers's "To the Stone-Cutters." Both poems show his belief in humanity's tenuous position versus nature, and both reveal his interesting view of art—that it is impermanent compared to nature's eternity but that nonetheless it outlives its makers to provide comfort and wisdom to future generations. "Hands," however, is a gentler poem than "To the Stone-Cutters," and it shows Jeffers's deep, lifelong respect for the cultures of Native Americans, whom he admired for living more closely to nature than modern man.

Robert Burns, OH, MY LOVE IS LIKE A RED, RED ROSE, page 128

Figures of speech abound in this famous lyric, similes (lines 1–2, 3–4), a metaphor (*sands o' life*, 12), overstatement (8 and 9, 10), and possibly another overstatement in the last line.

See other professions of love couched in hyperbole, among them Marvell's "To His Coy Mistress" and Auden's "As I Walked Out One Evening." Are the speakers in these poems mere throwers of blarney, whom no woman ought to trust?

For a discussion of this poem that finds more in it than figures of speech, see Richard Wilbur, "Explaining the Obvious," in *Responses* (New York: Harcourt, 1976). Burns's poem, says Wilbur, "forsakes the lady to glory in Love itself, and does not really return. We are dealing, in other words, with romantic love, in which the beloved is a means to high emotion, and physical separation can serve as a stimulant to ideal passion." The emotion of the poem is "self-enchanted," the presence or absence of the lady isn't important, and the very idea of parting is mainly an opportunity for the poet to turn his feelings loose. Absurd as this posture may be, however, we ought to forgive a great songwriter almost anything.

WRITERS ON WRITING

Robert Frost, THE IMPORTANCE OF POETIC METAPHOR, page 128

Frost made so many insightful and memorable observations about poetry that it is difficult to select just one passage. Rather than reprint one of his more famous comments, we have selected this fascinating but little-known passage from an address he gave at Amherst College in 1930.

In this brief excerpt Frost speculates on the general value of a literary education. He observes how studying poetry trains us to understand metaphors and other figures of speech. Metaphors pervade all types of discourse, Frost says, and they are used in all walks of life. An education in poetry helps us judge metaphors critically—to see how far they apply to a situation truthfully and where they "break down."

MyLiteratureLab Resources. Biography, critical overview, and bibliography for Frost.

7
Song

Singing and Saying

"Song" is an unusual chapter. It approaches poetry in ways different from most other textbooks. We urge new instructors to try this chapter. Most students who write comments about this book say this chapter is the most appealing. "It shows that poetry isn't all found in books," is a typical comment; and many students are glad to see song lyrics they recognize. Most important, the chapter talks to them about poetry by using songs—a context they know a great deal about. It also encourages them to hear poems in a way that they might never have done before if their entire experience was seeing poems on the printed page.

Even if there is not time for a whole unit on song, the instructor who wishes to build upon this interest can use at least some of this chapter to introduce the more demanding matters of sound, rhythm, and form (treated in the chapters that follow). Some instructors take the tack that lyric poetry begins with song, and they begin their courses with this chapter, supplemented by folk ballads elsewhere in the text.

Besides Ben Jonson's classic nondrinking song, many other famous poems will go to melodies. The tradition of poems set to music by fine composers is old and honorable. For lists of such poems with musical settings (and recordings), see *College English* for February 1985 and December 1985.

Ben Jonson, To Celia, page 132

Students may not know that in line 2 *I will pledge* means "I will drink a toast." Also, *I would not change for thine* (line 8) in modern English becomes "I would not take it in exchange for yours."

To demonstrate that "To Celia" is a living song, why not ask the class to sing it? Unfortunately, you can no longer assume that the tune is one that everyone knows, so you may need to start them off.

Anonymous, The Cruel Mother, page 133

Some versions of this ballad start the narrative at an earlier point in time, with a woman discovering that she is pregnant by the wrong man when she is about to marry another. See Alan Lomax's Notes to *The Child Ballads*, vol. 1, Caedmon TC 1145, an old LP record, which contains an Irish version.

If the instructor cares to discuss the bottomless but student-spellbinding topic of archetypes, this ballad will serve to illustrate an archetype also visible in the stepmother figure of many fairy tales.

William Shakespeare, O MISTRESS MINE, page 134

Here Shakespeare wrote in the most popular song form of his era. How many popular song lyrics look this good after four hundred years? Shakespeare had the brevity of the madrigal form working to his advantage; singers busy with elaborate counterpoint didn't need the extended lyrics found in such simpler strophic forms as the ballad. Although this song was presumably sung by a single voice (the clown, Feste, in *Twelfth Night*), it employs the madrigal form usually associated with three or more voices. Madrigals could take flexible forms ranging from four to thirteen lines.

In "Music in Shakespeare," an essay in his collection *The Dyer's Hand*, W. H. Auden says of "O mistress mine": "Taken by themselves, the songs in this play are among the most beautiful Shakespeare wrote. . . . But in the contexts in which Shakespeare places them, they sound shocking. Taken playfully, such lines as [lines 9–12] are charming enough. . . . Taken seriously, these lines are the voice of elderly lust, afraid of its own death. Shakespeare forces this awareness on our consciousness by making the audience to the song a couple of seedy old drunks."

MyLiteratureLab Resources. Photographs, biographical information, and bibliography for Shakespeare. Longman Lecture on "The Theme of Love in the Sonnets."

Edwin Arlington Robinson, RICHARD CORY, page 136
Paul Simon, RICHARD CORY, page 136

This pair sometimes provokes lively class discussion, especially if someone in the class maintains that Simon converts Robinson into fresh, modern terms. Further discussion may be necessary to show that Robinson's poem has a starkly different theme.

Robinson's truth, of course, is that we envy others their wealth and prestige and polished manners, but if we could see into their hearts we might not envy them at all. Simon's glib song does not begin to deal with this. The singer wishes that he too could have orgies on a yacht, but even after he learns that Cory died a suicide, his refrain goes right on, "I wish that I could be Richard Cory." (Live rich, die young, and make a handsome corpse!)

Some questions to prompt discussion might include:

1. In making his song, Simon admittedly took liberties with Robinson's poem. Which of these changes seem necessary to make the story singable? What suggestions in the original has Simon picked up and amplified?

2. How has Simon altered the character of Richard Cory? Is his Cory a "gentleman" in Robinson's sense of the word? What is the tone of Simon's line, "He had the common touch"? Compare this with Robinson: "he was always human when he talked." Does Robinson's Cory have anything more than "Power, grace and style"?

3. In the song, what further meaning does the refrain take on with its third hearing, in the end, after the news of Cory's suicide?

4. What truth about life does Robinson's poem help us see? Is it merely "Money can't make you happy" or "If you're poor you're really better off than rich people"? Does Simon's narrator affirm this truth, deny it, or ignore it?

Frank J. D'Angelo has noticed that the name Richard Cory is rich in connotations. It suggests Richard Coeur de Lion, and other words in Robinson's poem also point to royalty: *crown*, *imperially*, *arrayed*, *glittered*, *richer than a king*.

MLL *MyLiteratureLab Resources*. Longman Lecture and critical essay on "Richard Cory."

BALLADS

Anonymous, BONNY BARBARA ALLAN, page 137

Despite the numerous versions of this, the most widespread of all traditional ballads in English, most keep the main elements of the story with remarkable consistency. American versions tend to be longer, with much attention to the lovers' eventual side-by-side burial, and sometimes have Barbara's mother die of remorse, too! Commentators since the coming of Freud have sometimes seen Barbara as sexually frigid, and Robert Graves once suggested that Barbara, a witch, is killing Sir John by sorcery. An Irish version makes Barbara laugh hideously on beholding her lover's corpse.

To show how traditional ballads change and vary in being sung, a useful recording is *The Child Ballads*, vol. 1, Caedmon TC 1145, containing performances collected in the field by Alan Lomax and Peter Kennedy. Six nonprofessional singers are heard in sharply different versions of "Barbara Allan," in dialects of England, Scotland, Ireland, and Wales.

Dudley Randall, BALLAD OF BIRMINGHAM, page 140

Randall's poem is an authentic broadside ballad: it not only deals with a news event, it was once printed and distributed on a single page. "I had noticed how people would carry tattered clippings of their favorite poems in their billfolds," the poet has explained, "and I thought it would be a good idea to publish them in an attractive form as broadsides" (Interview in *Black World*, Dec. 1971). "Ballad of Birmingham" so became the first publication of Randall's Broadside Press, of Detroit, which later expanded to publish books and issue recordings by many leading black poets, including Gwendolyn Brooks, Don L. Lee, and Nikki Giovanni.

The poem seems remarkably fresh and moving, though it shows the traits of many English and Scottish popular ballads (such as the questions and answers, as in "Edward," and the conventional-sounding epithets in stanza 5). Randall presents without comment the horror of the bombing—in the mother's response and in the terrible evidence—but we are clearly left to draw the lesson that if the daughter had been allowed to join the open protest, she would have been spared.

Four black girls were killed in 1963 when a dynamite blast exploded in Birmingham's Sixteenth Street Baptist Church. In September 1977, a Birmingham grand jury finally indicted a former Ku Klux Klansman, aged 73, on four counts of first degree murder.

Blues

Bessie Smith with Clarence Williams, Jailhouse Blues, page 142

No one knows exactly who wrote this blues song. Authorship is assigned to Smith and Williams because they recorded it in 1923, but their version owes much to a traditional folk blues that survives in several versions. The concept of authorship in a conventional sense has little meaning in an oral tradition like early blues. Singers took songs they heard and transformed them into material for their own performance. One interesting feature of "Jailhouse Blues" is that the singer addresses the *blues* itself and converses with it.

W. H. Auden, Funeral Blues, page 143

Auden's poem not only uses many blues elements (especially hyperbolic figures of speech to depict sadness); these lines were also originally written for music. The first two stanzas (followed by different third and fourth stanzas) appeared in *The Ascent of F6*, a play that Auden wrote with Christopher Isherwood in 1936. Set to music by the young Benjamin Britten, the words lamented the death of the play's visionary hero. A few years later Auden and Britten rewrote both the words and the music as a cabaret song. (The poem was later set to music again by the American composer Ned Rorem.)

In the process of revision, the song changed from a dirge for a lost political savior to a personal lament for a dead lover. A careful reader will note how the imagery becomes less public and civic in the final two stanzas.

Auden keeps the exaggerated imagery of traditional blues and the flamboyant emotionalism. He also rimes in couplets, as blues songs conventionally do, but he drops the standard repetition of the first line. "Funeral Blues" therefore employs the mood and style of traditional blues but varies the metrical form.

"Funeral Blues" has long been one of Auden's more popular "songs" (a category the author used in his *Collected Poems*), but thanks to its inclusion in the film *Four Weddings and a Funeral*, it has become one of the most widely known modern love poems.

Rap

Run D.M.C., from Peter Piper, page 144

One reason we chose this excerpt from among many rap lyrics was its density of allusion. "Peter Piper" contains as many literary references as Milton's "Lycidas," but most students don't find them intimidating because they come from popular culture and children's literature. It might be helpful to work through the allusions and discuss how they shape the lyrics' effect on the listener; then use this as a model of how allusions to myth and literature work in traditional poetry. (It's nice to see King Midas in a Run D.M.C. lyric.) Rap is a form of oral poetry, and it's interesting to note how these lyrics incorporate many pieces of the central English-language classic of oral poetry—*Mother Goose*.

A metrical note: notice how once the rap settles into its regular rhythm (line 12) it bounces along in a four-stress line, the standard measure of English-language oral poetry from the Anglo-Saxons till today.

FOR REVIEW AND FURTHER STUDY

John Lennon and Paul McCartney, ELEANOR RIGBY, page 145

"Eleanor Rigby," we think, is a poem. Although swayed by the superstition that priests are necessarily lonely because celibate, McCartney's portraits of Father McKenzie and of Eleanor have details that reflect life. Both music and words contain an obvious beat, and if students pick out those syllables in long lines 4 and 7, 14 and 17, and 24 and 27, they will be getting into the subject of meter. (Each of the lines contains a stressed syllable followed by four anapests.)

Bob Dylan, THE TIMES THEY ARE A-CHANGIN', page 146

Bob Dylan's folk song became one of the definitive political anthems of the 1960s, and decades later it holds up extraordinarily well, even on the page. Seen from such a distance, "The Times They Are a-Changin'" is remarkable for its lack of specific topical issues. None of the key political issues of the era is mentioned by name—not even Civil Rights or pacifism. There are a few topical allusions embedded in the text. The lines "Don't stand in the doorway / Don't block up that hall," for example, refer to Governor George Wallace's defiant action to stop school integration in Alabama. But no listener needs to catch that now oblique allusion to get the broader sense of the lines because Dylan has so thoroughly universalized his images. In fact, except for the first line of stanza three with its references to senators and congressmen, there are no specifically American references in the song, which otherwise could apply equally to England, Italy, India, or China.

The song's imagery seems more informed by the Bible than the newspaper. The rising waters, the raging battle, the falling old order have an openly prophetic ring to them. (The lines "And the first one now / will later be last" directly allude to the Gospels—Matthew 19:30, Mark 10:31, Luke 13:30.) The poet/songwriter announces himself as the prophet of a new generation that intends to refashion society in direct confrontation with its elders, but no program of reform is offered by the speaker. The nature of this new order is left almost entirely up to our imagination. Perhaps one reason this song proved so powerful and popular was that each listener could project whatever vision of a new society he or she preferred.

Aimee Mann, DEATHLY, page 148

In the film *Magnolia*, the song "Deathly" is related to Claudia, the adult, drug-addicted daughter of a television quiz-show host, who maintains that she was sexually abused by her father. The song's lyrics describe her reaction—an instinctive defensiveness and unwillingness to be drawn out emotionally—to meeting a lonely, kindhearted police officer who is immediately and protectively attracted to her. The text works fairly successfully on the page (although when separated from its musical setting and forced to stand alone, it is metrically a bit wobbly in places), and lines 30–33 are particularly striking; but the loveliness of the melody—enhanced by the purity of Mann's voice—mitigates the harshness of the statement and adds dimensions of complexity and ambiguity that not only enrich the experience of "Deathly" but are quite appropriate to the character of Claudia and to the film's larger themes.

WRITERS ON WRITING

Paul McCartney, CREATING "ELEANOR RIGBY," page 149

McCartney's comments to the interviewer reveal a great deal about the creative process—how one idea grows unexpectedly out of another. It is interesting to imagine that this song was nearly titled "Daisy Hawkins."

8
Sound

Sound as Meaning

Alexander Pope, True Ease in Writing comes from Art, not Chance, page 153

Nowadays, looking at the pages of an eighteenth-century book of poetry, we might think the liberal capitalization and use of italics merely decorative. But perhaps Pope wished to leave his readers little choice in how to sound his lines. Most of his typographical indications seem to us to make sense—like a modern stage or television script with elements underlined or capitalized, lest the actors ignore a nuance.

Line 12 is deliberately long: an alexandrine, or twelve-syllable line, that must be spoken quickly in order to get it said within the time interval established by the other shorter, pentameter lines.

William Butler Yeats, Who Goes with Fergus?, page 155

Originally a song in Yeats's play *The Countess Cathleen*, this famous lyric overflows with euphony. Take just the opening question (lines 1–3): the assonance of the various *o*-sounds; the initial alliteration of *w*, *d*, and *sh*; the internal alliteration of the *r* in *Fergus*, *pierce*, and *shore*—musical devices that seem especially meaningful for an invitation to a dance. The harsh phrase *brazen cars* seems introduced to jar the brooding lovers out of their reveries. Unless you come right out and ask what brazen cars are, not all students will realize that they are brass chariots. In ancient Ulster, such chariots were sometimes used for hunting deer—though how you would drive one of them through the deep woods beats us.

If you discuss meter, what better illustration of the power of spondees than "And the WHITE BREAST of the DIM SEA?"

The last line of the poem, while pleasingly mysterious, is also exact. The personification "dishevelled wandering stars" makes us think of beautiful, insane, or distracted women with their hair down: Ophelia in Olivier's film *Hamlet*. That they are wandering recalls the derivation of the word *planet:* Greek for "wanderer." In what literal sense might stars look disheveled? Perhaps in that their light, coming through the atmosphere (and being seen through ocean spray) appears to spread out like wild long hair. For comparable figures of speech, see Blake's "Tyger," in which the personified stars weep and throw spears.

MyLiteratureLab Resources. Biography, critical overview, and bibliography for Yeats. Interactive reading of "Who Goes with Fergus?"

EXERCISE: *Listening to Meaning*, page 155
John Updike, RECITAL, page 155
William Wordsworth, A SLUMBER DID MY SPIRIT SEAL, page 156
Emanuel di Pasquale, RAIN, page 156
Aphra Behn, WHEN MAIDENS ARE YOUNG, page 156

"Recital" shows off Updike as one of America's virtuosos of light verse. The whole poem seems written in imitation of the trochaic "oom-pah" of a tuba, and every line ends in a thumping celebration of the near rime between Mr. Bobo's surname and his chosen instrument. Onomatopoeia is heard even more obviously in Behn's *hum-drum*. In di Pasquale's lines, the *s*-sounds fit well with our conception of rain, and *hushes* is an especially beautiful bit of onomatopoeia. By the way, di Pasquale's poem is particularly remarkable in view of the fact that the poet, born in Sicily, did not learn English until he was sixteen. Di Pasquale is now a professor of English at Middlesex Community College in New Jersey; his first collection of poems, *Genesis*, was published in 1989, and he has since published a sequence of love poems, *Escapes the Night* (2001).

In Wordsworth's Lucy poem, sound effects are particularly noticeable in the first line (the soporific *s*'s) and in the last two lines (the droning *r*'s and *n*'s). If students go beyond the sound effects and read the poem more closely, they might find problems in the first stanza. Is the poet's slumber a literal sleep or a figurative one? That is, is Wordsworth recalling some pleasant dream of Lucy (whether the living Lucy he used to know, or the dead Lucy in Eternity), or is he saying that when she was alive he was like a dreamer in his view of her? If so, he was deluded in thinking that she would always remain a child; he had none of the usual human fears of death or of growing old. However we read the poem, there is evidently an ironic contrast between the poet's seeing Lucy (in stanza 1) as invulnerable to earthly years and his later view that she is affected, being helplessly rolled around the sun once a year with the other inanimate objects. And simple though it looks, the poem contains a paradox. The speaker's earlier dream or vision of Lucy has proved to be no illusion but an accurate foreshadowing. Now she is a "thing," like rocks and stones and trees, and she cannot feel and cannot suffer any more from time's ravages.

Aphra Behn was the first English woman to earn a living by her pen. *Oroonoko* (1688), a tale of slavery in Surinam, is sometimes called the first true English novel. Her colorful life, mostly spent in London's literary bohemia, included a hitch in Holland as a spy for the Crown. In her destitute late years she was pilloried in lampoons ("a lewd harlot"), perhaps because she remained faithful to the Stuarts. She was buried in Westminster Abbey under her poetic pen name, Astrea Behn. Nowadays she seems to be enjoying a respectful dusting-off. See the extensive treatment given her in *Kissing the Rod: An Anthology of 17th Century Women's Verse*, ed. Germaine Greer and others (London: Virago, 1988) 240–60.

MyLiteratureLab Resources. Student paper for "Recital." Biography, critical overview, and bibliography for Wordsworth. Critical essay on "A Slumber Did My Spirit Seal."

ALLITERATION AND ASSONANCE

A. E. Housman, EIGHT O'CLOCK, page 158

The final *struck* is a serious pun, to which patterns of alliteration, begun in the opening line *(st . . . st, r)* and continued through the poem, have led up. The ticking effect of the clock is, of course, most evident in *the clock collected*.

Compare Housman's strapped and noosed lad with the one in Hugh Kingsmill's parody of Housman, "What, still alive at twenty-two?"

MyLiteratureLab Resources. Biography, critical overview, and bibliography for Housman.

James Joyce, ALL DAY I HEAR, page 158

This poem is the first of two "tailpieces" added to the sequence of love lyrics called *Chamber Music*, Joyce's first book publication. In these early, admittedly minor (but still highly accomplished) verses, Joyce already shows the excellent ear that would produce such stunning aural effects in *Ulysses* and *Finnegans Wake*. The alliterations in the second, third, and fifth lines are all on relatively soft consonants, in keeping with the melancholy and generally muted tone of the poem. All nine of the poem's rime words (at the ends of lines 2, 4, and 6; 3, 7, and 11; and 8, 10, and 12), along with *cold* (line 7), stress the long *o* sound, knitting the entire text together into an echo of the moan of the waters and the mood they evoke in the speaker.

MyLiteratureLab Resources. Biography, critical overview, and bibliography for Joyce.

Alfred, Lord Tennyson, THE SPLENDOR FALLS ON CASTLE WALLS, page 159

If read aloud rapidly, this famous lyric from Tennyson's *The Princess* will become gibberish; and the phrase *Blow, bugle, blow*, a tongue twister. But if it is read with any attention to its meaning, its long vowels and frequent pauses will compel the reader to slow down. Students may want to regard the poem as mellifluous nonsense, but they may be assured that the poem means something, that it is based on a personal experience of the poet's. Visiting the lakes of Killarney in 1848, Tennyson heard the bugle of a boatman sound across the still water, and he counted eight distinct echoes. "The splendor falls" is the poet's attempt to convey his experience in accurate words.

MyLiteratureLab Resources. Photographs, biography, critical overview, and bibliography for Tennyson. Audio clip for "The splendor falls on castle walls."

RIME

William Cole, ON MY BOAT ON LAKE CAYUGA, page 160

This is one of a series of comic quatrains, "River Rhymes," first printed in *Light Year '85* (Case Western Reserve U: Bits Press, 1984).

James Reeves, ROUGH WEATHER, page 162

This wise and lovely sonnet by the late British poet James Reeves deserves to be better known. (Perhaps it has been anthologized in the UK, but we have not seen it in an American collection.) The poem is technically notable for at least two reasons. First, the entire sonnet consists of a single sentence carefully developed to advance a complex and moving argument about how two lovers survive a difficult separation. Second, "Rough Weather" begins and ends with striking feminine rimes, but it modulates in the middle into masculine rimes.

The theme of the poem is how strongly the speaker's love persists—and indeed thrives—despite the absence of his beloved. The exact circumstance of their separation is never stated. The phrase "this rough, divisive weather" hints perhaps at some problem, and the speaker's later admission "And tell myself I want you to be free" suggests that the lover's absence may be voluntary—perhaps even a desertion. But the speaker stands steadfast in his affection and marvels at how strong memory proves in fostering love. Intelligence, as well as the physical senses, can nourish and sustain genuine love.

Hilaire Belloc, THE HIPPOPOTAMUS, page 163

This amusing short poem requires no commentary. Instructors and students alike might enjoy exploring more of Belloc's light verse, to be found in anthologies such as Kingsley Amis's *The New Oxford Book of English Light Verse* (New York: Oxford UP, 1978).

Ogden Nash, THE PANTHER, page 163

Extremely popular in his day, Nash may now be somewhat of an acquired taste. The first couplet of "The Panther" is clever, but not in a unique way; the second is likely to make the reader say Ouch; but the third exemplifies the kind of linguistic lunacy—exquisite or excruciating, depending on one's point of view—that produced the following complete poems, among many others: "The Bronx? / No, thonx!" and (referring to a risqué revue of the 1920s) "In the Vanities / No one wears panities."

William Butler Yeats, LEDA AND THE SWAN, page 164

The deliberately awful off-rime *up / drop* ends the sonnet with an appropriately jarring plop as the God-swan discards the used Leda and sinks into his post-ejaculatory stupor.

Other questions that can be raised:

1. What *knowledge* and *power* does Yeats refer to in line 14?
2. Do the words *staggering* (line 2) and *loosening* (line 6) keep to the basic meter of the poem or depart from it? How does rhythm express meaning in these lines? (It staggers on *staggering* and loosens on *loosening*.)
3. Compare this poem to Donne's sonnet "Batter my heart." Is the tone of Yeats's sonnet—the poet's attitude toward this ravishing—similar or dissimilar?

For an early draft of the poem, see Yeats's *Memoirs*, ed. Denis Donoghue (New York: Macmillan, 1973) 272–74.

MyLiteratureLab Resources. Biography, critical overview, and bibliography for Yeats. Critical essay on "Leda and the Swan."

Gerard Manley Hopkins, GOD'S GRANDEUR, page 164

Students who think Hopkins goes too far in his insistence on rimes and other similar sounds will have good company, including Robert Bridges, William Butler Yeats, and Yvor Winters. Still, it is hard not to admire the euphony of the famous closing lines—that ingenious alternation of *br* and *w*, with a pause for breath at that magical *ah!*—and the cacophony of lines 6–8, with their jangling internal rimes and the alliteration that adds more weight to *smeared*, *smudge*, and *smell*. For Hopkins, of course, sound is one with meaning, and the cacophonous lines just mentioned are also, as John Pick has pointed out, "a summary of the particular sins of the nineteenth century." For a brilliant demonstration that sound effects in Hopkins's poetry have theological meaning, see J. Hillis Miller, *The Disappearance of God* (Cambridge: Harvard UP, 1963) 276–317. Miller finds the poet's theory revealed in his sermons and journals: "Any two things however unlike are in something like"; therefore, "all beauty may by a metaphor be called rhyme."

In the text, it seemed best not to bury the poem under glosses but to let the instructor decide how thoroughly to explicate it. Here are a few more glosses in case they seem necessary:

Line 7, *man's smudge:* the blight of smoke and ugliness cast over the countryside by factories and mines. As a student for the priesthood in North Wales and as a parish priest in London and Liverpool, Hopkins had known the blight intimately. Another suggestion in the phrase: nature is fallen and needs to be redeemed, like man, who wears the smudge of original sin. Line 12, *morning . . . springs:* The risen Christ is like the sun at dawn. Eastward is the direction of Jerusalem, also of Rome. (Hopkins cherished the hope that the Church of England and the Pope would one day be reconciled.) Lines 13–14, *bent / World:* Perhaps because of its curvature the earth looks bent at the horizon; or perhaps the phrase is a transferred epithet, attributing to the earth the dove's bent-over solicitude. (And as the world seems to break off at the horizon, line 13 breaks at the word *bent*.) Line 14, *broods:* like a dove, traditional representation of the Holy Ghost.

For still more suggestions, see Pick, *Gerard Manley Hopkins, Priest and Poet*, 2nd ed. (Oxford: Oxford UP, 1966) 62–64; Paul L. Mariani, *Commentary on the Complete Poems of Gerard Manley Hopkins* (Ithaca: Cornell UP, 1970); and (not least) the poet's "Pied Beauty."

A sonnet by Wordsworth also begins "The world is," and Hopkins no doubt knew of it. In their parallel (though different) complaints against trade and commerce, the two deserve to be compared. Both poets find humanity artificially removed from nature: this seems the point of Hopkins's observation in lines 7–8 that once soil was covered (with grass and trees) and feet were bare, and now soil is bare and feet are covered. Clearly we have lost the barefoot bliss of Eden, but in answer to Wordsworth, one almost expects Hopkins to cry, "Great God! I'd rather be a Christian." (Wordsworth by *world* means "worldliness.")

MyLiteratureLab Resources. Photographs and biographical information for Hopkins.

Fred Chappell, NARCISSUS AND ECHO, page 165

Fred Chappell is best known as a novelist and short story writer, yet his poetry is exceptionally fine. He has often experimented with old verse forms (like Anglo-Saxon stress meter). In "Narcissus and Echo," he revived a virtually defunct form called "Echo Verse," which had not received much attention since the Renaissance. (Note that "Echo Verse" is described in the footnote to the poem.) To complete his *tour de force*, he uses the form to dramatize the plight of the nymph Echo.

Chappell takes the Echo Verse form one difficult step further than most earlier poets and makes his echoes form a vertical poem down the right-hand side of the page. (Students will usually miss that aspect of the poem unless you point it out to them.) Likewise, Narcissus's speech can be read in isolation, so there are essentially three different poems in this text: Narcissus's self-absorbed solo, Echo's plaintive response, and the pair's lopsided dialogue.

Robert Frost, DESERT PLACES, page 166

Possible answers to the questions following the poem:

1. *What are these desert places that the speaker finds in himself? (More than one theory is possible. What is yours?)* Terrible pockets of loneliness.

2. *Notice how many times, within the short space of lines 8–10, Frost says* lonely *(*or loneliness*). What other words in the poem contain similar sounds that reinforce these words?* The word *snow*, occurring three times. Other *o*-sounds occur in *oh, going, showing, no, so,* and *home*. The *l* of *lonely is* echoed by alliteration in *looked, last,* and *lairs*.

3. *In the closing stanza, the feminine rimes* spaces, race is, *and* places *might well occur in light or comic verse. Does "Desert Places" leave you laughing? If not, what does it make you feel?* It makes us feel a psychic chill! Yet the feminine rime lightens the grim effect of what is said and gives it a kind of ironic smirk.

For an intriguing if far-out appreciation of this poem that makes much of the sibilant *s*-sounds, see Marie Boroff, "Sound Symbolism as Drama in the Poetry of Robert Frost," *PMLA* 107 (1992): 131–144.

 *MyLiteratureLab Resources*. Biography, critical overview, critical articles, and bibliography for Frost.

Reading and Hearing Poems Aloud

Many poets spend their energies in writing poems and are not effective public speakers. Here is a comment by William Stafford on why certain poets read their poems with apparent carelessness. Unlike the Russian poet Andrei Voznesensky, a great performer, Stafford says,

> Most of the poets I know would feel a little guilty about doing an effective job of reading their poems. They throw them away. And I speak as one who does that. It feels fakey enough to be up there reading something as though you were reading it for the first time. And to say it well is just too fakey. So you throw it away. (Interview in *The Literary Monitor* 3.3–4 [1980])

This comment raises provocative questions for discussion. What is the nature of a poetry reading? Should it be regarded as a performance or as a friendly get-together?

For a symposium on poetry readings, with comments by Allen Ginsberg, James Dickey, Denise Levertov, and twenty-nine other poets, see *Poets on Stage* (New York: Some/Release, 1978).

A catalogue of over 800 radio broadcasts on cassette and CD, including a rich variety of programs featuring contemporary poets such as John Ashbery, Gwendolyn Brooks, John Ciardi, Rita Dove, Allen Ginsberg, Anthony Hecht, Colette Inez, Philip Levine, and many others reading and talking about their work, is available from New Letters on the Air, University of Missouri-Kansas City, 5100 Rockhill Road, Kansas City, MO 64110, phone (816) 235–1159. Or, go to <www.newletters.org>.

Exercise: *Reading for Sound and Meaning*, page 168
Michael Stillman, In Memoriam John Coltrane, page 168
William Shakespeare, Full fathom five thy father lies, page 169
Chryss Yost, Lai with Sounds of Skin, page 169
T. S. Eliot, Virginia, page 169

In Michael Stillman's tribute to the great jazz saxophonist, *coal train* is not only a rich pun on Coltrane's name, it also becomes the poem's central image. The poet has supplied this comment:

> One thing about that poem which has always pleased me beyond its elegiac strain—is the way the technique of the lines and phrases corresponds to a musical effect in Coltrane's playing. He was known for his ability to begin with a certain configuration of notes, then play pattern after pattern of variations. The repetition of "Listen to the coal . . . listen to the . . . listen to . . . listen" was one way to capture a feature of his playing. The image of the coal train disappearing into the night comes, particularly, from a place on the James River, west of Richmond, where I happened to be when I heard of Coltrane's death. Like all jazz musicians, I felt the loss very deeply.

Shakespeare's song contains an obvious illustration of onomatopoeia (the bell's sound), obvious alliteration in the *f*-full first line, and (less obviously) internal alliteration (note the *r* and *n* sounds) and assonance galore. Like a drowned man's bones, ordinary language becomes something "rich and strange" in this song.

The central metaphor of Chryss Yost's poem is weaving, and the author has woven an extraordinarily beguiling fabric of sound. Although the poem is only sixteen short lines long, students will be hard-pressed to find devices of sound Yost does not use. Rime, assonance, alliteration, enjambment, stress pattern, syllable count, and repetition are all present. Although the metrical scheme is syllabic, Yost also repeats patterns of stressed and unstressed syllables. Note, for example, how the stress pattern of the first line echoes in the opening line of the second stanza.

The *lai* (or more precisely, *lai nouveau*) is a French form of sixteen lines divided into two eight-line stanzas. Each line has a set syllable count of either two or five syllables. Students can discover the pattern by analyzing Yost's poem. The form is rarely used in English—probably because of the difficulty of rhyming sixteen lines with only three sounds. (The *a* rhyme must be used twelve times!) Amazingly, Yost not only handles the form in the most natural way but creates a gentle yet deeply expressive lyric poem in which the language of weaving becomes a metaphor for the motions of making love.

Chryss Yost has provided the following commentary on her poem:

> The lai, while short, is a deceptively difficult beast to master for at least three reasons. First, unlike most metrical forms in English which count the stressed syllables, the lai measures the syllables in each line. Second, the syllable count is extremely short, just five or two syllables per line. Finally, each stanza uses just two rhymes (*aabaabaa*). In combination with the short lines, this means that the poem must depend on relatively few sounds. A poem with short words and lots of repetition risks falling into obvious, overused rhyme (like *love* and *dove*). I wanted the poem to celebrate the interlocking, tightly-woven form, and I couldn't resist the pun on lai. I went hunting for beautiful and unusual words and discovered *weft*—the threads woven to make fabric. *Weft* has a soft, lingering sound and the meaning seemed to fit the form. *Weft* led to *heft*, *warp*, and *skein*. The technical language of weaving gave me the tools I needed to create an untraditionally sensual poem from a rather restrictive traditional form.

Eliot's "Virginia" is an experiment in quantitative verse, according to George Williamson (*A Reader's Guide to T. S. Eliot* [New York: Noonday, 1957]). You might read aloud "Virginia" and Campion's quantitative "Rose-cheeked

Laura" and ask the class to detect any similarity. Ted Hughes has written of "Virginia" with admiration. How is it, he wonders, that Eliot can create so vivid a landscape without specific images? "What the poem does describe is a feeling of slowness, with a prevailing stillness, of suspended time, of heat and dryness, and fatigue, with an undertone of oppressive danger, like a hot afternoon that will turn to thunder and lightning" (*Poetry Is* [New York: Doubleday, 1967]).

MyLiteratureLab Resources. Photographs, biographical information, and bibliography for Shakespeare. Biography, critical overview, and bibliography for Eliot.

Writers on Writing

T. S. Eliot, The Music of Poetry, page 170

Eliot's remarks on poetic music are full of significant distinctions—most notably his observation that poetic music does not exist apart from poetic meaning. He also bases poetry firmly in speech ("one person talking to another") and assumes that all poetic music will emerge in some way from the sound and rhythms of conversation.

9
Rhythm

STRESSES AND PAUSES

In the first section of this chapter, rhythm is discussed with as few technicalities as possible. For the instructor wishing to go on to the technicalities, the second part of the chapter, "Meter," gives the principles of scansion and the names of the metrical feet.

Except for one teacher at the University of Michigan, James Downer, who would illustrate the rhythms of Old English poetry by banging on his desk for a drum, we have never known anyone able to spend entire classes on meter without etherizing patients. Meter, it would seem, is best dealt with in discussing particular poems.

EXERCISE: *Get with the Beat*, page 175

Browning's four-beat anapestic lines vigorously capture the speed of the scene they describe.

Keeler's loose ballad meter seems suitably rollicking for his down-home subject and tone.

Finch's rhythm is itself an homage to her subject. She has borrowed the hymn stanza that Dickinson used so frequently. Likewise, Finch has deliberately imitated the clear syntax and sonorous cadences of the church hymns to present her images. Although Finch arranges her poem in couplets, the rime scheme and syntax fall into Dickinsonian quatrains.

Eisler's lines describing a newspaper photo of Marilyn Monroe have three strong stresses per line, but Eisler creates a different rhythm in each line by varying the number of unstressed syllables. The effect is a jazz-like syncopation. (The first line also has strong secondary stresses on the compound words *newsprint* and *moonprint* that make this especially evocative line read slowly.)

Shakespeare's songs were sung in the theater. Among other things, they provided a break from the iambic pentameter of most characters' speech. This song from *The Tempest* has a loosely iambic rhythm, but the line lengths differ. They follow a lost melody rather than a strict metrical scheme. The rollicking, unpredictable rhythm seems very appropriate to the mood and setting of the song.

Gwendolyn Brooks, WE REAL COOL, page 177

The poet might have ended every line with a rime, as poets who rime usually do:

> We real cool.
> We left school.

The effect, then, would have been like a series of hammer blows because there are so many short end-stopped lines and so many rimes in quick succession. But evidently Brooks is after a different rhythm. What is it? How to read the poem aloud? Let members of the class take turns trying, and compare their various oral interpretations. If you stress each final *We*, then every syllable in the poem takes a stress; and if, besides, you make even a split-second pause at every line break, then you give those final *We*'s still more emphasis. What if you don't stress the *We*'s but read them lightly? Then the result is a skipping rhythm, rather like that of some cool cat slapping his thighs.

After the class has mulled this problem, read them Brooks's own note on the poem (from her autobiography, *Report from Part One* [Detroit: Broadside, 1972] 185), which is reprinted in the "Writers on Writing" section at the end of this chapter.

As a student remarked about the tone and theme of this poem, "She doesn't think they're real cool, she thinks they're real fool—to die so young like that."

Brooks recorded her own reading of the poem for *The Spoken Arts Treasury of 100 Modern American Poets*, vol. 13, SA 1052.

MyLiteratureLab Resources. Biography, critical overview, and bibliography for Brooks. Interactive reading, student paper, and critical essay on "We Real Cool."

Alfred, Lord Tennyson, Break, Break, Break, page 178

Tennyson's plangent poem displays an interesting rhythmic design. It is written in accentual meter in which the author counts the number of strong stresses per line (rather than in the more conventional accentual-syllabic measure in which one counts both syllables and stresses). The normative line of Tennyson's poem has three strong stresses (though later in the poem, it occasionally broadens to four stresses). By varying the syllable count, Tennyson is able to create all sorts of interesting effects. (It may be worth pointing out to students that Tennyson employs exactly the same technique as Rap in this regard.)

The opening stanza should be scanned as follows:

/ / /
Break, break, break,

U U / U / U /
On thy cold gray stones, O Sea!

U U / U U / U / U
And I would that my tongue could utter

U / U U / U /
The thoughts that arise in me.

Note how Tennyson's accentual meter can stretch the line from 3 to 9 syllables.

MyLiteratureLab Resources. Biography, critical overview, and bibliography for Tennyson.

Ben Jonson, SLOW, SLOW, FRESH FOUNT, KEEP TIME WITH MY SALT TEARS, page 178

O sounds slow the opening line, whose every word is a monosyllable. Further slowing the line, eight of the ten monosyllables take heavy beats. "Drop, drop, drop, drop" obviously racks up still more stresses, as do the spondees that begin lines 4, 5, and 6. The entire effect is that we are practically obliged to read or sing the poem slowly and deliberately—as befits a lamentation.

EXERCISE: *Two Kinds of Rhythm,* page 179
Sir Thomas Wyatt, WITH SERVING STILL, page 179
Dorothy Parker, RÉSUMÉ, page 180

These two poems differ in their rhythm: Wyatt compels a heavy pause only at the end of every quatrain, while Parker end-stops every line. Students may be shown that pauses and meanings go together. Both poems are cast in two sentences, but Wyatt develops one uninterrupted statement throughout the entire poem (in sonnet fashion: first the summary of the speaker's problem in the opening three stanzas, then the conclusion beginning with "Wherefore all ye"). "Résumé," as its punctuation indicates, makes a new self-contained statement in every line.

A question on meaning: Must light verse necessarily be trivial in its theme? State Parker's theme in "Résumé." Surely it isn't trivial. At least in theme, the poem seems comparable to Hamlet's soliloquy "To be or not to be . . . ."

After *Not So Deep as a Well,* her collected poems of 1936, Parker brought out no more poetry collections. "My verses," she insisted to an interviewer. "I cannot say poems. Like everybody was then, I was following in the exquisite footsteps of Miss Millay, unhappily in my own horrible sneakers" (*Writers at Work: The Paris Review Interviews,* 1st ser. [New York: Viking, 1959]). Parker's wit, acerbic and sometimes macabre, is as clear from "Résumé" as it is from her celebrated remark on being informed that Calvin Coolidge had just died: "How could they tell?"

MyLiteratureLab Resources. Photographs and biographical information for Parker. Video clip for "Résumé."

METER

XJK used to think of meter as a platonic ideal norm from which actual lines diverge, but J. V. Cunningham's essay "How Shall the Poem Be Written?"

changed his mind. Metrical patterns (in the abstract) do not exist; there are only lines that poets have written, in which meters may be recognized. "Meter," declares Cunningham, "is perceived in the actual stress-contour, or the line is perceived as unmetrical, or the perceiver doesn't perceive meter at all" (*The Collected Essays of J. V. Cunningham* [Chicago: Swallow, 1976] 262).

Max Beerbohm, ON THE IMPRINT OF THE FIRST ENGLISH EDITION OF *THE WORKS OF MAX BEERBOHM*, page 180

John Updike has paid tribute to this brilliant bit of fluff:

> The effortless a-b-a-b rhyming, the balance of "plain" and "nicely," the need for nicely in pronouncing "Iambically" to scan—this is quintessential light verse, a twitting of the starkest prose into perfect form, a marriage of earth with light, and quite magical. Indeed, were I a high priest of literature, I would have this quatrain made into an amulet and wear it about my neck, for luck. ("Rhyming Max," a review of Beerbohm's collected verse, reprinted in *Assorted Prose* [New York: Knopf, 1965])

Thomas Campion, ROSE-CHEEKED LAURA, COME, page 186

Campion included this famous lyric in his polemic *Observations on the Art of English Poesie* (1602), in which he argued that English poets ought to adopt the quantitative meters of Greek and Latin. "This cannot be done in English," says John Hollander, "with its prominent word stress, save by assigning Latin vowel lengths to the written English, and simply patterning what amounts to a typographical code which cannot be heard as verse. . . . 'Rose-cheekt Laura' is therefore merely an unrhymed English trochaic poem, perfectly plain to the ear" (Introduction to *Selected Songs of Thomas Campion*, selected by W. H. Auden [Boston: Godine, 1973]).

EXERCISE: *Meaningful Variation*, pages 186–187

Aside from minor variations from a metrical norm (such as the substitution of a trochee for an iamb), the most meaningful departures in these passages seem to occur in these words or phrases:

1. Dryden: *deviates*. (Now there's a meaningful deviation!)

2. Pope: the spondees *snakes*, *drags*, and *slow length*.

3. Byron: the last line of Byron's stanza is two syllables (or one iambic foot) longer than the earlier lines. These extra syllables give the stanza a strong sense of closure.

4. Stevens: *spontaneous*, *casual*, *ambiguous*.

EXERCISE: *Recognizing Rhythms*, page 187

Edna St. Vincent Millay, COUNTING-OUT RHYME, page 187
Jacqueline Osherow, SONG FOR THE MUSIC IN THE WARSAW GHETTO, page 188
A. E. Housman, WHEN I WAS ONE-AND-TWENTY, page 188
William Carlos Williams, SMELL!, page 189
Walt Whitman, BEAT! BEAT! DRUMS!, page 189
Langston Hughes, DREAM BOOGIE, page 190

Probably it is more important that students be able to recognize a metrical poem than that they name its meter. The Millay and Housman poems are thoroughly metrical. The Whitman and Williams are not, but they include metrical lines in places: in Whitman's poem, besides the refrain (lines 1, 8, and 15) there are primarily iambic lines that end each stanza; the Williams poem grows rhythmically insistent in places where the speaker berates his nose for its omnivorous and indecorous curiosity. The first and third stanzas of the Osherow poem have a ballad-like near regularity, but the middle of the second stanza contains two lines of iambic pentameter: perhaps the author strives to avoid a repetitive singsong rhythm that might seem to undermine the gravity of the subject. Hughes's "Dream Boogie" starts out with a metrical beat, then (deliberately) departs from it in the italicized interruptions.

MyLiteratureLab Resources. Biography, critical overview, and bibliography for Millay, Housman, Williams, Whitman, and Hughes. Critical essay on "Dream Boogie."

David Mason, SONG OF THE POWERS, page 190

Another powerful poem written in accentual meters: there are two strong stresses in each line. Since nursery rhymes are usually written in accentual meters, and Mason's poem uses the children's game of Scissors, Paper, Stone as its unifying metaphor, the meter is especially appropriate to the subject. But Mason also uses the rough-edged quality of accentual meter to convey the raw, uncompromising nature of his protagonists. Each character (Stone, Paper, Scissors) speaks in turn, announcing its power, pride, and position. As the poem progresses, these symbolic speakers reveal how unrestrained ambition and desire destroy human relations and community.

WRITERS ON WRITING

Gwendolyn Brooks, HEARING "WE REAL COOL," page 191

Brooks's remarks on her poem suggest how she consciously uses rhythm as an instrument of meaning. By placing *we* at the end of each of the first seven lines—in contrast to a more conventional placement at the beginning of each line—she forces the reader to stop and think more probingly about what the lines mean. In the interview, she also stresses that her lineation was not trying to copy a colloquial rhythm but to express her attitude toward the protagonists in her poem—a significant and provocative distinction.

Kilroy, as students may need to know, was a fictitious—even mythical—character commemorated in graffiti chalked or penciled by U.S. soldiers wherever they traveled in World War II. KILROY WAS HERE was even scrawled in the sands of Anzio, a small testimonial that the graffitist is a person.

10
Closed Form

Beginning students of poetry have often had a hard time appreciating either a sonnet or a poem in open verse because they have yet to distinguish one variety of poetry from the other. On first meeting an unfamiliar poem, the experienced reader probably recognizes it as metrical or nonmetrical from its opening lines—and perhaps can tell at a glance from its look on the page (compact sonnet or spaced-out open verse). Such a reader then settles down to read with appropriate expectations, aware of the rules of the poem, looking forward to seeing how well the poet can play by them. But the inexperienced reader reads mainly for plain prose sense, unaware of the rhythms of a Whitmanic long line or the rewards of a sonnet artfully fulfilling its fourteenth line. Asked to write about poetry, the novice reader may even blame the sonnet for being "too rigid," or blame William Carlos Williams for "lacking music" (that is, lacking a rime scheme) or for "running wild." Such readers may have their preferences, but they say nothing about a poem or the poet's accomplishments.

That is why this chapter and the following one seem to us essential. To put across to students the differences between the two formal varieties, it isn't necessary to deal with every last fixed form, either. One can do much by comparing two poems (closed and open) on the theme of sorrow: Edna St. Vincent Millay's fine sonnet "What lips my lips have kissed" and Stephen Crane's astonishing "The Heart." Before taking up closed form, you might care to teach some song lyrics or a couple of traditional folk ballads. That way, the student isn't likely to regard fixed forms as arbitrary constructions invented by English teachers. A stanza, you can point out, is the form that words naturally take when sung to a tune; that is how stanzas began. Sing a second round of a song, and you will find yourself repeating the pattern of it.

Formal Patterns

John Keats, This Living Hand, Now Warm and Capable, page 195

After Keats's death, these grim lines were discovered in the margin of one of his manuscripts. Robert Gittings has pointed out that the burden of the poem is much like that of two letters Keats wrote late in life to Fanny Brawne, charging her conscience with his approaching death and blaming her for enjoying good health. "This," says Gittings, "marks the lowest depths of his disease-ridden repudiation of both love and poetry" (*John Keats* [Boston: Atlantic-Little, 1968] 403). To discuss: can a repudiation of poetry nevertheless be a good poem?

MLL *MyLiteratureLab Resources.* Photographs, biographical information, critical overview, and bibliography for Keats.

Robert Graves, Counting the Beats, page 197

At mid-century, Robert Graves was generally considered one of the major English poets of the Modern era. Then shortly before his death he fell out of critical favor. His work almost vanished from the anthologies. Now his reputation is slowly but surely on the rise. Poet, novelist, critic, autobiographer, Graves stands as a diverse and original (if also often eccentric) literary talent—the one surviving British poet of the First World War to achieve a major literary career.

"Counting the Beats" has received almost no critical attention, but it has been a favorite among poets since its first appearance. The poem has an almost hypnotic rhythm. The stanza pattern of the poem is original. The meter is accentual. Each four-line stanza begins with a short two-beat line. The next line has three beats. The long third line of each stanza has five stresses. The stanza then ends with another short two-beat line.

The rime scheme is equally noteworthy and original. Each stanza ends with an *l*-sound, but the first three lines of each stanza repeat a single word as an end-rime. This gives each stanza the effect of the two speakers repeating, refining, and qualifying their ideas as they converse.

Readers interested in learning more about Graves might want to consult the scholarly journal *Focus on Robert Graves and His Contemporaries*, edited by Richard Schumaker and published by the Department of English at the University of Maryland.

John Donne, Song ("Go and catch a falling star"), page 198

Maybe it is worth pointing out that, in bringing together short stanzas to make one longer one, Donne hasn't simply joined quatrain, couplet, and tercet like a man making up a freight train by coupling boxcars. In sense and syntax, each long stanza is all one: its units would be incomplete if they were separated.

Phillis Levin, Brief Bio, page 200

Levin's poem is, of course, an acrostic. The first letter of each line spells out the hidden subject of the poem—*BUTTERFLY.* The title also contains a double pun. First, the poem contains a brief biography of the butterfly's life (*bio* means *life* in Greek); second, the butterfly's life is brief. Levin provides this note about her poem:

> Poetry is intimately bound up with the unknown, and so to write a riddle is to begin from the reverse of our condition, and to mirror the condition of the reader. In a riddle, as in life, we do not know what will follow, what will surprise, and yet we remain engaged, because the riddle catches us. The tension and expectations arise from the encountering of a form—for if it closes, both in time and space, we expect it to disclose itself finally.

If a butterfly always seems to be moving somewhere, we must follow it, as one must follow the lines, the thread of thought and images, to find the answer to the riddle. Thus, the butterfly is an icon of passing, of the ethereal nature of presence. To compose a poem whose answer is the butterfly is to make an encomium to ephemeral beauty and eternal form. To write an acrostic is to commit oneself to a rather arbitrary journey, without rhyme or reason: one must first accept the fact of the letters that form the word, and from there make one's way into the poem, believing one's imagination will flower to meet the pressures and limitations imposed by the pattern accepted from the start.

But the very form of a riddle suggests an answer just out of reach, promising in time to be attainable. A riddle poses the possibility of knowing, of grasping; and in the case of a butterfly, the riddle's answer, when grasped, is the fulfillment of holding in one's mind the image of something that cannot be held in one's hand—without destroying the object. Perhaps the subject of the riddle, which I alighted on by chance, is really a paradigm of the poet's desire: to hold what cannot last, except in memory or in works that create a realm enacting the vividness of memory, and thereby making it possible to share what is usually limited to the boundary of individual consciousness. The poem is in the movement, not the answer, though that need for an answer, heightened by the growing sense of the as-of-yet unrecognized familiar noun, propels the reader, just as the delight in finding associations and clues that bring the reader closer is what moves the poet.

"Brief Bio" is also, of course, my elliptical, elided biographical note—a brief life, or a brief summation of one, an *ars poetica* in miniature. To be what one is, pure movement inseparable from one's form, the unity of rhythm and design—that is what I want my poems to embody, and that is what a butterfly seems to say of itself in its act of being itself. Its being is transitive, subject and object cannot be distinguished.

The profile of the butterfly is inscribed in the poem's shape (whose contours can be traced on the right side), just as the letters spelling its identity are traced on the vertical axis of the left-hand margin. If there is nothing less "concrete" than a butterfly, still we relish its brief moments of stillness, voyeurs to its constant sequence of change, the freedom of its detachment, to suddenly rise and then dip down, sipping nectar from a flower—as if in the same gesture it were eating and praying before passing on.

The Sonnet

William Shakespeare, Let me not to the marriage of true minds, page 201

Shakespeare's enormously popular Sonnet 116 is a meditation on ideal love and romantic fidelity. As one would expect of any famous work by Shakespeare, the meaning of every line in the poem has been debated. Most modern critical discussions have centered on whether the speaker really believes that perfect human constancy is possible or whether the poem is subtly skeptical about its own romantic idealism.

A crucial notion to point out in a classroom discussion is that Shakespeare's poem discusses a spiritual union ("the marriage of true minds," not of bodies). He acknowledges that physical youth and beauty are victim to the ravages of Time. Spiritual love even endures bodily death, the poem asserts, and lasts until Doomsday.

 *MyLiteratureLab Resources*. Photographs, biographical information, and bibliography for Shakespeare. Critical essay on "Let me not to the marriage of true minds."

Michael Drayton, SINCE THERE'S NO HELP, COME LET US KISS AND PART, page 202

Nay, yea, wouldst, and *mightst* are the only words that couldn't equally well come out of the mouth of a lover in the twenty-first century.

There seems to be an allegorical drama taking place, as Laurence Perrine has pointed out in "A Drayton Sonnet," *CEA Critic* 25 (June 1963): 8. Love is also called Passion, and apparently his death is being urged along by the woman's infernal Innocence.

Edna St. Vincent Millay, WHAT LIPS MY LIPS HAVE KISSED, AND WHERE, AND WHY, page 202

Millay's originality has been insufficiently appreciated by critics. Too often she has been portrayed as a sentimental traditionalist removed from the mainstream of Modernist innovation. Millay's diction was very traditional, and her devotion to metrical forms such as the sonnet seemed conservative when compared to the experimentalism of Pound and Williams. And yet Millay's tone and subject matter were revolutionary in their time, and her strong feminist voice remains powerful. The sexual candor and moral freedom of this 1923 sonnet hardly seem reactionary or conservative.

The female speaker of the sonnet recalls her many lovers but—significantly—only in a general sense. They are too numerous for her to individualize. She displays no traditional guilt for her amours. Her only specific remorse concerns her own aging. (By implication, she longs to be young and in love again.)

The sestet of Millay's sonnet explicitly recalls Shakespeare's sonnet "That time of year thou mayst in me behold"—another poem in which an aging lover regrets the passing of youth and the approach of old age. Millay boldly appropriates Shakespeare's metaphor of the winter tree and develops it for her own ends. In her excellent essay "Love's 'Little Day': Time and the Sexual Body in Millay's Sonnets" (in *Millay at 100: A Critical Appraisal*, edited by Diane P. Freedman, Carbondale: Southern Illinois UP, 1995), Stacy Carson Hubarb comments:

> The aging speaker as songless tree is an abject figure, one that we might be tempted to read as a prototype of abandoned womanhood, pathetic and powerless, if it were not for the powerful alliance that such abjectness establishes between Millay's speaker and Shakespeare's. The speaker of Shakespeare's sonnet makes a spectacle of his abjection by way of persuasion; so, too, does Millay's, but with the further motive of authorizing herself through

poetic echo. To read such self-abjection without a view to literary history would be to mistake it for mere self-pity, a sentimental attachment to the figure of woman as victim, rather than the bold poetic affiliation that Millay surely intends it to be.

MyLiteratureLab Resources. Photographs and biographical information for Millay. Video clip and student paper for "What lips my lips have kissed, and where, and why."

Robert Frost, Acquainted with the Night, page 203

This poem first appeared in *West-Running Brook* (1928), Frost's fifth volume, which some critics felt marked a turning in his work toward dark, personal themes. One might argue whether Frost's turn to dark themes began here, but it is true that many of his grimmer early poems were cast in a seemingly impersonal narrative form.

"Acquainted with the Night" shows many of the features we associate with Frost's darkly introspective side. Not only is the speaker solitary and alienated from the human community surrounding him; he fatalistically accepts this isolation. The poem begins and ends with the same line, which emphasizes the inescapable quality of the speaker's destiny, though by now *night* has acquired a metaphorical as well as a literal meaning.

Although the poem is written in a direct first-person voice, it confides very little to the reader. We know the speaker's desperate isolation but, as William Pritchard observes in his superb study *Frost: A Literary Life Reconsidered* (New York: Oxford UP, 1984), the poem provides "no clues or provocation to significant action." We know what is happening in the poem but not why. Noting that the poem was written in *terza rima*, Randall Jarrell commented that it possessed "Dante's own form . . . with some of Dante's own qualities." We might elaborate on Jarrell's passing remark by saying that one reading of the poem would describe it as the speech of a lost soul wandering in his own private hell.

It is worth noting that the moody Frost was a compulsive walker whose late night rambles were legendary, though he liked them best with friends.

MyLiteratureLab Resources. Biography, critical overview, critical articles, and bibliography for Frost. Longman Lecture on "Acquainted with the Night."

Kim Addonizio, First Poem for You, page 204

Anyone who thinks the sonnet form forces a writer into old-fashioned themes should look at this sexy and surprising poem. Addonizio creates a totally contemporary situation and language, and yet she also touches subtly on ancient, indeed primal poetic themes—the impermanence of flesh, the unpredictability of sexual passion, and the mysterious relationship between body and soul.

An interesting question to ask in class: what do the images the speaker's lover has tattooed onto his (or possibly her) body suggest about the person's character? The tattoos depict lightning and blue swirls of water out of which a serpent faces a dragon. These are the only specific images we have of the otherwise unseen lover.

Mark Jarman, UNHOLY SONNET: HANDS FOLDED, page 204

Mark Jarman has provided the following note.

> John Donne's Holy Sonnets are the models for my Unholy Sonnets. His poems are urgent declarations of faith and appeals for mercy, despite the obvious realities of sin and death. Donne applies terrific pressure to form and metaphor, and both at times come close to collapse. Still, he works from Anglo-Catholic, Christian assumptions widely disseminated and shared in his time. It is almost impossible to work from such assumptions today. My aim in the Unholy Sonnets has been to work against any assumption or shared expression of faith, to write a devotional poetry against the grain. At the same time I have tried to write traditional sonnets without sticking to any one traditional form. So far (the project is ongoing) the Unholy Sonnets includes English, Italian, Spenserian, composite, and nonce forms. Calling them Unholy is a way of warding off piety but not, I hope, ultimately, belief.

From the list of sonnet forms that Jarman provides in his comment, the one that fits "Hands Folded" is *composite*: the first eight lines resemble a Petrarchan octave in their *a b a b* rime scheme (though lines 5–8 do not repeat the rime words of the first four lines); the last six lines replicate a Shakespearean quatrain and concluding couplet. "All the people" are, of course, the eight fingers (excluding thumbs) of the two hands clasped together as alluded to in the familiar rhyme this poem is based on: "Here is the church, / Here is the steeple, / Open the doors, / And see all the people." If there is a turn of thought, it comes with the "But" at the beginning of line 11, where the poem moves from a fanciful description of two entangled hands to an implicit comment on human relationships.

Twenty "Unholy Sonnets" appear in Jarman's collection *Questions for Ecclesiastes* (Brownsville: Story Line, 1997).

Timothy Steele, SUMMER, page 205

Steele's sonnet carefully uses language that evokes—to rearrange his own words—the voluptuous plenty of summer. Most of the images are deliberately still or static: windless lakes, dense orchards, slow creeks, and the person "supine" in the meadow grass. The poem also contrasts nature's immense abundance with the poor striving of humankind. Faced with summer's magnificence, the thoughtful person simply surrenders to it. In this sense, Steele's sonnet works in the tradition of the *carpe diem* poem, but in Steele's world the consciousness of death is entirely absent. He suggests that we seize the day simply because it is so beautiful.

Instructors may want to note that Horace's original *carpe diem* ode is found in the "Translation" chapter along with three translations of it.

A. E. Stallings, SINE QUA NON, page 205

Note the ways in which Stallings combines the traditional features of the sonnet form with unusual variations of her own in order to achieve the subtle and moving effects of "Sine Qua Non." The rime scheme presents a variation on the Shakespearean sonnet: there are three quatrains riming *abba*, followed by a concluding couplet, but there are no full stops at the ends of lines 4 and 12; the text presents a linked, flowing set of separate ways of making the same central point, rather than approaching the subject from a different perspective in each four-line unit. In its appearance on the page, "Sine Qua Non" more closely resembles a Petrarchan sonnet, yet the turn, such as it is, at line 9 is actually more of a *re*turn to the poem's opening, with its repetition of the poem's first five words. The movement from octave to sestet is perhaps best perceived as a movement from implicit statement in the first eight lines to a more explicit approach in the last six, especially in line 12.

R. S. Gwynn, SHAKESPEAREAN SONNET, page 206

This is a Shakespearean sonnet in both form and content, inspired by newspaper TV-show plot summaries that had, for purposes of satiric inspiration, the double felicity of being laughably insipid and in perfect iambic pentameter. With that line as his *donnée*, Gwynn proceeds to perform similarly banal reductions of *Romeo and Juliet; Macbeth; A Midsummer Night's Dream; Richard III; Julius Caesar; Henry IV, Part 1; Othello; Henry V; Twelfth Night; As You Like It; King Lear; Coriolanus;* and *Antony and Cleopatra*.

Of the prominent formalist poets writing today, Gwynn may be the keenest satirist. He has written a wonderful extended satire on contemporary poets and poetry in the great tradition of Pope's *Dunciad: The Narcissiad* (New Braunfels, TX: Cedar Rock P, 1981). He frequently reviews poetry for *Texas Review, Sewanee Review*, and other literary journals, and he is currently a professor of English at Lamar University in Beaumont, Texas.

THE EPIGRAM

Alexander Pope, EPIGRAM ENGRAVED ON THE COLLAR OF A DOG, page 207

Students may be asked: What's the point? Pope makes a devastating comment on society. With few exceptions (such as His Royal Highness), every man is a dog: owned by somebody, accepting handouts, licking his master's hand, learning to heel.

Sir John Harrington, Robert Herrick, William Blake, E. E. Cummings, Langston Hughes, J. V. Cunningham, John Frederick Nims, Stevie Smith, Brad Leithauser, Dick Davis, Anonymous, Hilaire Belloc, Wendy Cope, A SELECTION OF EPIGRAMS, pages 207–209

Highly various, these thirteen examples illustrate the persistence of the epigram. Whether the form of an epigram is closed or open, its essence consists of brevity and a final dash of wit.

Besides writing "Of Treason," called the best epigram in English, Harrington has another claim to immortality: he invented the water closet.

Blake offers a definition of the epigram, written as epigrams.

Cunningham, the American master of the verse epigram in our time, has had few recent rivals. Instructors who seek further examples of this fixed form will find many to quote in his *Collected Poems and Epigrams* (Chicago: Swallow, 1971).

Nims, the closest rival to Cunningham, collected his epigrams, including "Contemplation," in *Of Flesh and Bone* (New Brunswick: Rutgers UP, 1967). When first printed, in the *New Yorker,* this poem was called "A Thought for Tristram"—suggesting that *you* means Isolde, betrothed of King Mark, with whom Tristan/Tristram shares a love potion.

If the haiku-like brevity of epigrams tempts you to ask your class to write a few, resist the temptation. Even from a bright class the results are likely to depress you. A successful epigrammatist needs, besides the ability to condense, the ability to deliver that final rapier thrust of nastiness. A talented creative writing class, after tackling poems in a few of the less demanding forms (ballads, villanelles, sestinas), might try epigrams, either rimed or rimeless.

If you do decide to challenge your class with writing an epigram, you might suggest they try the Wendy Cope approach and either update or revise an existing epigram. You'll be surprised how personal some revisions can become.

The Clerihew

As for the "conventional subject matter" of the clerihew, you should find a hint in the following example by E. C. Bentley:

> The Art of Biography
> Is different from Geography.
> Geography is about Maps,
> But Biography is about Chaps.

Other Forms

Robert Pinsky, ABC, page 210

The title of Robert Pinsky's short poem suggests its form: an abecediary, a poem which uses the order of the alphabet as its structural principle. Exactly twenty-six words long (not counting the equal sign in the last line), the poem offers one word for each letter of the alphabet in strict order from A to Z. Pinsky turns what might merely be a word game into a concise and evocative meditation on death. The meditation acquires a strange force because it seems to push against the arbitrary limitations of the form. Each new word feels hard-won, a fragment of meaning achieved against the odds. Without the poem's demanding form, Pinsky could easily achieve a more fluent statement of his theme, but that difficult articulation and urgent economy would vanish.

Dylan Thomas, Do not go gentle into that good night, page 211

No mere trivial exercise (as a villanelle tends to be), Thomas's poem voices his distress at the decline and approaching death of his father. At the time, the elder Thomas was a semi-invalid, going blind, and suffering from the effects of tongue cancer. As a teacher of English at Swansea Grammar School, the poet's father had ruled his class with authority; but those who knew him only in his last years knew a different, humbled man. (See Constantine FitzGibbon, *The Life of Dylan Thomas* [Boston: Atlantic-Little, 1965] 294–95.)

Like many other Thomas poems, this one contains serious puns: *good night*, *grave*. "Another assumption in this poem," says Amy Mulvahill (in a student paper written at Tufts), "may be Thomas's own self-destructive drive that led him to drink himself to death. It's possible that he preferred to taunt death with his boisterous life—to go down unrepentant and brawling."

Repetitious as a villanelle is, the form suits this poem, making its refrains sound like prayers said over and over. If you have any student poets, you might challenge them to write villanelles of their own. The hard part is to make the repeated lines occur naturally, to make them happen in places where there *is* something to be said. But the repetitious form is helpful; write the two refrain lines and already your labors are eight-nineteenths over.

For another instance of Thomas's fondness for arbitrary, demanding forms, see the poem "Prologue" at the beginning of Daniel Jones's edition of *The Poems of Dylan Thomas* (New York: New Directions, 1971). A poem of 102 lines, its first and last lines rime with each other, as do lines 2 and 101, 3 and 100, 4 and 99, and so on, until two riming lines collide at the poem's exact center. Except for that inmost pair of lines, however, no reader is likely to notice the elaborate rime scheme—rimes so far apart they can't be heard; but apparently it supplied the poet with obstacles to overcome and a gamelike pleasure.

MyLiteratureLab Resources. Interactive reading and critical essay on "Do not go gentle into that good night."

Robert Bridges, Triolet, page 211

The triolet is a form usually associated with light verse, but Bridges's poem demonstrates that it can convey heavier emotional loads if used with sufficient skill. Bridges's triolet could be offered as an example of a short lyric—compressed, evocative, musical, and personal. He also manages to make the opening lines acquire considerable additional force by the end of the poem. We now know both that the couple fell into their passion unawares (they "did not guess") and that their love was not only difficult but irretrievably disastrous. Is there a more moving triolet in English?

Elizabeth Bishop, Sestina, page 212

We would answer the questions following the poem like this:

1. That some terrible loss—a death in the family?—causes the grandmother to weep seems a guess that fits the poem. The old woman tries to hide her grief from the child (lines 6, 10, 31–32); she thinks it was somehow foretold (9).

2. We have no authority to read this poem as autobiography, but the figure of the grandmother—the most important person in Bishop's early life—and the stormy setting (such as we might find in a village on the Nova Scotia coast) invite us to do so. The source of grief may have been the death of the poet's father (hence, an irony that the child draws a man with tear-shaped buttons) or it may have been the illness of her mother, hospitalized several times for a mental disorder. When Bishop was eight months old her father died, and according to Robert Giroux, "The first real home Elizabeth knew was in the coastal town of Great Village, Nova Scotia, where her widowed mother returned in order to be with her parents" (Introduction to Bishop's *Collected Prose* [New York: Farrar, 1984]). When the poet was five, her mother had a final breakdown, leaving the girl in the care of her grandmother. Apparently Bishop looked back to her days in Nova Scotia with affectionate yearning. When she was six, her father's wealthy parents moved her to Worcester, Massachusetts, for a less happy stay.

3. Small round pieces of paper. Almanacs (such as *The Old Farmer's*) come with punched holes to make them easy to string and hang on a hook or a nail.

4. The playful ingenuity of the sestina, like that of the villanelle, tempts a poet to wax clever; yet Bishop is writing a deeply felt, moving poem in it. The tone is lightly serious, compassionate—yet with touches of gentle humor: the Little Marvel Stove, the child's drawings. Irony, too, informs the poem: a contrast between the grandmother's sorrow and the child's innocent ignorance.

5. Nims's comment seems an apt description of "Sestina." In the six repeated words, we are given the setting *(house)* the characters *(grandmother, child)*, and key symbols *(Stove, almanac, tears)*. "Sestina" weaves all six into a subtle relationship. This poem is full of things that suggest magic: the prophetic almanac, the teacup (with which fortune-tellers divine), the "marvellous stove." It also is full of secret-keepers: the grandmother, the almanac with its powers of prophecy, the concluding reference to the "inscrutable house." The repetitions are worth tracing: *tears*, in particular, accumulates an effect. In stanza 2 the tears arrive like an equinoctial storm; in 3, the kettle also weeps; in 4, tea is tears; in 5, the man in the child's drawing wears tears; in 6, the almanac weeps paper tears; and finally, in the envoy, tears are flowers. "Time to plant tears" may be a literal quotation from the almanac, *tears* being (if memory serves) the name of a small white flower favored by rock gardeners.

Bishop's *Complete Poems* contains another intriguing sestina, "A Miracle for Breakfast." At the time it was written Bishop remarked (in a 1937 letter to Marianne Moore):

> It seems to me that there are two ways possible for a sestina—one is to use unusual words as terminations, in which case they would have to be used differently as often as possible—as you say, "change, of scale." That would

make a very highly seasoned kind of poem. And the other way is to use as colorless words as possible—like Sidney, so that it becomes less of a trick and more of a natural theme and variations. I guess I have tried to do both at once. (Quoted by Nims in his essay cited in question 5.)

In the later "Sestina," the terminal words seem to be deliberately usual ones.

For the poet Eavan Boland's insightful comparison of "Sestina" and Bishop's poem "One Art," please see the notes on the latter poem in this manual.

MyLiteratureLab Resources. Biography, critical overview, and bibliography for Bishop.

Exercise: *Urgent Repetition*, page 213

This experiment just might leave you surprised at the quality of some of its results. Whoever writes a sestina has a powerful ally—the form—on his or her side.

In a *tour de force*, a student in a poetry workshop at Tufts once wrote a fairly successful sestina taking *one, two, three, four, five*, and *six* for its repeated words. The result seemed only mildly boring and mechanical!

Writers on Writing

A. E. Stallings, On Form and Artifice, page 214

Stallings makes the important observation that *artificial* is not a dirty word; *art, artifice*, and *artificial*, after all, are all linguistically related. A true artist works—with insight, discipline, and skill—to create the desired effect, which is far from the same thing as spontaneously setting down one's thoughts and feelings. A writer wishing, for example, to communicate the thrill and ache of first love could hardly do worse than transcribe an actual phone conversation, in all of its tedium and banality, between two smitten teenagers. "It seems an obvious point for art," as she says, but these days it also seems to be a point that needs to be made.

11
Open Form

Denise Levertov, ANCIENT STAIRWAY, page 217

This poem is discussed fairly extensively in the text. It may be a useful piece to use to generate a discussion about the nature of poetry. Particularly if you have just spent class time emphasizing the conventions of closed forms as they are discussed and illustrated in the previous chapter, you might begin by asking something like, "Given the absence of rime and meter, and of all the conventions of traditional poetical form, what is particularly poetic about this piece? What makes it a poem?"

E. E. Cummings, BUFFALO BILL 'S, page 221

Cleanth Brooks and Robert Penn Warren have taken this poem to be an admiring tribute to William Cody (*Understanding Poetry*, 3rd ed. [New York: Holt, 1960]). But Louis J. Budd, in an interesting dissent, thinks Cummings is satirizing the theatricality of the old sideshow straight-shooter and finds Mister Death "a cosmic corporal gathering up defunct tin-gods and stuffed effigies" (*The Explicator* 11 [June 1953]: item 55).

 *MyLiteratureLab Resources*. Photographs and biographical information for Cummings. Audio clip and critical essay on "Buffalo Bill 's."

W. S. Merwin, FOR THE ANNIVERSARY OF MY DEATH, page 221

W. S. Merwin's poem is written in unpunctuated free verse. The lines tend to end on natural speech pauses, but without conventional punctuation the reader cannot know if a phrase or sentence ends until he or she says the line aloud (or reads it carefully) and proceeds to the next line. The effect is one of discovering the full meaning of the lines only as they unfold. The phase "Tireless traveler," for example, is initially ambiguous in syntactical terms. Does it refer to the speaker or the silence of death? Only by going on to the next line ("Like the beam of a lightless star") does the reader understand that the phrase stands in apposition to *silence*. Merwin's lack of punctuation, therefore, both slows down one's reading of the poem and endows its language with an appropriate sense of mystery.

The central idea of the poem is itself a mystery—the exact date of the speaker's death. This question is a universal one because it is a mystery that every human faces. Merwin uses the occasion of his quandary to meditate on his mortality and to praise the beauty of the world in religious terms, though his spiritual impulse reflects the mystery of existence. The speaker bows "not knowing to what." Ultimately, Merwin's "For the Anniversary of My Death" is a contemporary version of the Roman poet Horace's *carpe diem* ode, in which the speaker acknowledges the impossibility of knowing the exact time of one's inevitable death and so resolves to seize the day by living fully.

William Carlos Williams, THE DANCE, page 222

Scanned, the poem is seen to abound in pairs of unstressed syllables. The result is a bouncing rhythm—anapestic or dactylic, depending on where one wishes to slice the lines into feet. This rhythm seems appropriate to a description of frolicking dancers and helps establish the tone of the poem, which is light, however serious. Williams severs his units of sense again and again in midphrase, placing his line breaks after *and, the, about, thick, those, such.* In this poem run-on lines predominate, and this is not only a technical device but a way of underlining the poem's meaning. Williams conveys a sense of continuous movement in a syntax that keeps overflowing line units.

By repeating its opening line, the poem, like Brueghel's dancers, comes round in a circle to where it began. Another metaphor is possible: like a painting enclosed in a frame, the poem encloses its central scene in a frame of words.

Williams first saw Brueghel's painting in Vienna in 1924, but he wrote this poem in 1942, some eighteen years later. A French critic, Jacqueline Saunier-Ollier, has speculated on the curious fact that the poem, in describing a vividly colorful tableau, omits all color images. Her work on Williams's Brueghel poems is summed up in *William Carlos Williams: Man and Poet*, ed. Carroll F. Terrell (Orono: National Poetry Foundation, 1983) 528–29.

MyLiteratureLab Resources. Biography, critical overview, and bibliography for Williams.

Stephen Crane, THE HEART, page 223
Walt Whitman, CAVALRY CROSSING A FORD, page 223

These two nineteenth-century American poems seem comparable mainly in their brevity and use of narration. The assonance and internal alliteration in Whitman's phrase *silvery river* are echoed in the poem's opening line: the assonance of the *i*-sound in *line, wind, islands;* the internal alliteration of the *r* in *array, where, green.* But any line of this short poem will repay such inspection. Crane's "The Heart" is obviously less heavy on verbal music, although *Held his heart in his hands* is heavily alliterative; and the second stanza favors the letter *b.* There is rime, too: *it/bitter, bitter/heart.*

Whitman seems to lambaste his poem with sound effects in his enthusiasm for his grand military spectacle. Crane cares for music, too, and yet his is a subtler, harsher one. Although longer in words, Whitman's "Cavalry" contains fewer pauses than "The Heart" (fifteen compared to Crane's seventeen, if every comma and line-end counts as a pause). The result is, in Crane's poem, a much more hesitant, start-and-stop movement—appropriate, perhaps, to a study of self-immolation. Whitman apparently wants an expansive, continuous progress in his syntax, as in his cavalry.

MyLiteratureLab Resources. Biography, critical overview, and bibliography for Whitman. Interactive reading and critical essay on "Cavalry Crossing a Ford." Biography, critical overview, and bibliography for Crane.

Ezra Pound, SALUTATION, page 224

Ezra Pound is best known for his formidably allusive Modernist epic, *The Cantos*, which he worked on for over fifty years. Less well known are Pound's early London poems, which are often funny, tender, and direct. This poem from *Lustra* (1915) attacks the bourgeoisie for its snobbery, materialism, and concern with appearance. In the poem's hierarchy of values, the fish, who are furthest from these failings, are the happiest. This celebration of simplicity may seem a bit odd coming from so fiercely cultured and mannered a figure as Pound, but you will notice that, in this context, the speaker is canny enough to rank himself near the bottom of the happiness scale.

Wallace Stevens, THIRTEEN WAYS OF LOOKING AT A BLACKBIRD, page 224

Suggestive as blackbirds may be, the theme of the poem is, "Pay attention to physical reality." Stevens chides the thin ascetic men of Haddam who would ignore good blackbirds and actual women for golden phantasms. He also chides that asinine aristocrat who rides about Connecticut (of all places) in a glass coach as if thinking himself Prince Charming. The poem ends in a section whose tone is matter-of-fact flatness, rather as though Stevens were saying, "Well, here's the way the world is; if you don't like it, go read newspapers." Taken as a series of notes for an argument for literalism, this much-discussed poem seems to have unity and to lead to a definite conclusion. For another (and more complicated) view of it, see Helen Vendler, *On Extended Wings* (Cambridge: Harvard UP, 1969).

Way-of-looking number 5 recalls Keats's "Grecian Urn": "Heard melodies are sweet. . . ."

Way number 10 eludes final paraphrase. Are the "bawds of euphony" supposed to be, perhaps, crass ex-poets who have sold out their Muses, who utter music to please the box office instead of truth? But blackbirds flying in a green light are so strikingly beautiful that even those dull bawds would be moved to exclaim at the sight of them.

MyLiteratureLab Resources. Biography, critical overview, and bibliography for Stevens.

Prose Poetry

Carolyn Forché, The Colonel, page 227

It is possible to argue either way on whether "The Colonel" is a prose poem or a short prose piece, but the stronger case is that it is a poem in prose. Why? First, "The Colonel" displays the compression we usually associate with poetry (prose fiction would unfold more leisurely). Second, by the end of the piece, it becomes apparent that the organization is as much lyric as narrative (the image of the ears pressed to the ground harks back to the *heard* in the opening line and to the auditory images throughout). Third, the density of literary effect (imagery, description, metaphor) has the feel of poetic language. The absence of poetic rhythms and lineation isn't enough to offset these qualities.

The rhetoric of Forché's piece deserves some attention. The effect of the poem depends heavily on the opening sentence ("What you have heard is true."). If we do not—at least initially—accept Forché's piece as reportage, then the poem loses a great deal of its impact. Forché understands this assumption clearly: notice how she dates the incident at the end to increase its verisimilitude. Some critics have questioned whether the episode truly happened as Forché presents it. That is a legitimate historical query, but, in poetic terms, it hardly matters; she has convincingly created the appearance of reality. The exaggerations seem no less credible than the bizarre incidents that fill the newspapers because Forché has captured the tone of factuality.

MyLiteratureLab Resources. Student paper for "The Colonel."

Charles Simic, The Magic Study of Happiness, page 227

This piece takes its title from a poem by the great nineteenth-century French poet Arthur Rimbaud (1854–1891), who was himself a pioneer in the art of the prose poem, and whose work—unsurprisingly, given the fact that all his poetry was written while he was still in his teens—deals frequently with themes of childhood and youth. Rimbaud's lines (from "Ô saisons, ô châteaux!") are: "J'ai fait la magique étude / Du bonheur, qu'aucun n'élude" ("I have made the magic study / Of happiness, which no one escapes"). Rimbaud biographer Graham Robb says of this and other, related poems: "Rimbaud attaches his songs to a concept which had fascinated him in the works of nineteenth-century illuminists: that behind the stage-set of sensory impressions lies a pure, absolute reality. . . . This ultimate truth can be glimpsed only in fleeting moments when the senses are no longer separate from the objects of perception, when the personality evaporates. . . ."

"The Magic Study of Happiness" appears in Simic's *Dime-Store Alchemy* (1992), a book about the reclusive American collage artist Joseph Cornell (1903–1972) that is itself a collage of sorts, combining biography, analysis, and Simic's own imaginative responses to Cornell's work. Cornell's miniature boxes often contain startling juxtapositions of objects and photographs through which he seeks, not unlike Rimbaud, to transcend rational perception and evoke a childlike sense of wonder. In an interview with the journal *Artful Dodge* shortly after the publication of *Dime-Store Alchemy*, Simic said:

> I really think that language cannot say or produce or convey the complexity, the depth of an experience, of heightened consciousness. When you feel exceptionally lucid, when you feel truly present to yourself and you see the world and you see yourself watching the world, there's a kind of plenitude of consciousness. So you step away from yourself and say "My God, I exist!" But, saying I exist is an impoverishment. There is so much more there; the experience itself is much larger than whatever words you have uttered. So I always feel that language does not quite equal the intensity of experience—that words are approximations. But this is a very complicated subject. The paradox that occurs is that attempts through words, through language, cannot instantly, simultaneously convey experience. One attempts by manipulating words in some fashion to find a way in a poem to recreate what the experience felt like originally. But it's no longer the same thing. It's coming to it in a very different way.

In that same interview, Simic rejects the interviewer's description of the pieces in *Dime-Store Alchemy* as prose poems; nonetheless, he allowed "The Magic Study of Happiness" to be included in David Lehman's anthology *Great American Prose Poems: From Poe to the Present* (2003). It is also worth noting that Simic is far from dismissive of the concept of the prose poem, either in general or in his own work: in 1989 he published *The World Doesn't End: Prose Poems*, which was awarded the 1990 Pulitzer Prize for poetry.

VISUAL POETRY

For more examples of graphic poetry, see the anthologies edited by Klonsky and Kostelanetz cited in footnotes to this chapter. Other useful anthologies include Emmett Williams's *Anthology of Concrete Poetry* (New York: Something Else, 1967), Eugene Wildman's *Chicago Review Anthology of Concretism* (Chicago: Chicago Review, 1967), Mary Ellen Solt's *Concrete Poetry: A World View* (Bloomington: Indiana UP, 1969), and Emmett Williams's selection of "Language Happenings" in *Open Poetry: Four Anthologies of Expanded Poems*, ed. Ronald Gross and George Quasha (New York: Simon, 1973).

George Herbert, EASTER WINGS, page 228
John Hollander, SWAN AND SHADOW, page 229

The tradition of the shaped poem, or *Carmen figuratum*, seems to have begun in Renaissance Italy, and the form flourished throughout Western Europe in the seventeenth century. English practitioners of the form, besides Herbert, included Robert Herrick (in "The Pillar of Fame") and George Puttenham.

Of "Easter Wings," Joan Bennett has remarked, "The shape of the wings on the page may have nothing but ingenuity to recommend it, but the diminuendo and crescendo that bring it about are expressive both of the rise and fall of the lark's song and flight (Herbert's image) and also the fall of man and his resurrection in Christ (the subject that the image represents)" (qtd. by F. E.

Hutchinson in his edition of Herbert's *Works* [Oxford: Oxford UP, 1941]). Visual shape and verbal meaning coincide strikingly when the second stanza dwindles to *Most thin*.

Like Herbert, Hollander clearly assumes that a word-shape has to have a meaningful relation to what is said in it. His reflected swan is one of twenty-five shaped poems collected in *Types of Shape* (New York: Atheneum, 1969). Other graphic poems in the book include a car key, a goblet, a beach umbrella, an Eskimo Pie, and the outline of New York State. Paul Fussell, Jr., discussing "Easter Wings" and Hollander's shaped poems, expresses reservations about this kind of poetry. Most shaped poems, he finds, are directed more to eyes than ears—"or better, we feel that the two dimensions are not married: one is simply in command of the other." But the greatest limitation in the genre is that there are few objects that shaped poems can effectively represent: "their shapes can reflect the silhouettes of wings, bottles, hourglasses, and altars, but where do we go from there?" (*Poetic Meter and Poetic Form* [New York: Random, 1965] 185–87). Students might be told of Fussell's view and asked to comment. A further disadvantage of most shaped poetry is that it cannot be heard aloud without loss.

MyLiteratureLab Resources. Critical essay on "Easter Wings."

Terry Ehret, from PAPYRUS, page 230

Terry Ehret comments on her poem:

> Why the hieroglyph?
>
> I had felt provoked for some time to do a mistranslation, or free-associative translation, of the Papyrus Harris 500 Text, and in January of 1991, busy with a new house, new town, two small children and a newborn, while the jets bombed Iraq and Rodney King took his serial beatings, I sat down each night after the household was asleep to find out what I was thinking. I'd pull out the text, select a glyph (or sometimes a sequence of glyphs) that suited my mood, and then free-associated from the image toward some part of my life I couldn't directly see.
>
> I often suspect my native language isn't language at all, at least not words, but rather rhythm and image. Most poems arise out of these impulses. Pictograms and hieroglyphs, being close to their origins in gesture and object, seem to speak very directly to that place where feelings lie but where words can't entirely go.
>
> During the Middle Kingdom when the original Papyrus text was written, the hieroglyphs had come to represent phonetic sounds. The particular glyph I was working with for this poem was a combination of T (breadloaf) and TH (unknown). Studying it awakened in me a haunting grief, a feeling of exile, of someone stirring uneasily in sleep, and I tried to catch these feelings/images in the words of the prose poem. As the series grew each night, a narrative evolved, each glyph revealing a different part of the drama. I stopped writing when I felt I had come to the end of the story, and selected 18 of them to arrange in the sequence *Papyrus: A Temporary Journey*. The glyph serves as title, or more accurately, as parallel text. I think of them as two versions of the same thing.

Dorthi Charles, CONCRETE CAT, page 231

This trifle first appeared in the second edition of *An Introduction to Poetry* and has been retained out of loyalty to the past. While hunting for an illustration of the sillier kind of concrete poem that simply and unfeelingly arranges words like so many Lincoln Logs, XJK found the very thing in one of William Cole's anthologies of humorous poetry: "Concrete Poem" by the British wit Anthony Mundy. Mundy's work repeats *miniskirt* several times in the form of a miniskirt and tacks on a couple of *leglegleglegleglegs*. No doubt he was parodying concrete poetry, too. But the cheapskate in XJK rebelled at the thought of paying for permission to reprint such a simple doodad, so he decided to cut and paste together a homemade specimen. While constructing the cat, he had some fun with it, making the tongue a *U*, and so on. As far as we know, however, the pun in the cat's middle stripe (tripes) is the only place where language aspires toward poetry and becomes figurative.

FOUND POETRY

Ronald Gross, YIELD, page 232

Fitting together drab and prosaic materials, Gross leaves them practically unaltered. What he lends them are patterns that seem meaningful. By combining traffic-sign messages in "Yield," he implies that the signs insistently pressure us with their yips and barks. "Yield" states its theme implicitly: we are continually being ordered to conform, to give in, to go along with laws laid down for us. We must heed the signs in order to drive a car, but perhaps it is chilling to find their commands so starkly abstracted. Students might want to discuss whether it is reading too much into the poem to suspect that this theme applies to other areas of our lives, not only to driving.

A discussion of Gross's work may be one of those rare sessions that end with the students' realization that to remove speech from its workaday contexts and to place it into lines is, after all, what most poets do. Many poems, not only found poems, reveal meanings by arranging familiar things into fresh orders.

Nancy Adams Malone of Mattatuck Community College in Waterbury, Connecticut, contributes an insight about "Yield": "Everybody seems to think it's a comment on social conformity, but it seems to me easier and more fun to read it as a seduction."

Jacob Korg of the University of Washington passes on a class assignment that enjoyably makes its point. He asks his students to bring in whatever found poems they can discover. "The best one," he reports, "was the juxtaposition of two shop signs: ADULT ENTERTAINMENT and LIVE BAIT."

EXPERIMENT: *Finding a Poem*, page 233

Timothy F. Walsh, of Otero Junior College in Colorado, discovered another found poem in an earlier edition of this book:

"The sonnet,"
quipped Robert Bly,

"is where old professors
go to die."

"It was fun," he writes, "to discuss found poems following my students' reading about them and then point to one I found in the previous chapter." (The Bly quotation is on page 203 of the current edition.)

SEEING THE LOGIC OF OPEN FORM VERSE

E. E. Cummings, IN JUST-, page 233

Cummings's poem is one of his "Chansons Innocentes," little songs for children. In it, however, we meet a poet who is familiar with the classics and who naturally associates spring with goat-footed Pan. In Greek mythology, the god's pipes heralded the return of Persephone and caused birds and beasts to start up at his call. In Cummings's view, he seems a kind of Pied Piper who brings children running.

Line breaks and capital letters in the poem seem designed to emphasize particulars. *Just-spring*, capitalized, is the name of a holiday: the moment when spring begins. Dividing its name with a line break gives it more importance, perhaps; and *mud - / luscious* similarly takes emphasis. Why are the children's names telescoped *(eddieandbill, bettyandisbel)?* So that these names will be spoken rapidly, pell-mell, the way their owners run and the way children speak about their friends. And when the lame balloonman completes his transformation into Pan, the word *goat-footed* is framed with white space on a line by itself. Except by putting it in capitals, the poet could hardly have thrown more weight on it.

MLL *MyLiteratureLab Resources*. Photographs and biographical information for Cummings. Audio clip for "in Just-."

Carole Satyamurti, I SHALL PAINT MY NAILS RED, page 234

Satyamurti's poem demonstrates that there are other means than meter for organizing poetic language. In this case, syntax gives the poem a linguistic structure as formal as that of a sonnet. One might also say the poem has another structure—that of a list, a common genre but not one we usually associate with poetry (though we can upgrade it to the venerable literary device of the *catalogue*, as in Homer's catalogue of Greek ships in *The Iliad*). Notice that Satyamurti's lines are grammatically incomplete, unless we read them in conjunction with the title.

All this formal discussion shouldn't blind us to Satyamurti's provocative content. "I Shall Paint My Nails Red" does something that poetry should: it makes us think deeply about a part of our everyday world. It asks questions about something we might otherwise take for granted.

Alice Fulton, FAILURE, page 234

In an interview that appeared in the Spring 2005 issue of the journal *Folio*, Alice Fulton says:

> We're so used to the gentle, fringed appearance of the right margin in poems that a right-justified margin seems hard-edged, obdurate. The silence of the margin is formalized; the white space seems to solidify. . . . My poem "Failure". . . uses right-justified stanzas to suggest a sense of being up against It.

The layout on the page reinforces the poem's thematic commitment—bred by repeated, frustrating attempts to attain the unattainable—to "the dung / and starspit of what-is."

Another of Fulton's comments in that interview provides an interesting perspective on an earlier section of this chapter: "Poets are so lucky to have the line as a way of making meaning. I think it's why I've never been interested in writing 'prose poetry.' I don't want to give up the possibilities of the line."

WRITERS ON WRITING

Walt Whitman, THE POETRY OF THE FUTURE, page 235

Although Whitman created one of the main traditions of American free verse, he had surprisingly little to say about the verse technique he fostered. In this interesting passage from the 1876 preface to the reissue of *Leaves of Grass*, Whitman focuses on two different sorts of innovation—free expression of emotion and direct presentation of character. He sees these features of attitude, tone, and subject leading American poetry into the future.

12
Symbol

T. S. Eliot, THE *BOSTON EVENING TRANSCRIPT*, page 239

To help a class see the humor of Eliot's poem, try reading it aloud and pronouncing the name of the newspaper slowly and deliberately, in the dullest tones you can muster. This small gem can serve effectively to introduce an early, longer Eliot poem of spiritual desolation, "The Love Song of J. Alfred Prufrock."

MyLiteratureLab Resources. Biography, critical overview, and bibliography for Eliot.

Emily Dickinson, THE LIGHTNING IS A YELLOW FORK, page 240

Perhaps the poet would have added more punctuation to this poem had she worked longer on it; a rough penciled draft is its only surviving manuscript. Students may ask, Isn't the fork a symbol? No, it is the other half of a metaphor: what the lightning is like. The lightning (like most literary symbols) is a physical thing or event, reportedly seen. The Apparatus of the Dark (neither fork nor lightning) is whatever dimly glimpsed furniture this cosmic house may hold. The fork seems too simple an instrument to deserve the name of Apparatus. The lightning is doing the revealing, not itself being revealed.

MyLiteratureLab Resources. Biography, critical overview, and bibliography for Dickinson.

Thomas Hardy, NEUTRAL TONES, page 241

Students usually like to sort out the poem's white, gray, washed-out, and ashy things. Can anyone think of a more awful description of a smile than that in lines 9–10? The God in line 2 seems angry and awe-inspiring. He has chided or reproved the sun and caused it to turn pale in fear (like a schoolboy before a stern headmaster).

Line 8 is a stickler. In Hardy's first draft it read, "On which was more wrecked by our love." Both versions of the line seem awkward, and the present version is obscure, but probably the sense of this and the previous line goes: we exchanged a few words about the question, Which one of us had lost (suffered) the more by our love affair? (That is, after *which* we should mentally insert "of the two of us.")

For speculation about the facts behind "Neutral Tones," see Robert Gittings's fine biography *Young Thomas Hardy* (Boston: Little, 1975) 86–93. Much has been guessed about the possible love affair between young Hardy and his cousin Tryphena Sparks; but if the woman in "Neutral Tones" was indeed real, no one has identified her for sure.

Similar in imagery to "Neutral Tones" is this horrific line from Hardy's novel *The Woodlanders*, chapter 4, when a poverty-stricken woman, Marty South, sees her last hopes expire: "The bleared white visage of a sunless winter day emerged like a deadborn child" (cited by F. B. Pinion in *A Commentary on the Poems of Thomas Hardy* [New York: Barnes, 1977]).

MyLiteratureLab Resources. Biography, critical overview, and bibliography for Hardy. Critical essay on "Neutral Tones."

Matthew, THE PARABLE OF THE GOOD SEED, page 242

"The Parable of the Good Seed" is one of three parables that Jesus tells to the crowd describing the "kingdom of heaven" in the thirteenth chapter of Matthew. After Jesus and the disciples leave the crowd and go into a house, the disciples ask him to explain this particular parable. Jesus obliges them with an explication. (We paraphrase the reply in the book following the text of the parable.) Here is his answer from Matthew:

> He answered and said unto them, "He that soweth the good seed is the Son of Man; the field is the world; the good seeds are the children of the kingdom; but the tares are the children of the wicked one; the enemy that sowed them is the devil; the harvest is the end of the world; and the reapers are the angels. As therefore the tares are gathered and burned in the fire; so shall it be in the end of this world. The Son of Man shall send forth his angels, and they shall gather out of his kingdom all things that offend, and them which do iniquity; and shall cast them into a furnace of fire; there shall be wailing and gnashing of teeth. Then shall the righteous shine forth as the sun in the kingdom of their Father. Who hath ears to hear, let him hear." (Matthew 13:37–43)

The special importance of this parable is that Jesus clearly states his own interpretation of the tale. He intends it, therefore, as an allegory with one consistent equivalent meaning assigned to each narrative element. Not all Gospel parables can be so easily allegorized. Some, such as "The Parable of the Prodigal Son," are so subtly complex as to allow multiple interpretations. Jesus himself told the disciples that his parables allowed two interpretations—one purely narrative reading open to the general public and another, deeper allegorical interpretation available to those who have been initiated in "the mysteries of the kingdom of heaven" (Matthew 13:10–23).

George Herbert, THE WORLD, page 243

The controlling image is established in the poem's opening phrase, "Love built a stately house"; we might liken this house, as the title suggests, to the world itself, with particular emphasis on our earthly existence and the soul's tenure in the body. In each of the poem's first three stanzas, a bad builder—Fortune, Pleasure, and Sin, respectively—causes the house to be flimsy and in danger of collapse, until the damage is repaired by a better craftsman. The razing of the house in the last stanza signifies the end of the world, and the "braver Palace" is, of course, heaven.

Edwin Markham, OUTWITTED, page 244

Broadly speaking, the circle in this poem symbolizes a fence or a barrier that draws a distinction between what it encloses and what it excludes. The symbol functions the same way both times; the difference lies in what is enclosed or excluded in each instance. So precise and traditional is Markham's use of the circle that we can describe it as a conventional symbol, perhaps even as an allegory—except, of course, for the poem's extreme brevity and lack of narrative.

The Wagner College Library has a large Edwin Markham Archive, some of which is available online. You can access the archive and hear a recording of Markham reading this poem by starting a search at <http://www.wagner.edu/library/embio>.

John Ciardi, A BOX COMES HOME, page 244

As a gunner on a B-29, John Ciardi flew 16 combat missions over Japan during the Second World War. Then, through the recommendation of a friend who knew that Ciardi was a widely published poet, he was appointed in April 1945 to write applications for awards and decorations, as well as letters of condolence to the families of men killed or missing in action. According to Ciardi's biographer, Edward Cifelli,

> The challenge was to make each letter sound as though the general had personally known each soldier, and Ciardi agonized over the work: "I did the best I could. But it was a bland kind of tinkering with tragedy. It tore me up. Some woman somewhere might treasure that lousy manufactured letter for the rest of her life . . . . " Then, in one of those ironic, not to say grisly, twists of fate that Ciardi was so aware of, his former plane and crew went down over Tokyo Bay on the third mission they flew without him. They took a direct hit in the wing gas tank, "and the plane just blew up, disintegrated in midair." In the incredible chanciness of war, Ciardi had been spared because he had been called upon to write letters of condolence—which he then had to write to the families of his own crew.

For many people, the phrase "the United States of America" might immediately call up an image of the symbol of the nation, the American flag. For the speaker of "A Box Comes Home" the phrase seems to link immediately to an image of that flag draped over the coffin of a serviceman, Arthur—whose relationship to the speaker is unspecified—who was killed in battle. From its title on, the poem is informed by the attitude expressed by Ciardi in the above passage—that our official rites and commemorations are "a bland kind of tinkering with tragedy," gestures thoroughly inadequate to the demands made of these young men by their country and the totality of their sacrifice in response to those demands. The fourth stanza implies that Arthur in life, his uniform, represented his country more nobly than it has represented him in death—although, of course, the United States is hardly singled out in this regard, as the second and third stanzas make clear. The last two stanzas call for an America that will not fail or betray Arthur and so many others like him, but will live up to its own ideals as heroically as Arthur did. Even so, the speaker has a sufficiently strong sense of history that he states this wish as a hope, not an expectation.

A great deal of scholarship on Ciardi was published in the nineties, much of it done by Edward Cifelli of the County College of Morris, New Jersey. Cifelli published *The Selected Letters of John Ciardi* (Fayetteville: U Arkansas P, 1991). His full-length biography, *John Ciardi*, appeared in 1997 along with a new edition of *The Collected Poems* (both from Akansas). These books present the life and work of the first major Italian American poet.

Robert Frost, THE ROAD NOT TAKEN, page 245

Stanley Burnshaw writes, in *Robert Frost Himself* (New York: Braziller, 1986), that Frost often said "The Road Not Taken" was about himself combined with Edward Thomas, a Welsh poet and good friend. Knowing this, Burnshaw confessed, didn't contribute much to his understanding of the poem. Still, the story is tantalizing. In *Robert Frost: The Years of Triumph* (New York: Holt, 1970) biographer Lawrance Thompson tells about the "excruciations through which this dour Welshman [Thomas] went each time he was required to make a choice." This amused Frost, who once said to Thomas, "No matter which road you take, you'll always sigh, and wish you'd taken another." "The Road Not Taken" (originally called "Two Roads") was apparently written to poke quiet fun at this failing. When Frost sent the poem in a letter to Thomas, the Welshman apparently missed the joke. He assumed, as have many readers since, that the speaker in the poem was Frost himself. Disappointed, Frost (according to Thompson) "could never bear to tell the truth about the failure of this lyric to perform as he intended it."

Despite the ambiguity that surrounds the poet's intent, the poem succeeds. The two roads are aptly symbolic of the choices we have to make almost every day of our lives. Still, perhaps the poem's essential playfulness is evident in the dramatic "sigh" with which the speaker expects some day to talk about his choice, and in the portentousness of the last line, which seems a bit exaggerated considering that the two roads were "really about the same."

A hardworking introduction to symbolism in poetry is that of Paul Hawkes of East Stroudsburg University. In a published article, he describes his classroom version of the TV game show "Family Feud," in which teams of students try to guess which meanings of certain symbols have occurred to most of the class. His aim is to show that a symbol, which may have widely familiar and traditional associations, can mean more or less the same to everyone; its meanings aren't the property of one reader alone. Then, to put this insight to use, he takes up "The Road Not Taken."

"I use this poem," he explains, "because it is simple and straightforward, offering little resistance to any student I may ask to summarize the paraphrasable content of the poem." He asks, "What statements in the poem, what choices of diction, suggest that the two roads are to be understood as something more than literal paths in the woods?" And students tend to reply, "A person wouldn't 'sigh' about a choice made years ago unless it was important," or, "The speaker wouldn't regret it 'ages hence' if it were only a path," or, "Why else would he say the decision 'has made all the difference' unless that decision were life-changing?" (We're paraphrasing and condensing Mr. Hawkes's examples.)

Someone will usually guess that the choice of roads suggests Frost's personal choice of careers: Should he or should he not become a poet? Hawkes then encourages the class to speculate on other possible life choices: marriage, children, a job, relocation. Perhaps this poem is about decision-making; perhaps the nature of the roads need not be specified. As in *Pilgrim's Progress*, a road or a journey on it is a traditional and conventional symbol for life; a fork or crossroads, a decision or turning-point. "The poem," he concludes, "suggests regret not for the way life has turned out but for the severe limitations life imposes on our desire to explore its possibilities." (See "Fire, Flag, Feud, and Frost: Teaching the Interpretation of Symbols," *Exercise Exchange* [Spring 1991] 6–11.)

MyLiteratureLab Resources. Biography, critical overview, critical articles, and bibliography for Frost. Critical essay on "The Road Not Taken."

Christina Rossetti, UPHILL, page 246

This allegorical poem develops a conventional simile: life is like a journey (shades of *Pilgrim's Progress!*). The road is the path of life; the day, a lifespan; the inn at the end of the road, the grave; other wayfarers, the dead; the door, the mouth of the grave (or perhaps the gate of Heaven); the beds, cold clay (or perhaps Heavenly rest). The title suggests another familiar notion: that life is a struggle all the way.

One possible way to paraphrase line 14: "You'll find the end result of your lifelong strivings: namely, death and the comfort of extinction." A more happily Christian paraphrase is possible, for Rossetti professed herself a believer: "Your labor shall bring you to your goal, the sight of the Lord." Without admitting the possibility of such a faith, the poem will seem grimmer and more cynical than it is.

Do these two characters seem individual persons? Not in the least. This is a straight question-and-answer poem, a dialogue between two stick figures.

Christian Wiman, POŠTOLKA, page 246

As the speaker is in Prague, the words he is learning are presumably words of the Czech language. The kestrel, a reddish-gray falcon, seems to him to be "a concentration of its light" willed by "the red dusk"; this sense of there being something willed or even fated in the falcon's arrival is underlined by the fact that "pane by pane it eyed / the stories facing ours / but never looked inside," but later it directly meets the speaker's gaze. Among innumerable superstitions, the appearance of a red bird may signify good luck, or the arrival of any bird at one's window might be an evil omen—which would seem to be the case here, to judge by the shiver that seizes the speaker's companion. Either way, one should make a wish on it, whether to take advantage of the opportunity or to neutralize the foreboding. He is urged to do so by his companion, in whose cheek a reddish "bloom of blood" appears and then disappears, coming and going like the moment, like the bird itself, and like the "almost love" that the bird symbolizes.

For Review and Further Study

Exercise: *Symbol Hunting*, page 247

William Carlos Williams, The Term, page 247
Ted Kooser, Carrie, page 248
Jane Hirshfield, Tree, page 248
Jon Stallworthy, An Evening Walk, page 249
Lorine Niedecker, Popcorn-can cover, page 249
Wallace Stevens, Anecdote of the Jar, page 250

"The Term" should be taken literally; its key phrase is "Unlike a man," suggesting that it would be pointless to look for symbolic meaning in the sheet of paper, since its resemblance to a man is superficial and irrelevant. "Carrie" presents dust in its traditional role as a symbol for human mortality (although Kooser uses the symbol in a charmingly original way). Jane Hirshfield's "Tree" spells out its symbolism fairly directly: the "house" contains "your life," which is represented by "this clutter of soup cans and books"; in contrast, the "great calm being" of the redwood tree embodies "immensity"; will you attune yourself to this larger life spirit or lose yourself in the petty details of day-to-day existence? In "An Evening Walk," the author explicitly makes the unanswered ringing telephone, with "[i]ts dark voice welling up," a symbol of "animal grief," a grief intensified by the pain and frustration of trying and failing to connect with someone else; all of these feelings are compounded by the simile in the poem's last line. "Popcorn-can cover" uses literal language in a manner reminiscent of Williams, but the title image of the popcorn-can cover screwed to the wall can be taken as a symbol of the house dweller's poverty and pragmatism. Niedecker does not force the symbolism of the image, yet it is there for our notice. "Anecdote of the Jar" contains central symbols.

Students familiar with Stevens sometimes reason, "The jar is a thing of the imagination, that's why it's superior to the wilderness—it makes order out of formless nature, the way Stevens thinks art is supposed to do." But Stevens is constantly warning us of the dangers of the mind divorced from the physical world, and we think he means this gray, bare, dominion-taking jar to be ominous. Who could think a wilderness *slovenly* before it came along? Some critics take the phrase *of a port in air* to mean a portal, "an evanescent entry . . . to order in a scene of disorder" (Ronald Sukenick, *Wallace Stevens: Musing the Obscure* [New York: New York UP, 1967]). We read it differently: *portly*, imposing, pompous. Although it is true that Stevens frequently raises the same philosophic or aesthetic questions, from poem to poem he keeps supplying very different answers. See the brilliant essay on Stevens by J. Hillis Miller in *Poets of Reality* (Cambridge: Harvard UP, 1965).

Jerald Bullis has written an intriguing poem in response to "Anecdote of the Jar." Thanks to Peter A. Fritzell of Lawrence University for discovering it.

Buck It

Take a shot-up bucket in a swale of woods—
For years "things" have been adjusting to it:
The deer have had to warp their whylom way
Through the fern to honor the order in their blood
That says not to kick it; the visiting woodcock

Probably take it for some kind of newfangled stump,
And doubtless welcome any addition that offers
Additional cover—especially if its imposition
Provides a shelving stay for worm-rich mulch;
A rivulet of breeze low-eddying the swale
Breaks around it much the way a stress's
Flow gets an increment of curvature
From encounter with an old Singer
Sewing machine; the ferns thereabout have turned
A bit more plagiotropic; if it's upright
And the lid's off it's an urn for leaves, bark-bits,
Bird droppings; but in the scope of the whole
Forty-acre woodpatch is it likely
To take dominion everywhere? no more
Than a barbed-wire tangle of words or a good jar.

MyLiteratureLab Resources. Biography, critical overview, and bibliography for Stevens. Interactive reading of "Anecdote of the Jar."

Writers on Writing

W. B. Yeats, Poetic Symbols, page 250

Symbols are central to Yeats's poetics. They are not arbitrary creations of the writer but primal forms of human communications—arising like Carl Jung's universal archetypes from the unconscious. For Yeats, therefore, the symbol is in some sense independent of the poet and carries "numberless meanings" beyond the often narrow intentions of the author.

13
Myth and Narrative

This chapter was revised in recent editions to make it more accessible to students. Although the chapter still begins with a discussion of what constitutes myth, there is now an attempt to relate the idea of myth to students' experience with popular culture, especially movies and television. This shift may initially annoy some instructors, but we hope that, if they stick with the chapter, they will discover that we have tried to show how similar myths permeate popular and literary culture. We want to make the material of this chapter less threatening to beginning students while still useful to instructors excited by the prospect of teaching Lawrence, Yeats, and Wordsworth.

Besides the poems in this chapter, other poems in the text will readily lend themselves to the study of myth and its pervasiveness in literature.

The story of Adam and Eve which figures in Frost's "Nothing Gold Can Stay" might be supplemented with Anthony Hecht's "Adam" (in "Poems for Further Reading").

Personal myths may be found in the poems of Blake, in Hardy's "Convergence of the Twain," and in certain poems of Yeats outside this chapter, such as "Leda and the Swan" and "Sailing to Byzantium."

Poems containing central references to familiar classical myths are Cummings's "in Just-," with its reincarnation of the Great God Pan, and Allen Ginsberg's "A Supermarket in California." Christian mythos is of course inseparable from the devotional poems of Donne and Herbert, from Hopkins's poems and G. K. Chesterton's "The Donkey," from Eliot's "Journey of the Magi" and Yeats's "The Magi," from Milton's sonnet on his blindness, and from many more.

In this chapter, Thomas Hardy (in "The Oxen") and William Wordsworth (in "The World Is Too Much with Us") sadly contemplate myths in decline.

Robert Frost, NOTHING GOLD CAN STAY, page 255

Many of your students may already be familiar with this popular poem. The relevant detail of the poem in this context is how much narrower its meaning would be if the reference to Eden were dropped. This single mythic allusion expands the resonance of the poem from the transience of spring's beauty to the transience of all perfection.

In his excellent study *Robert Frost: A Literary Life Reconsidered* (reissued with a new preface in 1993 by the University Press of New England), William Pritchard savors the poem's remarkable compression in the following way:

> The poem is striking for the way it combines the easy delicacy of "Her early leaf's a flower" with monumentalities about Eden and the transient fading

of all such golden things, all stated in a manner that feels inevitable. It is as if in writing "Nothing Gold Can Stay," Frost had in mind his later definition of poetry as a momentary stay against confusion. The poem's last word proclaims the momentariness of the "gold" that things like flowers and Eden, dawn and poems share. So the shortness of the poem is also expressive of its sense. (Quoted by permission of the author)

MyLiteratureLab Resources. Biography, critical overview, critical articles, and bibliography for Frost. Critical essays for "Nothing Gold Can Stay."

D. H. Lawrence, BAVARIAN GENTIANS, page 255

Written in 1929 when Lawrence was ill and nearing death, this splendid poem has been read as a kind of testament. As Keith Sagar has paraphrased it, "the poet's soul has been invited to the nuptials and accepts with joy." Dissolution offers not mere oblivion but the promise of renewed life, the cyclical rebirth of both the gentians and Persephone (*The Art of D. H. Lawrence* [Cambridge: Cambridge UP, 1966], 244–45). Another famous poem of Lawrence's last months, "The Ship of Death," may be read as a companion to this.

Why is "Bavarian Gentians" a better title for the poem than Lawrence's first thought, "Glory of Darkness"?

William Wordsworth, THE WORLD IS TOO MUCH WITH US, page 256

As its sense and its iambic meter indicate, the opening line calls for a full stress on the *with*.

Wordsworth isn't arguing for a return to pagan nature worship. Rather, like Gerard Manley Hopkins's blasting tirade in "God's Grandeur," he is dismayed that Christians, given to business and banking, have lost sight of sea and vernal woods. They should pay less heed to the world, more to the earth. What "powers" have they laid waste? The ability to open themselves to nature's benevolent inspirations. Modestly, the poet includes himself in the *us* who deserve reproof. The impatient outburst ("Great God!") is startlingly unbookish and locates the break in sense between octave and sestet in an unconventional place.

Compare Wordsworth's "Composed upon Westminster Bridge" for a somewhat similar theme.

MyLiteratureLab Resources. Biography, critical overview, and bibliography for Wordsworth.

H. D. [Hilda Doolittle], HELEN, page 257

What a cold, hate-inspiring queen H. D. portrays! She makes a sharp contrast with the lovable image of Helen as a child in Yeats's "Long-legged Fly."

Heather Burke's student essay on "Helen" at the end of this chapter provides an intelligent and fairly comprehensive close reading of the poem. For a few notes on recent scholarly activity on H. D., see the note on her poem "Heat" in this manual.

ARCHETYPE

Louise Bogan, MEDUSA, page 258

Bogan's chilling poem is a perfect example of how modern poets have used classical myths to new ends. Bogan presents Medusa quite faithfully to the Greek legend, but she employs the myth for distinctively modern psychological purposes—to portray a state of spiritual and emotional paralysis. The speaker is literally petrified in an eternal moment. Nothing will ever change. One curious feature of "Medusa" is that the speaker shows no surprise, no bitterness, no anger at the paralyzing Gorgon—only total resignation.

Bogan's biographer, Elizabeth Frank, believes the poem portrays the poet's mother as the paralyzing female monster. While there is no specific textual evidence for this interpretation, it is not inconsistent with the facts of Bogan's troubled past. This psychoanalytical/biographical interpretation, however, is not especially useful in reading "Medusa" as poetry. In fact, to reduce the poem to any single allegorical interpretation limits the powerful symbolic resonance of the central situation. The speaker's paralysis can be read with equal validity as emotional, spiritual, imaginative, or artistic. The poem invites us to interpret the speaker's dilemma beyond its literal narrative meaning, but the text does not demand any single construction.

John Keats, LA BELLE DAME SANS MERCI, page 259

This poem, unpublished in Keats's lifetime, was written in 1819, and some of its phrasing was later revised by Keats. While it is customary to accept an author's final version of a work as definitive, it is generally agreed that the original text of "La Belle Dame sans Merci" is fresher and more effective, and it is that text which we have printed here. The poem's title and basic situation are derived from a long French poem by Alain Chartier (c.1385–c.1433), translated into English by Sir Richard Ros around 1640.

Predilections for the ballad form, for medieval settings, and for supernatural themes were all characteristic of one strain of English Romanticism, as exemplified earlier (at about the time of Keats's birth) in the work of Samuel Taylor Coleridge, most notably in "Christabel" and "The Rime of the Ancient Mariner," and Robert Southey. Notice how many of the attributes of the medieval folk ballad Keats imitates here: lack of rime in the first and third lines of each quatrain; occasional metrical irregularities; pointless specificity ("kisses four"—compare "Nine bean-rows will I have there" in Yeats's "The Lake Isle of Innisfree"); shifting (and unidentified) speakers; and elliptical narration.

The season is clearly autumn, a time traditionally depicted as one of melancholy and decline, as is made clear through the descriptions provided by the unidentified speaker of the first three stanzas. Some have seen an autobiographical dimension in this melancholy and decline, speculating that Keats used the myth of the succubus-like fairy creature who enchants and seduces men, only to abandon them, as a way of expressing his complex feelings toward his fiancée, Fanny Brawne. The historical record, however, shows her to have been an intelligent young woman who reciprocated the depth and tenderness of his love—a far cry from the shallow and heartless flirt of legend toying with the affections of the tormented, dying poet.

MyLiteratureLab Resources. Photographs, biographical information, critical overview, and bibliography for Keats.

Personal Myth

William Butler Yeats, The Second Coming, page 261

The brief discussion in the book leaves several points untouched. Students may be asked to explain Yeats's opening image of the falcon and the falconer; to discuss the meaning of the *Blood-dimmed tide* and the *ceremony of innocence;* to explain how the rocking cradle at Bethlehem can be said to "vex" twenty centuries to nightmare; and to recall what they know about the sphinx.

In *A Vision,* Yeats sets forth his notion of the two eras of history (old and new) as two intertwined conelike gyres, revolving inside each other in opposing directions. He puts it succinctly in a note for a limited edition of his poem *Michael Robartes and the Dancer* (1921):

> The end of an age, which always receives the revelation of the character of the next age, is represented by the coming of one gyre to its place of greatest expansion and of the other to that of its greatest contraction. At the present moment the life gyre is sweeping outward, unlike that before the birth of Christ which was narrowing, and has almost reached its greatest expansion. The revelation which approaches will however take its character from the contrary movement of the interior gyre.

Students can be asked to apply this explanation to "The Second Coming." (In fact, this might be a writing assignment.)

For other evidence of Yeats's personal mythology, direct students to "Leda and the Swan" and "Sailing to Byzantium." For alternative versions of "The Second Coming," see Yeats's worksheets for the poem as transcribed by John Stallworthy in *Between the Lines: Yeats's Poetry in the Making* (Oxford: Oxford UP, 1963).

MyLiteratureLab Resources. Biography, critical overview, and bibliography for Yeats.

Gregory Orr, Two Lines from the Brothers Grimm, page 262

When he was twelve years old, Gregory Orr shot and killed his younger brother in a hunting accident. As he recounts in his memoir *The Blessing*, this event left him emotionally devastated and near-suicidal, and it had a severely damaging effect on the surviving members of his family, whose customary method of dealing with tragedy was silence and emotional detachment. Once one knows this history, it is almost impossible not to interpret the poem in light of it, and to see the "Hansel and Gretel"-like opening of the poem (and the horror-movie-like image in line 4) as Orr's response to the accident and its traumatic effect on his family and their relationships with one another. The poem also exemplifies—not through its content, but by virtue of its very existence—a central theme of Orr's memoir, the healing and transformative power of art.

If you choose to incorporate this information in your presentation of the poem, you might wish first to determine the most effective way of doing so; in this connection, you may find it helpful to reread Natasha Trethewey's poem "White Lies" and the discussion of it in both the anthology itself and this manual.

Diane Thiel, MEMENTO *MORI* IN MIDDLE SCHOOL, page 262

Diane Thiel has provided this note about her poem:

> For years, I wanted to write about this memory of an odd middle school project I presented on Dante's *Inferno*. The piece existed only as notes for some years. About twenty years after the childhood incident described in the piece, the poem finally came together and found its form as *terza rima* (the form Dante invented in the Middle Ages). I chose a rather loose interpretation of *terza rima* for the poem (varying the end-rhymes between exact rhymes, slant rhymes, and assonance) because the variation seemed to best suit the conversational diction and tone of the poem.
>
> I think of "*Memento Mori* in Middle School" as an echo-location, a multi-layered term I invented in the book, *Echolocations* (2001), which contains the poem, to refer to conversations with the past. In the case of this poem, the conversation is with both this work of art from a distant medieval past and the more immediate echoes of a childhood interpretation of the piece. The union of the *Inferno* with that trial-filled middle school age becomes a reflection of threshold crossings that burn themselves into our memories.
>
> *An Exercise for Students*:
> In my writing guide, *Writing Your Rhythm*, I include an exercise which asks students to respond to a poem (preferably choosing from a more distant century) using the form of the chosen piece. This approach helped "*Memento Mori* in Middle School" find its form.

MYTH AND POPULAR CULTURE

Charles Martin, TAKEN UP, page 265

"Taken Up" illustrates how a good poet can borrow potentially hackneyed material from popular culture and, by linking it to the underlying myth, transform it into genuine poetry.

Martin links the popular myth of flying saucers with the eternal human need for the divine. His golden aliens (whose bodies are so fine as to seem incorporeal) are almost godlike. What they offer the humans who waited for them is a version of heaven. (Notice that the aliens mention angels in factual terms; the spiritual and divine are real to them.) The situation of the poem on a hill deliberately recalls the Transfiguration and Ascension episodes of the Gospels. The aliens are science fiction versions of angels—perhaps even gods.

One way to start a classroom discussion on the poem is to ask if anyone has seen Spielberg's *Close Encounters of the Third Kind* and encourage someone to describe the film's ending. Then compare it to the poem and discuss from what mythic sources they both draw their inspiration.

Andrea Hollander Budy, SNOW WHITE, page 266

"The story of the prince" makes Snow White's experience seem unique and inaccessible, and thus it serves as a convenient cover story to keep other, frustrated women from trying to horn in on her good thing. The reference to "the footprints of your own / children" calls up images of women with gangs of children underfoot, a detail suggestive of a life whose grind and "plainness" they would be only too glad to escape by fleeing into the forest to be made much of by seven attentive little men.

Anne Sexton, CINDERELLA, page 267
WRITERS ON WRITING
Anne Sexton, TRANSFORMING FAIRY TALES, page 270

"Cinderella" was part of Sexton's fifth collection, *Transformations* (Boston: Houghton, 1971). This volume consisted of seventeen long poems that retold fairy tales in idiosyncratic versions. Although earlier poets such as Auden and Jarrell had published revisionist fairy tale poems, Sexton's book proved extremely influential by claiming the fairy tale as the special territory of feminist poets. Some critics (as well as Sexton's editor, Paul Brooks) felt these poems represented a falling off from her more compressed earlier poetry, and there is some truth in that criticism. But the poems have remarkable narrative energy and originality.

"Cinderella" begins like a lyric poem with a series of four rags-to-riches stories that seem gleaned from the tabloids. But just when it might seem that Sexton would wrap up her short poem, she leaps into an extended narrative. Her version of Cinderella is very close to the Perrault original, although she spices it up with contemporary images and large doses of irony. Then, as the story comes to its conclusion, Sexton emphasizes the violent aspects of the original so that it overwhelms the romance. In the last stanza, Sexton resumes the original structure of the poem with a bitterly ironic version of "happily ever after."

To use an overworked term, Sexton "deconstructs" the happy ending of a fairy tale; marriage, in her view, is no solution to Cinderella's problems but the beginning of new ones.

The two letters included in "Writers on Writing"—one to her publisher, the other to a fellow writer—describe Sexton's intentions in turning popular fairy tales to her own ends. She wants to make the stories "as wholly personal as my most intimate poems." This attitude may surprise students who don't yet understand how an artist's treatment can transform borrowed material (like myth or legend) into something unique and idiosyncratic.

14
Poetry and Personal Identity

"Poetry and Personal Identity" provides students with an introduction to the ways in which a poet's race, gender, cultural background, age, and other factors influence his or her writing. The chapter explores the different ways that poets have defined their personal, social, sexual, and ethnic identities. It also examines the problematic relationship between the author and the poem.

The first section focuses on autobiography and explores the idea of "confessional" poetry. Having drilled students earlier in this book that poems cannot be read as direct autobiography, we now relax a bit and let them think about the tricky relationship between life and art through Sylvia Plath's brilliant but harrowing "Lady Lazarus." This issue usually generates lively classroom discussion. The challenge will be to keep the discussion on track by focusing on the specific text under examination.

We then broaden the discussion by showing how autobiography includes issues of culture, race, age, and gender. Two compelling poems on minority identity—by Rhina Espaillat and Claude McKay—show different approaches toward ethnic writing. With Samuel Menashe and Francisco X. Alarcón we see poems about Jewish and Mexican American identity. The coming-of-age poems by Judith Ortiz Cofer and Amy Uyematsu draw on their authors' Hispanic and Asian backgrounds.

Anne Stevenson's short poem "Sous-Entendu" focuses on gender in terms that students should understand from their everyday life, while Adrienne Rich's poem explores it in more general, archetypal terms. Yusef Komunyakaa's powerful Vietnam poem raises questions of identity that transcend racial categories; he is a black veteran, but he seems to speak for all Vietnam vets without losing his personal identity (reflected in the Vietnam Veterans Memorial's black stone). With Donald Justice's striking "Men at Forty," we begin looking at issues of age; these questions are explored—with merciless honesty—in Philip Larkin's "Aubade," a poem that will disturb everyone. Andrew Hudgins's poem explores both religion and the gap between generations. Shirley Geok-lin Lim's poem portrays the ambivalent emotions of the immigrant caught between cultures.

Sylvia Plath, LADY LAZARUS, page 278

This poem was written over seven days in late October 1962 about two weeks after the composition of "Daddy" (in the "Poems for Further Reading" chapter). On February 11, 1963, Plath committed suicide by putting her head in a gas oven.

In her 1989 biography of Plath, *Bitter Fame*, Anne Stevenson describes "Lady Lazarus" as a "merciless" self-projection of the author, who cast herself as "the central figure of her mythic world." Considering several of the poems written that final October, Stevenson continues:

> The poems are extraordinary *performances*—not only in their consummate poetic skill, but in that their central figure is giving a performance as though before a single quelled spectator or in a fairground . . .

Stevenson concludes:

> These poems, penetrating the furthest reaches of disdain and rage, are bereft of all normal "human" feeling. Hurt has hardened to hate, and death is omnipresent.

Surely the dark anger and aching death-wish are tangible in "Lady Lazarus." This poem is spoken by a voice beyond hope. If Plath is a performer, she performs only a script of her own merciless invention.

One stylistic note: "Lady Lazarus" (like "Daddy") is full of German tags. You might ask students why she uses German so much in these late poems. The Nazi connection will be easy for them to see, but it may be worthwhile to mention that Plath's father, Doctor Otto Plath (Ph.D. in entomology), was a German immigrant who spoke with a heavy accent. In other words, there is something to interest both formalist and biographical critics in this chilling late poem.

MyLiteratureLab Resources. Longman Lecture on "Lady Lazarus."

Rhina Espaillat, BILINGUAL / BILINGÜE, page 281

Espaillat's poem is an excellent demonstration of the famous dictum of William Carlos Williams, "No ideas but in things." How better to demonstrate the challenges and frustrations of shuttling between two languages (and two cultures) than to employ both languages in the statement itself? The use of both English and Spanish also vividly underscores the daughter's inability to maintain the divisions that her father insists on, divisions that he hopes will prevent his daughter from becoming Americanized to the point where she will be alienated from their heritage and even from him. Removing the Spanish phrases would indeed change the poem, and significantly for the worse. The speaker's heart is one in its ability to cherish both parts of her identity, but the strain of doing so is evident throughout the text.

CULTURE, RACE, AND ETHNICITY

Claude McKay, AMERICA, page 282

McKay was one of the first of many black American writers who emigrated from the West Indies. (Students might write an interesting comparison between McKay's sonnet and the later Caribbean poet Derek Walcott's "The Virgins," to be found in the "Poems for Further Reading" chapter.) McKay was born in Jamaica in 1891 and immigrated to the United States in 1912. Although shaped by black experience, "America" reaches for—and indeed achieves—universality of expression; it articulates the frustrated dreams and overpowering desires of any young immigrant. The speaker in this poem defines himself not by his ethnic identity but by his existential identity—as an outsider—in a heartless, if vital society.

Samuel Menashe, THE SHRINE WHOSE SHAPE I AM, page 283

Menashe's poem defines Jewishness in a mystical biological way. "Breathed in flesh by shameless love," he was born from his parents' bodies, and his body contains the history of his people. "There is no Jerusalem but this" means, among other things, that his Jewishness is not found in a geographical place but in himself: his body is the lost temple ("the shrine") of his people, his bones the hills of Zion. This poem may seem difficult to students at first, but once they understand the central metaphor, they usually find it fascinating. A good place to start discussing the poem is its title, which contains the central idea.

Menashe's short, compressed poems have been repeatedly praised by leading critics such as Stephen Spender, Donald Davie, Kathleen Raine, and Hugh Kenner, but his work remains little known. Menashe lives in New York City in a cold-water flat. His most recent work is *New and Selected Poems* (2005), for which he won the first Neglected Masters Award from the Poetry Foundation.

Francisco X. Alarcón, THE X IN MY NAME, page 284

Alarcón's poem is about the relation between one's name and one's identity. On a literal level, the X in Alarcón's name stands presumably as an abbreviation for Xavier (a name that almost always identifies one as being of Catholic background and most commonly Hispanic descent, though many an Irishman bears it, too). But Alarcón sees the letter as a symbol for the X an illiterate peasant must sign on the legal documents that control his or her life. Ultimately, Alarcón also implicitly uses the X (in a way perhaps influenced by Malcolm X) as an algebraic symbol for the elements of his identity lost or repressed in America.

Francisco X. Alarcón teaches at the University of California at Davis. He publishes poetry in both Spanish and English.

Judith Ortiz Cofer, QUINCEAÑERA, page 284

Cofer creates a wonderfully detailed speaker for this coming-of-age poem—a young woman on the brink of adulthood only half cognizant of the mysteries of her new identities. Still partly a child, the speaker embraces her new self with a mixture of awe, fear, and pride. Her childhood is symbolized by the dolls put in the chest "like dead / children." The fifteen-year-old now stands in a middle ground between childhood and marriage. Her new status is represented most clearly by the menstrual blood that privately confirms her new status as an adult woman at least partially independent from her mother (who will no longer wash her clothes and sheets). Although on one level the poem presents a universal female situation, the title, images, and mythology are distinctly Latin Catholic. Cofer's poem demonstrates that a poem does not necessarily lose universality by being embodied in a specific cultural framework. As William Stafford observed, "All events and experiences are local, somewhere."

Amy Uyematsu, Deliberate, page 285

Without knowing that the author is a sansei (third-generation Japanese American), one might assume, from the Los Angeles setting and other details, that the speaker—who, along with her friends, dreads being mistaken for white, the quintessence of the uncool—is Hispanic. Awareness of the author's (and presumably the speaker's) Asian heritage gives another layer of meaning to the title, with its implication of assuming styles of dress and behavior that do not come out of one's own culture. The reference to "Daddy's muddy gardening shoes," which evokes traditional mainstream American attitudes toward the Japanese and suggests how badly these girls wish to escape the burden of those attitudes, also stirs the intriguing possibility that what they are doing, essentially, is exchanging one stereotype for another.

Yusef Komunyakaa, Facing It, page 286

This powerful poem requires little commentary. One feature of the poem wants special mention because students may overlook it: the *entire* poem describes what the speaker sees on the polished black granite of the Vietnam Veterans Memorial. What he witnesses there is the combination of the memorial itself and what the mirror-like stone reflects. *Reflection* (line 6) is therefore the key word in the poem, a word the author uses in both senses, for, as the speaker studies the name on the stone, he reflects on his wartime experience and flashes back to the death of a fellow soldier. The way the stone both mirrors and transforms the reality around it is the external symbol for the speaker's internal experience.

Gender

Anne Stevenson, Sous-Entendu, page 287

Students will have no trouble understanding the situation of this poem, but you may need to push them to explore the role of language between the two people. Not only does everything the people say (and don't say) have two meanings—one literal, the other sexual—but the words they speak metaphorically become part of the clothes they remove.

Emily Grosholz, Listening, page 288

The speaker of Emily Grosholz's poem is an expectant mother. The listener is the unborn child in her womb. The speaker develops the idea of how words connect mother and child in a series of metaphors and allusions. She will weave her new son "a birthplace" out of words. Likewise, language will "re-create the gardens of the world," including perhaps the original Garden of Eden, a landscape of pure grace and innocence. Language is also called a "cradle" for the child. All of these images are positive and sustaining. The unborn son "still on his stalk" is implicitly compared to a flower—a part of creation that lacks language. (The stalk is also perhaps a more specific metaphor for the umbilical cord that connects mother and son.) The mother will give him the gift of language "to draw him out" into his full being.

Students might enjoy comparing Grosholz's images and metaphors with those in Sylvia Plath's "Metaphors," which addresses a similar subject.

EXERCISE: *Donald Justice*, MEN AT FORTY, page 289
Adrienne Rich, WOMEN, page 289

As anyone who tries to translate the images and metaphors of either poem into the voice of the opposite gender discovers, both of these poems are embedded in the sexual identity of the speaker. But the experiences they describe still speak to the opposite sex. The poems' structures do survive the translation, which demonstrates that good art can be both specific and universal.

For an example of how a skilled poet translated one set of these images across genders, here is a poem by Andrea Hollander Budy from her award-winning *House Without a Dreamer* (Brownsville: Story Line, 1993):

Women at Fifty
after Donald Justice

All of their doors
Have closed and their daughters'
Rooms betray a familiar faint perfume
That says *I'll not be back*.

They pause sometimes
At the top of the stairs
To stroke the bannister,
Its perfect knots.

They invite other women now
Only to clean. And like queens in fairy tales
They turn their heads from mirrors
That hold secrets they've kept

Even from themselves,
As they look into their husbands' faces
When their husbands say
They only look.

Women at fifty
Corner a cricket with a broom
And do not kill it, but shoo it out of the house
Into the abundant silence.

(Poem reprinted by permission of the author and Story Line Press.)

For Review and Further Study

Shirley Geok-lin Lim, Learning to love America, page 290

The title of this poem may immediately suggest the speaker's ambivalence about her situation: her love for America is not immediate and instinctive, but must be acquired through a learning process. Complex feelings are shown throughout the text. Lines 2–4 suggest the necessity of letting go of what is past and cannot be regained, along with an acceptance of the newfound land that sounds grudging at best; lines 15–16 also point to the immense difficulties involved in uprooting oneself and one's family and trying to put down roots in a new place. Many other details point to more positive aspects of the experience of assimilation: a sense of inclusion (line 5), personal integration and wholeness (lines 9–11), and freedom (line 12). The last five lines reinforce the complexity of the speaker's responses, telling us that while the love of a new country, or the sense of belonging in the place where one has come, may not be a spontaneous and rapturous response, it is in the end a necessary and inevitable one.

Lim, who was born and educated in Malacca, Malaysia, earned her Ph.D. in English at Brandeis. For years she taught at Westchester Community College in New York. She is currently a professor at the University of California at Santa Barbara.

Andrew Hudgins, Elegy for My Father, Who Is Not Dead, page 290

Hudgins's poem explores religious identity—and, by extension, a generation gap. He and his father see death differently. The father has a devout Christian's faith in an afterlife; the speaker, by contrast, is not sure. The son is not against his father's religion; he simply doesn't share its consolations.

Students can compare the father's vision of death in this poem with the bleak view of the speaker in Philip Larkin's "Aubade" at the end of the chapter.

Alastair Reid, Speaking a Foreign Language, page 291

Alastair Reid is a Scottish poet who has lived all of his adult life abroad—in Spain, the United States, and now the Dominican Republic. Although he is best known as a translator of Neruda, Borges, and other Latin American authors and as a *New Yorker* contributor, Reid is a superb poet. "Speaking a Foreign Language" brings a double perspective to the challenge of communicating in a second tongue: Reid portrays the roles of both speaker and listener. "What faith / we rest in one sentence," Reid writes, "hoping a smile will follow," as he portrays the role of the speaker. Then in the second stanza he shifts perspective from the speaker to the listener ("And yet, to hear . . .") and affirms how our common humanity helps translate "syntax into love."

Philip Larkin, AUBADE, page 292

"Aubade" was the last substantial poem that Philip Larkin wrote. Except for a few minor short poems and occasional verses, he produced no more poetry in his remaining eight years. "I didn't abandon poetry," he later remarked, "it abandoned me." In this context, it's hard not to see "Aubade" as a kind of summing up—and if so, what a chilling summation!

"Aubade" is a confessional poem about old age and the fear of death. Larkin's poems often begin in observation and only midway move into a personal tone. "Aubade" begins with a surprising personal confession ("I work all day and get half drunk at night"). Waking alone in bed in the middle of the night, the speaker confronts his own mortality and discovers he has no defenses—neither philosophical ("No rational being / Can fear a thing it will not feel" he notes ironically) nor religious ("That vast moth-eaten musical brocade / Created to pretend we never die"). Larkin sees death without any illusions and can barely survive the vision. Ultimately, he can only resolve to meet it when he must ("Death is no different whined at than withstood").

The British critic John Bayley sees Larkin's ability to confront this frightening subject so candidly in poetry as a kind of moral victory. Larkin, Bayley claims, "goes on to descant with an almost joyful eloquence on the fear of death and the terror of extinction. The fear is all too genuine but the fact of the poetry overcomes it."

Students may want to compare this poem to Andrew Hudgins's "Elegy for My Father, Who Is Not Dead." In Hudgins's poem, religious faith banishes the fear of death for the father. It would be hard to find a starker contrast in tone or images between the two visions of death.

WRITERS ON WRITING

Rhina Espaillat, BEING A BILINGUAL WRITER, page 293

This passage from the Afterword to *Where Horizons Go* (1998), Rhina Espaillat's second book of poems, is not only an excellent gloss on her poem "Bilingual / Bilingüe" but also an intriguing and enlightening discussion of the dilemma of the bilingual writer. Espaillat shows us how the choice of a language involves so many other, larger choices between cultures and even loved ones, leading to difficulties that are made even more complex by the fact that pure choice—the father's insistence on an absolute division between the world inside the family's apartment and the larger alien world that surrounds it—is impossible when one lives in a foreign culture. Instead, one must endlessly negotiate between the two worlds, in a process that brings inevitable stress, confusion, and pain. But in this excerpt, as in the poem, Espaillat stresses her ultimate reconciliation of her two cultures, along with deeper discoveries that this reconciliation provides. As she says elsewhere in the Afterword, "There is a sense in which every poet is bilingual, and those of us who are more overtly so are only living metaphors for the condition that applies to us all."

15
Translation

Is Poetic Translation Possible?

World Poetry

Li Po, Drinking Alone Beneath the Moon, page 298

The small unit on Li Po (pronounced Lee-Bo) offers a brief introduction to the pleasures and challenges of Chinese poetry, perhaps humanity's longest thriving poetic tradition. The T'ang Dynasty writer Li Po is traditionally considered, with his contemporary Tu Fu, one of China's two greatest poets. We have presented one of his most famous poems in four versions—Chinese characters, phonetic transcription, literal translation, and literary translation. (Note how the original Chinese rhymes, with a regular number of syllables and characters per line.) The central image of the lonely drinker and the moon has a special poignancy in the Chinese literary tradition since the hard-drinking Li Po legendarily died trying to embrace the reflection of the moon in a river.

There are a great many English translations of Li Po. Having read through many alternatives, we chose Arthur Waley's famous version, "Drinking Alone by Moonlight." Quietly lyrical and deftly modulated, Waley's translation reads beautifully as a poem in English. No other translation seems equally faithful to the original or so expressively realized in English. This translation also has a substantial claim to historical importance because Waley (1889–1966), who worked in the Oriental Prints and Drawings department of the British Museum, was perhaps the most influential translator of Chinese poetry in the twentieth century. More even than Ezra Pound, Waley created the English-language conventions by which most subsequent work has been translated.

Comparing Translations

Horace, "Carpe Diem" Ode, page 300

Quintus Horatius Flaccus, whom we remember as Horace, was the son of a freed slave. Although his father was a poor man, he sacrificed a great deal to give his talented son an excellent education in Rome and Athens. Having served as a soldier on the losing side of the Roman civil wars, Horace returned to find his father dead and their small farm confiscated. He managed to find work as a minor financial clerk and gradually established his reputation as a poet. By the end of his life in 8 B.C. he was one of the most honored authors in the Roman empire. He has never lacked readers since.

This famous short ode created a tradition of lyrics we call *carpe diem* poems. Although later poets often use the *carpe diem* line to woo their reluctant lovers, Horace's original is more strictly philosophical. We do not know how long our lives will last, and death is inevitable, so let us enjoy the time we have. (Horace's clear-eyed stoic acceptance of death contrasts interestingly with Larkin's nihilistic terror in "Aubade" in the preceding chapter.) Horace finds joy and meaning in life's uncertainty. No wonder it became the framework for later playful poems such as Marvell's "To His Coy Mistress" and Herrick's "To the Virgins, to Make Much of Time."

Edwin Arlington Robinson, James Michie, A. E. Stallings, TRANSLATIONS FROM HORACE, pages 301–302

All three translations are excellent—but in different ways. The Robinson (done when he was barely out of school) is straightforward and classical in its approach. The Michie emphasizes the lyric and intimate elements of the Latin. A. E. Stallings's recent version of Horace updates the ancient Roman images into *au courant* equivalents with Psychic Friends, the millennium, and the purported Y2K computer crash all making appearances in her wittily rhymed lines.

Some of the best student poems ever seen by one of the editors of this anthology came from an assignment to "translate this poem into a contemporary American setting, preferably somewhere where you yourself have lived." (None of the students knew Latin, so they worked with a literal translation plus two poetic versions.) The results were outstanding, and the students were astounded at how many settings appeared to work equally well.

Omar Khayyam, RUBAI, page 302

The phonetic transcription of the Persian may confuse students slightly, if they study the rime scheme, because in this poem all four lines rime (rather than the usual *aaba* scheme).

But it seems worthwhile to let them study the original of the best-known rubai in English (and almost equally famous in Persian). You might point out to the class the poem's final word in Persian—*soltani*, a word that exists virtually unaltered in English as *sultan*.

Edward FitzGerald, Robert Graves and Omar Ali-Shah, Dick Davis, TRANSLATIONS FROM OMAR KHAYYAM, page 303

FitzGerald's rubaiyat are so intoxicating that we couldn't resist including a few more at the end. But their music should not distract you entirely from Dick Davis's ingeniously faithful version, which even duplicates the original's quadruple rime. (Davis teaches Persian literature at Ohio State University and is a considerable poet in his own right.) By comparison, the Graves/Ali-Shah version seems stiff and unidiomatic.

Parody

Ezra Pound, in his *ABC of Reading*, urges students of poetry to write parodies of any poems they find ridiculous, then submit their parodies to other students to be judged. "The gauging pupil should be asked to recognize what author is parodied. And whether the joke is on the parodied or the parodist. Whether the parody exposes a real defect, or merely makes use of an author's mechanism to expose a more trivial content."

Anonymous, We four lads from Liverpool are, page 305

The origin of this jingle among children who sang it (to the familiar tune of "We Three Kings of Orient Are") on the streets of Edinburgh, about 1963 when the Beatles became popular, is attested to by the folklorist James T. R. Ritchie in *The Singing Street* (Edinburgh and London: Oliver & Boyd, 1964). Clearly, even Christmas carols are fair game to jejune British parodists. Another classic, current at the time of the abdication of Edward VIII in 1936, goes, "Hark, the herald angels sing: / Missus Simpson's pinched our king!"

Wendy Cope, from Strugnell's Rubaiyat, page 305

Wendy Cope has written about how her father would recite FitzGerald's *Rubaiyat* to his family. Having loved the poems since childhood, Cope turned her considerable powers of parody to exorcising these resonant poems from her psyche. To parody the old song, "You always hurt the poems you love."

Jason Strugnell is a second-rate poet invented by Cope. Strugnell leaps on every fashionable and unfashionable bandwagon—thereby allowing Cope endless opportunities for parody. All of the FitzGerald originals parodied by Cope can be found in the translation section of this chapter.

Hugh Kingsmill, What, still alive at twenty-two?, page 306

Kingsmill's insistence on dying young suggests "To an Athlete Dying Young," but the parodist grossly exaggerates Housman's hint of nihilism. Like bacon, Kingsmill's lad will be "cured"—of the disease of life. (And how often Housman himself says *lad* by the way.) His metaphysical conceit of ink and blotting pad coarsens Housman's usual view of night and day. (Some comparable Housman lines, from "Reveille": "Wake: the silver dusk returning / Up the beach of darkness brims, / And the ship of sunrise burning / Strands upon the eastern rims.")

Bruce Bennett, The Lady Speaks Again, page 306

Bennett's quatrain shows students a different use of parody. Bennett is not making fun of Emma Lazarus's sonnet (the original appears in the next chapter, "Recognizing Excellence"); instead, he uses Lazarus's poem as a departure point for his own satire on how contemporary America has fallen short of the ideals articulated by Lazarus's democratic vision.

Gene Fehler, IF RICHARD LOVELACE BECAME A FREE AGENT, page 306

The target of Fehler's satire has only become more vulnerable since 1984. Professional baseball has lost its innocence. Although there is no less joy in Mudville, a baseball-addicted poetry lover will find much pleasure in the work of Gene Fehler, the poet laureate of American baseball, whose work often appears in baseball journals and anthologies. His collection *Center Field Grasses: Poems from Baseball* (Jefferson, NC: McFarland, 1991) is especially delightful for its parodies of sixty classic poems, including "A Certain Slant of Curve," "On First Looking at a Mantle Homer," "A Noiseless Patient Owner," "The Lead Rises, the League Falls," and "Song of the Open Base."

Aaron Abeyta, THIRTEEN WAYS OF LOOKING AT A TORTILLA, page 307

Abeyta's Latino parody of Wallace Stevens's Modernist classic may invite your students to try their hand at a similar revision—perhaps even as an in-class writing assignment. One thing Abeyta's parody demonstrates is the strength of great syntax and form. Even rewritten with entirely new images, Stevens's original form carries the new meanings strongly along.

WRITERS ON WRITING

Arthur Waley, THE METHOD OF TRANSLATION, page 309

Waley's comments, like those of many another translator, provide for the rest of us—who might otherwise tend to assume that translation is a simple matter of word-by-word substitution—an interesting glimpse into the actual complexities of translation, especially of poetry. After reading the translations in this chapter, would you agree with Waley that "the restrictions of rhyme necessarily injure either the vigor of one's language or the literalness of one's version"?

16
Poetry in Spanish: Literature of Latin America

Sor Juana, Asegura la Confianza de que Ocultura de Todo un Secreto (She Promises to Hold a Secret in Confidence), translated by *Diane Thiel*, page 314

One might find it surprising that Sor Juana, a Catholic sister, wrote such a great volume of love poetry. As discussed in the prose excerpt by Stephanie Merrim at the end of the chapter, there are a variety of conjectures about her choice of this subject matter. The intensity of the passion in these poems is extraordinarily memorable, though.

In "She Promises to Hold a Secret in Confidence," one feels the passion of the speaker and also the weight of the confidence which must be kept. The speaker's passion is especially evident in the fact that she not only tears up the secret, but swallows it. She doesn't want it taken from her chest. The secret has become literally a part of her.

Sor Juana's poetry often uses elaborate wordplay, as can be seen in the play of "tore" and "be torn" in this poem and in the husk and the chestnut in "A Simple Gift Made Rich by Affection." This wordplay, as well as the tight rimes, is common to the baroque style of her era. But while much poetry in this style can feel stilted or outdated, Sor Juana's verse has an intensity of emotion brimming beneath the surface.

Sor Juana, Presente en que el Cariño Hace Regalo la Llaneza (A Simple Gift Made Rich by Affection), translated by *Diane Thiel*, page 314

As noted in the discussion of the preceding poem, Sor Juana's characteristic wordplay is also quite evident in this text. The husk in the poem seems to be the thorny self, the exterior that contains the chestnut. Perhaps the chestnut is the love the speaker has to give, or the speaker's spirit, while the husk represents the difficult aspects of the speaker's nature, of which she is well aware. Both Sor Juana poems included here feel like correspondences, either missives actually sent or love poems with a specific recipient.

Note that in both of these poems, the translator has chosen to re-create the wordplay in English and has also re-created the tight rhyme schemes characteristic of Sor Juana's work and her era. One might ask students about different translators' choices throughout the chapter.

Pablo Neruda, MUCHOS SOMOS (WE ARE MANY), translated by *Alastair Reid*, page 315

"Muchos Somos" is not merely one of Neruda's most famous poems, it is also among his most deeply characteristic. It reveals his open, exuberant, and personable poetic voice. One can see the influence of Walt Whitman in this poem. Compare Neruda's multiple personalities to Whitman's famous confession in *Song of Myself*: "Do I contradict myself? / Very well then I contradict myself / (I am large, I contain multitudes.)"

Alastair Reid's translation wonderfully captures the verve of the Spanish, but it remains important that we hear the poem in the original language. For classroom discussion, ask a student to read the Spanish aloud. (If you have native Spanish speakers in class, don't miss the chance to let them recite it.) The sonorous resonance of Neruda's language will be obvious even to students who have no Spanish.

It might also be worthwhile to ask if students have seen the Italian film *Il Postino* (*The Postman*), an Academy Award nominee for best film in 1995. Although fictionalized, the film presents Neruda's political exile in Italy. Students may well have seen the film without remembering the poet's name. *Il Postino* did a marvelous job of portraying Neruda's life-affirming, imaginative exuberance.

Pablo Neruda, CIEN SONETOS DE AMOR (V) (ONE HUNDRED LOVE SONNETS (V)), translated by *Stephen Tapscott*, page 317

Pablo Neruda, though known for the politics in his poetry, is perhaps best known for his love poetry. In this love poem, the merging of images of the body with images of the land is particularly potent: "you are my dark familiar clay: touching your hips, / I touch the wheat in its fields again." The end of the poem continues this connection: Love is a land of "kisses and volcanoes." The last line reverberates with the intensity of "volcanoes" and surprises somewhat in the poem. It leaves the reader shaken by the assertion.

Jorge Luis Borges, AMOROSA ANTICIPACIÓN (ANTICIPATION OF LOVE), translated by *Robert Fitzgerald*, pages 318–319

The premise of Borges's poem is both simple and ingenious. His speaker imagines his beloved (whom he has not yet known—and perhaps never will know—physically as a lover) after they have made love. As he imagines her sleeping, his thoughts are hardly carnal, but instead deeply emotional and in the end virtually spiritual in his love. As Neruda does in "One Hundred Love Sonnets (V)," Borges uses the landscape to speak about love. In this poem, the speaker, addressing his love, refers to the "shore of your life" and "that ultimate beach of your being" which he will see for the first time if they ever become lovers in a physical sense. The poem is one of renewal, of seeing one's love with new eyes. The reference to becoming "virgin again" in sleep supports this reading of renewal. The end of the poem has a note of sadness, however, as the speaker thinks of his love "free from love," free from himself.

Jorge Luis Borges, LOS ENIGMAS (THE ENIGMAS), translated by *John Updike*, pages 319–320

The poem itself feels like the subject matter—puzzling, enigmatic. The speaker looks to the day of his own death, which he sees as a kind of immortality but also as a condition of never having existed. The rimes of the sonnet form lend themselves to the subject matter as well. One might ask students about Updike's translation, which doesn't carry over many of the rimes. Is anything lost in this choice of a way of translating the poem? Note that Updike does retain some of the lyricism and ends the poem on an eloquent rime: "oblivion" and "been."

Octavio Paz, CON LOS OJOS CERRADOS (WITH EYES CLOSED), translated by *Eliot Weinberger*, page 321

This short poem by the Nobel laureate Octavio Paz is simple enough that anyone with basic Spanish can follow it in the original. (The original text will also give any native Spanish speakers in your class a chance to show off their bilingual abilities.) The poem explores a paradoxical conceit: in shutting oneself off from physical light, one can experience an inner light. Becoming a "blind stone" to the outside, "you light up within." The second stanza turns the metaphor erotic, although Paz is deliberately ambiguous about whether the lovers are together or apart. "Night after night" the speaker recreates his love with his eyes shut—perhaps carving her features from memory or perhaps touching her with his hands. The final stanza celebrates how the lovers enlarge their existence by knowing one another "with eyes closed".

Octavio Paz, CERTEZA (CERTAINTY), translated by *Charles Tomlinson*, page 321

This short poem by Paz speaks simultaneously about his consideration of the artistic process and about the fleeting nature of our lives, where what is said vanishes as it is spoken. Why "parentheses," one might wonder. Are the words captured there, in their cage of parentheses? Parentheses seem to be a symbol for what is written/recorded, as opposed to what vanishes in speech.

SURREALISM IN LATIN AMERICAN POETRY

César Vallejo, LA CÓLERA QUE QUIEBRA AL HOMBRE EN NIÑOS (ANGER), translated by *Thomas Merton*, pages 323–324

Vallejo's poem is an extraordinary example of surrealism, where sense is made by that which doesn't make sense. The progression of anger breaking a man into children, which break into birds and then eggs, sets up the reader's expectations in the poem. One feels the intensity of "anger," the manifestation of which often has precisely such a surreal quality; it breaks a person down into pieces.

Students might be asked what kind of meaning they glean from such bizarre, surreal images and assertions. Do they "feel" the poem even as they struggle to make sense of it?

CONTEMPORARY MEXICAN POETRY

José Emilio Pacheco, ALTA TRAICIÓN (HIGH TREASON), translated by *Alastair Reid*, page 325

Pacheco is a Mexican poet who has chosen to work in the United States, and he currently teaches at the University of Maryland. He writes in Spanish, but he collaborated with the noted poet-translator Alastair Reid (himself an immigrant from Scotland) on the English versions of his poems. Pacheco's presence in the anthology (along with the inclusion of writers such as Octavio Paz, Rhina Espaillat, Emanuel di Pasquale, Derek Walcott, and Claude McKay—not to mention Alastair Reid) highlights the importance of immigrants and foreign expatriates in our literary culture.

Pacheco's poem should require little gloss, but the effective and subtle irony of the opening probably deserves a moment's consideration in class to show how irony can be used rhetorically. By saying "I do not love my country" in a poem that celebrates his love for his homeland, Pacheco effectively qualifies the nature of his affection. It is not conventional patriotism but love for its particulars.

It is worth noting that although the poem presumably celebrates Mexico, its images are deliberately universal. It could be describing Finland or China. The title of this poem is also ironic: Pacheco's treason is a personal love for his country.

Francisco Hernández, BAJO CERO (BELOW ZERO), translated by *Carolyn Forché*, pages 325–326

The portrait of the mind of a suicide that this poem presents could be described as chilling in both the physical and the emotional connotations of the term. In the opening lines, Hernández rejects the common assumption that a person on the verge of self-destruction suffers from a mind that is feverishly spinning out of control. The feeling of icy emptiness is conveyed not only by the sensory descriptions, but also by the constant recurrence of negative terms (*not, nor, never, nothing, neither, no one*), patiently fashioning the sense of a mind beyond any claim life can make—whether in the form of a lover, one's children, or any other earthly attachment or emotion—and coldly sealed in its own focused isolation.

It may seem odd at first that a Mexican poet would invest a text with such wintry imagery, but as we read we come to realize that heat and passion are here implicitly associated with life, a connection that is memorably reinforced in the poem's last two lines.

Tedi López Mills, CONVALECENCIA/CONVALESCENCE, page 326

"Convalescence" comes closer than most of the poems in the anthology to the condition of "pure poetry"—that is, poetry which essentially uses imagery to create a mood or convey a sensation with little, if anything, in the way of larger thematic intent, thus fulfilling Archibald MacLeish's famous dictum that begins his "Ars Poetica": "A poem should not mean / But be." With a series of auditory images intended to produce an effect equivalent to that of chalk screeching on a blackboard, López Mills conveys the heightened sensitivity and irritability of someone recovering from an illness, for whom the common noises of the daily round—as hinted at by the epigraph from the great Spanish poet Antonio Machado—become almost unendurable assaults. The insistently repeated *first* is intended, of course, to communicate the raw newness of each offense to the nerves, before the senses have an opportunity to accommodate and adjust to the intrusion.

WRITERS ON WRITING

Octavio Paz, IN SEARCH OF THE PRESENT, page 327

In this excerpt from Paz's 1990 Nobel Lecture, he focuses on the influence of different cultures that affects writers, with Latin American writers as a vital example. The very language has been "transplanted," and Latin American writers feel simultaneously European yet not European. Languages grow and are transformed over the years and via their different uses. Paz is interested in the dialogue that is formed as a result of the recognition of this multilayered history.

WRITERS ON TRANSLATING

Alastair Reid, TRANSLATING NERUDA, page 327

Reid's illuminating memoir of translating Neruda gives us an intimate glimpse of how one poet translates another. Reid's entire memoir, which also discusses his long working relationship as a translator of Jorge Luis Borges, is well worth reading. It originally appeared in the June 24, 1996, issue of the *New Yorker*.

17
Recognizing Excellence

Ezra Pound long argued for the value of bad poetry in pedagogy. In his *ABC of Reading*, Pound declared that literary education needs to concentrate on revealing what is sham so that the student may be led to discover what is valid. It is a healthy gesture to let the student see that we don't believe everything contained in a textbook to be admirable. Begin with a poem or two so outrageously awful that the least sophisticated student hardly can take it seriously—some sentimental claptrap such as Cook's "The Old Arm-Chair." From these, you can proceed to subtler examples. It is a mistake to be too snide or too self-righteous toward bad poems, and it is well to turn quickly to some excellent poetry if the classroom starts smelling like a mortuary. There is a certain sadness inherent in much bad poetry; one can readily choke on it. As Allen Tate has said, the best attack upon the bad is the loving understanding of the good. The aim in teaching bad poetry has to be the admiration of good poetry, not the diffusion of mockery.

One further suggestion on bad poetry: a program of really execrable verse orated with straight faces by a few students and members of the faculty can be, with any luck, a fine occasion. For bad poems to work on besides those offered in this chapter, see the dustier stacks in a library for the following anthologies: *Heart Throbs* and *More Heart Throbs*, ed. Joe Mitchell Chapple (New York: Grosset, 1905 and 1911, respectively; many later editions); *The Stuffed Owl: An Anthology of Bad Verse*, ed. D. B. Wyndham Lewis and Charles Lee (London: Dent, 1930; reprinted in the United States by Capricorn paperbacks); *Nematodes in My Garden of Verse*, ed. Richard Walser (Winston-Salem: Blair, 1959); *The Worst English Poets*, ed. Christopher Adams (London: Wingate, 1958); *Pegasus Descending: A Book of the Best Bad Verse*, ed. James Camp, X. J. Kennedy, and Keith Waldrop (New York: Macmillan, 1971); and *The Joy of Bad Verse*, ed. Nicholas T. Parsons (London: Collins, 1988).

Anonymous, O MOON, WHEN I GAZE ON THY BEAUTIFUL FACE, page 331

Glorious behind seems inexact, and so does *boundaries* for "boundlessness."

Grace Treasone, LIFE, page 331

Treasone's poem develops a central metaphor, but its language is wildly imprecise. Is the tooth "that cuts into your heart" one's own or somebody else's? (It is probable that the poet means not tooth but "toothache.") Anatomically, the image seems on a par with the "heart's leg" of the tradesman poet quoted by

Coleridge. Through the murk of her expression, however, the poet makes clear her theme: the familiar and sentimental notion that life is really all right if you see it through (or have a competent dentist).

Treasone's item first adorned a Dover, New Jersey, newspaper column of local poets called "This Way to Parnassus."

Emily Dickinson, A DYING TIGER – MOANED FOR DRINK, page 331

This is not, by any stretch of the critical imagination, a good poem. Besides the poet's innocent lack of perception that *His Mighty Balls* suggests not eyeballs but testicles, the concluding statement (that the fact that the tiger was dead is to blame) seems an un-Dickinsonian failure of invention. Perhaps the poet intended a religious allegory (Christ the Tiger). Her capitalization of *He* in the last line doesn't seem sufficient proof of such intent, for her habits of capitalization cannot be trusted for consistency.

The failures of splendid poets are fascinating. As in this case, they often seem to result from some tremendous leap that sails over and beyond its object, with the poet crashing to earth on the other side.

EXERCISE: *Ten Terrible Moments in Poetry*, pages 332–333

J. Gordon Coogler, a printer by trade, was said to have displayed a sign in the window of his print shop in Columbia, South Carolina: "POEMS WRITTEN WHILE YOU WAIT."

For Byron's rousing lines, we have to thank Walter H. Bishop of Atlanta, for whom this discovery won first prize in a contest to find the worst lame verse by a well-known poet, conducted by John Shelton Reed in *Chronicles*. (The results were reported in the magazine's issue of November 1986.)

Mattie J. Peterson has attracted fierce partisans, some of whom see her battling Julia A. Moore for the crown of Queen of American Bad Verse. Richard Walser has brought out a modern facsimile of her 1890 book, *Little Pansy, A Novel, and Miscellaneous Poetry* (Charlotte: McNally & Loftin, 1967).

Francis Saltus Saltus is the rediscovery of Nicholas T. Parsons in *The Joy of Bad Verse* (London: Collins, 1988). We lifted the two excerpts from Parsons's splendid anthology, and it was a temptation to lift a third:

> Oh! such a past can not be mute,
>   Such bliss can not be crushed in sorrow,
> Although thou art a prostitute
>   And I am to be hanged tomorrow.

Saltus regarded himself as a rakehell. As C. T. Kindilien has observed, "Although he idealized cigarette-smoking women, looked for pornography in the Bible, and honored Baudelaire, Gerard de Nerval, and Le Marquis de Sade, he never escaped the tone of the boy who expected any moment to be caught smoking behind the barn" (*American Poetry in the Eighteen-Nineties* [Brown UP, 1956] 188–89).

Rod McKuen, THOUGHTS ON CAPITAL PUNISHMENT, page 334
William Stafford, TRAVELING THROUGH THE DARK, page 335

McKuen is still popular with some students, and any dogmatic attempt to blast him may be held against you. There may be value in such a confrontation, of course; or you can leave evaluation of these two works up to the class. Just work through McKuen's effusion and Stafford's fine poem, detail by detail, in a noncommittal way, and chances are good that Stafford will win the contest.

It may not be apparent that Stafford's poem is ordered by a rime scheme from beginning to end: *abcb* stanzas and a final couplet. Stafford avoids obvious rimes in favor of the off-rimes *road / dead* and *engine / listen* and the cutoff rimes *killing / belly*, *waiting / hesitated*, and *swerving / river*—this last a device found in some folk ballads. McKuen's poem announces an obvious rime scheme but fails to complete it. Unlike Stafford, he throws rime out the window in the end, with the effect that his poem stops with a painful inconclusiveness.

Stafford contributes a long comment on his poem to *Reading Modern Poetry: A Critical Introduction*, Paul Engle and Warren Carrier, eds. (Glenview: Scott, 1968).

Wallace McRae, REINCARNATION, page 336

If any recent cowboy poem deserves the name of classic, it's "Reincarnation," probably the most widely recited work by one of the best-known poets of the cowboy school. McRae is a cattle rancher from Forsyth, in eastern Montana, an area where his family settled five generations ago.

"Reincarnation" is no simple thing to evaluate. Its theme of the organic continuity of life seems straight out of *Hamlet:* "Thus may a king pass through the guts of a beggar." But the poem turns out to be a shaggy-dog meditation that leads up to an insulting joke: "Slim, you always were a horse's turd, and you still are." Still, most of us will probably enjoy being taken in. Perhaps we feel relief when a ponderous meditation on life and death turns into a mere comic kick in the teeth.

The poem's language wavers inconsistently between plain speech and bookishness: "life's travails," "rendered mound," "yer vegetative bower." In retrospect, McRae's bookish, ornate phrasings may seem ironic, for apparently even the poet doesn't take them in earnest. They exist only to be punctured with a bang in the last line.

Short of attending the annual Cowboy Poetry Gathering in Elko, Nevada (if you can get a room), the next-best introduction to the field may be two anthologies edited by Hal Cannon: *Cowboy Poetry* and *New Cowboy Poetry* (Salt Lake City: Peregrine Smith Books, 1985 and 1990). *American Cowboy Poetry*, published in Idaho, is a magazine whose motto might well be "Git along, little doggerel, git along." (We are grateful for the advice and a bibliography provided by Jim Hoy of Emporia State University.)

RECOGNIZING EXCELLENCE

William Butler Yeats, SAILING TO BYZANTIUM, page 338

Has XJK implied that this poem is a masterpiece so far beyond reproach that no one in his right mind can find fault with it? That is, of course, not the truth. If the instructor wishes to provoke students to argument, he or she might read them the withering attack on Yeats's poem by Yvor Winters (*Forms of Discovery* [Chicago: Swallow, 1967] 215–16).

This attack really needs to be read in its entirety. Winters is wrong, we believe, but no one can begin to answer his hardheaded objections to the poem without being challenged and illuminated.

Other discussions of the poem, different from XJK's and also short, appear in Richard Ellmann's *Yeats: The Man and the Masks* (New York: Macmillan, 1949) and John Unterecker's *A Reader's Guide to William Butler Yeats* (New York: Noonday, 1959). Those who wish to go deeper still and to read a searching examination (informed by study of Yeats's manuscripts) can be directed to Curtis Bradford, "Yeats's Byzantium Poems," *PMLA* 75 (Mar. 1960): 100–25. For those interested in alternatives, John Stallworthy reprints nearly all the legible manuscript versions in *Between the Lines: Yeats's Poetry in the Making* (Oxford: Clarendon, 1963) 87–112.

A deconstructionist reading of "Sailing to Byzantium," subjecting the poem to relentless questioning, showing where it fails to make sense and how it doesn't work, is offered by Lawrence I. Lipking in "The Practice of Theory" (in *Profession 83: Selected Articles from the Bulletins of the Association of Departments of English and the Association of Departments of Foreign Languages*, MLA, 1983). But in his role as a poststructuralist, Lipking confesses himself "a sheep commissioned to say something sympathetic about wolves." He finds that deconstructionist tactics offend his students, especially the bright, idealistic ones who expect their teachers to show them why certain works are great, and who wish poems to "make sense" and to relate to their own lives.

Jean Bauso has used a writing assignment to introduce this challenging poem. "I want you to pretend that you're an old person—someone in his or her eighties," she tells a class. "You've got arthritis, so buttoning or zipping your clothes is slow. Now you will write for ten minutes nonstop in the voice of this old person that you've made yourself into. You want to follow your person's stream of consciousness as he or she sits there thinking about the human condition, about the fact that we human beings have to die." After the students free-write for ten minutes, they read a few of the results, and she picks up on any comments about wishing for immortality. Then she asks for responses to the name "Byzantium," perhaps holding up pictures of the Santa Sophia mosaics. She then reads "Sailing to Byzantium" aloud, gives out reading sheets with points for reading it alone, and dismisses the class. For Bauso's detailed account of this lesson plan and her reading sheets, see "The Use of Free-Writing and Guided Writing to Make Students Amenable to Poems," *Exercise Exchange* (Spring 1988).

MLL *MyLiteratureLab Resources*. Biography, critical overview, and bibliography for Yeats. Critical excerpts on "Sailing to Byzantium."

EXERCISE: *Two Poems to Compare*, page 340

Arthur Guiterman, ON THE VANITY OF EARTHLY GREATNESS, page 340
Percy Bysshe Shelley, OZYMANDIAS, page 340

The title of Guiterman's bagatelle playfully echoes that of a longer, more ambitious poem: Samuel Johnson's "The Vanity of Human Wishes." If Guiterman's achievement seems smaller than that of Shelley's "Ozymandias," still, it is flawless. "Ozymandias," although one of the monuments of English poetry, has a few cracks in it. Many readers find line 8 incomplete in sense: the heart that fed what, or fed on what? From its rime scheme, we might think the poem a would-be Italian sonnet that refused to work out.

Nevertheless, Shelley's vision stretches further than Guiterman's. Ozymandias and his works are placed at an incredibly distant remove from us. The structure of the poem helps establish this remoteness: Ozymandias's words were dictated to the sculptor, then carved in stone, then read by a traveler, then told to the first-person speaker, then relayed to us. Ironies abound, more subtle than Guiterman's. A single work of art has outlasted Ozymandias's whole empire. Does that mean that works of art endure (as in "Not marble nor the gilded monuments")? No, this work of art itself has seen better days, and soon (we infer) the sands will finish covering it. Obviously, the king's proud boast has been deflated, and yet, in another sense, Ozymandias is right. The Mighty (or any traveler) may well despair for themselves and their own works, as they gaze on the wreckage of his one surviving project and realize that, cruel as Ozymandias may have been, time is even more remorseless.

What are the facts behind Shelley's poem? According to the Greek historian Diodorus Siculus, Ozymandias was apparently a grand, poeticized name claimed for himself by the Egyptian pharaoh Rameses II. Diodorus Siculus saw the king's ninety-foot-tall statue of himself, carved by the sculptor Memnon, in the first century B.C. when it was still standing at the Ramesseum in Thebes, a mortuary temple. Shelley and his friend Horatio Smith had read a description of the shattered statue in Richard Pococke's *Description of the East* (1742). Smith and Shelley wrote sonnets expressing their imagined views of the wreckage, both of which Leigh Hunt printed in his periodical the *Examiner* in 1818. This is Smith's effort, and students might care to compare it with Shelley's:

On a Stupendous Leg of Granite, Discovered Standing by Itself in the Deserts of Egypt

In Egypt's sandy silence, all alone,
    Stands a gigantic leg, which far off throws
    The only shadow that the desert knows.
'I am great Ozymandias,' saith the stone,
    'The king of kings: this mighty city shows
The wonders of my hand.' The city's gone!—
    Nought but the leg remaining to disclose
The site of that forgotten Babylon.

We wonder, and some hunter may express
Wonder like ours, when through the wilderness,
    Where London stood, holding the wolf in chase,
He meets some fragment huge, and stops to guess
    What powerful but unrecorded race
    Once dwelt in that annihilated place.

For more background to the poem, see H. M. Richmond, "Ozymandias and the Travelers," *Keats-Shelley Journal* 11 (1962): 65–71.

MyLiteratureLab Resources. Audio clip for "Ozymandias."

Robert Hayden, The Whipping, page 341

Hayden's poem chillingly depicts the cycles of family and social violence. The old woman beats the boy to avenge the "lifelong hidings / she has had to bear." The narrator stands outside the action of the poem, but the boy's tears trigger his own memories of being beaten by—in a frightening synecdoche—"the face that I / no longer knew or loved." Notice that Hayden deliberately leaves the relationship between "the boy" and "the old woman" unstated. Is she mother, grandmother, aunt, babysitter, foster mother? It doesn't matter in the poem. She is large and powerful while the boy is small and helpless. One might assign this poem together with Hayden's "Those Winter Sundays," for contrasting views of domestic life.

MyLiteratureLab Resources. Biography, critical overview, and bibliography for Hayden.

Elizabeth Bishop, One Art, page 342

Like Thomas's "Do not go gentle," this villanelle manages to say something that matters while observing the rules of a tricky French courtly form. (For remarks on the villanelle and on writing it, see the entry on Thomas's poem in this manual.) A similar feat is performed in Bishop's ingenious recollection of childhood, "Sestina."

Question: What varieties of loss does the poet mention? (She goes from trivial loss—lost door keys—to lost time, to losing beloved places and homes, to loss of love.)

In recalling that she has lost a continent, the poet may be speaking personally: she lived in Brazil for many years, and wrote this poem after returning to America. Early in life, Bishop knew severe losses. Her father died when she was eight months old; when she was five, her mother was confined to an institution.

Perceptively, the Irish poet and critic Eavan Boland has likened "One Art" to Bishop's "Sestina," remarking that "it is obvious that [the poet] entrusted some of her deepest implications of loss to two of the most intricate game forms in poetry." However, she finds differences between the two works: "'Sestina' is packed with desolate halftones, dropped hints, and the incantatory shadows of nursery rhymes. It manages to convey, at one and the same time, that there is sorrow, yes, and loss, yes, but that they are imperfectly understood. Therefore the poem operates at two different levels. Within it a terrible sorrow is happening. But the teakettle keeps boiling, the cup is full of tea, the stove is warm. Only we, outside the poem, get the full meaning of it all. 'One Art' is quite different. . . . The tone, which is both casual and direct, is deliberately worked against the form, as it is not in 'Sestina.' Once again, Bishop shows that she is best able to display feeling when she can constrain it most." (We quote from her fine essay on Bishop's work, "Time, Memory, and Obsession," *PN Review* [Nov.–Dec. 1991] 18–24.)

MyLiteratureLab Resources. Biography, critical overview, and bibliography for Bishop. Longman Lecture on "One Art."

W. H. Auden, SEPTEMBER 1, 1939, page 343

It seems fitting that only months before writing "September 1, 1939," W. H. Auden composed his justly celebrated elegy for William Butler Yeats, since this poem, like Yeats's "Easter 1916," shows a magnificent poet working at the height of his powers, writing with sureness and authority, creating a profound meditation on the relationship between our private natures and our public life. The speaker sits "Uncertain and afraid" as years of compromise and appeasement have reached their inevitable end in the unleashing of a war that is certain to have catastrophic effects for the world (although few could have predicted the full horror of that catastrophe). Some have understood the reference to Linz (line 16) to ascribe the roots of Nazism to Hitler's unhappiness and isolation as a child. Some have understood lines 21–22 to refer to the punitive terms of the Treaty of Versailles or to the inevitable response by the Allies to the German invasion of Poland; whatever specific application of these lines one may make in the context of 1939, it can hardly be doubted that every day's newspapers furnish new proofs, on both the global level and the personal, of the general truth of Auden's observation.

The third and fourth stanzas address "the lie of Authority / Whose buildings grope the sky" (lines 82–83), just as the fourth, fifth, and sixth stanzas analyze "The romantic lie in the brain / Of the sensual man-in-the-street" (lines 80–81). As the poet and critic John Fuller points out, "September 1, 1939" is "centered upon the need to establish the Just Society. . . . The basis of such a society is a universal love, the Christian Agape indeed, which appears to be denied by the Eros of the individual corrupted by sin." While seemingly impervious himself to "[t]he windiest militant trash / Important Persons shout" (lines 56–57), the speaker nonetheless recognizes that he, like all others, must rise above the Eros and the dust that constitute the lower part of his nature, so that he may approach and, he hopes, attain the universal love which he sees as the only possible salvation for a morally diseased world. Only on this basis can we show the "affirming flame" that is needed as desperately now as in 1939.

MyLiteratureLab Resources. Biography, critical overview, and bibliography for Auden.

Walt Whitman, O CAPTAIN! MY CAPTAIN!, page 346

This formerly overrated poem is uncharacteristic of Whitman in its neatly shaped riming stanzas and in its monotonously swinging observation of iambic meter, so inappropriate to a somber elegy. The one indication that an excellent poet wrote it is the sudden shift of rhythm in the short lines that end each stanza—particularly in line 5, with the unexpected turning-on of heavy stresses: "Oh heart! heart! heart!"

MyLiteratureLab Resources. Biography, critical overview, and bibliography for Whitman.

EXERCISE: *Reevaluating Popular Classics*, page 348

Paul Laurence Dunbar, WE WEAR THE MASK, page 348

Nowadays, Paul Laurence Dunbar is perhaps most frequently perceived as the author of a great deal of conventional and undistinguished verse in standard English and of ballads in African American dialect that are sometimes labored, often mawkish, and, to some, cringe-inducing. According to this view, his popularity in his own time was inflated by shallow standards and by allowances made for him because of his race, and contemporary interest in him is based more on historical and ethnic considerations than on aesthetic ones.

While there may be some truth to this (admittedly exaggerated) characterization, it is ultimately unfair to Dunbar. His 1902 novel, *The Sport of the Gods*, is a strong, well-written book which, though it has been reprinted several times, is still underappreciated. And amid the mass of his verse are some genuinely solid achievements—including, most notably, the poem at hand. There may be a couple of small blemishes in "We Wear the Mask": "torn and bleeding hearts" in line 4 is a bit of a cliché, and "guile" might not have been used in the preceding line if not for the necessity of the rime. But these slight weaknesses are far outweighed by the poem's strengths: Dunbar adheres strictly to a very demanding form—the rondeau—with almost no visible strain, and in doing so he displays a great deal of organization, control, and, for the most part, restraint. The artistry shown here is satisfying in itself, and it persuades the reader that the treatment has done justice to the theme.

Emma Lazarus, THE NEW COLOSSUS, page 349

Most Americans know at least a line or two of this famous sonnet carved on the pedestal of the Statue of Liberty, but surprisingly few can name the author of the poem. The poem and its author have vanished from most anthologies and textbooks. Yet Lazarus's sonnet seems that rare thing—a truly successful public poem. The images are clear and powerful, the language is memorable, and the sonnet avoids the chief danger of public poetry—prolixity. The contrast between the original colossus of the ancient world, which represented might, and the new colossus, which represents freedom, is both an original and effective means of dramatizing the difference between the Old World of European despotism and the New World of American democracy, a popular theme of nineteenth-century patriotic poetry, but one rarely so well expressed.

Edgar Allan Poe, ANNABEL LEE, page 350

Students usually adore this poem. Most modern critics hate it. There is some truth in both camps.

Let's catalogue the faults of the poem first. The poem is sentimental: it asks the reader to be sad while reveling in the beauty of the sadness. The poem is also heavy-handed. When Poe gets a nice line or image going, he can't resist repeating it—more often for the sake of sound than sense. (These repetitions make most of the stanza patterns go awry.) The language is abstract and literary (*angels*, *kingdom*, *highborn kinsmen*, *sepulcher*, *maiden*, etc.). It may be unfair to say that these are not authentic *American* images, but, more to the point, the words seem borrowed from a book rather than observed from life.

And yet, with all its faults neatly noted, the poem remains weirdly beautiful. The very irregularity of the stanzas keeps the form of the poem subtly surprising, despite the bouncy anapestic meter. The abstract quality of the language used in this hypnotic meter—all drenched in emotion—eventually gives the poem a dreamlike reality. That placeless "kingdom by the sea" now begins to resemble the world of memory, and the poem lures us back into our own emotion-drenched childhood memories. ("*I* was a child and *she* was a child," as more than one psychological critic has noted, places the poem in a presexual stage; Annabel Lee is a bride only in the future tense.) The childlike innocence of the language and emotions somehow carry the poem into a sphere where adult critical concerns seem less relevant. "Annabel Lee" somehow marries the style and meter of light verse to the themes of elegiac, if not quite tragic, poetry. Whatever its faults, American poetry would be poorer without it.

When told we were including this poem in a new edition, one instructor (a highly regarded critic adept in literary theory) said, "Be gentle. I love that poem. Critics keep showing me why it's awful, but I love it anyway." We hope she feels we've been gentle enough.

MyLiteratureLab Resources. Photographs, biographical information, critical comments, bibliography for Poe.

Writers on Writing

Edgar Allan Poe on Writing, A Long Poem Does Not Exist, page 351

Do you agree or disagree? If Poe is right, should we discard *The Odyssey*, *The Divine Comedy*, and "Lycidas"? If he is wrong, then how do you account for the fact that certain long poems contain patches of deadly dullness?

18
What Is Poetry?

This chapter is not designed to answer the question of its title in any definitive sense. Instead, we have attempted to create an occasion for reflection and discussion after all the material covered earlier in the book. We have compiled a small anthology of quotations by writers on the nature of poetry. You may want to supplement our list with others you have discovered.

Archibald MacLeish, ARS POETICA, page 353

This compressed and vividly drawn Modernist manifesto rewards careful reading couplet by couplet. Many people remember the famous closing lines—probably the most widely quoted formulation of modern poetry in English—but forget how finely realized the rest of the poem is. MacLeish manages a difficult trick in "Ars Poetica"—he creates a didactic poem in lyric form. Each rimed *vers libre* couplet contains an idea which is expressed in evocative lyric terms.

MacLeish plays upon a number of verbal paradoxes which students sometimes like to point out. He says a poem ought to be "mute," "dumb," and "wordless"; yet he is obviously writing a poem in speakable, audible words. As in some of the definitions of poetry quoted elsewhere in this chapter, MacLeish's poem understands that some truths can be expressed only as dynamic tensions between opposing forces or ideas. (Note, for example, Auden's definition of poetry—"the clear expression of mixed feelings.")

The poem contains a larger paradox, a potential topic for class argument. "A poem should not mean / But be," declares the poet. But is his poem pure being? Is it not heavy on meaning?—a tendency that an *ars poetica*, a poem that tells us how poetry should be written, can hardly be expected to avoid.

Ha Jin, MISSED TIME, page 356

We end the pedagogic portion of the poetry book with Ha Jin's simple, direct, and moving "Missed Time," a poem the average reader can appreciate on first hearing. Poems need not be complex or challenging to matter. What they need be is expressive, true, and beautiful—though no lover of literature will confuse the beautiful with the merely pretty or decorous.

19
Two Critical Casebooks: Emily Dickinson and Langston Hughes

This chapter offers a representative cross-section of two major American poets, Emily Dickinson and Langston Hughes—one author drawn from the nineteenth century, the other from the twentieth. The selections found in this chapter can be supplemented by additional poems from these two writers elsewhere in the text. There are now 21 Dickinson poems and 17 Hughes poems in the volume as well as substantial prose passages from each author. We have also incorporated visual information into the book, with author and documentary photographs relevant to the poems and the historical periods. Finally, a critical casebook on each poet's work provides a variety of analytical approaches for the student.

This chapter gives instructors the additional flexibility of using the material for in-depth classroom examinations of the individual poets. The casebooks provide students with some background—including author biographies and criticism—to prepare essays and term papers, though many instructors may want students to supplement their reading and research in the library or on our textbook Web site.

Emily Dickinson

This selection of Dickinson's poems spans her entire career. We have presented many of her most famous poems because students should know these classic works, but we have also included a few lesser-known ones to add variety and, we hope, surprise.

MyLiteratureLab Resources. Biography, critical overview, and bibliography for Dickinson.

Emily Dickinson, Success is counted sweetest, page 358

When the first collection of Dickinson's *Poems* (1890) was published—four years after her death—by Mabel Loomis Todd and T. W. Higginson, they placed this poem on the first page. The editors implicitly saw that it represents an important theme in the poet's work. They may also have used the poem to symbolize Dickinson's lifelong obscurity. Ironically, this was one of only seven poems Dickinson actually published in her lifetime. It appeared anonymously in 1878 (two decades after its inception) in Helen Hunt Jackson's anthology, *A Masque of Poets*.

The poem articulates one of Dickinson's central themes—how suffering heightens perception and understanding. The nature of success, the poem argues, is best "comprehended" by someone who has tried to secure it but failed. The central image of the poem is the defeated, dying soldier who hears the distant sounds of a victory he will never share. (Some critics—even the learned Judith Farr—comment that the military image is borrowed from the Civil War, which inspired so many poems from Dickinson, but the dating of the poem's first appearance in two manuscripts from 1859 makes such a connection impossible.)

In a lecture on Dickinson delivered in 1959 at the bicentennial celebration of the town of Amherst, Richard Wilbur made a cogent case that the poem goes beyond the conventional ideas of compensation ("the idea that every evil confers some balancing good, that through bitterness we learn to appreciate the sweet"). Wilbur speculated that Dickinson's poem

> is arguing for the *superiority* of defeat to victory, of frustration to satisfaction, and of anguished comprehension to mere possession. What do victors have but victory, a victory which they cannot fully savor or clearly define? They have paid for their triumph by a sacrifice of awareness; a material gain has cost them a spiritual loss. ("Sumptuous Destitution," reprinted in *Responses: Prose Pieces 1953–1976* [New York: Harcourt, 1976])

Emily Dickinson, I TASTE A LIQUOR NEVER BREWED, page 358

This joyful lyric is a most unusual nature poem—a hymn to the world's beauty in a form reminiscent of a drinking song. The first stanza celebrates a liquor that doesn't exist in the literal sense—it is never brewed but definitely intoxicating. An "Inebriate of Air" (what a gorgeous phrase!) and "Debauchee of Dew," the speaker draws her ecstasy from the everyday world around her rather than from the distant and seemingly romantic "Vats upon the Rhine." As in a good drinking song, the speaker brags about her great capacity to drink in the third and fourth stanzas. She cannot stop imbibing this "liquor never brewed."

In his superb essay on Dickinson, "Sorting Out," J. V. Cunningham quarrels with the traditional efforts to read the poet's work biographically. So much Dickinson criticism and textual scholarship, he observes, tries to create "a reconstructed history of the poet's emotional life." Such an approach obscures the actual surface meaning of the poem—"History would destroy the text to attain the fact." Cunningham then remarks:

> And so it is amusing that one of the best known poems of these [supposedly autobiographical works], "I taste a liquor never brewed" (214), has been until quite recently read as a self-portrait of Legendary Emily, that

> "Debauchee of Dew," that "little Tippler / Leaning against the – Sun." But it seems more likely that the speaker is not Emily at all, but a hummingbird; that the poem is, as many similar nature poems are, a riddle; and we have long missed the answer, not knowing "Guess Who?" was being asked. (*The Collected Essays of J. V. Cunningham* [Chicago: Swallow, 1976])

Questions the class might ask include whether the poem is indeed a riddle and whether Cunningham's interpretation is entirely inconsistent with traditional readings. Could the speaker not be both a hummingbird and the poet herself—or, more precisely, be the hummingbird as an allegory for the poet?

"I taste a liquor never brewed," one of the very few of her nearly 1800 poems to be published in her lifetime, appeared in a newspaper, the Springfield (Massachusetts) *Republican*, on Saturday, May 4, 1861. Here is the text of the poem as first printed, which is of interest for its demonstration of the ways in which Dickinson's earliest editors "normalized" her work to make it acceptable to the taste of the times. The poem is supplied with a (somewhat misleading) title; the first stanza is rewritten to provide an exact rhyme (though "Frankfort berries" is Dickinson's own phrase, from an alternative draft); and, most damaging of all, the extraordinary concluding image is flattened out to something quite conventional.

The May-Wine

I taste a liquor never brewed,
From tankards scooped in pearl;
Not Frankfort berries yield the sense—
Such a delirious whirl.

Inebriate of air am I,
And debauchee of dew;—
Reeling through endless summer days,
From inns of molten blue.

When landlords turn the drunken bee
Out of the Fox-glove's door,
When butterflies renounce their drams,
I shall but drink the more;

Till seraphs swing their snowy hats,
And saints to windows run,
To see the little tippler
Come staggering toward the sun.

Emily Dickinson, WILD NIGHTS – WILD NIGHTS!, page 359

It is worth noting that this famous love poem contains almost nothing explicitly about romantic love. And yet the text radiates erotic passions—mostly through suggestive word choice and imagery.

The first stanza begins with a fantasy of the "wild nights" the speaker would enjoy if she were with her beloved. (We know she speaks to her beloved because of the "Heart" metaphor in the second stanza.) The sexual element of the fantasy is also suggested by the associations of *luxury*, which originally meant *lust* or *lasciviousness*. (Remember the ghost of Hamlet's father admonishing his son: "Let not the royal bed of Denmark be / A couch for luxury and damnèd incest.") Although the word had also acquired its modern meaning by Dickinson's time, the echo of the original sense still remained. Finally, the nocturnal setting of the poem also suggests the obvious setting for the consummation of sexual love.

The second stanza introduces a metaphorical situation that continues through the rest of the poem—a boat in port. The speaker, however, realizes that this metaphor is still fantasy. She both imagines herself a boat in harbor (lines 6–9) and sees herself in her real situation (lines 11–12) as merely longing to "moor" herself to her beloved.

One more interesting word in this poem is *Eden*. The image of "Rowing in Eden" suggests that fulfillment of the speaker's romantic longings is paradisiacal. The metaphor of Eden further suggests that the speaker's longings—however erotic—are innocent of sin. Eden, the lost paradise, permitted a sexual freedom unknown to the post-lapsarian world. (Dickinson knew her Milton.) The speaker, therefore, longs for erotic fulfillment in a way that harmonizes body and soul in an idealistic, Edenic fashion.

MyLiteratureLab Resources. Audio clip for "Wild Nights—Wild Nights!"

Emily Dickinson, I FELT A FUNERAL, IN MY BRAIN, page 359

There are at least two ways of approaching this stark and powerful poem. We can read it either as a poem about death—the speaker's mental vision of her own extinction—or as a poem that uses death as the central metaphor in an allegory of an unstated psychological anguish.

The poem has an explicit narrative structure. It describes a funeral service and burial. The speaker describes the event simultaneously from two different but related perspectives (a characteristic Dickinsonian device). She places the funeral inside her brain, but she also experiences the ceremony as if she were inside the coffin at the service. Trapped in the coffin, she cannot see the events, only hear them. To borrow a phrase from Judith Farr (whose 1992 study, *The Passions of Emily Dickinson*, places the poet in the context of mid-nineteenth-century American sensibility), the poem is "staged to describe the sensations of lost perception."

Emily Dickinson, I'M NOBODY! WHO ARE YOU?, page 360

Small and simple, this poem is nonetheless memorable. It illustrates some classic Dickinsonian verbal devices—especially her gift of using everyday words (like *nobody* and *somebody*) in unusual but revelatory ways. Students might enjoy comparing this poem to E. E. Cummings's "anyone lived in a pretty how town," which uses the same verbal device in a more elaborately sustained manner.

Emily Dickinson, I DWELL IN POSSIBILITY, page 360

Given the fact that its keynote is "Possibility," this little poem makes very effective use of contrast and ambiguity in its treatment of the theme. From the first two lines, it is clear that if it is in contrast to "Prose," then "Possibility" must signify poetry and/or the imagination. It makes sense that there would be more windows in the house of Possibility, and one might at first assume that the superiority of its doors would also mean that there are more of them; but then we see that this house, however limitless its roof may be, is solidly constructed and "Impregnable of Eye," which would suggest that the life of poetry and the imagination is an exclusive, even hermetic one—which it certainly was, as practiced by Dickinson herself. After the nice play on the word "Occupation"—suggesting both residency and employment—the last two lines are suitably rich in possibility: the speaker seems to say that the poet's art will be both her way of comprehending the mysteries of existence and her means of achieving salvation.

Emily Dickinson, THE SOUL SELECTS HER OWN SOCIETY, page 360

"The Soul selects her own Society" is about both solitude and companionship. It is ultimately a love poem, though it does not initially seem so. The first two stanzas are written in the third person. The speaker views the "Soul" from a distance, though it will eventually seem it is her own soul she describes. The "Soul" chooses her "Society," which proves in the final stanza (now spoken in the first person) to be a single other person. This "divine Majority" of two suffices for the speaker, who then cares little for the rest of the world. She becomes "Like Stone." Even an Emperor kneeling at her doorstep leaves her unmoved.

Emily Dickinson, SOME KEEP THE SABBATH GOING TO CHURCH, page 361

This celebration of natural religion was one of the seven poems Dickinson actually published during her lifetime. It appeared in the March 12, 1864, issue of *The Round Table*, a New York weekly published by a relation. (It appeared there under the title "My Sabbath," which may have been Dickinson's own suggestion.)

In the original Massachusetts colony, Sunday church attendance was legally mandatory. By Dickinson's time it was merely a social obligation—but a serious one. Although Dickinson was deeply (if also unconventionally) religious, she stopped attending church by her thirtieth birthday. This poem was published a few years thereafter. The poem makes a clear and cogent case for worshipping God not by attending a church service but by being attentive to God's creation. The poem has a simple rhetorical structure: the speaker contrasts her own practices (what the *I* does) with the customs of *some*. A useful question for class discussion is to ask how each of Dickinson's natural images suitably matches (or exceeds) the ecclesiastic person or object it replaces—chorister, dome, surplice, bell, sexton, and clergyman.

Emily Dickinson, AFTER GREAT PAIN, A FORMAL FEELING COMES, page 361

The meaning of the poem depends heavily on the first three words, "After great pain." All of the subsequent description and rationale originate as consequences of this suffering. If "outlived," the poem suggests, great pain transforms one.

Like many other Dickinson poems, "After great pain" contains images and suggestions of death—tombs, the "hour of Lead," the "Freezing persons" losing consciousness in the snow. In this poem, however, the implied protagonist has survived the possible brush with death. (It is, in fact, possible to interpret the poem as describing a sort of spiritual resurrection—in contrast to the metaphorical reading of "I felt a Funeral, in my Brain" as describing a spiritual or emotional death and disintegration.)

The style and form of the poem are worth noting. Although it feels intimately personal, the poem is spoken in the third person. The speaker seemingly distances herself from the intensity of emotion she has painfully lived through. The middle stanza is arranged as irregular (5 lines versus the two 4-line stanzas that surround it). Heard aloud, however, the two irregular lines (7 and 8) combine into a metrically standard tetrameter line. Dickinson probably arranged the written text in an irregular fashion to slow the reader down and to emphasize the ideas presented in the lines.

Emily Dickinson, THIS IS MY LETTER TO THE WORLD, page 361

This memorable short poem begins with a characteristic Dickinsonian twist, "This is my letter to the World / That never wrote to Me." As Richard B. Sewall remarks in his detailed volume *The Life of Emily Dickinson* (Cambridge: Harvard UP, 1980), this poem "too often regarded as a tearful complaint about being neglected is actually a statement . . . of the difficulty of conveying what she calls the 'Message' of Nature." The "Her" in line 5 is clearly nature, but to whom do the "Hands" belong in line 6? It is possible to interpret these hands as belonging to posterity—probably the "countrymen" of line 7 whose tender judgment she implores.

If this poem is not specifically a complaint about being neglected, it is nonetheless a call to posterity. Whatever else it might mean, the poem is also an address to her posthumous audience. She may humbly position herself merely as Nature's messenger, but she does claim authorship as the transcriber of that message. She also implicitly confides an uncertainly about her own achievement and hopes that her audience will be tender in its judgment.

Emily Dickinson, I HEARD A FLY BUZZ – WHEN I DIED, page 362

Plump with suggestions, this celebrated fly well demonstrates a symbol's indefiniteness. The fly appears in the room—on time, like the Angel of Death—and yet it is decidedly ordinary. A final visitor from the natural world, it brings to mind an assortment of suggestions, some of them offensive (filth, stenches, rotting meat, offal, and so forth). But a natural fly is a minor annoyance, and so is death, if one is certain of Eternity. Unsure and hesitant in its flight, the fly buzzes as though faltering. It is another failing thing, like the light that comes through the windows and through the eyes (which are, as a trite phrase calls them, "the windows of the soul").

Most students will easily identify "Eyes around" as those of surrounding friends or relatives, and "that last Onset" as death throes. Is "the King" Death or Jesus? It seems more likely that the friends and relatives will behold death. What is the speaker's assignable portion? Physical things: keepsakes bequeathed to friends and relatives; body, to the earth.

Discussion will probably focus on the final line. It may help students to remember that the speaker is, at the present moment of the poem, in Eternity. The scene she describes is therefore a vision within a vision. Perhaps all the last line means is (as John Ciardi has argued), "And then there was no more of me, and nothing to see with." But the last line suddenly thrusts the speaker to Heaven. For one terrible moment she finds herself, with immortal eyes, looking back through her mortal eyes at a blackness where there used to be light.

MyLiteratureLab Resources. Audio clip for "I heard a Fly buzz—when I died."

Emily Dickinson, I STARTED EARLY – TOOK MY DOG, page 362

It would be unfortunate if students were to regard this poem as nothing more than a sexual fantasy. Handled with frankness and tact, it can be an excellent class-awakener. The poet expresses feelings for the natural world so intense that, like a mystic choosing erotic imagery to speak of the Beatific Vision, she can report her walk on the beach only in the language of a ravishing. The humor of the poem is essential: the basement-dwelling mermaids, the poet's picturing herself as a mouse.

Emily Dickinson, BECAUSE I COULD NOT STOP FOR DEATH, page 363

QUESTIONS FOR DISCUSSION

1. *What qualities does Dickinson attribute to death? Why is Immortality going along on this carriage ride?* For the poet, death and immortality go together. Besides, Dickinson is amplifying her metaphor of Death as a gentleman taking a woman for a drive: Immortality, as would have been proper in Amherst, is their chaperone.

2. *Is the poem, as the poet wrote it, in some ways superior to the version first printed? Is* strove *perhaps a richer word than* played? *What is interesting in the phrase* Gazing Grain? *How can grain "gaze"?* Grain has kernels like eyes at the tips of its stalks. As the speaker dies, the natural world—like the fly in "I heard a Fly buzz"—is watching. *What is memorable in the rhythm and meaning of the line "The Dews drew quivering and chill"?* At *quivering*, the rhythm quivers loose from its iambic tetrameter. The image of cold dampness foreshadows the next stanza, with its images of the grave.

3. *What is the Carriage? What is the House?*

4. *Where is the speaker at the present moment of the poem? Why is time said to pass more quickly where she is now?* Eternity is timeless.

5. *What is the tone of the poem?* Complicated!—seriousness enlivened with delicate macabre humor? Surely she kids her own worldly busyness in the opening line.

William Galperin reads the poem as a feminist affirmation. Not death, he finds, but immortality is Dickinson's subject. In the end the poet asserts a triumph possible only because she has renounced the proposal of Death, that threatening gentleman caller who might have married her ("Emily Dickinson's Marriage Hearse," *Denver Quarterly* Winter 1984: 62–73).

Emily Dickinson, THE BUSTLE IN A HOUSE, page 363

This evocative short poem perfectly illustrates one of Dickinson's greatest imaginative methods—the interpenetration of the domestic and the religious realms. The first stanza describes in clinical terms the busy activity in a house after the death of a loved one. The activity is "solemnest," but the living continue their work. The second stanza, however, reveals a radical shift—first into a symbolic mode and then into a religious one. The domestic activities of the first stanza are now allegorized into emotional symbols—the Heart and Love. The last two lines affirm trust in Eternity (not always the case in Dickinson's work) and close the poem with an epigrammatic click.

Emily Dickinson, TELL ALL THE TRUTH BUT TELL IT SLANT, page 363

Critics have traditionally seen this poem as Dickinson's clearest explanation of her poetic method, and it does remind us of her indirect procedures. Note that the *Truth* is associated with images of light. The poet's job is to make the light illuminating rather than blinding, to ease the viewer into seeing truth gradually. (Even the word *Delight*, which Dickinson wonderfully qualifies with *infirm* to describe the human capacity for truth, contains a possible play on the word *light*.) Likewise, the inability to grasp the truth—to see the light, in the metaphoric world of this poem—is characterized as blindness.

EMILY DICKINSON ON EMILY DICKINSON

Emily Dickinson, RECOGNIZING POETRY, page 364

It may be worth pointing out to students that this famous passage from Dickinson does not exist in any of her writing. It comes from a letter that T. W. Higginson, a critic and novelist who befriended Dickinson after she wrote him, mailed to his wife during a visit to Amherst. Higginson took notes on his conversation with the poet to share with his wife; these brief notes provide a vivid description of both her genius and her eccentricity. (We have reprinted the statement in its full original context in the "Critics on Emily Dickinson" section which follows.)

Questions for Discusssion

1. Is Dickinson right about recognizing poetry? Is there any other way to recognize it than by experiencing physical sensation?
2. What poem in the anthology affects you in the way that Dickinson describes? Can you relate the sensations you experience to any particular words or images in the poem?

Emily Dickinson, Self-Description, page 365

Few letters in literature have generated more commentary—and wild speculation—than Dickinson's April 25, 1862, response to Thomas Wentworth Higginson. Virtually every sentence has been offered several interpretations. The letter is often excerpted, but we have included the whole text to give an accurate impression of Dickinson's unique epistolary style.

Here Dickinson lists her poetic influences—Keats and the two Brownings. For prose she lists Ruskin and Browne, two notably gorgeous and ornate stylists, as well as Revelation, a revealing choice among the books of the Bible. It is worth noting that all of these choices remain respectable a century and a half later. Dickinson recognized truly good writing in both verse and prose. And amusingly she admits she has never read Whitman because she has been "told that he was disgraceful."

Critics on Emily Dickinson, pages 367–373

We have offered five interesting and diverse critical views of Emily Dickinson. The first is **Thomas Wentworth Higginson**'s extensive account of meeting her in 1870. He not only provides a number of superb observations, he also quotes her remarks extensively. Students will note that Dickinson's famous statement on recognizing poetry ("I feel physically as if the top of my head were taken off") came not from the poet's own letters but from Higginson's account. "I never was with any one who drained my nerve power so much," Higginson remarks at the end of his letter.

Thomas H. Johnson provides an account of discovering Dickinson's manuscripts—one of which we have reproduced. This background will help students understand the unusual nature of the texts of her poems—not an unimportant aspect of interpreting her work. **Richard Wilbur** offers a compelling psychological and biographical portrait of the poet. **Cynthia Griffin Wolff** discusses Dickinson's obsessive central theme, death, and provides a reading of "Because I could not stop for Death," while **Judith Farr** gives a reading of "My Life had stood – a Loaded Gun" that addresses issues of power, gender, and love.

Langston Hughes

Our selection of Hughes's poetry tries to represent the considerable range of his work—in mood, form, and genre. His special gift of combining traditional and innovational impulses is especially apparent. The juxtaposition with Dickinson's work in this chapter also opens up some interesting comparisons in style and approach that might be used for student essays.

MLL *MyLiteratureLab Resources.* Biography, critical overview, and bibliography for Hughes.

Langston Hughes, The Negro Speaks of Rivers, page 374

This remarkable poem was written by Hughes while still in his teens. The influence of Walt Whitman and Carl Sandburg, two early models, is evident, but the poem already demonstrates Hughes's characteristic voice. A good discussion question to ask is why Hughes chooses each of the four specific rivers to tell his story of the Negro race. The Euphrates is traditionally seen as the original center of human civilization. By invoking it, Hughes places the Negro at the dawn of humanity. The Congo is the center of black African culture. The Nile represents the source of the most celebrated African culture, and Hughes claims for the Negro a role in building this great civilization. Finally, the Mississippi becomes a symbol of the Negro in America, though Hughes selects a joyous moment to represent the race's turbulent place in our history.

Langston Hughes, Mother to Son, page 375

This stark, naturalistic poem contains (and half conceals) a transcendent central symbol—a stairway. While the mother has not spent her life climbing a "crystal stair," she has nonetheless felt confident she was ascending a stairwell. This more mundane stairway is badly maintained, poorly lit, and slightly dangerous, but the mother has had the drive and courage to climb it. And she insists that her son show the determination to do so, too.

The spare, conversational free verse of "Mother to Son" provides an interesting contrast to the extravagantly syncopated jazz rhythm of "The Weary Blues" or the rich formal measures of "Song for a Dark Girl." Hughes's poems show a wonderful prosodic range.

Langston Hughes, Dream Variations, page 375

This poem, according to Hughes's biographer, Arnold Rampersad, was written in response to the poet's 1923 trip to Africa. Presenting a vision of racial harmony, the poem contrasts the "white day" and the gentle dark night in a dream of joyous and unproblematic co-existence. The poem's now famous last line served as the title of John Howard Griffin's *Black Like Me* (1961), an exposé of American racial prejudice and discrimination.

Langston Hughes, I, TOO, page 376

This poem represents Hughes's admirable ability to critique American race relations and yet maintain a hopeful tone. The speaker's identity is crucial to the symbolic structure of the poem. He is a brother, a spurned darker brother but nonetheless a member of the family who knows he has an unquestioned right to live in the home. The symbolic segregation of being forced to eat in the kitchen obviously reflects the social realities of Southern segregation in that era. The speaker, however, knows his day will come soon—"tomorrow" in line 8—when he will claim his rightful place at the table, confident of his strength and beauty. But, as the last stanza reminds us, it isn't only the threat of the speaker's strength that will intimidate the others but the justice of his cause. They will "be ashamed" of their previous oppression.

The title and opening line is probably an allusion to Walt Whitman's famous passage in part 52 of "Song of Myself":

> I too am not a bit tamed . . . I too am untranslatable,
> I sound my barbaric yawp over the roofs of the world.

Langston Hughes, THE WEARY BLUES, page 376

"The Weary Blues" is a poem of rhythmic bravado. Hughes starts with a basic four-beat line ("Droning a drowsy syncopated tune"). He then flamboyantly varies it with jazz-like syncopations and contrasts it with interpolated short lines. As in "Song for a Dark Girl," he also incorporates allusive quotations from a traditional song—in this case the blues song of the poem's title. ("The Weary Blues" was published, after all, in the twenties—the same decade as T. S. Eliot's allusive *The Waste Land* and Ezra Pound's *A Draft of XVI Cantos*. Hughes was a populist Modernist but a Modernist nonetheless.)

There are two key characters in "The Weary Blues"—the speaker and the piano-playing blues singer. The poem is a recollection by the speaker of the performance he recently heard in Harlem. (Lenox Avenue was one of the main streets of Harlem nightlife in the twenties. It has since been renamed Malcolm X Boulevard, so Hughes's once famous setting has become a historical footnote.) The speaker is of unstated race, but the blues singer is repeatedly identified as a Negro. The singer and his song ultimately become a symbol for the sorrows of the modern African American. ("Sweet Blues! / Coming from a black man's soul. / O Blues!") The expression of the blues seems not only cathartic to the singer but almost annihilating. After singing all night, he goes home to sleep "like a rock or a man that's dead."

Hughes's biographer, Arnold Rampersad, has called "The Weary Blues" a work "virtually unprecedented in American poetry in its blending of black and white rhythms and forms." In his autobiographical book *The Big Sea* (1940), Hughes commented, "It was a poem about a working man who sang the blues all night and then went to bed and slept like a rock. That was all." Most readers will find much more in the poem than that summary suggests.

MLL *MyLiteratureLab Resources*. Longman Lecture on "The Weary Blues."

Langston Hughes, SONG FOR A DARK GIRL, page 377

One of the most impressive things about Hughes's massive *Collected Poems* is the stylistic diversity of his work. Written in regular rimed quatrains, "Song for a Dark Girl" shows the tight formal but evocatively modernist side of Hughes's style. The poem uses an ironic, allusive refrain borrowed from Daniel Decatur Emmet's famous minstrel song "Dixie's Land," which during the Civil War became a marching song for Confederate troops and then a nostalgic rallying cry for the lost Southern cause. Hughes quotes the song lyric, which is spoken in the faux-black voice of the minstrel, to underscore the reality that the black experience in "de land ob cotton" is not so joyful. The Christ-like imagery associated with the lynched young man is important to note.

Langston Hughes, PRAYER ("GATHER UP"), page 377

This lovely little poem shimmers with the compassion for the downtrodden that is so large a component of Hughes's work. Notice the movement in the second stanza from "pity" (which inherently suggests a distance between those who pity and the objects of their pity) to the much more intimate "love." Notice too the nice ambiguity of the poem's last word: it is not only God's mercy that "All the scum / Of our weary city" have despaired of, but also the mercy of those who foolishly regard themselves as superior.

Langston Hughes, BALLAD OF THE LANDLORD, page 378

This ingenious ballad begins to tell its story in the traditional way but then presents an innovative turn midway. The ballad starts in the voice of a black tenant who complains about his negligent landlord. As the poem progresses, the reader realizes that the speaker is arguing with his landlord, who is actually present. The argument heats up until the speaker threatens to hit the landlord (in line 20). Suddenly and unexpectedly, the voice of the poem shifts to outside observers, who condemn and overtly misrepresent the tenant. (Note how Hughes also abruptly shifts his meter and lineation once the voices change.) The poem ends with three isolated but sequential newspaper headlines in all capital letters. Hughes's mixture of auditory prosody and visual prosody in this poem is extremely interesting and demonstrates his use of Modernist techniques in seemingly populist works.

Langston Hughes, KU KLUX, page 378

In his discussion of its concluding stanza, the critic Bart Brinkman offers an interesting interpretation of the larger implications of this seemingly simple poem:

> In order for the black man to look in the white man's face, the latter must remove his KKK hood—his sustaining marker of whiteness—and reveal himself as an individual. The white man's demand becomes a desperate

plea: he is begging for the black man to acknowledge some essential whiteness that is not dependent on an oppressive dialectic, but is biologically inherent and assured. We do not get the black man's response to this last question (unless we consider it to be the poem itself) and we do not know his fate. But we are left with an impression of "whiteness" as fragile and poorly constructed, to be questioned even by a man under torture. Hughes's poem interrogates the history of oppression based on race and calls into question the very category of race itself.

Langston Hughes, END, page 379

This unusually stark poem presents a chilling vision of death. Hughes's images of death go one step beyond the conventional depictions. Time has not merely stopped; there is no time. Shadows have not fallen; there are no shadows. There is not only no light but also no dark. There is not even a door to exit. There is, by implication, nothing at all. This free verse, imagistic, and consciously impersonal poem demonstrates a different side of Hughes's talent—a darker and colder side—yet its immediacy and accessibility remain characteristic.

Langston Hughes, THEME FOR ENGLISH B, page 379

This poem demonstrates how a great writer in his maturity can turn a routine homework assignment into a memorable piece of literature. If youth is wasted on the young, so perhaps are writing assignments.

Hughes is so convincing a storyteller that you will probably have to remind students—repeatedly—that this poem is not autobiographical. Hughes was not born in Winston-Salem, but in Joplin, Missouri. He did not go to school in Durham, but in Lawrence, Kansas, and Cleveland, Ohio. He did attend Columbia (where, by implication, the poem takes place), but he left after a year to travel. (He later completed his college education at Lincoln University in Pennsylvania.) He was nearly fifty when he wrote this poem, not twenty-two as the narrator is.

Langston Hughes, SUBWAY RUSH HOUR, page 380

In this compressed but vivid depiction of rush hour in the subway, the poet seems to send an optimistic message: that were blacks and whites ever to mingle closely with one another on equal terms, there would be "no room for fear." Notable in the poem is Hughes's imagery. Within his sixteen-word limit he evokes three of the five senses: smell, touch, and sight.

Langston Hughes, SLIVER, page 380

"Sliver" provides another example of how Hughes employs a direct, song-like structure to create a richly evocative lyric. Hughes enjoyed contrasting the visual arrangement of his poems to the auditory shape. In "Sliver" he prints the two rhymed quatrains as a single, eight-line stanza to underscore the tight imagistic unity of the poem. Note, for example, how the "sliver of the moon" unexpectedly becomes the weapon to slit the man's throat.

Langston Hughes, HARLEM [DREAM DEFERRED], page 381

Simile by simile, Hughes shows different attitudes, including violent protest, that blacks might possibly take toward the long deferral of their dream of equality. Students might be asked what meaning they find in each comparison. Also worth noting are the strong, largely unpleasant verbs used to characterize the types of decay caused by deferring the dream: *dry up*, *fester*, *run*, *stink*, *crust and sugar over*, and *sags*. No wonder an explosion is likely to follow.

Hughes's poem supplied the title for Lorraine Hansberry's long-running Broadway play, *A Raisin in the Sun* (1958), in which the Youngers, a family descended from five generations of slaves, seek to move out of a Chicago ghetto in hopes of fulfilling their dream.

Donald Ritzhein has written a moving account of what the poem has meant to him, starting when his mother cut it out of a newspaper and pasted it to his bedroom door. "By the time I got to high school . . . I still didn't know a lot about the misery of deferred dreams . . . I knew a little more about them when I heard Martin Luther King, Jr. talk about dreams in Washington. I finally felt a little of what it's like to defer dreams when John F. Kennedy was killed" ("Langston Hughes: A Look Backwards and Forwards," *Steppingstones*, Harlem, Winter 1984: 55–56). Have you any student who would care to write about what the poem has meant to her or him?

Langston Hughes, AS BEFITS A MAN, page 381

Each of the poem's first two stanzas begins with the line "I don't mind dying." The speaker, unlike a great many others, is calmly reconciled to the inevitable end of his own existence. What does concern him is not how or when he will die, or even how much he will suffer, but how he will be remembered and mourned—and, "as befits a man," what that means to him is how he will be remembered and mourned by the women in his life. As shown in the third stanza, he wants the richness and fullness of his life to be commemorated by appropriate fanfare and display at his funeral.

You may find it useful to have your students compare and contrast this poem with Gwendolyn Brooks's "Southeast Corner": while Brooks seems disapproving of the Madam's superficiality and complacency, there is no sense here that Hughes is anything but admiring of his speaker's gusto and *joie de vivre*.

LANGSTON HUGHES ON LANGSTON HUGHES

Langston Hughes, THE NEGRO ARTIST AND THE RACIAL MOUNTAIN, page 382

Hughes's essay "The Negro Artist and the Racial Mountain" was the key manifesto of the younger African American artists associated with the Harlem

Renaissance. This crucial article originally appeared in the *Nation* as a response to George Schuyler's dismissive article "The Negro-Art Hokum." Hughes's proud assertion of black identity and the unabashed celebration of jazz and the blues struck a responsive chord among many members of the new generation of African American artists and intellectuals. The new artists saw their role, in the words of Arnold Rampersad, "to assert racial pride and racial truth in the face of either black or white censure or criticism."

Langston Hughes, THE HARLEM RENAISSANCE, page 383

In his autobiography, *The Big Sea* (1940), Hughes gave a vivid account of the Harlem Renaissance. This passage describes both the cultural excitement and the racial tension of Harlem's nightlife after white people began patronizing the local clubs. This profitable influx of white customers led to bizarre situations such as the famous Cotton Club and other nightspots, banning African Americans except as performers and staff—"barring their own race," as Hughes indignantly puts it. But Hughes also celebrates the talent and vitality of the club scene in a way that conveys the African American side of the Jazz Age.

CRITICS ON LANGSTON HUGHES, pages 385–392

The critical selections on Langston Hughes offer a range of approaches. **Arnold Rampersad**, Hughes's most distinguished biographer, discusses the innovative aspects of the early poetry, which blended both black and white literary traditions. **Rita Dove** and **Marilyn Nelson** examine Hughes's role as spokesman for African Americans. **Darryl Pinckney** analyzes in both historical and reader-response terms how Hughes connected with his early African American readers. **Peter Townsend** analyzes how Hughes used jazz influences and speculates on the social impact of his jazz poetry during his long career. Finally, **Onwuchekwa Jemie** provides a highly sensitive reading of Hughes's most famous poem, "Dream Deferred" (also published under the title "Harlem").

20 Critical Casebook: T. S. Eliot's "The Love Song of J. Alfred Prufrock"

As the first poem in T. S. Eliot's first published volume, and therefore the first poem in every subsequent selected and collected edition of his poetry, "The Love Song of J. Alfred Prufrock" has been the introduction to Eliot's work for many readers over the nearly one hundred years since it was first published. To this day, "Prufrock" remains an ideal text for young people to make their first acquaintance with Eliot. It is substantial enough to communicate some of his major themes and techniques, without being daunting in its length or complexity. It can still seem strange and in places even shocking to those who have not encountered it before, and thus it can still suggest to contemporary readers the radical innovations of Modernism, while proving at the same time to be absorbing and accessible. And, despite all indications to the contrary, many adolescents and young adults will still sympathize, and even empathize, with the poem's preoccupation with such concerns as loneliness, self-consciousness, fear of the opposite sex, the desire to live meaningfully in a trivializing culture, and pervasive feelings of futility and failure.

The poem's enduring popularity with readers has recently been reaffirmed in an extraordinary fashion. David Lehman, editor of the new *Oxford Book of American Poetry* (2006), selected the ten poems from that anthology that he considered the most popular, and readers were asked to vote for their favorite from the list. "Prufrock" was the clear winner, beating out such warhorses as Walt Whitman's "Song of Myself," Robert Frost's "Stopping by Woods on a Snowy Evening," Edgar Allan Poe's "The Raven," and Emma Lazarus's "The New Colossus."

In addition to "The Love Song of J. Alfred Prufrock," this chapter presents a number of supplemental texts and images selected to enrich your students' understanding of the poem, to enable them to view it in the context of its own time, and to help them understand why it is a work for all time. "Publishing 'Prufrock'" recounts—with excerpts from Ezra Pound's letters to Harriet Monroe, the editor of *Poetry* magazine—Pound's often frustrating but untiring efforts to get "Prufrock" into print. A selection of excerpts from the reviews, in both Britain and America, of *Prufrock and Other Observations* (1917) gives a vivid sense of both the dismissive incomprehension and the discerning appreciation of some of the poem's earliest readers. Passages from Eliot's own critical writings communicate some of his poetic theories and techniques as they bear directly on the poem. A cross-section of some of the best critical discussions of the poem over the last several decades helps to illuminate some difficult passages and other significant aspects of the text—and concludes with observations by two distinguished poet-critics, John Berryman and M. L. Rosenthal. Rosenthal's reminiscence of what

"Prufrock" meant to him in his own adolescence should prove to be of particular interest to young readers involved in their own first encounter with Eliot's poem.

T. S. Eliot, THE LOVE SONG OF J. ALFRED PRUFROCK, page 395

Given the wealth of supplemental material presented in the chapter, an extended commentary on the poem seems superfluous, if not presumptuous. But we would like to offer a few questions to start the classroom discussion.

QUESTIONS FOR DISCUSSION

1. *Why the epigraph from Dante? What expectations does it arouse?* Perhaps that this "song" will be the private confession of someone who thinks himself trapped and unredeemable, and thinks it of his hearer, too; also, that he is emboldened to speak only because he feels that his secrets will be kept.

2. *What facts about J. Alfred can we be sure of? His age, his manner of dress, his social circles? What does his name suggest? Can you detect any puns in it?* A prude in a frock—a formal coat.

3. *What do you make of the simile in lines 2–3? What does it tell us about this particular evening? Etherized* suggests fog, also submission, waiting for something grim to happen—his insides are going to be exposed and examined. *What does it tell you about Prufrock's way of seeing things?* "A little sick," some students may say, and with reason.

4. *What gnaws at Prufrock?* Not just his sense of growing old, not just his inability to act. He suffers from Prufrock's Complaint: dissociation of sensibility. In line 105, unable to join thought and feeling, he sees his own nerves existing at one remove from him, as if thrown on a screen by a projector.

5. *Who are "you and I" in the opening line? Who are "we" at the end?* Some possibilities: Prufrock and the woman he is attending. Prufrock and the reader. Prufrock and Prufrock—he's talking to himself, "you" being the repressive self, "I" being the timid or repressed self. Prufrock and the other eggheads of the Western world—in this view, the poem is Eliot's satire on the intelligentsia.

6. *What symbols do you find and what do they suggest? Notice those that relate to the sea, even* oyster-shells *(line 7)*. XJK points out blatantly that water has connotations of sexual fulfillment, and quotes "Western Wind." Eliot hints that, unlike Prufrock, the vulgar types who inhabit cheap hotels and fish shops have a love life.

7. *Try to explain the last three lines.*

8. *Now summarize the story of the poem. What parts does it fall into?* Part one: Prufrock prepares to try to ask the overwhelming question. Then in lines 84–86 we learn that he has failed to ask it. In 87–110 he tries to justify himself for chickening out. From 111 to the end he sums up his static present and hollow future.

A few other points worth making:

That Eliot may have taken the bones of his plot from Henry James's "Crapy Cornelia" (1909) is Grover Smith's convincing theory. "This is the story of White-Mason, a middle-aged bachelor of nostalgic temperament, who visits a young Mrs. Worthington to propose marriage but reconsiders owing to the difference in their worlds" (*T. S. Eliot's Poetry and Plays* [Chicago: U of Chicago P, 1960] 15).

"The meter of 'Prufrock' is peculiar," observes John Heath-Stubbs. "It is not simply free verse, as in [Eliot's] earlier Laforgueian pieces, but in its lines of irregular length, many but not all of which rhyme, suggests a free version of the Dantesque Canzone." This suggestion, and the poem's epigraph from the *Inferno,* point to Eliot's growing preoccupation with Dante ("Structure and Source in Eliot's Major Poetry," *Agenda* [Spring-Summer 1985]: 24).

Cleanth Brooks has written an essay full of wisdom and practical advice, "Teaching 'The Love Song of J. Alfred Prufrock,'" which you can find in *Eliot's Poetry and Plays,* one of the MLA's valuable "Approaches to Teaching" series (1988).

T. S. Eliot Reading His Poetry (Caedmon recording TC 1045) includes the poet's rendition of "Prufrock." There are also recordings of the poem spoken by Alec Guinness (*Sir Alec Guinness Reads T. S. Eliot*) and Ted Hughes (*T. S. Eliot: The Waste Land and Other Poems*).

MyLiteratureLab Resources. Biography, critical overview, and bibliography for Eliot. Student paper on "The Love Song of J. Alfred Prufrock."

PUBLISHING "PRUFROCK," page 399

This selection is intended to give some sense of the poem's original appearances—including the tangled bibliography of Eliot's first three poetry chapbooks—and to demonstrate the eternal nature of the issues involved. The excerpts from Ezra Pound's letters to Harriet Monroe convey the flavor of Pound's explosive and often arrogant personality, especially in defense of the writers and the artistic principles that he strongly believed in, and they illustrate the age-old clash between the artist's uncompromising integrity and the editor's audience-pleasing instincts. Pound's expostulations, in his letter of January 31, 1915, against what he perceived as Monroe's desire to have "Prufrock" end "on a note of triumph" may put you in mind of the famous witticism about "the ultimate *Reader's Digest* article: 'New Hope for the Dead.'" It should interest students to discover that many works now regarded as classics encountered a good deal of difficulty in achieving publication, and to learn how much perseverance is often needed in the face of obstacles to success.

THE REVIEWERS ON *PRUFROCK AND OTHER OBSERVATIONS*: 1917–1918, pages 402–404

The three British reviews excerpted here were all published anonymously, as was the custom of the times with such publications. The judgments expressed were no doubt intended to sound magisterial and absolute, rather than being presented for what they were, the opinions of fallible—and at times, it would seem from the internal evidence, unqualified—individuals. From the tone of these passages it can be seen how seriously those publications took themselves as "guardians of the faith," to borrow a sarcastic phrase from another of the poems in the *Prufrock* volume. The reviewer for the *Times Literary Supplement* (who was F. T. Dalton, an assistant editor of the *TLS* from 1902 to 1923) seems serene in his conviction that what he considers trivial and unenjoyable will strike most others in the same way; rather more surprising is his description of Eliot's poems as "untouched by any genuine rush of feeling," until one considers the gush of hyperbolic sentiment displayed in so much of the verse of that period. The author of the notice in the *Literary World* assumes, as was common in such circumstances, that what he cannot understand is deliberate nonsense, intended as a hoax by its author; his astuteness in maintaining that "[a]ll beauty has in it an element of strangeness" makes his overall obtuseness all the more peculiar. The writer in the *New Statesman* seems considerably more discerning than his colleagues, but his tone is somewhat patronizing overall, and, as May Sinclair suggests, it is uncomprehending, if not offensive, to exalt "The *Boston Evening Transcript*" at the expense of "Prufrock."

More perceptive were the reactions of Eliot's fellow Americans (and fellow poets). One would expect a favorable review from **Conrad Aiken,** given his friendship with Eliot; less expected, perhaps, is the mingling of a bit of blame ("the trivial") with the praise, showing Aiken's concern to demonstrate the objectivity of his judgment—though the phrase "the adorers of free verse" shows his own commitment to traditional verse techniques. Like Aiken, **Babette Deutsch** emphasizes Eliot's great technical skill and his cleverness. Of the three, it is **Marianne Moore** who most clearly communicates the depth and seriousness of Eliot's achievement in the *Prufrock* volume.

This recognition of Eliot's true value is even more directly displayed in the review by the British novelist **May Sinclair**. In the midst of excoriating the *New Statesman* review, she uses the word "masterpieces" to describe the poems and refers several times to Eliot's "genius." Among all the reviewers represented in this sampling, she is the one who shows the greatest awareness of the implications of Eliot's work for the future development of poetry.

T. S. Eliot on Writing

T. S. Eliot, Poetry and Emotion, page 405

This passage from the seminal essay "Tradition and the Individual Talent" addresses a number of concerns. In taking issue with William Wordsworth's classic definition of poetry as "the spontaneous overflow of powerful emotion recollected in tranquility," Eliot is a bit puckish in describing it as "an inexact formula," since he disputes every term of the phrase he quotes—and surely would have disputed "spontaneous" as well, had he quoted the entire comment. Eliot also supplies a useful corrective to some strivers after novelty when he says that it is not poetry's mission "to seek for new human emotions to express." The most famous passage in the excerpt is the last two sentences; in the light of facts about Eliot's personal life revealed after his death, it is fashionable among some to interpret these remarks in a narrowly personal manner—an unavoidable and, to some extent, valid response, but ultimately an insufficient engagement of the full implications of what Eliot is saying.

T. S. Eliot, The Objective Correlative, page 406

Here is Eliot's famous definition of a term of his own devising, a formulation that has become as much a part of the critical discourse as Keats's "negative capability" and Coleridge's "willing suspension of disbelief."

T. S. Eliot, The Difficulty of Poetry, page 406

Eliot's remarks on the subject of difficulty in poetry are well worth attending to, not only because his own poetry is frequently branded "difficult," but especially because of the good sense in what he has to say. As he points out, there are different ways in which a poem can be difficult and different reasons for such difficulty, and some of these are more worthy of respect than others. Two points made in this excerpt are particularly worth emphasizing to students: (1) there are times when a poem must be difficult, when its being otherwise would entail an injustice to the complexity or even the intractability of the material and/or the author's vision; (2) one should read poetry, especially difficult poetry, not in a state of anxiety to determine "what the author is trying to bring out"—that is, to impose an understanding on the text, sum up the theme, and move on as quickly as possible—but, instead, with a relaxed openness and receptivity, to experience the poem on all of its levels, not just that of paraphrasable content.

Critics on "Prufrock," pages 408–416

We begin with the commentary by **Denis Donoghue,** even though it is the most recent of our critical excerpts, because his speculations on the possible meanings of the epigraph provide an entranceway into discussion of the text. Your students may also appreciate Donoghue's description of his discovery of "Prufrock" in his adolescence and his immediate awareness that it was "memorable" and "fully achieved," without any concern for what critics had to say on the subject.

Speaking of speculations and entrances into the poem, **Christopher Ricks** considers a range of implications arising from the poem's title—not only the odd coupling of its two halves, but especially the speaker's name and the assumptions that it provokes; then, having done this, he is just deconstructionist enough to question the legitimacy of the procedure.

In his comments on the referents of the pronouns in "Prufrock," **Philip R. Headings** understandably gives most of his attention to the unidentified "you" of line 1; he valuably supplies the source for Eliot's well-known coy observations on the subject, though Headings's own conclusion about the identity of "you" is certainly open to challenge.

By considering the ways in which time functions in the poem, **Maud Ellmann** provides an illuminating analysis of Prufrock's use of tenses; from there, she addresses the larger issue of what it is that he is expressing when he expresses himself.

Burton Raffel employs the word "indeterminacy" to describe Eliot's frequent use of allusions that are not fully explained in context. He takes up two instances—Prufrock's intention to "wear the bottoms of my trousers rolled" and the "overwhelming question"—and decides that, while these references may not be presented with pinpoint precision, they are clear enough in context to satisfy all but the most insecure readers.

As a poet, **John Berryman** cultivated a notoriously compressed and difficult style, and his prose can also be demanding. But it is worth grappling with here for the illuminations that it affords regarding four central historical and fictional figures that Prufrock invokes in the course of his monologue. Especially rewarding is Berryman's analysis of one of the strangest and most difficult passages in the poem, the "pair of ragged claws" couplet.

Bringing us full circle, **M. L. Rosenthal** recalls his own discovery of "Prufrock" in the 1930s and muses on the reasons why Eliot's early poetry has a perpetual appeal for adolescents.

21
Poems for Further Reading

Anonymous, LORD RANDALL, page 419

Students might be asked to read the information about ballads in the chapter "Song," either before or after reading this ballad. "Lord Randall" exhibits many of the qualities of the traditional folk ballad, including a certain roughness in places, as with the meter in line 19. But, as demonstrated by the shift in the refrain halfway through, it demonstrates a certain degree of literary sophistication as well.

QUESTIONS FOR DISCUSSION

1. The basic situation in this ballad is slow to unfold. Is this an effective technique here, or do you think that the poem would have benefited by opening with more of a "grabber"?

2. Do you find the repetitiousness of the refrain a hindrance to your enjoyment of the poem? What is gained (or lost) by changing the refrain in the sixth stanza?

3. What is the value to the poem of the question-and-answer method of storytelling? Is the ending of the poem surprising, or do you see it coming from a long way off?

4. What else could the author have told us about Lord Randall's "true-love" and their relationship? Do you find it troublesome that she does what she does without our knowing why? Might the poem have suffered if the author had more deeply explored her motivations?

Anonymous, THE THREE RAVENS, page 420
Anonymous, THE TWA CORBIES, page 421

QUESTIONS FOR DISCUSSION

1. In "The Three Ravens," what is suggestive about the ravens and their conversation? How are the ravens opposed in the poem by the hawks and the hounds? (The ravens are selfish eaters of carrion, but the hawks and hounds are loyally standing guard over their dead master's body. Their faithfulness also suggests that of the fallow doe.)

2. Are you persuaded by Friedman's suggestion (quoted in the note under "The Three Ravens") that the doe is a woman who is under some enchantment? What other familiar fairy tales or stories of lovers transformed into animals do you recall?

3. Do you agree that "The Twa Corbies" is "a cynical variation of 'The Three Ravens,'" as it has been called? Compare the two poems in their comments on love and faithfulness.

4. For all the fantasy of "The Three Ravens," what details in the ballad seem realistic reflections of the natural world?

Anonymous, LAST WORDS OF THE PROPHET (NAVAJO MOUNTAIN CHANT), page 421

This valediction is part of the Mountain Chant of the Navajo translated by Washington Matthews, one of the pioneering linguistic anthropologists. His work helped broaden appreciation for the genius of Native American poetry. The Mountain Chants were performed by the Navajo under the direction of a shaman and contain many archaic words whose meanings were lost even to the priesthood.

Matthew Arnold, DOVER BEACH, page 422

Arnold and his family did such an efficient job of expunging the facts of his early romances that the genesis of "Dover Beach" is hard to know. Arnold may (or may not) have been in love with a French girl whom he called Marguerite, whose egotistic gaiety made her difficult. See Lionel Trilling's discussion of the poem and of Arnold's Marguerite poems in his biography *Matthew Arnold* (New York: Columbia UP, 1949). Marguerite, Trilling suspects, viewed the world as much more various, beautiful, and new than young Arnold did.

A sympathetic reading of "Dover Beach" might include some attention to the music of its assonance and alliteration, especially the *s*-sounds in the description of the tide (lines 12–14). Line 21 introduces the central metaphor, the Sea of Faith. Students will probably be helped by a few minutes of discussion of the historical background of the poem. Why, when the poem appeared in 1867, was religious faith under attack? Darwin, Herbert Spencer, and Victorian industrialism may be worth mention. Ignorant armies (line 37) are still with us. Arnold probably had in mind those involved in the Crimean War of 1853–1856, perhaps also those in the American Civil War. For sources of the poem, see C. B. Tinker and H. F. Lowry, *The Poetry of Matthew Arnold* (New York: Oxford UP, 1940) 173–78.

A dour view of the poem is taken by Donald Hall in "Ah, Love, Let Us Be True" (*American Scholar*, Summer 1959). Hall finds "love invoked as a compensation for the losses that history has forced us to sustain," and adds, "I hope there are better reasons for fidelity than disillusion. . . . Like so many Victorian poems, its negation is beautiful and its affirmation repulsive." This comment can be used to provoke discussion. A useful counterfoil to "Dover Beach" is Anthony Hecht's satiric poem "The Dover Bitch," in his collection *The Hard Hours* (New

York: Atheneum, 1960) and in many anthologies. For other critical comment, see William E. Cadbury, "Coming to Terms with 'Dover Beach,'" *Criticism* 8 (Spring 1966): 126–38; James Dickey, *Babel to Byzantium* (New York: Farrar, 1968) 235–38 (a good concise general essay); and A. Dwight Culler, *Imaginative Reason: The Poetry of Matthew Arnold* (New Haven: Yale UP, 1966).

John Ashbery, AT NORTH FARM, page 423

It is never easy to decide what an Ashbery poem "means." This one is rich with suggestions about which students may be invited to speculate. Who is this threatening catlike "someone" for whom we set out milk at night and about whom we think "sometimes, / Sometimes and always, with mixed feelings"? Is it the grim reaper? And yet Death always knows where to find the person he's looking for. And what are we to make of lines 7–11? How can the granaries be "bursting with meal, / The sacks of meal piled to the rafters" if "Hardly anything grows here"? The poet hints at a terrible sterility underlying the visible abundance at North Farm. Perhaps the farm can be regarded as, among other things, a paradigm of the world, rich in material things but spiritually empty. But that is to reduce the poem to flat words. Because such paraphrases tend to slip from Ashbery's poems like seals from icebergs, this poet's work is a favorite of critics. It challenges them to make subtler and stickier paraphrases.

Margaret Atwood, SIREN SONG, page 423

Atwood's "Siren Song" is a wonderfully tricky poem that seduces the reader as cleverly as it does its doomed listener. The reader doesn't realize that he or she has been taken in, until it is too late.

The poem is in three parts. The first section (lines 1–9) recounts the sirens and their deadly songs. Many readers will recognize the legendary monsters (half bird, half woman) from Book XII of *The Odyssey*. "Siren" has become a synonym for a dangerously alluring woman. The second section (lines 10–24) switches gears suddenly, as one of the sirens confesses to us her unhappy plight. She offers to tell us the secret of her irresistible song, but mainly she talks about herself and cries for our help. Then, without knowing it until too late, we are in the final section (the last three lines), where we realize that we have been lured into the siren's emotional grasp.

Feminist poets have often retold famous myths and legends with a twist; Atwood's "Siren Song" is surely a model of this genre.

You can listen to a recording of Margaret Atwood reading "Siren Song" at <http://www.poetryarchive.co.uk/poetryarchive/trackListing.do?poetId=96> and watch a video clip in which Atwood discusses the significance of myth at <http://www.pbs.org./moyers/faithandreason/media_players/atwoodpreview.html>.

W. H. Auden, AS I WALKED OUT ONE EVENING, page 425

This literary ballad, with its stark contrast between the innocent song of the lover and the more knowing song of the clocks, affords opportunities to pay close attention to the poet's choice of words. Auden selects words rich in connotations: the *brimming* of the river (which suggests also the lover's feelings), the *crooked* neighbor (with its hint of dishonesty and corruption as well as the denotation of being warped or bent by Time, like the "diver's brilliant bow"). Figures of speech abound: the opening metaphor of the crowds like wheat (ripe and ready to be scythed by Time the Reaper), the lover's extended use of hyperbole in lines 9–20, the personifications of Time and Justice, the serious pun on *appalling* in line 34 (both awe-inspiring and like a pall or shroud, as in Blake's "London"), the final reconciliation in metaphor between the original "brimming river" and the flow of passing Time. Auden's theme appears to be that as young lovers grow old, their innocent vision is smudged and begrimed by contact with realities—and yet "Life remains a blessing" after all.

The lover's huge promises in stanzas 3 and 4 ("I'll love you Till China and Africa meet . . .") have reminded Richard Wilbur of the hyperbolic boasts of the speaker in Burns's "Oh, my love is like a red, red rose." Burns speaks for the romantic lover, wrapped in his own emotions, but Auden's view of romantic love is skeptical. "The poem then proceeds to rebut [the lover's] lines, saying that the human heart is too selfish and perverse to make such promises" (*Responses* [New York: Harcourt, 1976] 144).

This poem may appear to have too little action in it to resemble folk ballads in more than a few touches. Auden himself, according to Monroe K. Spears, did not call this a ballad but referred to it as "a pastiche of folk-song."

"As I Walked Out One Evening" is one of the "Five Lyrics" included in *W. H. Auden Reading* (Caedmon recording TC 1019). For comparison with the poet's own modest delivery, *Dylan Thomas Reading*, vol. 4 (Caedmon TC 1061), offers a more dramatic rendition.

MLL *MyLiteratureLab Resources*. Biography, critical overview, and bibliography for Auden.

W. H. Auden, Musée des Beaux Arts, page 427

In Breughel's *Landscape with the Fall of Icarus* (reproduced with this poem), students may need to have their attention directed to the legs disappearing in a splash, one quarter inch below the bow of the ship. One story (probably apocryphal) is that Breughel's patron had ordered a painting on a subject from mythology, but the artist had only this landscape painting completed. To fill the order quickly, Breughel touched in the little splash, gave the picture a mythological name, and sent it on its way. Question: How does that story (if true) make Breughel seem a shallower man than Auden thinks he is?

Besides the *Landscape*, Auden apparently has in mind two other paintings of Pieter Breughel the Elder: *The Census*, also called *The Numbering at Bethlehem* (Auden's lines 5–8), and *The Massacre of the Innocents* (lines 9–13). If the instructor has access to reproductions, these works might be worth bringing in; however, the *Landscape* seems central to the poem. This painting seems indebted to Ovid's *Metamorphoses*, but in Ovid the plowman, shepherd, and fisherman looked on the fall of Icarus with amazement. The title of Auden's poem, incidentally, is close to the name of the Brussels museum housing the *Landscape*: the Musées Royaux des Beaux Arts.

Edward Mendelson has remarked on the poem in *Early Auden* (New York: Viking, 1981):

> The poetic imagination that seeks out grandeur and sublimity could scarcely be bothered with those insignificant figures lost in the background or in the crowd. But Auden sees in them an example of Christianity's great and enduring transformation of classical rhetoric: its inversion of the principle that the most important subjects require the highest style. If the sufferings of a carpenter turned preacher mattered more to the world than the doom of princes, then the high style, for all its splendor, was a limited instrument. . . . These casually irregular lines make none of the demands for action and attention that marked Auden's earlier harangues on the urgency of the times, yet beneath the apparent surface disorder a deeper pattern of connectedness gradually makes itself felt. The unassertive rhymes, easily overlooked on a first reading, hold the poem together.

Yet another device of language helps bring unity to Auden's meditation, in P. K. Saha's view. Four clauses begin with *how*, and one phrase begins with *anyhow* (line 11). These *hows* vary in meaning; still, the repeated *how* is the crucial word in the linguistic pattern of the poem ("Style, Stylistic Transformations, and Incorporators," *Style* 12 [1978]: 18–22).

MyLiteratureLab Resources. Biography, critical overview, and bibliography for Auden.

Elizabeth Bishop, FILLING STATION, page 428

QUESTIONS FOR DISCUSSION

1. *What is the poet's attitude toward the feeble attempts at beautification detailed in lines 23–33? Sympathy, contempt, or what? How is the attitude indicated?* The attempts are doomed, not only by the gas station's being saturated with oil, but by the limitations of the family, whose only reading appears to be comic books and whose tastes run to hairy plants and daisy-covered doilies. In line 20, *comfy* is their word, not the poet's own. But the tone of the poem seems to be good-humored amusement. The sons are "quick and saucy"—likable traits. The gas station can't be beautiful, but at least its owners have tried. In a futile gesture toward neatness, they have even arranged the oil cans in symmetry.

2. *What meanings do you find in the last line?* Somebody has shown love for all motorists by arranging the oil cans so beautifully that they spell out a soothing croon, such as what one might say over and over to an agitated child. But the somebody also suggests Somebody Up There, whose love enfolds all human beings—even this oil-soaked crew.

3. *Do you find any similarity between "ESSO—SO—SO—SO" in "Filling Station" and "rainbow, rainbow, rainbow!" in "The Fish"?* Both lines stand late in their poems and sound similar; both express the speaker's glimpse of beauty—or at least, in "Filling Station," the only beauty the people can muster and the poet can perceive.

Helen Vendler, discussing the poem in *Part of Nature, Part of Us* (Cambridge: Harvard UP, 1980), takes the closing statement to mean "God loves us all." But Irvin Ehrenpreis disagrees: "The '—SO—SO—SO' of overlapping labels on stacked cans is supposed to comfort automobiles as if they were high-strung horses, i.e., like a mother, not a god." Doily and begonia indicate that some absent woman has tried to brighten up this gas station for her husband and her sons (review of Vendler's book in *New York Review of Books*, 29 Apr. 1980).

Edward Cifelli, County College of Morris, passes along an insight from his student Joseph Grana. The message "ESSO—SO—SO—SO" may be an SOS from the same "somebody" who embroidered the doily and waters the plant. Professor Cifelli adds, "The pitiable woman who tries to put traces of beauty into a filthy filling station is unconsciously calling out for help, for rescue. Now *that* engages me!"

Robert Pinsky has also written of "Filling Station" with high esteem. He calls the poem a kind of contest between "the meticulous vigor of the writer" and "the sloppy vigor of the family," both filling a dull moment and scene with "an unexpected, crazy, deceptively off-hand kind of elegance or ornament." He particularly admires the poet's choice of modifiers—including the direct, honest-seeming *dirty*. "Adjectives," he notes, "according to a sound rule of thumb for writing classes, do not make 'good descriptions.' By writing almost as though she were too plain and straightforward to have heard of such a rule, Bishop loads characterizations of herself and her subject into the *comfy* dog, the *dim* doily, the *hirsute* begonia; the quietest possible virtuoso strokes" (*The Situation of Poetry* [Princeton: Princeton UP, 1976] 75–77).

"I've sometimes thought 'Filling Station' would make a good exercise for acting students," observes critic and teacher David Walker, "given the number of different ways the first line—and much of the rest—might be stressed. Is the opening exclamation solemn and childlike, or prissy and fastidious, or enthusiastic? All we can identify with certainty, I think, is the quality of fascination, the intent gaze on the filling station's pure oiliness." Walker is reminded of Frost's "Design" in that both poets seek to discover "a meaningful pattern in apparently random details"—but while Frost points toward a sinister architecture in what he observes, Bishop finds beauty and harmony ("Elizabeth Bishop and the Ordinary," *Field* [Fall 1984]).

Brad Leithauser has admired the poem's ingenious sound effects. At its end, "the cans of oil are arranged like cue cards to prompt that concluding sentence, the SO—SO—SO grading toward that 'Somebody loves us all.' Neatly, the message in the oil cans is reinforced by both the 'so' and the 'softly' in the fourth line from the end" ("The 'Complete' Elizabeth Bishop," *New Criterion* [Mar. 1983]: 38).

MLL *MyLiteratureLab Resources*. Biography, critical overview, and bibliography for Bishop.

William Blake, THE TYGER, page 430
William Blake, THE SICK ROSE, page 431

"The Tyger," from *Songs of Experience*, is a companion piece to "The Lamb" in *Songs of Innocence*. But while "The Lamb" poses a relatively easy question ("Little lamb, who made thee?") and soon answers it, "The Tyger" poses questions that remain unanswerable. Alert students may complain that some of Blake's questions have no verbs—what dread hand and what dread feet did *what?* While the incompleteness has been explained by some critics as reflecting the agitated tone of the poem, it may have been due to the poet's agitated habits of composition. Drafts of the poem in Blake's notebook show that, after writing the first three stanzas, he began the fourth stanza with the line "Could fetch it from the furnace deep," which would have completed the question in line 12. But then he deleted it and wrote stanza four almost as it stands now. (See Martin K. Nurmi, "Blake's Revision of 'The Tyger,'" *PMLA 71* [1956]: 669–85.) Other useful discussions include that of E. D. Hirsch, Jr., *Innocence and Experience* (New Haven: Yale UP, 1964), who thinks the stars are the rebel angels who threw down their spears when they surrendered; and John E. Grant, "The Art and Argument of 'The Tyger'" in *Texas Studies in Literature and Language 2* (1960): 38–60.

In "The Sick Rose," why is the worm, whose love is rape, *invisible?* Not just because it is hidden in the rose, but also because it is some supernatural dweller in night and storm. Perhaps the worm is unseen Time, that familiar destroyer—is the rose then mortal beauty? Those are usual guesses. For an unusual guess, see E. D. Hirsch, Jr.: "The rose's sickness, like syphilis, is the internal result of love enjoyed secretly and illicitly instead of purely and openly." In Hirsch's view, the poem is social criticism. Blake is satirizing the repressive order, whose hypocrisy and sham corrupt the woman who accepts it. Still, like all the best symbols, Blake's rose and worm give off hints endlessly, and no one interpretation covers all of them. We noted with interest that "The Sick Rose" is rightly included in *The Faber Book of Seduction* (London, 1988).

MyLiteratureLab Resources. Photographs and biographical information for Blake. Audio clip for "The Tyger."

Eavan Boland, ANOREXIC, page 432

Boland's poem is spoken in the voice of an anorexic. Although self-inflicted starvation is the controlling idea, the anorexia is expressed in two clusters of images. The first set of images evokes a witch being burned at the stake (her flesh consumed away in punishment for her heresy). The second set of images relates to claustrophobia and presents a series of small enclosures. Boland counterpoints these two sets of images in a feverishly quick pace. The speaker aspires to be "sinless, foodless," though she destroys her body in the process.

The image of the witch also appears in Anne Sexton's poem "Her Kind." Sexton's use of the witch affords interesting parallels to Boland's poem. Both speakers assume the witch's identity to express forbidden aspects of their troubled selves.

Gwendolyn Brooks, THE MOTHER, page 433

This powerful, direct poem is controversial for many readers, but it so memorably addresses an important contemporary issue that it is worth risking an overheated classroom discussion. Students will easily become polarized according to their moral positions on abortion, so it will help if you focus the discussion on the poem itself rather than broader social, legal, and theological issues. What does this troubling poem say?

First of all, point out that the poem is not spoken by Brooks about herself, that it employs two voices—first a narrator who speaks to another character ("The Mother" of the title), then the Mother's voice itself. Recognizing this literary distancing device will in itself depoliticize the discussion and allow you to focus on the poem's complex and at times almost contradictory argument. Second, point out the crucial division in the poem. In the first stanza the mother is the *you*. Another voice describes her situation. (This voice can be seen as either an outsider or part of the mother's divided self.) In the second stanza, however, the mother suddenly becomes the *I* and describes her own thoughts, fears, and memories. The *you* now becomes the unborn children. This switch is quiet but startling.

The form of "The Mother" is interesting and unusual—rimed free verse. Brooks usually rimes her free verse lines in couplets, but in a few places she varies the pattern. A good question to ask students is what effect does the form have on the poem's tone?

MLL *MyLiteratureLab Resources*. Biography, critical overview, and bibliography for Brooks. Longman Lecture on "The Mother."

Gwendolyn Brooks, THE PREACHER: RUMINATES BEHIND THE SERMON, page 434

In reading this poem, one might be reminded of the quip attributed to Voltaire and others, "God created man in his own image, and man returned the favor." As he ruminates in his heart of hearts, expressing private thoughts that do not find their way into his sermon, Brooks's preacher imagines an anthropomorphic God, one, he thinks, whose exalted position, and the barriers that that position creates between him and all others, may very well create feelings of loneliness and emptiness within. But of course we understand God to be all-sufficient unto himself, never to suffer such human afflictions as loneliness and need. Preachers, however, might feel isolated by their exalted positions and by expectations that they are superior beings who do not have to contend with the same weaknesses and problems that others do, and such preachers may very well unconsciously identify with a God onto whom they project their own longings and needs.

For an interesting comparison, you might read your class "Was He Married?" by Stevie Smith, a poem that explores the God-man relationship from a different—one might say opposite—perspective: the principal speaker in Smith's poem sees the humanly imagined Christ as an inadequate model because, as God, he cannot understand or feel the doubts and fears that lie at the heart of the human experience.

MyLiteratureLab Resources. Biography, critical overview, and bibliography for Brooks.

Elizabeth Barrett Browning, HOW DO I LOVE THEE? LET ME COUNT THE WAYS, page 435

Dropping this famous sonnet from a previous edition broke more than one teacher's heart. The many requests for this poem, "My Last Duchess," "Mending Wall," "Death be not proud," and Poe's work remind us how much students enjoy reading famous poems—works that an educational theorist like E. D. Hirsch would claim have "cultural utility." They are poems that are still frequently quoted in newspapers, conversation, and electronic media. Anthologists eager for novelty too often forget that these famous poems are novel to every new generation.

This is the penultimate sonnet of forty-four constituting Elizabeth Barrett Browning's *Sonnets from the Portuguese*, a book that Ezra Pound once called "The second: that is, a sonnet sequence surpassed in English by one other alone. I would argue for that." The sonnets document the poet's growing love for Robert Browning, whom she married, in defiance of her father's wishes, in her fortieth year. "My little Portuguese" was a pet name Robert often used for Elizabeth: hence the title of her book.

Teachers not opposed to biographical interpretations might direct their students to the notes on both Brownings in the "Lives of the Poets" chapter.

MyLiteratureLab Resources. Audio clip for "How Do I Love Thee? Let Me Count the Ways."

Robert Browning, SOLILOQUY OF THE SPANISH CLOISTER, page 435

The "Soliloquy" is a poem especially valuable for combating the notion that poetry can deal only in love and gladness. Here the subject is a hatred so intense that the speaker seems practically demented. In the last stanza, he almost would sell his soul to the Devil in order to blight a flowering shrub. A little background information on abbeys, their organization, and the strictness of their rules may help some class members. From the internal evidence, it is hard to say whether this is a sixteenth-century cloister or a nineteenth-century one; Barbary corsairs (line 31) plied their trade from about 1550 until 1816. The business about drinking in three sips (lines 37–39) may need explaining: evidently it refers to a symbolic observance, like crossing knife and fork.

It might be stressed that the person in this poem is not the poet: the tone isn't one of bitterness but of merriment. Comedy is evident not only from the speaker's blindness to his own faults, but from the rollicking rhythm and multisyllable comic rimes (*abhorrence/Lawrence; horsehairs/corsairs; Galatians/damnations; rose-acacia/Plena gratia*).

Questions: With what sins does the speaker charge Brother Lawrence? (Pride, line 23—monogrammed tableware belonging to a monk!; lust, 25–32; and gluttony, 40.) What sins do we detect in the speaker himself? (Envy, clearly, and pride—see his holier-than-thou attitude in stanza 5. How persuasive are his claims to piety when we learn he secretly owns a pornographic novel?) "Soliloquy" abounds in ironies, and class members can spend a lively few minutes in pointing them out.

MyLiteratureLab Resources. Photographs and biographical information for Browning.

Geoffrey Chaucer, MERCILESS BEAUTY, page 437

It can be great fun for students to learn (well, more or less) how to pronounce Chaucer's English, provided one has the time and strength to help them make the attempt. One does much better by Chaucer's lines if one puts on an Irish brogue. (A couple of Guinness stouts before class usually help.)

Some scholars doubt that Chaucer himself wrote this poem, but if he did not, someone who thoroughly knew Chaucer's work probably did.

"Since I escaped from love, I've grown so fat . . ." is a crude modernization of another poem from the "Merciles Beaute" series. Carlos Baker offers another modern American version of it in his book of poems *A Year and a Day* (Nashville: Vanderbilt UP, 1963).

G. K. *Chesterton*, THE DONKEY, page 438

QUESTIONS FOR DISCUSSION

1. *Who is the speaker—some particular donkey?* No, the generic donkey, looking back over the history of his kind.

2. *To what prehistoric era does Chesterton refer in lines 1–3?* To the original chaos out of which the world was made. The poet apparently imagines it in bizarre, dreamlike imagery: fish with wings, walking forests, fig-bearing thorn. Chesterton was fascinated by the book of Genesis "because of its beginning in chaos," comments Garry Wills in his introduction to a reprint edition of Chesterton's novel of 1908, *The Man Who Was Thursday* (New York: Sheed, 1975). The novel hints at a playful God who enjoys returning things to chaos every now and then. Writing about the world of dream in a newspaper article in 1904, Chesterton remarked, "A world in which donkeys come in twos is clearly very near to the wild ultimate world where donkeys are made."

3. *Whose "ancient crooked will" is meant? The will of the devil in perversely designing the donkey, or the donkey's own venerable stubbornness?* We're not certain.

4. *What fools does the donkey chide in the last stanza?* Anybody who ever abused a donkey, or who thinks donkeys contemptible.

5. *Explain how the allusion in the last stanza is essential to the meaning of the poem.*

6. *What devices of sound contribute to the poem's effectiveness?*

Lucille Clifton, HOMAGE TO MY HIPS, page 439

Lucille Clifton's poetry exults in everyday images—often viewed from an unusual angle that reveals some transcendent aspect. Her work is also terse and compressed, as in this short but definitely not petite poem. Clifton's exuberant poem is, first of all, a dramatic monologue. The speaker celebrates her own hips ("*these* hips" is a repeated phrase). Written in free verse, the poem divides its lines into natural speech units, often short declarative sentences. Another interesting feature of the poem is Clifton's personification of the hips: "They go where they want to go / they do what they want to do." The poem is so conversational that students may easily miss Clifton's sly figures of speech.

Samuel Taylor Coleridge, KUBLA KHAN, page 440

The circumstances of this poem's composition are almost as famous as the poem itself, and, for the convenience of instructors who wish to read to their students Coleridge's prefatory note, here it is:

> In the summer of the year 1797, the author, then in ill health, had retired to a lonely farmhouse between Porlock and Linton, on the Exmoor confines of Somerset and Devonshire. In consequence of a slight indisposition, an anodyne had been prescribed, from the effects of which he fell asleep in his chair at the moment that he was reading the following sentence, or words of the same substance, in *Purchas's Pilgrimage*: "Here the Khan Kubla commanded a palace to be built, and a stately garden thereunto. And thus ten miles of fertile ground were inclosed with a wall." The author continued for about three hours in a profound sleep, at least of the external sense, during which time he had the most vivid confidence that he could not have composed less than from two to three hundred lines; if that indeed can be called composition in which all the images rose up before him as *things*, with a parallel production of the correspondent expressions, without any sensation or consciousness of effort. On awaking he appeared to himself to have a distinct recollection of the whole, and taking his pen, ink, and paper, instantly and eagerly wrote down the lines that are here preserved. At this moment he was unfortunately called out by a person on business from Porlock, and detained by him above an hour, and on his return to his room, found, to his no small surprise and mortification, that though he still retained some vague and dim recollection of the general purport of his vision, yet, with the exception of some eight or ten scattered lines and images, all the rest had passed away like the images on the surface of a stream into which a stone has been cast, but, alas! without the after restoration of the latter!

It is clearly a vulgar error to think the poem a mere pipe dream which anyone could have written with the aid of opium. The profound symbolism of "Kubla Khan" has continued to intrigue critics, most of whom find that the pleasure-dome suggests poetry, the sacred river, the flow of inspiration, or instinctual life. About the *ancestral voices* and the *caves of ice* there seems less agreement, and students might be invited to venture their guesses. For a valuable modern reading of the poem, see Humphry House, "Kubla Khan, Christabel and Dejection" in *Coleridge* (London: Hart-Davis, 1953), also reprinted in *Romanticism and Consciousness*, ed. Harold Bloom (New York: Norton, 1970).

Some instructors may wish to bring in "The Rime of the Ancient Mariner" as well—in which case it may be a temptation to go on to Jung's theory of archetypes and to other dreamlike poems such as Yeats's "The Second Coming." A fine topic for a term paper might be, after reading John Livingston Lowes's classic source study *The Road to Xanadu* (Boston: Houghton, 1927), to argue whether it is worth trying to find out everything that may have been going on in the back of a poet's mind, and to what extent such investigations can end in certainty.

MyLiteratureLab Resources. Audio clip, student essay, and critical essay on "Kubla Khan."

Billy Collins, CARE AND FEEDING, page 441

The equation that this poem turns on—that one year of a human being's life is equal to seven years in the life of a dog—is usually expressed the other way around, as when, in answering a friend's question about the age of a pet dog, we might say something like: "Harlow is nine, which makes her sixty-three in human years." Here, on the eve of his sixtieth birthday, the speaker begins by calculating his age in dog years, and through the rest of the poem he imagines himself as both dog and master. He is an adult human being who is mature and responsible, as befits both the dignity of his age and his status as a higher being; at the same time, he sees himself as a dog in the simple, playful side of his nature, prompted entirely by instinct and affection. As the title suggests, he must see to the care and feeding of his inner dog (which, thanks to such care, has become "venerable") and must nurture that side of himself in order to stay as fully alive, in every sense of the word, as he can.

MyLiteratureLab Resources. Biography, critical overview, and bibliography for Collins.

Hart Crane, MY GRANDMOTHER'S LOVE LETTERS, page 442

Diane Thiel, a poet and professor of English, has contributed this commentary:

> In his correspondence, Hart Crane speaks of the trials of writing this early poem after the initial inspiration. He longs for the "silence" he feels is necessary to properly address his subject. The poem becomes a poignant example of the poet's process, of the surprising turns a work might take, and of the possible inability to fully embrace certain endeavors at various points in one's life.
>
> Early in the poem, the speaker tries to chart the constellation of his grandmother's life, via love letters discovered in the "corner of the roof." Yet already in the first two stanzas, the images suggest that the speaker feels the tug of impermanence: the old letters "are brown and soft / And liable to melt as snow." Crane continues to evoke an elegiac tone with such images in the third stanza: "It is all hung by an invisible white hair." In contrast to the impermanence is the rain, constant throughout the space of the poem.
>
> It is "the loose girdle of soft rain" that helps to create the music of the poem. The piece has a generally iambic current, but it is indeed "loose" and "soft," with an "echo" of meter, rather than a tight pattern. The rhymes as well are "gentle" and "soft": these two words themselves are repeated in the poem. In Crane's music, the words "enough," "Elizabeth," "roof" and "soft" provide a light touch of rhyme. Such delicacy makes his exact rhymes all the more intense when they appear: "the invisible white hair" alongside the "birch limbs webbing the air." He leads his "grandmother by the hand / Through much of what she would not understand."
>
> The poem ends with the rain on the "roof" gently rhyming its "laughter" at the poet's attempts to inhabit the past, via his grandmother's love life. The poem, which initially tried to explore the world of those letters, now recognizes the difficulty of the poet's role as translator of certain experiences. In

his correspondence, after recounting his difficulties with the subject matter, Crane states that the finished poem was "shorter than [he] had planned."

When the speaker asks himself if his fingers are "long enough to play / Old keys that are but echoes" and longs for the silence to be able to hear the music, one senses not only the longing for his grandmother's experience, but a longing to feel such a love himself. The speaker seems to wonder at his own ability to love. The poem becomes a quiet harbinger of his later "Voyages": "Permit me voyage, love, into your hands." The rain's "gently pitying laughter" suggests a realization of the distance the speaker feels, not only from the grandmother's experience, but from his own ability to inhabit the "greatness of such space." In its longing, the poem, itself, feels like a love letter—to his grandmother, to her life, and to his own desire to "carry back the music to its source."

E. E. Cummings, SOMEWHERE I HAVE NEVER TRAVELLED,GLADLY BEYOND, page 443

Why is this exquisite love poem so rarely anthologized? Cummings surely ranks as one of the great love poets in American literature, and this evocative lyric is one of his finest efforts. Many readers prize it greatly. We recently received a wedding announcement that reprinted the poem, and Woody Allen included the entire poem at a pivotal moment in *Hannah and Her Sisters.* The striking last line is one of the most famous in modern American poetry, and it serves as epigraph to Tennessee Williams's *The Glass Menagerie.*

The central image of the poem is a rose which the speaker equates with himself. (If one adopts a biographical strategy by which to interpret the text, it is worthwhile to note that Cummings wrote the poem for Anne Barton, an artist's model, whom he married in 1929 and divorced in 1932 after she left him for a wealthy New York surgeon. The interesting aspect of a biographical view is that Cummings's speaker uses the flower image, traditionally a female image, for himself, and it becomes a symbol of sexual and emotional awakening in the presence of his beloved.)

The poem moves via paradox and synesthesia. Eyes are "silent." The speaker cannot touch things because "they are too near." Fragility is portrayed as "intense." The effect is to endow the situation with strangeness and mystery. Words are used oddly, the lover's looks *unclose* the speaker. Punctuation is employed for expressive purposes, and normal word order is changed to heighten its musical and semantic effect, as in the lovely lines "you open always petal by petal myself as Spring opens / (touching skilfully,mysteriously)her first rose." All of these effects are used subtly and unexpectedly. Cummings carefully avoids repeating any verbal trick too often in this poem. Even the form of the poem is alluringly elusive. Many lines slip into iambic pentameter, but the poem never falls into a predictable rhythmic pattern. There are also rhymes hidden throughout the poem, but only in the last stanza do they appear conventionally at the ends of the lines. The sheer density of beautifully employed poetic effects and the constant shifting from one effect to another create an intoxicating, almost hypnotic spell on the listener.

MyLiteratureLab Resources. Photographs and biographical information for Cummings.

Marisa de los Santos, PERFECT DRESS, page 444

Dr. Johnson famously described remarriage as "the perpetual triumph of hope over experience," an adage with some applicability to "Perfect Dress." "Today in the checkout line," says the speaker, "I felt the old pull, flare / of the pilgrim's twin flames, desire and faith." Everyone, of course, feels desires of one kind or another, but it is faith—the belief that these desires can be fulfilled in just the ways that we want them to be—that distinguishes the speaker of this poem, and faith that the speaker finds impossible to relinquish. When she was fifteen, she "reached for polyester satin, / machine-made lace, petunia- and Easter-egg-colored, / brilliant and flammable. Nothing *haute* about this / *couture* but my hopes for it"—and yet those hopes are enough for the believer, "despite all we know." Even toward the end of the poem, she is still willing to credit at least the possibility that such hopes may be realized: "Silly maybe or maybe // I was right, that there's no limit to the ways eternity / suggests itself . . ." Despite the occasional ruefulness of tone earlier in the poem, this commitment seems, on the surface at least, uncomplicated by irony.

It might be interesting to read and discuss this poem in the context of several other texts in the anthology: Jane Martin's play *Beauty* (for the theme that physical beauty is everyone's secret desire) and Margaret Atwood's poem "Siren Song" (for the suggestion that, despite knowing better, we can't help falling for the same old lures every single time).

John Donne, DEATH BE NOT PROUD, page 445

During the Renaissance, when life was short, a man of the cloth like Donne would have surprised no one by being on familiar terms with death. Still, "Death be not proud," one of Donne's "Holy Sonnets," is an almost startling put-down of "poor death." Staunchly Christian in its sure expectation of the Resurrection, Donne's poem personifies death as an adversary swollen with false pride and unworthy of being called "mighty and dreadful." (For another bold personification, see "Batter my heart, three-personed God," another of the "Holy Sonnets," in which Donne sees God as ravisher.)

In "Death be not proud" the poet accuses death of being little more than a slave bossed around by "fate, chance, kings and desperate men"—a craven thing that keeps bad company, such as "poison, war, and sickness," and is itself powerless without their assistance. Finally Donne taunts death with a paradox: "death, thou shalt die."

Of interest, though perhaps of less than immediate usefulness in the classroom, are the articles on Donne's religious poetry by Helen Gardner, Louis L. Martz, and Stanley Archer in *John Donne's Poetry: Authoritative Texts, Criticism*, ed. A. L. Clements (New York: Norton, 1966). All three explore the extent to which Jesuit methods of meditation might have influenced the "Holy Sonnets."

It might be instructive for students to compare two personifications of death: Donne's and Emily Dickinson's in "Because I could not stop for Death," where death appears in the guise of a courtly gentleman who stops by to take the poet for a pleasant ride.

MyLiteratureLab Resources. Biography, critical overview, and bibliography for Donne. Audio clip for "Death be not proud."

John Donne, THE FLEA, page 446

This outrageous poem is a good class-rouser on a dull day, but we don't urge you to use it unless the class seems friendly. (Some women students tend to be offended by Donne's levity; men tend to be put off by his ingenuity.)

A little familiarity with a seventeenth-century medical notion may help make Donne's metaphor clear. Conception, it was thought, took place when the blood of men and women mingled during intercourse. That is why Donne declares in line 11 that "we almost, yea more than married are." Bitten by the flea containing his blood, the woman may already be pregnant.

Instructors fond of Donne's knotty poems will be grateful for Theodore Redpath's valuable crib-book *The Songs and Sonets of John Donne* (London: Methuen, 1956; also New York: University Paperbacks, 1967). Redpath works through the poems line by line, explicating difficulties. He explains line 18: The woman would commit "three sins in killing three" in that she'd commit murder in killing him, suicide in killing herself, and sacrilege in killing the flea. Why sacrilege? Because she would be attacking a "marriage temple" and symbol of the Trinity.

Patricia Meyer Spacks has treated the poem to scrutiny in *College English* 29 (1968): 593–94.

MLL *MyLiteratureLab Resources*. Biography, critical overview, and bibliography for Donne.

John Donne, A VALEDICTION: FORBIDDING MOURNING, page 446

In his *Life of Donne*, Izaak Walton tells us that Donne wrote this poem for his wife in 1611, when he was about to depart on a diplomatic mission to France.

Much of the meaning of the poem depends upon the simile of the compasses in the last three stanzas. There is probably no better way to make sure students understand it clearly than to bring in a draftsman's compass—even the Wal-Mart variety—and to demonstrate the metaphor with it. There'll always be someone who thinks Donne means the kind of compass that indicates north.

QUESTIONS FOR DISCUSSION

1. *What is a* valediction *anyway? What is a high school "valedictorian"?*

2. *Why does the speaker forbid mourning? Do lines 1–4 mean that he is dying? Explain this simile about the passing away of virtuous men.* As saints take leave of this world—so sweetly and calmly that one hardly knows they're gone—let us take leave of each other.

3. *In lines 7–8, what is suggested by the words with religious denotations?* Profanation *(the desecration of a sacred thing)*, the laity. *What is the idea?* Love seems to the speaker a holy mystery. He and his wife are its priests or ministers.

4. *Explain the reference to astronomy in the third stanza.* Earthquakes shake, rattle, and roll; Ptolemaic spheres revolve gently and harmlessly. This takes us to the notion of *sublunary* lovers in stanza 4. In the medieval cosmos, the heavenly bodies are fixed and permanent, while everything under the moon is subject to change.

5. *Paraphrase stanza 4.* Unlike common lovers, bound to their earthly passions, we have less need of those things that serve sensual love: namely, bodies.

6. *Why is beaten gold an appropriate image in the sixth stanza? What connotations does gold have?* Refined, precious, durable, capable of being extended without breaking.

7. *Comment on the word* hearkens, *line 31.* As a draftsman's compass will illustrate, the fixed central foot leans forward when the compass is extended, as if, in Donne's comparison, eager for its mate's return.

 *MyLiteratureLab Resources.* Biography, critical overview, and bibliography for Donne.

John Dryden, To the Memory of Mr. Oldham, page 448

With the aid of Dryden's great short poem (and the selections in the book from Swift, Pope, and Johnson), one at least can acquaint students with a little neoclassical poetry. The directness and plainness of Dryden's poem are clear from its very opening, and in teaching it one can question the assumption that neoclassical poetry is written only in bookish and Latinate words.

In teaching Dryden's poem, one can also mention (and define) the elegy and refer students to other famous elegies in the text.

A. E. Housman's "To an Athlete Dying Young" may be likened to Dryden's poem in that both poets favor classical conventions: footraces with laurels as crowns and the dead hero's descent into the underworld. Both poets find that premature death can confer benefits. What would Oldham have gained had he survived? More polish as a poet, yet he would have lost much of his force. In reading Housman's poem, students can be helped to recognize its metaphors: the comparison in the first two stanzas of victor's chair and dead lad's coffin, the comparison in line 5 of all human life to a footrace with death at the finish line. Students might be asked if they know of any living proof of Housman's observation that sometimes the name dies before the man (a truth often shown by the wistfulness of old football players at alumni weekends).

T. S. Eliot, Journey of the Magi, page 448

The speaker is a very old man ("All this was a long time ago . . .") looking forward to his death. As his mind roves back over the past, it is mainly the discomforts and frustrations of his journey that he remembers, and when he comes to the part we have been waiting for, his account of the Nativity, he seems still mystified, as though uncertainly trying to figure out what had happened—"There was a Birth, certainly." Apparently the whole experience was so devastating that he prefers to omit all further details. His plight was to recognize Christ as God and yet to be unable to accept Christ as his savior. Being a king, he did not renounce his people, but they henceforth seemed alien to him, clutching their discredited gods like useless dolls.

The passage beginning "Then at dawn" (lines 21–28) is full of foreshadowings, both hopeful and sinister. Besides the symbolic white horse, the vine leaves suggest Christ, who said to his disciples, "I am the vine, ye are the branches" (John 15:5). The tavern customers suggest the Roman soldiers who will drink and cast dice at the cross.

Although Eliot's dissatisfied Magus isn't one of the kings portrayed by Yeats in "The Magi"—being dissatisfied for different reasons—it is curious that Eliot may have taken the dramatic situation of his poem from one of Yeats's stories. In "The Adoration of the Magi" in Yeats's prose collection *Mythologies* (reprinted in 1925, two years before Eliot first published his poem), three old men call on the storyteller and, drawing close to his fire, insist on telling him of a journey they had made when young, and of a vision of Bethlehem. Like Eliot's speaker, who repeats "set down / This set down / This," they demand that their story be taken down word for word.

Among the useful discussions of Eliot's poem are Elizabeth Drew's in *T. S. Eliot: The Design of His Poetry* (New York: Scribner, 1949) 118–22, and Grover Smith's in *T. S. Eliot's Poetry and Plays* (Chicago: U of Chicago P, 1960) 121–25. More recently, Daniel A. Harris has characterized the Magus as a primitive Christian with a "baffled consciousness of mystery." See his article "Language, History, and Text in Eliot's 'Journey of the Magi,'" *PMLA* 95 (1980): 838–56. But Harris's opinions are questioned by William Skaff in a letter in *PMLA* 96: (1981) 420–22: "In 'Journey' Eliot adopts the dramatic mask of the Magus in order to express his own struggles with literal belief, his real 'religious position of 1927.'"

MLL *MyLiteratureLab Resources*. Biography, critical overview, and bibliography for Eliot.

Louise Erdrich, INDIAN BOARDING SCHOOL: THE RUNAWAYS, page 450

For discussion: Have you ever been somewhere you wanted to run away from? If so, how does your memory of that experience compare with that of the speaker in this poem?

This poem is long on wounds: the railroad tracks are scars (6), the runaways' old welts are like roads (15), the names they wrote in wet cement and the leaves they pressed into the sidewalk before it dried recall "delicate old injuries" (22–24). All these things carry powerful connotations of being wounded, mistreated, beaten down—like the runaways themselves.

Jacklight (New York: Holt, 1984), the collection in which this poem appears, contains several other realistic poems of Indian life. Since the success of *Love Medicine* (1984), *The Beet Queen* (1986), and *Tracks* (1988), Louise Erdrich is best known as a novelist, but we think her poetry warrants attention too.

Erdrich, born in Little Falls, Minnesota, grew up in Wahpeton, North Dakota, and now lives in New Hampshire.

B. H. Fairchild, A STARLIT NIGHT, page 451

The opening stanza of "A Starlit Night" (the first three words of the poem, actually) establishes the universality, as Fairchild sees it, of the theme he is developing.

All over America, at what is perhaps that part of the day most likely to lead us into reflectiveness and longing, men pause and think in the middle of a totally mundane activity. The equation of the memory of one's first sexual experience with taxes and broken faucets may seem a bit odd at first: why would such recollections have the same nagging, insistent quality as the other two more obvious irritants? As is suggested by the phrase "the stars rushing, rushing away," the answer might be a pervasive feeling of disappointment, a feeling that nothing—including the very things we thought would do so—has ever really healed the emptiness inside us.

The remaining three stanzas focus on a particular couple, especially the wife lying in bed watching her husband, who presumably stands at the closet with his pants over his arm, as examples of that universal condition. The details of her life—unmade bed, piled dishes in the sink, great gray sea of the kitchen's linoleum floor—surround her and threaten to overwhelm her, while the music coming from the radio downstairs takes her back to her own childhood and her father's constant praise and encouragement of her playing despite the fact, significant in the larger context of the poem, that she never quite got the piece right. The lovely, ghostly image of the moon sliding over the lacquered piano top "as if it were something / that lived underwater, something from far below," very effectively knits the poem's two main strands, as it symbolizes both the subterranean longings of the human soul (compare the "board games / with missing pieces" of lines 20–21) and the relentless passage of time (the "sunburst clocks in the kitchen / that made them, each morning, a little sad" in lines 21–22).

The last two lines are quite striking, especially the last five words. On the surface, "and now they have it" would seem to suggest a state of satisfaction, and yet, in the context of everything that has gone before, the couple in "A Starlit Night" seem in the end to be as isolated and unfulfilled as the people in an Edward Hopper painting.

Robert Frost, BIRCHES, page 451

"Birches," according to Lawrance Thompson, was written during a spell of homesickness in 1913–1914, when Frost and his family were living in Beaconsfield, Buckinghamshire, England (*Robert Frost: The Years of Triumph* [New York: Holt, 1970] 37, 541).

Students may be led to see the poem as much more than a nostalgic picture of boyhood play. From line 43 on, the poem develops a flamboyant metaphor. Richard Poirier has given us a good summary of the poem's theme: "While there are times when the speaker [of "Birches"] would 'like to get away from earth awhile,' his aspiration for escape to something 'larger' is safely controlled by the recognition that birch trees will only bear so much climbing before returning you, under the pressure of human weight, back home" (*Robert Frost: The Work of Knowing* [Oxford: Oxford UP, 1977] 172).

One line in "Birches" meant most to Frost, the line about feeling lost in the woods, facing too many decisions about which way to go. He pointed it out to audiences on several occasions: "It's when I'm weary of considerations" (line 43). Reading the poem at Bread Loaf in July 1954, he remarked of the line, "That's when you get older. It didn't mean so much to me when I wrote it as it does now" (*Robert Frost: A Living Voice*, ed. Reginald Cook [Boston: U of Massachusetts P, 1974] 51). Radcliffe Squires has written interestingly of the birch tree as a path toward heaven fraught with risk, suspense, even a kind of terror. The climbing boy performs his act of birch-bending gracefully, but in doing so goes almost too far, like one filling a cup "even above the brim" (*The Major Themes of Robert Frost* [Ann Arbor: U of Michigan P, 1963] 55–56).

Sidelights on the poem: Frost wrote to his friend Charles Madison in 1950, "'Birches' is two fragments soldered together so long ago I have forgotten where the joint is." Can anybody find it? . . . A particular word he congratulated himself on finding was *crazes* in line 9: "cracks and crazes their enamel" (Cook, 230). Frost's concern for scientific accuracy is well known. He sought evidence to confirm his claim that birches bend to left and right. "With disarming slyness, he said: 'I never go down the shoreline [from Boston] to New York without watching the birches to see if they live up to what I say about them in the poem.' His birches, he insisted, were *not* the white mountain or paper birch of northern New England (*Betula papyrifera*); they were the gray birch (*Betula populifolia*)" (Cook, 232).

MyLiteratureLab Resources. Biography, critical overview, critical articles, and bibliography for Frost. Audio clip for "Birches."

Robert Frost, MENDING WALL, page 453

This familiar poem is often misread or loaded with needless symbolism. Some possible notions you might meet:

1. That the poem is an allegory: the wall stands for some political barrier such as segregation, immigration quotas, or the Iron Curtain. But can the text of the poem lend such a notion any support? Frost, according to Louis Untermeyer, frowned on all attempts to add to the wall's meaning: "He denies that the poem says anything more than it seems to say" (Note in *Robert Frost's Poems* [New York: Washington Square P, 1964]).

2. Frost's theme is that fences should be destroyed. Up with communal land, away with private property! But as Radcliffe Squires points out, none of Frost's other poetry supports such a left-wing view. Neither does "Mending Wall" support it, "for the poet-narrator himself cooperates with the wall-builder, replacing the stones in the spring even as he protests in spirit" (*The Major Themes of Robert Frost* [Ann Arbor: U of Michigan P, 1963]).

3. The maxim "Good fences make good neighbors" is just a smug platitude for which the speaker has only contempt. This view would make him out to be a cynic. Yet, by cooperating in the wall-mending, the speaker lends the maxim some truth. Although limited in imagination, the neighbor isn't an idiot. (Frost is portraying, by the way, an actual farmer he liked: the cheerful Napoleon Guay, owner of the farm next door to the Frosts' farm in Derry, New Hampshire. See *New Hampshire's Child: The Derry Journals of Leslie Frost* [Albany: State U of New York P, 1969].)

At the center of the poem is a contrast between two ways to regard mending a wall. The speaker's view is announced in the first line; the neighbor's is repeated in the last. "The opposing statements," says Untermeyer, "are uttered by two different types of people—and both are right." Students may be asked to define the very different temperaments of speaker and neighbor. A hard-working farmer to whom spring means walls to mend, the neighbor lacks fancy and frivolity. Spring is all around him, yet he *moves in darkness*, as though blind. Lines 30–40 compare him to a man of the Stone Age. A conservative from habit, he mends walls mainly because his father did. The speaker, full of mischief and imagination, is presumably a poet who wants to do no more hard labor than he can help. The speaker enjoys having some fun with the neighbor, telling him that apple trees won't invade pines. Mending walls is a kind of spring ritual, and the speaker likes to pretend there is magic in it: using a spell to make stones balance, blaming the wear-and-tear of winter upon elves—or more exactly, upon some Something not to be offended.

MLL *MyLiteratureLab Resources*. Biography, critical overview, critical articles, and bibliography for Frost. Longman Lecture on "Mending Wall."

Robert Frost, STOPPING BY WOODS ON A SNOWY EVENING, page 454

Students will think they know this poem from their elementary school textbooks, in which it is usually illustrated as though it were about a little horse, but they may need to have its darker suggestions underlined for them. Although one can present a powerful case for seeing Frost as a spokesman for the death wish, quoting other Frost poems such as "Come In," "To Earthward," and "Into My Own," we think it best to concentrate on this familiar poem and to draw the class to state what it implies. The last stanza holds the gist of it. What would he do if he *didn't* keep his promises? There is sense, however, in an objection a student once made: maybe he'd just stay admiring the snow for another fifteen minutes and be late for milking. "People are always trying to find a death wish in that poem," Frost told an audience at the Bread Loaf Writers' Conference in 1960. "But there's a life wish there—he goes on, doesn't he?"

Ask students if they see anything unusual about the rime scheme of the poem (rimes linking the stanzas as in *terza rima* or as in Shelley's "Ode to the West Wind"), and then ask what problem this rime scheme created for the poet as the poem neared its end. How else would Frost have ended it if he hadn't hit upon that magnificent repetition? In 1950 Frost wrote to a friend, "I might confess the trade secret that I wrote the third line of the last stanza of 'Stopping by Woods' in such a way as to call for another stanza when I didn't want another stanza and didn't have another stanza in me, but with great presence of mind and a sense of what a good boy I was I instantly struck the line out and made my exit with a repeat end" (qtd. in Lawrance Thompson, *Robert Frost: The Years of Triumph* [New York: Holt, 1970] 597–98). On another occasion Frost declared that to have a line in the last stanza that didn't rime with anything would have seemed a flaw. "I considered for a moment winding up with a three line stanza. The repetend was the only logical way to end such a poem" (letter of 1923 to Sylvester Baxter, given by R. C. Townsend, *New England Quarterly* 36 [June 1963]: 243).

That this famous poem may be sung to the old show tune "Hernando's Hideaway" (from *The Pajama Game*) was discovered by college students working as waiters at the Bread Loaf Writers' Conference in 1960.

Paper topic: Read Lionel Trilling's speech at Frost's eighty-fifth birthday dinner, in which Trilling maintained, "I think of Robert Frost as a terrifying poet" ("A Speech on Robert Frost: A Cultural Episode," *Partisan Review* 26 [Summer 1959]: 445–52; also reprinted in *Robert Frost: A Collection of Critical Essays*, ed. James M. Cox [Englewood Cliffs: Prentice, 1962]). Referring to "Stopping by Woods" and other Frost poems, state to what extent you agree or disagree with Trilling's view.

Frost reads the poem on *An Album of Modern Poetry* (Library of Congress, PL 20) and on *Robert Frost Reading His Own Poems*, record no. 1 (EL LCB 1941, obtainable from the National Council of Teachers of English, 1211 Kenyon Road, Urbana, IL 61801). Both recordings also include "Fire and Ice."

MLL *MyLiteratureLab Resources*. Biography, critical overview, critical articles, and bibliography for Frost.

Allen Ginsberg, A SUPERMARKET IN CALIFORNIA, page 454

A comparison of this poem with Walt Whitman's work (e.g. "To a Locomotive in Winter") demonstrates the extent to which Ginsberg, in his tribute to Whitman, uses very Whitmanlike "enumerations." Ginsberg's long sentences, his use of free verse, parentheses, and fulsome phrases ("childless, lonely old grubber," "lonely old courage-teacher," etc.) are further indications that he is paying tribute to Whitman in part by echoing his style.

There is in "A Supermarket in California" as well a quality of surrealism that is Ginsberg's own. The existence of a "Neon fruit supermarket," the juxtaposition of past and present, the inclusion of the Spanish poet García Lorca (like Ginsberg and Whitman, a homosexual) "down by the watermelons," and the references to Charon and to the River Lethe all hover at the edges of dream.

Questions for discussion: What does Ginsberg mean when he speaks of "the lost America of love"? What does the poem say about loneliness? About death? (Whitman's death, in the poem, is as lonely a journey as Ginsberg imagines his life to have been.)

Thom Gunn, THE MAN WITH NIGHT SWEATS, page 455

Thom Gunn's particular genius was to embody the human and artistic contradictions of his age. Reading his extravagantly diverse *Collected Poems* (1994), one finds poems on LSD and San Francisco street hustlers next to lyrics on Catholic saints and Caravaggio—all of them recognizably drawn from the same imagination. Gunn is the crown prince of incongruity, a Romantic entranced by classical control, an experimentalist who never renounced rime and meter, and an anti-authoritarian ruled by mandarin standards.

When Gunn first came to California from England in 1954, he was only twenty-five but had already published a celebrated book of poems. Having won a writing fellowship to Stanford, the young gay poet with "a promiscuous love of experience" studied with the famously rigorous Yvor Winters. Gunn's already incisive style sharpened under Winters's formalist tutelage, yet his tone and subjects kept their rebellious edge. His second book may have begun with rimed iambic stanzas, but they described a motorcycle gang on the move.

Gunn's greatest moment as a poet came at his most difficult time—the AIDS epidemic. In a single month he lost four close friends. Out of this personal and public crisis grew *The Man with Night Sweats* (1992), which will probably stand as the finest poetic testament of those plague years. While most AIDS poetry relied on naked grief and raw emotion, Gunn's lucid but lyric meditations were simultaneously realistic and transcendent. He did not merely give voice to the lost—he gave them poetry, as in the title piece, which begins: "I wake up cold, I who / Prospered through dreams of heat / Wake to their residue, / Sweat, and a clinging sheet."

The speaker in Gunn's poem faces the certainty of his own impending death. The language is precisely phrased and classically balanced in the tradition of English death poems such as John Keats's "When I have fears that I may cease to be." This earlier poem would provide illuminating contrast for class discussion or possible student essays. What words would suffice to face one's own death?

Donald Hall, NAMES OF HORSES, page 456

Hall is apparently eulogizing not one horse but a long succession of them, each taking on its predecessors' duties through the years. The poem enumerates the everyday chores the horses had to do, "generation on generation," Sundays included. The "man, who fed you and kept you, and harnessed you every morning" represents not a single farmer, apparently, but all those on this New Hampshire farm who cared for and finally buried their horses in the time-honored way "for a hundred and fifty years." Like all dead animals (including people), the horses when they die become "soil makers," useful even in their graves.

The wonderful list in the poem's last line delivers what the title has promised, names of horses. The last one, Lady Ghost, is the most connotative. You might wish to have students explore its suggestions.

First published in the *New Yorker*, this poem later appeared in Hall's seventh book of poems, *Kicking the Leaves* (New York: Harper, 1978). The farm in New Hampshire where Hall lives was once a working farm run by his grandparents and, before them, his great-grandparents. Hall has written a prose memoir, *String Too Short to Be Saved* (Boston: Godine, 1981), about the boyhood summers he spent there with his grandmother and grandfather. "Names of Horses," too, seems to depend heavily on the poet's fond memories of the farm he still loves.

Thomas Hardy, THE CONVERGENCE OF THE TWAIN, page 457

The discovery in September 1985 of the well-preserved wreck of the *Titanic* in the North Atlantic, and the subsequent squabble over possession of it, gave this old favorite poem a certain immediacy. Most students will be familiar with the history of this great disaster from news reports or from the many popular films and books. Still, a few facts may need to be recalled. The fateful day was April 15, 1912. The pride of the British White Star lines, the *Titanic* was the world's largest ship in its day, celebrated for luxurious trappings (including Turkish baths and a fully equipped gym). Many of the unlucky passengers were wealthy and famous. One reason the *Titanic* sank with such cost of life was that the builders, smugly assuming the ship to be unsinkable, had provided lifeboats for fewer than half the 2,200 passengers. (Only 705 people survived.) Hardy wrote the poem for the souvenir program of a benefit show for the *Titanic* Disaster Fund (to aid survivors and the bereaved) given at Covent Garden, May 14, 1912.

Hardy has been seen as an enemy of science and industrialism, those spoilers of rural England, but Donald Davie argues that "The Convergence of the Twain" shows no such animosity. The poem censures vanity and luxury, "but not the technology which built the great ship and navigated her" (*Thomas Hardy and British Poetry* [Oxford: Oxford UP, 1972]). Although Hardy personally knew two victims of the disaster, the "Convergence," as J. O. Bailey points out, is not a personal lament; indeed, the drowned are hardly mentioned. The poem is a philosophic argument, with the Immanent Will punishing man for pride: "It acts like the Greek concept of Fate that rebukes *hubris*" (*The Poetry of Thomas Hardy* [Chapel Hill: U of North Carolina P, 1970]). Fate, however, seems personified in the poem as the Spinner of the Years, a mere agent of the Will.

Students can concentrate profitably on the poet's choice of words: those that suggest the exotic unnaturalness of the *Titanic's* furnishings (*salamandrine*, *opulent*, *jewels . . . to ravish the sensuous mind*, *gilded*). Diction will also point to the metaphor of the marriage between ship and iceberg: the *intimate welding* and the *consummation*. The late Allen Tate was fond of reading this poem aloud to his friends, with mingled affection and contempt, and remarking (according to Robert Kent) that it held "too many dead words, dead then as now, and all the more obtuse for having been long dead in Shelley. 'Stilly,' for example." From Hardy's original printed version of the poem, as given in *The Variorum Edition of the Complete Poems of Thomas Hardy*, ed. James Gibson (New York: Macmillan, 1979), it appears that he originally cast line 6: "The cold, calm currents strike their rhythmic tidal lyres." Isn't *thrid* an improvement, even though it is stiltedly archaic?

MyLiteratureLab Resources. Biography, critical overview, and bibliography for Hardy.

Thomas Hardy, THE DARKLING THRUSH, page 459

"The Darkling Thrush" comes out of the Romantic pastoral tradition, and through its first two stanzas Hardy pulls out all the stops in displaying the connection between the bleakness of the landscape and the bleakness of the speaker's mood. Virtually every line yields a word indicative of enervation and hopelessness: note "spectre," "dregs," "desolate," "weakening," "broken," and "haunted" in the first eight lines alone.

It is at the poem's midpoint that the thrush of the title makes his sudden and surprising appearance, a bird who is described as being as "frail, gaunt, and small" (line 21) as the speaker feels himself to be, and thus is presented as a figure with whom the speaker may readily identify, and with whose values and reactions he may therefore be willing to associate himself. And so a reader may be tempted—a temptation to which many students will almost certainly succumb—to characterize the poem's theme along these lines: I was suffering from gloom induced by the winter-afternoon dying-of-the-light blahs, until the joyous song of this little bird showed me how silly I was to feel that way.

But notice how muted the conclusion of the poem actually is. The speaker says that "I could think" (line 29) that the thrush knew something that he didn't, not "I *did* think." And the very end of the poem reminds us that, if there is any basis for hope, the speaker remains "unaware" of it. You might find it useful to have your students compare "The Darkling Thrush" with Hardy's own "The Oxen," in which the speaker describes his attitude to the pious legend of his youth as "hoping," not "persuaded." You might also discuss "The Darkling Thrush" in terms of Robert Frost's "The Road Not Taken," another poem whose subtleties are often overlooked by consolation-seekers who would reduce it to a sort of national anthem of rugged individualism.

MLL *MyLiteratureLab Resources*. Biography, critical overview, and bibliography for Hardy.

Thomas Hardy, HAP, page 460

This early poem summarizes Hardy's bleak view of existence. A lesser artist might have been crushed by this sense of hopelessness, but Hardy filled the theological gap with love, compassion, and humor. Students might compare this bitterly atheistic poem with the gentler "The Oxen." In "The Oxen" Hardy longs for the Christian faith he had as a child.

Two things are worth noting in the poem (since students sometimes overlook them). First, Hardy would rather have a cruel deity than none at all. It is not the pain of existence he bemoans, it is the meaninglessness of life without some guiding divine plan. Second, Hardy's worldview is so deeply religious that even when he claims there is no God, he ends up personifying the nothingness under which he suffers ("Crass Casualty" and "dicing Time," which he then groups as "purblind Doomsters").

The vocabulary of "Hap" is interesting. The title word means both a "happening" and "chance." *Hap* is not used much today but is still alive in common terms in "happenstance" and "hapless." *Casualty* is a word we are used to seeing primarily in accident reports and insurance forms. Hardy uses it here in its broader original sense of "chance" in the same way we still use "accident" in the neutral sense of a "chance event." Detective novel fans may know *Doomsters* from the title of Ross Macdonald's compelling novel; *doomster* is an archaic word for a judge (that survives in the family name Dempster). In Scottish courts the doomster not only read the sentence but also carried out the execution. Finally, you might quiz the class on *purblind*, a perfectly modern term that many of them won't know.

"Hap" is, by the way, a sonnet. Notice how neatly the meaning turns at the beginning of the sestet ("But not so."). Hardy uses the form so naturally that one might overlook it entirely.

MLL *MyLiteratureLab Resources*. Biography, critical overview, and bibliography for Hardy.

Robert Hayden, THOSE WINTER SUNDAYS, page 461

QUESTIONS FOR DISCUSSION

1. Is the speaker a boy or a man? How do you know?

2. Summarize the poem's theme—its main idea.

3. What do you understand from "the chronic angers of that house"?

4. How does this poet's choice of words differ from that of most writers of prose? Suggestion: Read the opening five lines aloud.

This brief poem, simple in the word's best sense, has a depth that rewards close reading. It appears that years have intervened between the speaker today and his previous self, the observing child. Now the speaker understands his father better, looks back on himself, and asks, "What did I know?"

The poem states its theme in its wonderful last line (worth quoting to anyone who distrusts abstract words in poetry). Students can miss Hayden's point unless they understand its vocabulary. *Austere* can mean stern, forbidding, somber, but it can also mean (as it does here) ascetic, disciplined, self-denying. To rise in the freezing house takes steely self-discipline. That the father's life is built on austerity we get from his labor-worn hands. What is an *office?* A duty, task, or ceremony that someone assumes (or has conferred on him): the tasks of shining shoes, of stirring banked fires in a furnace (or a coal-burning stove?). James Wright, a keen admirer of Hayden's poem, has spoken of it in an interview:

> The word *offices* is the great word here. *Office*, they say in French. It is a religious service after dark. Its formality, its combination of distance and immediacy, is appropriate. In my experience uneducated people and people who are driven by brute circumstance to work terribly hard for a living, the living of their families, are very big on formality. (*The Pure Clear Word: Essays on the Poetry of James Wright*, ed. Dave Smith [Urbana: U of Illinois P, 1982] 10)

Perhaps the "chronic angers" belong to the father: the boy gets up slowly and fearfully as though in dread of a tongue-lashing. Yet this reading does not seem quite in keeping with the character of the father as he emerges: stoic, patient, long-suffering, loving. Hayden does not invest these angers in the father exclusively. Perhaps any tenant of this bitterly cold house has reason to dread getting up in it.

When read aloud, the opening stanza reveals strong patterns of sound: the internal alliteration of the *k*-sound in *blueblack*, *cracked*, *ached*, *weekday*, *banked*, *thanked* (and, in the next stanza, in *wake*, *breaking*, *chronic*)—staccato bursts of hard consonants. Rather than using exact rime at the ends of lines, Hayden strengthens lines by using it internally: *banked/thanked* (line 5), *wake/breaking* (6); perhaps off-rime, too: *labor/weather* (4), *rise/dress* (8). Alliteration and assonance occur in *clothes . . . cold* (2), *weekday weather* (4). If you assign this poem early in your investigation of poetry, probably it matters more that students hear and respond to the rich interplay of repeated sounds than that they be able to give these devices labels.

"Those Winter Sundays" is the most often reprinted poem of Robert Hayden. A black poet who grew up in Detroit and who for many years was an English professor at the University of Michigan, he has written other poems apparently drawn from childhood and memory, among them "Obituary," another moving tribute to his father. Hayden's posthumous *Collected Poems* (New York: Norton/Liveright, 1985) belongs, we think, in every library.

MyLiteratureLab Resources. Biography, critical overview, and bibliography for Hayden.

Seamus Heaney, DIGGING, page 462

When Irish poet Seamus Heaney went to Lewiston, Maine, in 1986 to receive an honorary degree at Bates College, he read "Digging" aloud to the assembled graduates, parents, and friends. It seemed an appropriate choice. Some of the Maine students in his audience must have found expressed in Heaney's poem their own admiration for hardworking forebears whose course through life they had decided not to follow. Is the speaker in the poem uneasy about choosing instead to be a poet? It is clear that he admires the skill and strength his father and grandfather displayed in their work. But the poem ends on a positive note. The poet accepts himself for what he is.

In "Feeling into Words," an essay in his *Preoccupations* (New York: Farrar, 1980), Heaney likens the writing of poetry to digging up archaeological finds. Apparently it is a matter of digging a spade into one's past and unearthing something forgotten. "Digging," written in 1964, was his earliest poem in which it seemed that his feelings had found words. "The pen/spade analogy," he adds, "was the simple heart of the matter and *that* was simply a matter of almost proverbial common sense." As a schoolboy, he was often told to keep studying "because 'learning's easily carried' and 'the pen is lighter than the spade.'"

MyLiteratureLab Resources. Longman Lecture on "Digging."

Anthony Hecht, ADAM, page 463

"Adam" was the title poem (see line 26) of Anthony Hecht's Pulitzer Prize-winning collection, *The Hard Hours* (1967). The book is dedicated to Hecht's two sons, Jason and Adam. The poem's title, therefore, has a double resonance—one religious, the other personal. The poem memorably embodies one of the central teachings of the Judeo-Christian tradition, namely that human love emulates God's love for mankind. Hecht parallels God's love for His first "son," Adam, with the poet's love for his own son Adam.

The first stanza is spoken by the God of Genesis to Adam, who has been created but not yet awakened to find the world fashioned for him. The divine voice announces that "These very words you hear / Compose the fish and starlight." God's word, as the Judeo-Christian tradition believes, becomes reality. While not claiming divine power for his own words, the speaker of "Adam" asserts his right as a poet and father to use the power of language to bless and comfort his son.

It may be worth asking students about the dramatic situation of the poem. Where is the speaker's son when these fatherly words are spoken? (In the beginning of the third stanza, we learn that the son is in a foreign country and the poet speaks "to the empty air.")

Several other poems can be profitably compared to "Adam." To explore the human dimension, "Adam" can be compared to the two Robert Hayden poems in the book. "Those Winter Sundays," especially, provides a son's glimpse of a father to contrast with this father's view of a son. Finally, a dramatic contrast could be made with Weldon Kees's "For My Daughter," which is spoken by a man who feels he has no power to bless or protect his child.

George Herbert, LOVE, page 465

Herbert's poem is often read as an account of a person's reception into the Church; the eaten *meat*, as the Eucharist. Herbert's extended conceits or metaphors are also evident in "The Pulley."

For discussion: compare "Love" with another seventeenth-century devotional poem, Donne's "Batter my heart." What is the tone of each poem? Herbert may seem less intense, almost reticent by comparison. Douglas Bush comments, "Herbert does not attempt the high pitch of Donne's 'Divine Poems.' His great effects are all the greater for rising out of a homely, colloquial quietness of tone; and peace brings quiet endings—'So I did sit and eat'" (*English Literature in the Earlier Seventeenth Century* [New York: Oxford UP, 1945] 139).

Herbert, by the way, is an Anglican saint—the only one who does not also appear in the Roman Catholic calendar.

Robert Herrick, TO THE VIRGINS, TO MAKE MUCH OF TIME, page 466

Roses would have suited Herrick's iambic meter—why is *rose-buds* richer? Rosebuds are flowers not yet mature and therefore suggest virgins, not matrons. There may be a sexual hint besides: rosebuds more resemble private parts than roses. But in this poem, time flies, the rosebuds of line 1 bloom in line 3. *Rose-buds* is also rhythmically stronger than *roses*, as Austin Warren has pointed out: it has a secondary stress as well as a primary. Warren has recalled that when he first read the poem in college in 1917, he misread *rose-buds* as *roses*, kept misreading it ever after, and only a half-century later realized his mistake and found a new poem in front of him. "In untutored youth, the sentiment and the rhythm suffice: the exactness of the language goes unnoticed. And in later life a remembered favorite escapes exact attention because we think we know it so well" ("Herrick Revisited," *Michigan Quarterly Review* 15 [Summer 1976]: 245–67).

Question for discussion: What do you think of Herrick's advice? Are there any perils in it?

Gerard Manley Hopkins, SPRING AND FALL, page 466

Hopkins's tightly wrought syntax may need a little unraveling. Students may be asked to reword lines 3–4 in a more usual sequence ("Can you, with your fresh thoughts, care for leaves like the things of man?") and then to put the statement into more usual words. (An attempt: "Do you, young and innocent as you are, feel as sorry for falling leaves as for dying people?") Lines 12–13 may need a similar going over and rough paraphrase. ("Neither any human mouth nor any human mind has previously formed the truth that the heart and spirit have intuited.") "Sorrow's springs are the same"—that is, all human sorrows have the same cause: the fact that all things pass away. A world of constant change is "the blight man was born for": an earth subject to death, having fallen from its original state of a changeless Eden. The difficulties of a Hopkins poem result from a swiftly thoughtful mind's trying to jam all possible meaning into a brief space (and into words that are musical).

Wanwood is evidently a term the poet coined for pale autumn woods. W. H. Gardner, the editor of Hopkins's poems, finds in it also the suggestion of "wormwood"—bitter gall, also wood that is worm-eaten. The term *leafmeal* reminds him of "piecemeal," and he paraphrases line 8: "One by one the leaves fall, and then rot into mealy fragments."

MLL *MyLiteratureLab Resources*. Photographs and biographical information for Hopkins.

Gerard Manley Hopkins, No worst, there is none, page 467

Just from reading the title (and opening phrase) of this Petrarchan sonnet, one might get the impression that the thrust of the poem is consolatory, but as we read on, we come to see that the theme here is reflective of Edgar's famous aside in Shakespeare's great tragedy *King Lear*, "And worse I may be yet: the worst is not / So long as we can say 'This is the worst'"—in effect, that there is no conceivable limit to the depths of human suffering. As lines 2–4 suggest, earlier pangs of grief ("forepangs") do not cushion later ones by teaching us to cope with suffering; instead, deeper pains only make us suffer more deeply, and these sufferings are not alleviated or even diminished by the traditional consolations of religious belief.

As seen in line 6, the angst that the speaker suffers from is not merely particular to himself and his circumstances; it is a "world-sorrow," and his cries resound "on an age-old anvil": the suffering that he describes is universal, an unavoidable condition of being human. In keeping with the recurring motif of giving a momentary illusion of hope only to snatch it away a moment later, "Then lull, then leave off" at the beginning of line 7 seems at first to refer to the woe itself, but as we read on we come to see that it is only the cries themselves that leave off, not the griefs that cause them.

The beginning of the sestet follows the previously established pattern: "O the mind, mind has mountains" might seem to suggest an intellectual grandeur that can combat and perhaps overcome suffering; but no, Hopkins's point is that from such elevations steep falls are possible, even likely. The superficially baffling statement in lines 10–11 can be unknotted by straightening out the word order: "who ne'er hung there may hold them cheap," i.e., those lucky enough to have never experienced these terrors may not fully grasp how terrible such feelings are.

The ending of "No worst, there is none" may put you in mind of the conclusion of another famous sonnet by a religiously oriented British poet, John Donne's "Death be not proud." What chiefly distinguishes the two is the distance between them. Donne's witty argument is intended as a refutation of death's power over us, whereas Hopkins presents with us with comparatively scant consolation, the realization that just as sleep brings respite from pain at the end of every day, so death will bring us the peace of oblivion at the end of life. The near-despair of this poem is especially striking given the fact that Hopkins was a Jesuit priest, a man of profound religious sentiment and conviction; it serves to remind us that even the truest of believers are not exempt from the dark night of the soul.

MLL *MyLiteratureLab Resources*. Photographs and biographical information for Hopkins.

Gerard Manley Hopkins, THE WINDHOVER, page 467

"The best thing I ever wrote," said Hopkins. If your students have enjoyed "Pied Beauty" or "God's Grandeur" without too much difficulty, then why not try "The Windhover," despite its famous ambiguities? Some students may go afield in reading the opening line, taking *I caught* to mean that the poet trapped the bird; but they can be told that Hopkins, a great condenser, probably means "I caught a glimpse of."

Dispute over the poem often revolves around whether or not the windhover is Christ and around the meaning of *Buckle!* Most commentators seem to agree that the bird is indeed Christ, or else that Christ is like the bird. (Yvor Winters, who thought the poem "minor and imperfect," once complained, "To describe a bird, however beautifully, and to imply that Christ is like him but greater, is to do very little toward indicating the greatness of Christ.") Some read *Buckle!* as a plea to the bird to descend to earth; others, as a plea to all the qualities and things mentioned in line 9 *(Brute beauty, valor, act)* to buckle themselves together into one. Still others find the statement ending in *Buckle!* no plea at all, but just an emphatic observation of what the poet beholds. If Christ is the windhover (other arguments run), in what sense can he be said to buckle? Two of the answers: (1) in buckling on human nature and becoming man, as a knight buckles on armor; (2) in having his body broken on the cross. Students can be asked to seek all the words in the poem with connotations of royalty or chivalry—suggestive, perhaps, of Christ as King and Christ as noble knight or chevalier. Why the *sheer plod?* Hopkins reflects (it would seem) that if men will only buckle down to their lowly duties they will become more Christ-like, and their spiritual plowshares will shine instead of collecting rust. Hopkins preached a sermon that expressed a similar idea: "Through poverty, through labor, through crucifixion His majesty of nature more shines." The *embers*, we think, are a metaphor: moist clods thrown by the plow going down the sillion. Hopkins likes to compare things to hearth fire: for instance, the "fresh-firecoal chestnut-falls" in "Pied Beauty."

For detailed criticism, one might start with Norman H. MacKenzie, *A Reader's Guide to Gerard Manley Hopkins* (Ithaca: Cornell UP, 1981). MacKenzie provides facts from ornithology and his own kestrel-watching: no other birds are so expert in hovering, body horizontal, tail and head pointing down as they study the ground for prey. To hang stationary in the air over one spot, they must fly into the wind "with rapidly quivering (*wimpling*, line 4) wings, missing a few beats as gusts die, accelerating as they freshen"—responding to variations in the wind with nearly computer speed. Once in about every eight hovers, the kestrel will dive, not inertly but with wings held tense and high—it doesn't "buckle" in the sense of *collapse*. If it finds no victim, the bird swings and banks and takes an upward "stride," to hover once more. Hopkins's "how he rung upon the rein" doesn't mean that the kestrel climbs in a spiral. No gyring Yeats-bird, he.

An interesting view of the religious imagery informing this poem can be found in James Finn Cotter's study *Inscape: The Christology and Poetry of Gerard Manley Hopkins* (Pittsburgh: U of Pittsburgh P, 1972). Cotter, who is formidably learned in theology, examines traditional Christian writings to discover how they shaped Hopkins's sense of imagery. Cotter maintains that "Hopkins fashioned a myth of his own making," but that his private vision drew from a wide variety of philosophical and theological sources. In his long, careful reading of "The Windhover" Cotter observes:

> Circular motion and form dominate "The Windhover": the kestrel moves in slow, wide, sharp, and gliding circles which the rhythm and language perfectly mimic. Christ is present here as throughout the other sonnets, in the sun illuminating the scene; he is the dawn drawing the bird to a brilliant expression of itself and hence of its Lord.

Despite his fondness for Old and Middle English, Hopkins luckily refrained from calling the windhover by its obsolete name: *fuckwind* or *windfucker*. (No, that *f* is not a long *s*.) Thomas Nashe in *Lenten Stuffe* (1599) speaks of the "Kistrilles or windfuckers that filling themselves with winde, fly against the winde evermore." See *windfucker* in the *Oxford English Dictionary*. (For this dumbfounding discovery, thanks to David Lynch, who copyedited *Literature*, 4th ed.)

MyLiteratureLab Resources. Photographs and biographical information for Hopkins.

A. E. *Housman*, LOVELIEST OF TREES, THE CHERRY NOW, page 468

What is Housman's theme? Good old *carpe diem*. If you ask students to paraphrase this poem (it's not hard), a paraphrase might add, to catch the deeper implication, "Life is brief—time flies—I'd better enjoy beauty now."

Not part of the rough poem Housman began with, the second stanza was added last. Lines 9–10 originally read: "And since to look at things you love / Fifty times is not enough." What can be said for Housman's additions and changes? (These and other manuscript variations are given by Tom Burns Haber in *The Making of "A Shropshire Lad"* [Seattle: U of Washington P, 1966].)

MyLiteratureLab Resources. Biography, critical overview, and bibliography for Housman.

A. E. *Housman*, TO AN ATHLETE DYING YOUNG, page 468

For a comment on this poem, see the note earlier in this chapter on Dryden's "To the Memory of Mr. Oldham."

Randall Jarrell, THE DEATH OF THE BALL TURRET GUNNER, page 469

The speaker seems to be an unknown citizen like Auden's. Jarrell's laconic war poem is complex in its metaphors. The womb is sleep; the outside world, waking; and the speaker has passed from one womb to another—from his mother into the belly of a bomber. His existence inside the ball turret was only a dream, and in truth he has had no mature life between his childhood and his death. Waking from the dream, he wakes only to nightmare. In another irony, the matter-of-fact battle-report language of the last line contrasts horribly with what is said in it. How can the dead gunner address us? Clearly the poet had written his epitaph for him—and has done so as Jarrell said he wrote "The Woman at the Washington Zoo," "acting as next friend."

Robinson Jeffers, TO THE STONE-CUTTERS, page 470

If students will compare this poem with Shakespeare's sonnet "Not marble nor the gilded monuments," they'll be struck by a sharp difference of view. Shakespeare, evidently, is the optimist. For him, a poem can confer immortality and inspire love until doomsday. For Jeffers, poems will merely bring a little respite to "pained thoughts"—much as a spoonful of honey helps a hangover, according to one popular belief.

For a short assignment: Write a paraphrase of each of these two poems. Bring your work to class, ready to read it aloud. We'll discuss the poems, taking off from your work on them.

For another pessimistic view of monuments, direct students to Shelley's "Ozymandias." You might ask them to compare its theme with those of Shakespeare and Jeffers.

A sidelight on this poem: Any doubt he may have had that stone monuments last long didn't prevent Jeffers from building, with his own hands, a stone tower next to his home at the ocean's edge in Carmel, California.

Ben Jonson, ON MY FIRST SON, page 470

This heartbreaking poem from Jonson's *Epigrammes*, requested by several instructors, repays close reading. What is "the state he should envy"? Death. Why the dead child should be envied is made clear in the lines that immediately follow (7–8). The final couplet is difficult in its syntax, and it contains a pun on *like* in a sense now obsolete. The speaker vows, or prays (*vow*, along with *votive*, comes from the Greek *euchesthai*: "to pray"), that anyone whom he loves may not live too long. The seriousness of Jonson's wit is shown in this colossal pun: *like* meaning "thrive, do well, get on" as well as "to be fond." See *like* in the *OED* for other illustrations:

> SHALLOW TO FALSTAFF: "By my troth, you like well and bear your years very well." (*Henry IV, Part 2*, 3.2.92)
>
> "Trees generally do like best that stand to the Northeast wind." (Holland's Pliny, 1600)

"Poems Arranged by Subject and Theme" in this manual lists the book's other poems about fathers and children. In this section, see especially the father-and-son poems by Anthony Hecht, Robert Phillips, and James Wright ("Autumn Begins in Martins Ferry, Ohio").

Donald Justice, ON THE DEATH OF FRIENDS IN CHILDHOOD, page 471

There is more emotional distance and less grief in this poem than in Ben Jonson's. Nor does the speaker in "On the Death of Friends in Childhood" seem to be mourning one specific loss. The "Friends" he mentions suggests friends in general, perhaps other people's as well as his own. Yet, though time has softened the impact of long-ago losses, the narrator urges that we remember dead childhood friends and what was shared with them.

Brief as it is, this poem by one of the finest modern American poets displays the hallmarks of his work—the unerring sense of rhythm, the quiet beauty of the phrasing, the communication of powerful emotion through restrained statement. In its chiseled perfection, it would not be out of place in the *Greek Anthology*.

John Keats, ODE ON A GRECIAN URN, page 471

Why is the symbol of the urn so endlessly suggestive? It may help students to recall that Grecian urns are vessels for the ashes of the dead, and that their carved or painted figures *(Of deities or mortal, or of both)* depict a joyous afterlife in the Elysian fields. The urn being round, its design appears to continue endlessly. What greater image for eternity, or for the seamlessness of perfected art?

Most good discussions of the "Urn" confront a few of the poem's celebrated difficulties. Some questions to help speed the confrontation:

1. *Assuming that the urn is said to be* sylvan *because it displays woodland scenes, in what sense is it a* historian? *What history or histories does it contain, or represent?*

2. *How can unheard melodies be sweeter than heard ones?*

3. *Why are youth, lover and loved one, trees, and musicians so lucky to exist upon the urn?* (Lines 15–27.)

4. *What disadvantages do living lovers labor under?* (Lines 28–30.)

5. *In stanza four, the procession of thought turns in a new direction. What additional insight occurs to the poet?* That the urn, whose world had seemed perfect, is in some ways limited and desolate. The altar cannot be reached nor sacrifice fulfilled, nor can the unseen little town ever be returned to.

6. *Paraphrase the statement that the urn "dost tease us out of thought / As doth Eternity."* The urn lures us out of our habit of useless cogitation. Eternity also stops us from thinking because, for us mere mortals, it too is incomprehensible.

7. *How is the urn a "Cold Pastoral"?* Literally, it's lifeless clay; figuratively, it stands aloof from human change and suffering. Compare Stevens's "Jar."

8. *How then can a Cold Pastoral be called "a friend to man"?* It provides a resting place for human ashes; it inspires and delights; and, as the last lines attest, it teaches us.

MyLiteratureLab Resources. Photographs, biographical information, critical overview, and bibliography for Keats. Audio clip and student essay on "Ode on a Grecian Urn."

John Keats, WHEN I HAVE FEARS THAT I MAY CEASE TO BE, page 473

Students will see right away that the poem expresses fear of death, but don't let them stop there: there's more to it. Why does the poet fear death? Because it will end his writing and his loving. The poem states what both loving and writing poetry have in common: both are magical and miraculous acts when they are spontaneous. Besides favoring "unreflecting love" for its "fairy power," Keats would write "with the magic hand of chance." And—if you care to open up a profundity—what might the poet mean by those "huge cloudy symbols of a high romance"? Literal cloud shapes that look like Tristram and Isolde's beaker of love-potion, or what?

Note that this poem addresses not Keats's beloved Fanny Brawne, but "the memory of the mysterious lady seen in adolescence one brief moment at Vauxhall long ago in the summer of 1814," according to Robert Gittings in *John Keats* (Boston: Atlantic, 1968) 188. The poem is about a "creature of an hour." (Fanny, of course, occupied not one hour but many.)

Gittings has found in the poem echoes of two sonnets of Shakespeare, both about devouring time: #60 ("Like as the waves make towards the pebbled shore, / So do our minutes hasten to their end") and #64 ("When I have seen by Time's fell hand defaced"). In the copy of the *Sonnets* that Keats co-owned with his friend Reynolds, these two were the most heavily marked.

This poem has had a hefty impact on later poets, notably John Berryman, who took from it the title for an autobiographical collection of his own poems on ambition and desire: *Love and Fame* (1972).

MyLiteratureLab Resources. Photographs, biographical information, critical overview, and bibliography for Keats.

John Keats, TO AUTUMN, page 474

Although "To Autumn" proved to be the last of the poet's great lyrics, we have no evidence that Keats (full of plans and projects at the time) was consciously taking leave of the world. On September 21, 1819, three days after writing the poem, Keats in a letter to his friend John Hamilton Reynolds spoke of his delight in the season: "I never lik'd stubble fields so much as now—Aye better than the chilly green of the Spring. Somehow a stubble plain looks warm—in the same way that some pictures look warm—this strikes me so much in my Sunday's walk that I composed upon it."

Questions for Discussion

1. *In the opening stanza, what aspects of autumn receive most emphasis? To what senses do the images appeal?*

2. *In the first two stanzas, autumn is several times personified (lines 2–3, 12–15, 16–18, 19–20, 21–22). Who are its different persons?* Conspiring crony, careless landowner, reaper, gleaner, cider presser.

3. *In the third stanza, how does the tone change? Has there been any progression in scene or in idea throughout the poem?* Tone: calm serenity. In the first stanza, autumn is being prepared for; in the second, busily enjoyed, in the third, calmly and serenely contemplated. There is another stanza-by-stanza progression: from morning to noon to oncoming night. Like the *soft-dying day*, the light wind sometimes dies. The gnats in *wailful choir* also have funereal, mourning suggestions, but the stanza as a whole cannot be called gloomy.

4. *What words in stanza 3 convey sounds?* Songs, music, wailful choir, mourn, loud bleat, sing, treble, whistles, twitter. What an abundance of verbs! The lines convey a sense of active music making.

5. *Do you see any case for reading the poem as a statement of the poet's acceptance of the facts that beauty on earth is transitory and death is inevitable?* Surely such themes are present; the poem does not have to be taken to mean that the poet knows he himself will soon perish.

For an unusually grim reading of the poem, see Annabel M. Patterson, "'How to load . . . and bend': Syntax and Interpretation in Keats's 'To Autumn,'" *PMLA* 94 (1979): 449–58. Finding that the poem "undermines" our traditional notion of Autumn, Patterson argues that Keats subversively portrays the goddess as deceptive, careless, and demanding. Her proffered ripeness leads only to *last oozings* and *stubble-plains*—dead ends not to be desired. In the poet's view (as she interprets it), "Nature is amoral and not to be depended upon." Try this argument on the class. Do students agree? Whether or not they side with Patterson, they will have to examine the poem closely in order to comment.

For a good discussion of ways to approach Keats's poem with a class, see Bruce E. Miller, *Teaching the Art of Literature* (Urbana: NCTE, 1980) 75–84. Miller points out that not all students will know how cider is made, and he suggests asking someone to explain Keats's reference to the cider-press in stanza 2. He recommends, too, borrowing from your nearest art department some reproductions of landscape paintings: "Constable's work, which was contemporary with Keats, to my mind almost catches the spirit to 'To Autumn,' but it is a little more literal and photographic. . . ."

With this rich poem, you might well start a discussion of imagery, or review this topic if students have met it earlier. "The students," remarks Miller, "need not ask themselves as they read, 'What does it mean?' Rather they should continually ask, 'What do I see?' 'What do I hear and touch?' 'What do I feel?'"

MLL *MyLiteratureLab Resources.* Photographs, biographical information, critical overview, and bibliography for Keats.

Ted Kooser, ABANDONED FARMHOUSE, page 475

In the first major essay on Ted Kooser's poetry, Dana Gioia wrote in 1983:

> He offers no blinding flashes of inspiration, no mystic moments of transcendence. He creates no private mythologies or fantasy worlds. Instead he provides small but genuine insights into the world of everyday experience. His work strikes the difficult balance between profundity and accessibility, just as his style manages to be personal without being idiosyncratic. It is simple without becoming shallow, striking without going to extremes. He has achieved the most difficult kind of originality. He has transformed the common idiom and experience into fresh and distinctive poetry.

"Abandoned Farmhouse" is an excellent illustration of this analysis. Grounded thoroughly in common details and presented in straightforward statements, it captures the poignancy of failed efforts and ruined hopes by expressing it through the objects left behind. This poignancy is heightened by the consistent use of the past tense in describing the lives lived in the farmhouse and the present tense in communicating what each of the mute details "says": the people and their hopes and dreams are gone, but the sadness continues. Inevitably, one is reminded of certain poems by Robert Frost, most notably "The Need of Being Versed in Country Things," which also chronicle the difficulty and the desolation of life in rural America.

Also worth noting is the subtle artistry of "Abandoned Farmhouse." At first approach it seems to be written in free verse, and several readings may be required to perceive its underlying iambic rhythm and its use of mixed tetrameter and pentameter lines. The very bareness of statement and description throughout the poem gives added force to its single simile—"Its toys are strewn in the yard / like branches after a storm" (lines 21–22)—which itself reinforces the larger theme of living things ripped apart by the harshness of nature. Coupled with the poem's only rime, it creates what in this hushed context is virtually a crescendo effect, which is immediately resolved by the diminuendo of the poem's last sentence.

—Michael Palma

Philip Larkin, HOME IS SO SAD, page 476

Larkin's considerable achievement in "Home is so Sad" is that he so beautifully captures the ring of ordinary speech within the confines of a tight *a b a b a* rime scheme and iambic pentameter. Note the slant rimes in the second stanza: *as*, *was*, and *vase*.

In an interview, Larkin recalled a letter he received from a middle-aged mother who had read his poem: "She wrote to say her children had grown up and gone, and she felt precisely this emotion I was trying to express in the poem" ("Speaking of Writing XIII: Philip Larkin," [London] *Times* 20 Feb. 1964: 16). Bruce Martin finds the poem written not from a mother's point of view, but from that of a son who used to live in this house himself. The speaker projects his own sadness into it: it has remained pathetically changeless. What has changed is himself and others who once lived here (*Philip Larkin* [Boston: Twayne, 1978] 52).

DMK, taking a different view, thinks it quite possible to read the poem as though (as in Larkin's well-known "Mr. Bleaney" from the same collection, *The*

Whitsun Weddings) the former inhabitants of this house have died. The speaker is left unidentified, an impersonal seeing-eye. Your students, too, will probably come up with differing interpretations.

Is Larkin's poem sentimental? Hard-eyed and exact in its observations, aided by the colloquialism of line 7, "A joyous shot at how things ought to be," it successfully skirts the danger. Students might like to discuss the three words that follow: "Long fallen wide." Does Larkin mean that the home was an unhappy one, or merely ordinary in its deviation from the idea? Or is it that the arrow—the "joyous shot"—has fallen merely in the sense that, meant to be full of life, the home is now "bereft / Of anyone to please"?

Philip Larkin, POETRY OF DEPARTURES, page 477

The speaker wonders why he doesn't break with his dull, tame life, just walk out, chuck everything, launch into the Romantic unknown like a highwayman. What an appealing notion! Question: Have you ever yearned to do that very thing? (Who hasn't?)

Well, why doesn't he take off? Because he sees all too clearly and painfully that such a grandiose gesture would be ridiculous. Commenting on lines 25–27, in which the speaker imagines himself swaggering nut-strewn roads and crouching in the fo'c'sle, David Timms finds him "unconvinced by such daydreams, though sympathetic to the dreamers, for he is one himself." And so he dismisses his Romantic urge as too studied and belabored, ultimately false. Still, just because he sees through those dreams, he won't let himself feel superior. The dreams may be artificial, but so is his own tame life, his room, his specially chosen junk. As he is well aware at the end, his greatest danger is to be trapped in owning things and neatly arranging them: books, china, all fixed on shelves in an order "reprehensibly perfect." (We have somewhat expanded on Timms's paraphrase, from *Philip Larkin* [Edinburgh: Oliver & Boyd, 1973] 87.)

William H. Pritchard has remarked that Larkin himself expunged Romantic possibilities from his life, the better to entertain them in his writing ("Larkin's Presence," in *Philip Larkin: The Man and His Work*, ed. Dale Salwak [Iowa City: U of Iowa P, 1989] 74–75).

Irving Layton, THE BULL CALF, page 478

Sentimental poets frequently shed tears over concrete objects while (in their imagery and diction) failing to open their eyes to the physical world. Such is not the case of Layton's "The Bull Calf," in which the poet tells us that he weeps only after having portrayed the dead calf in exact detail ("one foreleg over the other").

Layton's poem develops a series of contrasts. In the first section, the calf's look of nobility ("the promise of sovereignty," "Richard II") is set against his immaturity. The "fierce sunlight," in an implied metaphor, is compared to the calf's mother: taking in maize, licking her baby. In line 14, the "empty sky," suggestive of the calf's coming death, seems the turning point of the poem. In the remainder, the calf, which had been portrayed at first as full of life and pride, becomes an inanimate object, "a block of wood," a numb mass that emits ugly sounds when handled ("a sepulchral gurgle"). But in the closing lines, introducing still another contrast, Layton seems to show the calf as a living sleeper, or perhaps a statue or finished work of art.

Probably the best-known living poet in Canada at the end of the twentieth century, Layton was born in Rumania and came to Montreal early in life. Situated outside both British and French communities, Layton often had the perspective of an outsider, a Jew, a satirist, and a revolutionary. *The Selected Poems of Irving Layton*, with an introduction by Hugh Kenner (New York: New Directions, 1977), was an attempt to widen his audience south of the border.

Denise Levertov, THE ACHE OF MARRIAGE, page 479

Despite its brevity, "The Ache of Marriage" gets at the heart of one of the most rewarding, demanding, and frustrating relationships that the majority of us ever experience. The speaker is clearly committed to this relationship, committed by vows, by love (the spouse is twice addressed as "beloved" in the first six lines), and by the desire to make the relationship work and to experience all that it has to offer ("looking for joy, some joy / not to be known outside it"). But as this desire is defeated, commitment comes to feel more like entrapment ("It is leviathan and we / in its belly"). This sense of confinement is somewhat moderated as the metaphor changes from the belly of the beast to an ark, with its suggestion of the voyage of survival and the search for a landfall where a better life may be found. Note the artistry of the poem, as echoes of phrasing and sound reinforce the complexities of theme: the isolation of "each and each" softens to the attempted communion of "two by two," but then "ark" immediately blends into "ache," bringing us back to the poem's title and first line and principal theme, underlining the circular and ultimately static nature of the situation.

Philip Levine, THEY FEED THEY LION, page 480

As with many another poet, the poem for which Philip Levine is best known is in many ways his least characteristic work. Levine's poems are customarily written in a straightforward, conversational style, and they often concern themselves with the lives of blue-collar workers, especially those in the automobile factories of his native Detroit. Its symbolic details, its multileveled use of language, and its almost apocalyptic urgency make "They Feed They Lion," the title poem of Levine's fifth collection, published in 1972, all but unique in his canon.

Levine has said that this poem was inspired by his return to Detroit after the race riots of 1967: "I had to go back to see what the city was like, and one of the things that I discovered was that it wasn't mine anymore." He has also said that "They Feed They Lion" takes its structure from a poem by Christopher Smart (an excerpt from Smart's poem is included later in this chapter under the title "For I Will Consider My Cat Jeoffry").

There is an especially interesting piece by Joe Jackson on "They Feed They Lion" in the *Explicator* 41:4 (Summer 1983) 56–58. Here are provocative thoughts from its opening and closing paragraphs:

> On a gloomy, greyly monochromatic night in a time and place deliberately left unspecified, the speaker is driving his car from "West Virginia to Kiss

My Ass" through the Appalachian wastelands of tin-roofed huts, junked autos, "black bean and wet slate bread." As he drives, his thoughts become a catalogue of both what he sees and what, through inference, he knows is outside the car window. . . . These observations pass in a frenzied rush, and the sense is that of pressure building at a threatening rate. The speaker does not understand this pressure on a conscious level. . . . As the poem ends, this building pressure finally bursts, and he knows.

. . .

Thus the poem is a litany for the oppressed, in the voice of the oppressed, as told by one of the threatened oppressors. . . . [There] is a constant switching between inanimate and animate, between the dead and the living. This becomes most important in the two stalled strophes on the butchered hog. Through his sacrifice, this hog almost assumes a property of rebirth ("From 'Bow Down' come 'Rise Up'"), which immediately transfigures into the image of a common laborer with a shovel at the end of strophe 4 ("The grained arm that pulls the hands"). Thus, the hog becomes an extended metaphor for the rising poor. . . . At the end of strophe 4, we finally discover what the poem is about; it is here, too, that the voice changes to first person. There is a minor, though pregnant pause. The speaker has also realized the poem's meaning and hurriedly leaves the scene before the threat becomes too real.

Shirley Geok-lin Lim, RIDING INTO CALIFORNIA, page 481

In "Riding into California," Shirley Geok-lin Lim emphasizes the isolation and alienation that are so much a part of the immigrant experience—although she is quick to make clear ("The veterans in the mobile home / park don't want to be there") that such feelings are not unique to immigrants. What is exclusive to the newcomer from a very different culture is a pervasive sense of dislocation, which can lead to some surprising attitudes (surprising, perhaps, even to their possessor): "So you're / grateful for familiarity, and Bruce Lee / becomes your hero"). In the last three lines, just as she does in "Learning to love America," Lim simultaneously stresses both the positive and—especially—the negative aspects of the experience.

You can see Shirley Geok-lin Lim read "Riding into California"—and briefly discuss the power and pleasure that can come from the writing of poetry—at <http://www.pbs.org/wnet/foolingwithwords/main_video.html>.

Robert Lowell, SKUNK HOUR, page 482

Students should have no trouble in coming up with the usual connotations of skunk, but they may need help in seeing that the title is a concise expression of Lowell's theme. This is an evil-smelling hour in the speaker's life; and yet, paradoxically, it is the skunks themselves who affirm that life ought to go on. After the procession of dying and decadent people and objects in the first four stanzas, the mother skunk and her kittens form a triumph: bold, fecund, hungry, impossible to scare. Although they too are outcasts (surrounded by their aroma as the poet is surrounded by his madness and isolation?), they stick up for their right to survival.

The poem is rich in visual imagery. In the mind's eye, there are resemblances between the things contained in stanza 5 (the Ford car and the hill's skull), and also between the objects set in fixed rows (love-cars, tombstones, beached hulls). Water and the sea (by their decline or absence) are to this poem what they are to Eliot's *Waste Land*. Even the Church is "chalk-dry"; its spire has become a spar like that of a stranded vessel.

This poem is intensively analyzed in *The Contemporary Poet as Artist and Critic: Eight Symposia*, ed. Anthony Ostroff (Boston: Little, 1964). Richard Wilbur, John Frederick Nims, and John Berryman comment on the poem, after which Lowell comments on their comments. Lowell calls the opening of the poem "a dawdling, more or less amiable picture of a declining Maine sea town. . . . Sterility howls through the scenery, but I try to give a tone of tolerance, humor, and randomness to the sad prospect." He sees the skunk hour itself as a sort of dark night of the soul and refers readers to the poem by St. John of the Cross. Lowell's night, however, is "secular, puritan, and agnostical." Lowell notes that the phrase *red fox stain* was intended only to describe the color of vegetation in the fall on Blue Hill, a mountain in Maine.

Elizabeth Hardwick, Lowell's wife when "Skunk Hour" was written, has affirmed that all the characters in the poem were actual—"were living, more or less as he sees them, in Castine [Maine] that summer. The details, not the feeling, were rather alarmingly precise, I thought. But fortunately it was not read in town for some time" (quoted by Ian Hamilton, *Robert Lowell: A Biography* [New York: Random, 1982] 267).

Sandra M. Gilbert, who sees the poem as "richly magical," reads it for its embodiment of myth. She explores it as a vision of Hell, pointing out that its events happen not on Halloween, but "somewhere in Hallowe'en's ritually black and orange vicinity." (The decorator's shop is "sacramentally orange.") The summer millionaire has departed in fall, like a vegetation deity—Osiris or Attis. Nautilus Island's witchlike hermit heiress is Circe, Hecate, Ishtar, Venus, "the goddess of love turned goddess of death in an All Soul's Night world" ("Mephistopheles in Maine: Rereading Lowell's 'Skunk Hour,'" *A Book of Rereadings*, ed. Greg Kuzma [Lincoln, NE: Pebble and Best Cellar, 1979] 254–64).

Andrew Marvell, To His Coy Mistress, page 483

Questions for Discussion

1. *"All this poet does is feed some woman a big line. There's no time for romance, so he says, 'Quick, let's hit the bed before we hit the dirt.'" Discuss this summary. Then try making your own, more accurate one. Suggestion: The poem is divided into three parts, each beginning with an indented line. Take these parts one at a time, putting the speaker's main thoughts into your own words.*
   There's a grain of truth to this paraphrase, rude though it be. We might question, however, whether Marvell's speaker is trying to hoodwink his loved one. Perhaps he only sums up the terrible truth he knows: that time lays waste to youth, that life passes before we know it. He makes no mention of "romance," by the way—that's the paraphraser's invention. A more nearly accurate paraphrase, taking the three divisions of the poem one by one, might go like this:

Lines 1–20: If we had all the room in the world and if we were immortal, then our courtship might range across the globe. My love for you could expand till it filled the whole world and I could spend centuries in praising your every feature (saving your heart for last). After all, such treatment is only what you deserve.

Lines 21–32: But time runs on. Soon we'll be dead and gone, all my passion and all your innocence vanished.

Lines 33–46: And so, while you're still young and willing, let's seize the day. Let's concentrate our pleasure into the present moment. Although we can't make the sun stand still (like Joshua in the Bible), we'll do the next best thing: we'll joyously make time fly.

Now, obviously, any such rewording of this matchless poem must seem a piddling thing. But if students will just work through Marvell's argument part by part, they may grasp better the whole of it.

2. *In part one, how much space would be "world enough" for the lovers? Exactly how much time would be enough time?* To point out the approximate location of the Humber and the Ganges on a globe (or a simple circle drawn on a blackboard) can drive home the fact that when the poet says *world enough,* he spells out exactly what he means. A little discussion may be needed to show that in defining "enough" time, Marvell bounds it by events (the conversion of the Jews), numbers the years, and blocks out his piecemeal adoration. Two hundred years per breast is a delectable statistic! Clearly, the lover doesn't take the notion of such slow and infinitely patient devotion seriously.

3. *What is the main idea of part two? How is this theme similar to that of Housman's "Loveliest of trees"?* Both Marvell and Housman in "Loveliest of trees" are concerned with the passage of time; they differ on what needs to be done about it. Marvell urges action; Housman urges filling one's youth with observed beauty. Of these two expressions of the *carpe diem* theme, Housman's seems the more calm and disinterested.

4. *Paraphrase with special care lines 37–44. Is Marvell urging violence?* In lines 37–44, Marvell's point seems to be that time works a gradual, insidious violence. It is like a devouring beast (*slow-chapped*), holding us in its inexorable jaws. Some students will find the imagery odd, even offensive in a love poem: *birds of prey* (who want to eat, not be eaten), the cannonball of strength and sweetness that batters life's iron gates. Violence is not the speaker's counsel, but urgency. His harsh images lend his argument intensity and force.

5. *Considering the poem as a whole, does the speaker seem playful, or serious?* This fifth question presents an easy dichotomy, but of course Marvell's speaker is both playful and serious. In making clear the tone of the poem, a useful poem for comparison is Marlowe's "Passionate Shepherd." What are the two speakers' attitudes toward love? Marvell's seems more down-to-earth, skeptical, and passion-driven: a lover in a fallen world, not (like Marlowe's shepherd) a lover in a pastoral Eden.

If later on, in teaching figures of speech, you want some great lines for illustrations, turn back to this inexhaustible poem. There's hyperbole in lines 7–20, understatement ("But none, I think, do there embrace"), metaphor, simile, and of course the great personification of chariot-driving time.

Telling a class that Marvell was a Puritan usually shakes up their overly neat assumptions. Some may be surprised to learn that one can be a Puritan and not necessarily be puritanical.

Defending the poem against charges that its logic is fallacious, a recent critic, Richard Crider, has shown that "the speaker's appeal is not merely to the lady's passion, . . . but to a more inclusive and compelling value—completion and wholeness." A good student of Aristotle's logic as well as Aristotle's ethics, Marvell's speaker calls on his listener to exercise all her human powers, among them reason. "Although no single net will capture all the resonances of the final couplet, near the heart of the passage is the thought of living life completely, in accordance with natural law" ("Marvell's Valid Logic," *College Literature* [Spring 1985]: 113–211).

Edna St. Vincent Millay, RECUERDO, page 484

There is probably not much to do with this delightful poem but leave it alone and let students discover it for themselves. The only thing we would find in it to discuss: Would that newspaper vendor really break down into tears of gratitude? We bet she is a mere literary convention here, and in real life would probably be one tough old egg.

Would this highly musical lyric make a good song? Might it be sung?

MyLiteratureLab Resources. Photographs and biographical information for Millay.

John Milton, HOW SOON HATH TIME, page 485

Traditionally this sonnet had been dated December 1631, the month of Milton's twenty-third birthday and therefore the end of his twenty-third year, but contemporary scholars—one of them stating "Simply put, Milton was no mathematician"—tend to see the poem as having been composed a year later. Whatever the date of its composition, "How soon hath time" is a true Petrarchan sonnet, not only by following the prescribed stanzaic structure and rime scheme but also by including a *volta*, a "turn" or thematic shift, at the beginning of the sestet. In the octave, the speaker laments the swift passage of time and his own failure meanwhile to achieve any accomplishment of note: "But my late spring no bud or blossom show'th" (line 4).

Lines 5–6 are customarily understood to refer to Milton's youthful appearance; it is elsewhere documented that in early and middle life he did in fact look much younger than his actual age. There has been considerable speculation as to the identities of the "timely-happy spirits," that is, those who have achieved more in their early careers than the speaker has: in addition to such obvious candidates as Edmund Spenser and Sir Philip Sidney, the names of several of Milton's contemporaries have been advanced, including Thomas Randolph, a fellow student at Cambridge University who wrote several highly admired verse dramas and died young, and the even more precocious Abraham Cowley, several years younger than Milton, who published his first collection of poetry at the age of fifteen. (Perhaps taking their cue from a presumed play on "measure"—that is, poetic meter—in line 10, most commentators have assumed that the true subject of the poem is achievement, or the lack thereof, in the field of poetry.)

After the seeming anxiety expressed in the octave, Milton resolves his theme with a sort of anti-*carpe diem* approach, maintaining in the last six lines that, however his destiny unfolds, whatever the level or amount of his achievement, it will all be in accordance with the will of God, who is of course the "great task-Master" of line 14, "if I have grace to use it so." The similarity of theme should be obvious between this sonnet and the following one, "When I consider how my light is spent."

John Milton, WHEN I CONSIDER HOW MY LIGHT IS SPENT, page 486

While this famous sonnet is usually taken to refer to the poet's lost eyesight, some critics have argued that it is not about blindness at all. The familiar title "On His Blindness" was given not by Milton, but by a printer a century later.

QUESTIONS FOR DISCUSSION

1. *If the poem is not about blindness, what might it be about?* Possible suggestions: Milton's declining powers of poetry; Milton's fame as a Puritan apologist.

2. *Is "talent" a pun referring to Milton's talent for writing poetry? What other meanings of the word seem appropriate in this poem?* In the New Testament parable (Matthew 25:14–30), the hidden talent is money that should have been earning interest. That Milton is thinking primarily of work and business can be plausibly argued; other words in the poem convey such connotations—*spent, true account, day-labor,* and perhaps *useless,* which suggests the Medieval Latin word for interest, *usura.*

The theme of frustration in life (and reconciliation to one's lot) is dealt with differently in Shakespeare's "When, in disgrace with Fortune and men's eyes."

Marianne Moore, POETRY, page 486

Marianne Moore was a singular poet both on the page and in real life. Her elaborate verse style, complex syllabic meters, and penchant for collage and quotation mirror in some mysterious way her carefully cultivated eccentricity and wry personal reticence. One peculiar feature of her work is that most of her poems—directly or indirectly—explore aesthetics, especially the nature of literary art. In this respect, "Poetry" occupies an important position in her work. This superbly observed and intellectually provocative poem also illustrates a central irony of her work—the more overtly abstract her poem appears, the more covertly personal it proves to be.

"Poetry" appears in several versions in Moore's various collections. Hardly had she first published the poem in 1921 than she began revising it. By the time she published her *Complete Poems* in 1967, Moore had grotesquely cut the poem down to only three lines. For this anthology we have reprinted her original version, which seems to us the finest and fullest one. (Instructors should make sure they compare our version to others they may have in different books.)

"Poetry" is both a defense of poetry as an important human enterprise and—to quote critic Helen Vendler—Moore's "indirect self-reproach for her painstaking absorption in 'all this fiddle.'" While eventually justifying the art of poetry for its heightened attention to genuine phenomena, the poem also admits its own skepticism about the elaborate "fiddle" of poetry and its recognition of the failure of "half poets" and "derivative" writers. Moore's aesthetic ideal is best summarized in her famous (and wondrously oxymoronic) image "imaginary gardens with real toads in them." Boldly the poet affirms the utility of poetry. Poetry is "useful" to Moore when it genuinely encompasses both external and internal reality.

The poet Donald Hall, who knew Moore, has commented in similar terms on the poem:

> In her well-known poem "Poetry," Miss Moore begins, "I too, dislike it." This line has been interpreted as ironic, as an attempt to disarm, or as evidence that she practices her art only half-seriously. Quite obviously, however, her reasoning is serious. She refers to a kind of poetry that is neither honest nor sincere but that has found fashionable approval by virtue of its very obscurity. (*Marianne Moore: The Cage and the Animal* [New York: Pegasus: 1970] 40)

The form of "Poetry" is also worth discussing. It might help to ask the class if the poem has a form—to see what features they discover on their own. Moore shaped the version of "Poetry" reprinted here into five complex syllabic stanzas of six lines each. Students can count out the syllables in each line to determine the stanza pattern. The stanzas also rime—although the rimes are more visible to the eye than audible in her run-on enjambed lines. The rime scheme is *abbccd*. The poem unfolds in the manner of an impassioned, learned conversation, and it employs prose rhythms in its elaborate syllabic pattern. Spoken aloud, it sounds like free verse; on the page, however, the reader sees how carefully wrought it is as formal verse.

Frederick Morgan, THE MASTER, page 487

Morgan's poem describes an actual painting, Han Kan's "Nightshining White," which is owned by the Metropolitan Museum of Art in New York. The painting is so fragile that it is not always on display, but it is so striking that, once seen, it is never forgotten.

Morgan's poem retells the legendary account of the painting's creation. Han Kan (who was active between 742 and 756) was a painter of the T'ang dynasty. His depiction of the Emperor Ming-huang's favorite charger is probably the most famous horse painting in Chinese art, considered a masterpiece since its creation. The actual painted scroll is covered with seals and commentaries by scholars.

The theme of Morgan's poem is the artist's dependence on actual experience. Arriving in the capital, Han Kan is invited to study with the imperial court painter. He chooses instead to study from nature itself in the emperor's stables.

Poetry, then, tends to inhere not in abstract editorial stands but in particulars. William Carlos Williams's brief poem about eating the plums in the ice box may not be great, but it is human and hard to forget. Sources of poems may lie before your eyes. Although poets can learn from reading other poets' work, they can also learn from the testimony of their own senses. In the best poems, as Morgan's poem reminds us, there is always a quality that cannot be distilled from schools and libraries: a freshness that comes only from contact with the living world.

Frederick Morgan was a well-known editor as well as a poet. In 1948 he was one of the founders of the *Hudson Review*, the distinguished journal which has been called "the last of the great quarterlies."

Marilyn Nelson, A STRANGE BEAUTIFUL WOMAN, page 488

This strange and beautiful short poem has the simplicity of a haiku—a single image doubled in a mirror followed by a single question also doubled. The poem's power rests in its suggestiveness, and it works—like the mirror—in two ways at once. The poem is affirmative in the speaker's recognition of her own beauty, but it is also subtly self-critical in noting that the speaker is insufficiently familiar with admitting her own beauty, which initially seems "strange" to her. In the same way, the speaker's surprised question—"Hey, / I said, / what you doing here?"—acquires a more disturbing existential quality when the reflection repeats it. What is the speaker doing, the image seems to ask, in and with her own life?

Howard Nemerov, THE WAR IN THE AIR, page 489

This poem can be understood by students who know very little about World War II, but explaining the many allusions will enrich their appreciation. During World War II, air force pilots and crew members suffered the highest mortality rates of any Allied service branch. Sometimes every member of a squadron would be killed in a single engagement. Nemerov, who served in both the Royal Canadian and American air forces, memorializes those who usually died far away and sometimes vanished into the sea or enemy territory.

Here are the major allusions woven into the poem—all of which would be familiar to veterans of the conflict. In praising the contributions of Allied pilots during the Battle of Britain, Winston Churchill famously told Parliament, "Never in the field of human conflict was so much owed by so many to so few." The inspirational Latin tag *per ardua ad astra* ("through difficult things to the stars") served as the motto of England's Royal Air Force. Mars is, of course, the god of war. "The Good War" was an Allied nickname for World War II. The pun on "for goodness' sake" (in line 14) is also worth noting to students. This seemingly straightforward elegy is full of wordplay, allusion, and wit.

Lorine Niedecker, POET'S WORK, page 489

Though she published five collections here and in Britain, Niedecker's work has seldom appeared in anthologies. But here and there, her life and distinctive work have won recognition. In 1985 the Jargon Society published her collected writing, *From This Condensery*. In 1989 *Niedecker*, a biographical play by Kristine Thatcher, had a successful Off-Broadway production.

The poet, who spent most of her quiet life on remote Blackhawk Island, Wisconsin, worked for a time as a cleaning person in a hospital. While far from literary capitals, she kept up a lively correspondence with Basil Bunting, Cid Corman, William Carlos Williams, Louis Zukofsky, and other innovative nonacademic poets of her day.

"Poet's Work" exemplifies its own content. Like much of Niedecker's work, it is a very short poem written in very short lines, condensed to its essence, with everything extraneous—including "a," "the," or "my" before "desk"—squeezed out (a condensery is a place for making condensed or evaporated milk). Equating the writing of poetry with a trade suggests her practical approach to her work, but the last three lines of the poem, especially "No layoff," will likely put you in mind of William Butler Yeats's "Adam's Curse": "Yet if it does not seem a moment's thought, / Our stitching and unstitching has been naught. / . . . / For to articulate sweet sounds together / Is to work harder than all these, and yet / Be thought an idler. . . . " The ironies inherent in Yeats's observation are no doubt fully endorsed by Niedecker.

Yone Noguchi, A Selection of Hokku, page 490

Yone Noguchi, the first Asian American poet of significant influence, was born in Tsushima, a small town near Nagaya, Japan. He became interested in English language and literature in public school. He later studied English at Keio University in Tokyo, but after two years he decided to immigrate to America. He arrived in San Francisco in December 1893, where he worked for a Japanese-language paper while studying American poetry. In 1896 he met the popular Western poet Joaquin Miller, who encouraged his literary ambitions. For three years Noguchi lived in a hut on Miller's hillside property above Oakland, and he associated with *Les Jeunes*, a group of young San Francisco writers including Gelett Burgess. Noguchi soon published two books, *Seen & Unseen* (1897) and *The Voice of the Valley* (1897), which showed the influence of Miller and Walt Whitman. Although written in slightly odd English, these early books were praised for their freshness. His next two collections of poetry, *From the Eastern Sea* (1903) and *The Summer Cloud* (1906), not only display more confidence and originality, they also incorporate more traditional Japanese elements of style and structure. *The Summer Cloud*, which presented sixty-two prose poems, also demonstrated Noguchi's early interest in literary modernism. In 1904 Noguchi returned to Japan—leaving behind his American lover, Leonie Gilmour, and their newborn son, Isamu Noguchi (who would become an internationally celebrated sculptor).

Noguchi corresponded with Ezra Pound and William Butler Yeats about Japanese literary aesthetics. He, therefore, played an important but little-known role in influencing the development of Imagism. He also helped popularize haiku as an English-language form. His volume *Japanese Hokkus* (1920), which was dedicated to Yeats, stills stands as a major early milestone in the American haiku tradition. Noguchi understood his unique role as a conduit between the Japanese and English-language literary traditions. "We must lose our insularity," he wrote hopefully of Japanese literature, but he could certainly have claimed to have helped broaden the perspective of American letters.

Sharon Olds, THE ONE GIRL AT THE BOYS' PARTY, page 491

This poem whimsically describes a talented little girl, "her math scores unfolding in the air around her," during a pool party at which all the other guests are boys. *They* in lines 2 and 15, *their* in lines 18 and 19 seem to refer only to the boys. In lines 5, 7, and 11, the word *they* apparently includes the girl. You might ask students to note the pairs of adjectives that affirm the child's strength and composure: she is "smooth and sleek" (line 3), her body is "hard and / indivisible as a prime number" (lines 5–6), her face is "solemn and / sealed" (lines 16–17). The adjectives make clear the narrator-mother's respect for her brilliant daughter. Notable too is the metaphor of wet ponytail (itself a by-now-dead metaphor!) as pencil (line 12). That and the "narrow silk suit / with hamburgers and french fries printed on it" remind us that she is in some ways a very typical little girl.

It is the mathematical figures of speech that make this poem unique. Why not ask students to point out and discuss them? Are they apt? Do they ever appear forced? Which ones succeed best?

Wilfred Owen, ANTHEM FOR DOOMED YOUTH, page 492

Metaphorically, this sonnet draws a contrast between traditional funeral trappings and the actual conditions under which the dead lie on the field of battle: with cannon fire instead of tolling bells, rifle bursts instead of the patter of prayers, the whine of shells instead of choirs' songs, the last lights in dying eyes instead of candle-shine, pale brows (of mourning girls, at home?) instead of shrouds or palls, the tenderness of onlookers (such as the poet?) instead of flowers—an early draft of the poem reads, "Your flowers, the tenderness of comrades' minds"—and the fall of night instead of the conventional drawing down of blinds in a house where someone has died.

For another Owen war poem, see "Dulce et Decorum Est." For other war poems, see in this manual "Poems Arranged by Subject and Theme."

The poet's revisions for this poem, in four drafts, may be studied in the appendix to C. Day Lewis's edition of Owen's *Collected Poems* (London: Chatto, 1963). In its first draft, the poem was called "Anthem for Dead [not Doomed] Youth," and it went, in our reading of the photographed manuscript:

> What minute bells for these who die so fast?
> Only the monstrous anger of our guns.
> Let the majestic insults of their iron mouths
> Be as the priest-words of their burials.
> Of choristers and holy music, none;
> Not any voice of mourning, save the wail
> The long-drawn wail of high, far-sailing shells.
> What candles may we hold for these lost souls?
> Not in the hands of boys, but in their eyes

Shall many candles shine, and [?] will light them.
Women's wide-spreaded arms shall be their wreaths,
And pallor of girls' cheeks shall be their palls.
Their flowers, the tenderness of all men's minds,
And every dusk, a drawing-down of blinds.

Linda Pastan, ETHICS, page 492

As a student, the narrator, like others in her class, found her teacher's ethical puzzler irrelevant. Now the mature woman pondering the "real Rembrandt" in the museum finds the question still remote from her vital concerns, but for different reasons. The approach of her own old age has shown her that nothing lasts, that with the onflow of years our choices, whatever they may be, fade into insignificance.

One way of entering the poem: students may be asked to sum up its theme. Is it *carpe diem?* Is the poet saying, with Housman in "Loveliest of trees," "Life is fleeting; I'd better enjoy beauty while I can"? No, for the poet seems not to believe in day-seizing. Is it *ars longa, vita brevis est?* No, for both art and life seem pitifully brief and temporary. The point, rather, is that all things pass away despite our efforts to hold on to them. But instead of telling them what the point is, you might ask students to paraphrase the poem's conclusion that "woman / and painting and season are almost one / and all beyond saving by children."

To discuss: In what ways does "Ethics" differ from prose? Pastan's language seems far more musical. She makes beautiful music of alliteration and assonance. Read the poem aloud. And central to "Ethics" is a huge metaphor: old woman, season, earth, painting, and poet become one—all caught in time's resistless fire.

In a previous Instructor's Manual, we wondered: How many times did the speaker have to repeat that ethics course? To our relief, on a recent visit to the University of Arizona in Tucson, Linda Pastan supplied an answer, reported to us by Ila Abnernathy of the Poetry Center. Pastan went to the Ethical Culture School in New York City, a private school run by the Ethical Culture Society and serving both elementary and high school students. The school's curriculum hits ethics hard: the poet was required to take once-a-week ethics classes for twelve years.

Linda Pastan chose "Ethics" to represent her in *The Poet's Choice*, an anthology of poets' own favorite poems, edited by George E. Murphy, Jr. (Green Harbor, MA: Tendril, 1980).

Robert Phillips, RUNNING ON EMPTY, page 493

Robert Phillips was born in Delaware. For many years he worked on Madison Avenue as a copywriter. During his advertising career, Phillips published over a dozen volumes of poetry, short stories, and criticism, and he edited several volumes by his late teacher, Delmore Schwartz. Phillips then joined the Creative Writing Department at the University of Houston. He has provided the following comment about his poem:

> "Running on Empty" is fairly autobiographical. I was stunned at how grudgingly my father let me use the family car once I'd obtained my driver's

> license at age 16. It seemed to me he withheld this symbol of my new freedom and attainment just as he withheld his affection. So when I finally had use of the car, I went hog-wild in celebration and release.
>
> The landscape is Sussex County, Delaware—extremely flat country bisected by Route 13 (nicknamed "The Dual" because it is composed of twin lanes dually parallel in an inexorable straight line). I was pushing my luck speeding and refusing to refuel in an act of rebellion against my father's strictness (which may explain why the 12th line reads "defying chemistry" rather than the more accurate "defying physics"—my father taught high school chemistry, and even in the classroom I was subject to his discipline).
>
> I'm rather pleased with the way the poem picks up rhythm and begins to speed when the car does (5th–7th stanzas). And I hope students relate to the central images of car and boy, one of which can be mechanically refueled and replenished, one of which cannot.

For us the word *chemistry* in line 12 carries additional meaning, as in "behavior or functioning, as of a complex of emotions" *(The American Heritage Dictionary)*. In this sense, too, the narrator was surely in defiance of his father's chemistry.

Sylvia Plath, DADDY, page 494

There are worse ways to begin teaching this astonishing poem than to ask students to recall what they know of Dachau, Auschwitz, Belsen (line 33), and other Nazi atrocities. "Every woman adores a Fascist"—what does Plath mean? Is she sympathizing with the machismo ideal of the domineering male, lashing his whip upon subjugated womankind? (No way.) For an exchange of letters about the rightness or wrongness of Plath's identifying with Jewish victims of World War II, see *Commentary* (July and October 1974). Irving Howe accuses Plath of "a failure in judgment" in using genocide as an emblem of her personal traumas.

Incredible as it seems, some students possess an alarming fund of ignorance about the Nazis, and some might not even recognize the cloven foot of Satan (line 53); so be prepared, sadly, to supply glosses. They will be familiar with the story of Dracula, however, and probably won't need much help with lines 71–79. Plath may be thinking of *Nosferatu*, F. W. Murnau's silent screen adaptation of Bram Stoker's novel *Dracula*, filmed in Germany in 1922. Hitler's propagandists seized on the Nosferatu theme and claimed that the old democratic order was drinking the country's blood. Plath sees Daddy as doing the same to his daughter.

Edgar Allan Poe, A DREAM WITHIN A DREAM, page 497

"A Dream within a Dream" is a poem that Poe kept coming back to; earlier versions of it, substantially different from the final one printed here, were published in 1827 and 1829. And the theme is certainly one that recurs frequently in Poe's verse; in a body of work that contains fewer than fifty completed poems, there are texts titled "A Dream," "Dreams," and "Dream-Land," as well as a number of other poems that treat the concept without using the word in their titles.

In his classic edition of Poe's complete poems, which inaugurated the Dell Laurel Poetry Series in 1959, the poet Richard Wilbur writes of "A Dream within a Dream":

> The hero of these poems is always separated from his love through betrayal, death, or "destiny." This poem begins with a farewell to a woman of the real world by a hero whose incompatible destiny it is to dream. His dreams are of his lost visionary past—of a past that was itself a dream; and he argues that the loss of a dream is as painful as the loss of a "reality," reality itself being only an "insubstantial pageant." . . . What appalls the poet in the last two lines is that dreams, though seemingly beyond time, are yet as subject to change, loss, and oblivion as any temporal thing.

MLL *MyLiteratureLab Resources.* Photographs, biographical information, critical comments, bibliography for Poe.

Alexander Pope, A LITTLE LEARNING IS A DANG'ROUS THING, page 497

This passage is an excerpt (lines 215–232) from Pope's "An Essay on Criticism," which he published when he was only twenty-three years old. It was this poem, which Joseph Addison immediately proclaimed "a Master-piece in its kind," that made Pope a literary celebrity.

Many teachers object to using excerpts from long works; such selections, they feel, betray the author's original intentions. In general, we agree; we favor including complete poems, so that each part of the work may be seen in relation to the whole. Pope, however, provides a special case. All of his greatest poems are too long to include in total. But it would seem too cruel to deny both teachers and students alike the pleasures of Pope's verse, so we have bent the rules several times to introduce this satiric master's work to a new generation. As every teacher knows, one sometimes needs to bend critical rules a bit.

As long as we are bending the rules, we should point out how much this excerpt from a long didactic poem looks like a self-standing lyric in its new form. Examining these eighteen lines in isolation, we see how carefully Pope arranged the images in each line to build toward a cumulative poetic as well as an intellectual effect. The final image of the weary traveler looking over the mountaintop at the endless Alps rising ahead is a brilliant stroke that seems closer to a romantic sensibility than a neoclassical one.

Ezra Pound, THE RIVER-MERCHANT'S WIFE: A LETTER, page 498

After the death of Ernest Fenollosa, a scholar devoted to Chinese language and literature, Pound inherited Fenollosa's manuscripts containing rough prose versions of many Chinese poems. From one such draft, Pound finished his own version of "The River Merchant's Wife." Fenollosa's wording of the first line was:

> My hair was at first covering my brows (child's method of wearing hair)

Arthur Waley, apparently contemptuous of Pound for ignoring dictionary meanings of some of the words of the poem, made a translation that began:

> Soon after I wore my hair covering my forehead . . .

Pound's version begins:

> While my hair was still cut straight across my forehead . . .

Pound, says the critic Waj-lim Yip, has understood Chinese culture while Waley has not, even though he understands his dictionary. "The characters for 'hair/first/cover/forehead' conjure up in the mind of a Chinese reader exactly this picture. All little Chinese girls normally have their hair cut straight across the forehead." Yip goes on to show that Pound, ignorant of Chinese as he was, comes close in sense and feeling to the Li Po original. (*Ezra Pound's Cathay* [Princeton: Princeton UP, 1969] 88–92.)

What is the tone of the poem? What details make it seem moving and true, even for a reader who knows nothing of Chinese culture?

Dudley Randall, A DIFFERENT IMAGE, page 499

Randall's memorable and concise poem bears examination from several angles. The poem is in two short stanzas. The first states the challenge in largely abstract terms (the need to create a new image of identity); the second stanza offers a specific solution (to replace a false slave-era stereotype with a majestic African image). Notice that there is nothing specifically African American in the first stanza, but the concluding stanza particularizes the abstract challenge of the opening. Don't forget to point out (or elicit from the class) the fact that a burnt-cork face minstrel would have been a white man wearing blackface in contrast to the authentic African face of a Benin sculpture. The form of the poem is also very interesting. The lines are iambic, but their length is not constant. (They range from two to eleven syllables.) Every line is also rimed but in no regular pattern. Randall's rimed iambic lines, therefore, resemble open form in some key respects.

Finally, there is one literary allusion embedded in "A Different Image." Randall's opening stanza deliberately echoes Ezra Pound's famous lines from *Hugh Selwyn Mauberly* (1921):

> The age demanded an image
> Of its accelerated grimace,
> Something for the modern stage,
> Not, at any rate, an Attic grace.

Randall refashions Pound's search for a meaningful vision of modern beauty in African American terms. Consequently, he returns not to classical Greece but to classical West Africa. Randall's lucidity and immediacy often lead critics to underestimate the sophistication and complexity of his work. He had a classical sensibility that prizes unity of design, economy of means, clarity of intention, and a governing sense of form. The poems contain intense emotion, but it is always held in balance by the total design.

John Crowe Ransom, PIAZZA PIECE, page 500

This weird and wonderful sonnet is both funny and disturbing. The old man by the rose trellis is hardly a model senior citizen but the proverbial dirty old man given an existential twist. The fun of the poem is how well it operates simultaneously on a mundane and mythic level. If the man in the dustcoat is an elderly masher, he is also a death figure who has wandered into the beautiful young lady's moonlit rose garden. The idyllic setting is a classic poetic and artistic archetype for youthful female sexuality and virginity (pervasive in love poetry from "The Song of Songs" to the present). There she waits until her "truelove" comes. In Renaissance painting one also sees this situation frequently—an Edenic pastoral landscape populated by young lovers. These pictures often have a skull hidden in the vines or bushes, bearing the Latin inscription "*Et in Arcadia ego*," which means "Even in Arcadia, am I [i.e. Death]."

The old man inhabits the same physical space as the young lady, but he sees the lovely setting as proof of their shared mortality. The roses on the trellis are "dying" and the moon's song is "spectral." He will "have [his] lovely lady soon" not because he will rape her in the mundane sense, but because, as Death, he will eventually possess her—no matter how much she ignores his words.

Since "Piazza Piece" is a sonnet, the sestet represents the turn of attitude and perspective. The young lady responds appropriately, affirming life and hope. She considers the old man's warnings and threats as "dry and faint as in a dream." By ordering him away, she also rightly asserts that for the time being at least, the garden belongs to her. Whatever her ultimate fate, she is for the present "a lady young in beauty waiting."

Southerners will probably be familiar with the slightly old-fashioned architectural term *piazza*, which means an open porch or balcony adjacent to a garden; but Yankees, Midwesterners, and Westerners may need some remedial instruction.

Henry Reed, NAMING OF PARTS, page 500

This is one of the most teachable poems ever written. There are two voices: the voice of the riflery instructor, droning on with his spiel, and the voice of the reluctant inductee, distracted by the springtime. Two varieties of diction and imagery clash and contrast: technical terms opposed to imagery of blossoming nature. Note the fine pun in line 24, prepared for by the rapist bees in the previous line. Note also the connotations of the ambiguous phrase *point of balance* (line 27)—a kind of balance lacking in the recruits' lives?

Students need to be shown the dramatic situation of the poem: the poor inductee, sitting through a lecture he doesn't want to hear. One would think that sort of experience would be familiar to students, but a trouble some instructors have met in teaching this poem is the yearning to make out of it a vast comment about Modern Civilization.

The poet himself has recorded the poem for *An Album of Modern Poets*, 1 (Library of Congress, PL 20). Dylan Thomas reads "Naming of Parts" even more impressively in his *Reading, Vol. IV: A Visit to America and Poems* (Caedmon, TC 1061).

Adrienne Rich, LIVING IN SIN, page 501

The title of Adrienne Rich's powerfully pensive poem may need explaining to some students nowadays, and it is essential that they understand the phrase because it sets up the narrative situation of the poem. As the title indicates, Rich's pair of lovers (who are referred to only as "he" and "she") are living together but not married—a bolder lifestyle in 1955 than today. The woman has expected their life together to be romantic and carefree—"no dust upon the furniture of love"—but the daily reality of housework and habitual intimacy proves dull and disillusioning. This deflation of romantic fantasy suggests the secondary meaning of the title—the Adam and Eve of her hoped-for lover's Eden have fallen from grace into the humdrum world of everyday disappointment.

Rich has neatly divided the two worlds of the protagonists' experience into night and day. The night remains romantic—if also diminished from the woman's original expectations—but the dawn brings only disappointment. The poem never directly states whether the woman's vacillating feelings will bring matters to a crisis, but the relative impact of each emotional state is suggested by the fact that the evening world of love receives three lines of treatment, whereas the daylight world of disillusionment gets twenty-three. These proportions give "Living in Sin" the feel of an Anton Chekhov short story in which the final outcome remains unstated but the narrative situation has been so carefully presented as to make the conclusion inevitable.

For this reason, "Living in Sin" would be a good poem to use in a classroom discussion of "Saying and Suggesting." Rich's poem leaves a great many important things unsaid but implicit. The images suggest conclusions the protagonist seems not yet able to articulate—like the "beetle-eyes" staring at her from the shelf. The poem also has an interesting point of view. Although narrated in the third person, the poem adopts the subjective point of view of the woman.

"Living in Sin" is an early Rich poem (published in 1955 in her second collection, *The Diamond Cutters*). It is tempting, therefore, to read the poem as a narrative that prefigures Rich's turn to feminism. "Living in Sin" certainly responds to such interpretation. The woman in the poem has mistakenly sought fulfillment by creating a domestic world designed to please her male lover. (The particulars of the apartment "had risen at his urging.") Now she begins to understand the mistaken idealism and unintentional subjugation of that decision. Some changes—some escape—must happen, even if the particular course of action has not yet been imagined. What must come next, to quote the title of a subsequent Rich volume, is "the will to change."

Edwin Arlington Robinson, MINIVER CHEEVY, page 502

"Miniver Cheevy" is one of Robinson's great character portraits. These miniature character studies (see also "Richard Cory") are a genre that Robinson perfected. Influenced by the dramatic and narrative poems of poets such as George Crabbe and Robert Browning, Robinson compressed the portrait poem into tighter, often lyric structures. His work, with its stark realism, bitter antiromanticism, and concise form, marks the true beginning of modern (but not Modernist) American poetry.

Mr. Cheevy of the title is a man unable to face reality. He lives in a fantasy world of "the days of old." Cheevy imagines he would have lived a more exciting and fulfilling life in an earlier age, but Robinson makes it clear that Cheevy's fantasies are pure self-deception. Robinson undercuts Cheevy's delusions with irony ("He missed the medieval grace / Of iron clothing").

Writing the introduction to Robinson's posthumous *King Jasper* in 1935, Robert Frost reminisced about reading "Miniver Cheevy" in London in 1913 with Ezra Pound. They laughed over the fourth *thought* in "Miniver thought, and thought, and thought / And thought about it." "Three 'thoughts' would have been 'adequate' as the critical praise-word then was," Frost remembered ". . . The fourth made the intolerable touch of poetry. With the fourth the fun began."

Theodore Roethke, ELEGY FOR JANE, page 503

By piling up figures of speech from the natural world, Roethke in "Elegy for Jane" portrays his student as a child of nature, quick, thin, and birdlike. A *wren*, a *sparrow*, a *skittery pigeon*, Jane has a *pickerel smile* and neck curls *limp and damp as tendrils*. She waits *like a fern, making a spiny shadow*. She has the power to make shade trees and (even more surprising) mold burst into song. For her, leaves change their whispers into kisses.

Then she dies. The poet acknowledges that for him there is no consolation in nature, in the "sides of wet stones" or the moss; his grief is not assuaged. Because he mourns the girl as teacher and friend, no more, he recognizes a faint awkwardness in his grief as he speaks over her grave:

> I, with no rights in this matter,
> Neither father nor lover.

Roethke, writing about this poem in *On the Poet and His Craft* (Seattle: U of Washington P, 1965) 81–83, reminds the reader that it was John Crowe Ransom (to whose "Bells for John Whiteside's Daughter" this poem has often been compared) who first printed "Elegy for Jane." Roethke discusses his use of enumeration, calling it "the favorite device of the more irregular poem." He calls attention to one "of the strategies for the poet writing without the support of a formal pattern," a strategy he uses in "Elegy for Jane": the "lengthening out" of the last three lines in the first stanza, balanced by the progressive shortening of the three lines at the poem's end.

Some readers have interpreted "Elegy for Jane" as the work of a man who never had children of his own; but in fact Roethke as a young man had fathered a daughter, for whom he felt great affection. Although "neither father nor lover" of Jane, he at least could well imagine a father's feelings.

Mary Jo Salter, WELCOME TO HIROSHIMA, page 504

Salter's poem is a meditation on the tragedy of Hiroshima that admits the foreigner's difficulty in understanding the exact nature of the event as the Japanese themselves experienced it. The speaker looks to understand the past cataclysm but repeatedly finds that the contemporary commercial reality impedes her comprehension. The ironic title is made even more mordant by being in English on a sign sponsored by Toshiba. One touristic observation after another distracts, surprises, dismays, or confuses the speaker, until an exhibit of a glass shard trapped in a woman's arm for three decades finally provides the mute but eloquent testimony of suffering and redemption on a tangibly human scale.

 *MyLiteratureLab Resources.* Longman Lecture on "Welcome to Hiroshima."

William Shakespeare, WHEN, IN DISGRACE WITH FORTUNE AND MEN'S EYES, page 506

Figures of speech are central to many Shakespearean sonnets, but they hardly enter into "When, in disgrace" until line 11, when the simile of the lark is introduced. The lark's burst of joy suggests that heaven, called *deaf* in line 3, has suddenly become keener of hearing. Critical discussion of the sonnets goes on: *Shakespeare's Sonnets*, edited with analytic commentary by Stephen Booth (New Haven: Yale UP, 1977) is especially valuable.

 *MyLiteratureLab Resources.* Photographs, biographical information, and bibliography for Shakespeare.

William Shakespeare, NOT MARBLE NOR THE GILDED MONUMENTS, page 507

To discuss: Is Shakespeare making a wild boast, or does the claim in lines 1–8 seem at all justified? (Time has proved him right. Here we are, still reading his lines, 500 years after they were written! Of course, the fact that he happened to be Shakespeare helped his prediction come true.)

For teaching this poem in tandem with Robinson Jeffers's "To the Stone-Cutters," see the entry on Jeffers in this manual.

MyLiteratureLab Resources. Photographs, biographical information, and bibliography for Shakespeare.

William Shakespeare, THAT TIME OF YEAR THOU MAYST IN ME BEHOLD, page 507

Shakespeare's magnificent metaphors will probably take some brief explaining. How is a body like boughs, and how are the bare boughs like a ruined choir loft? Students will get the general import, but they can be helped to visualize the images. "Consumed with that which it was nourished by" will surely require some discussion. Youth, that had fed life's fire, now provides only smothering ashes. The poet's attitude toward age and approaching death stands in contrast to the attitudes of poets (or speakers) in other poems of similar theme: admiration for the exultant sparrows in William Carlos Williams's "To Waken an Old Lady"; defiance in Yeats's "Sailing to Byzantium."

MLL *MyLiteratureLab Resources*. Photographs, biographical information, and bibliography for Shakespeare. Longman Lecture on "That time of year thou mayst in me behold."

William Shakespeare, MY MISTRESS' EYES ARE NOTHING LIKE THE SUN, page 508

Have students state positively each simile that Shakespeare states negatively, and they will make a fair catalog of trite Petrarchan imagery. Poking fun at such excessive flattery is a source of humor even today, as in an old wheeze: "Your teeth are like the stars—they come out at night."

MLL *MyLiteratureLab Resources*. Photographs, biographical information, and bibliography for Shakespeare. Longman Lecture on "The Theme of Love in the Sonnets."

Louis Simpson, AMERICAN POETRY, page 508

Simpson's brilliant short poem would make an excellent classroom assignment in a discussion that could also include Archibald MacLeish's "Ars Poetica" and Marianne Moore's "Poetry." All three are classic statements of modern poetics. Simpson's is both the most recent work (1963) and the only one specifically focused on what makes American poetry different from other literatures. The short imagistic poem combines odd and usually seemingly unpoetic items (rubber, coal, uranium) with more traditional literary elements (moons, poems). The final stanza develops this principle of contradictory assemblage into the surreal extended simile of the shark-like poem swimming through the desert uttering cries that are almost human. Clearly Simpson's poem is not conceptual and discursive but suggestive and symbolic. What does the shark symbolize? At the very least, the image suggests the restless, untamed, omnivorous, and even dangerous nature of American poetry. How does this vision of the art compare to Moore's or MacLeish's?

David R. Slavitt, TITANIC, page 508

In "The Convergence of the Twain," Hardy censures the vanity, luxury, and pride that prompted Fate to ram the *Titanic* into an iceberg. Slavitt's poem about the same tragedy takes another tack. He makes dying on the *Titanic* sound almost like fun—all aboard!

> If they sold passage tomorrow for that same crossing, who would not buy?

Slavitt's point is that, since we all have to die, it's certainly more glamorous, more desirable to do it "first-class" (note the double meaning of "go" in the last line) than to die less comfortably, in more mundane ways, and soon be forgotten.

Christopher Smart, For I will consider my Cat Jeoffry, page 509

Telling us more about cats than Carl Sandburg and T. S. Eliot (in "Prufrock," lines 15–22) put together, Smart salutes Jeoffry in one of several passages in *Jubilate Agno* that fall for a little while into some continuity. This fascinating poem, and the whole work that contained it, have come down to us in a jumble of manuscripts retrieved from the asylum, sorted out brilliantly by W. H. Bond in his edition of Smart's work (Cambridge: Harvard UP, 1954). Some of Smart's gorgeous lines seem quite loony, such as the command to Moses concerning cats (lines 34–35) and the patriotic boast about misinformation: the ichneumon (or *Icneumon*, line 63) is not a pernicious rat, but a weasel-like, rat-killing mammal.

Talking with Boswell of Smart's confinement, Dr. Johnson observed:

> I did not think he ought to be shut up. His infirmities were not noxious to society. He insisted on people praying with him; and I'd as lief pray with Kit Smart as with any one else. Another charge was, that he did not love clean linen; and I have no passion for it.

A possible paper topic: "Smart's Cat Jeoffry and Blake's Tyger: How Are These Poems Similar in View?"

William Jay Smith, American Primitive, page 511

We might expect a painter called an American primitive to be naive, unsophisticated, and childlike in his view. So is the speaker who draws this verbal scene. Not only do the references to Daddy seem juvenile, but so does the line "the screen door bangs, and it sounds so funny." (Smith, incidentally, has written much fine verse for children in addition to his more serious poetry, and he understands the way a child thinks and speaks.) There is, of course, an ironic distance between the speaker's point of view and the poet's. Irony is enforced, too, in the contrast between the grim event and the bouncy rhythm and use of feminine rimes.

Another possible way of looking at the poem is that Daddy himself is the primitive: the primal dollar-worshipping American. The capitalization of *Dollar* (as in the familiar phrase "the Almighty Dollar") may support this view. We are not told why Daddy died, an apparent suicide, but it is evident that riches did not buy him life. Besides inviting comparison with Sylvia Plath's ironic poem about the death of a terrible "Daddy," Smith's mock-elegy may be set beside Wallace Stevens's "The Emperor of Ice-Cream," with students asked to compare the two in tone and in subject matter.

Cathy Song, Stamp Collecting, page 512

Song's poem depends upon an original and illuminating conceit: the speaker views the countries of the world through the stamps they issue. Understanding that the subject of each stamp reflects in some way the culture and geography that produced it, the speaker speculates on the national vision and self-image behind her stamps. "Stamp Collecting" is a political poem, but it unfolds with such delicate observations and employs such ingenious language that it may be easy for students to miss the political content. Moreover, the poem has no specific ideological ax to grind. "Stamp Collecting" explains the concept of national self-identity rather than any particular political cause.

William Stafford, THE FARM ON THE GREAT PLAINS, page 513

In 1962—when Stafford still had three decades of life and poetry before him—he selected this poem, "The Farm on the Great Plains," for Paul Engle and Joseph Langland's *Poet's Choice* (New York: Dial, 1962), an anthology in which one hundred or so English-language poets selected their favorite among their own works and supplied a (usually) brief explanation of their choice. Stafford wrote the following note to accompany his poem:

> A glance at "The Farm on the Great Plains" jolts me with a succession of regrets about it, but these regrets link with reassurances as I confront and accept something of my portion in writing: an appearance of moral commitment mixed with a deliberate—even a flaunted—nonsophistication; an organized form cavalierly treated; a trace of narrative for company amid too many feelings. There are emergences of consciousness in the poem, and some outlandish lunges for communication; but I can stand quite a bit of this sort of thing if a total poem gives evidence of locating itself.
>
> And the *things* here—plains, farm, home, winter, lavished all over the page—these command my allegiance in a way that is beyond my power to analyze at the moment. Might I hazard that they signal something like austere hope? At any rate, they possess me. I continue to be a willing participant in the feelings and contradictions that led me to write the poem.

Wallace Stevens, THE EMPEROR OF ICE-CREAM, page 514

Choosing this poem to represent him in an anthology, Stevens once remarked, "This wears a deliberately commonplace costume, and yet seems to me to contain something of the essential gaudiness of poetry; that is the reason why I like it." (His statement appears in *Fifty Poets: An American Auto-Anthology*, ed. William Rose Benet [New York: Diffield, 1933].)

Some students will at once relish the poet's humor; others may discover it in class discussion. Try to gather the literal facts of the situation before getting into the poem's suggestions. The wake or funeral of a poor old woman is taking place in her home. The funeral flowers come in old newspapers, not in florists' fancy wrappings; the mourners don't dress up, but wear their usual street clothes; the refreshments aren't catered but are whipped up in the kitchen by a neighbor, a cigar-roller. Like ice cream, the refreshments are a dairy product. Nowadays it would probably be a sour cream chip-dip; perhaps in 1923 they were blocks of Philadelphia cream cheese squashed into cups for spreading on soda crackers. To a correspondent, Stevens wrote that *fantails* refers not to fans but to fantail pigeons (*Letters* [New York: Knopf, 1966] 341). Such embroidery seems a low-brow pursuit: the poor old woman's pathetic aspiration toward beauty. *Deal* furniture is cheap. Everything points to a run-down neighborhood, and to a woman about whose passing nobody very much cares.

Who is the Emperor? The usual guess is Death. Some students will probably see that the Emperor and the muscular cigar-roller (with his creamy curds) suggest each other. (Stevens does not say that they are identical.) Ice cream suggests the chill of the grave—and what besides? Today some of its connotations will be commonplace: supermarkets, Baskin-Robbins. To the generation of Stevens, ice cream must have meant more: something luxurious and scarce, costly, hard-to-keep, requiring quick consumption. Other present-day connotations may come to mind: sweetness, deliciousness, childhood pleasure. Stevens's personal view of the icecream in the poem was positive. "The true sense of 'Let be be finale of seem' is let being become the conclusion or denouement of appearing to be: in short, ice cream is an absolute good" (*Letters* 341). An absolute good! The statement is worth quoting to students who have doubts about the poet's attitude toward ice cream—as did an executive of the Amalgamated Ice Cream Association, who once wrote to the poet in perplexity (see *Letters* 501–2). If ice cream recalls sweet death, still (like curds) it also contains hints of mother's milk, life, and vitality.

On a visit to Mount Holyoke, XJK was told that, as part of an annual celebration, it is customary for the trustees and the seniors to serve ice cream (in Dixie cups) to the freshman class at the grave of Mary Lyon, founder of the college. In a flash he remembered Stevens's poem and embraced Jung's theory of archetypes.

MyLiteratureLab Resources. Biography, critical overview, and bibliography for Stevens.

Jonathan Swift, A DESCRIPTION OF THE MORNING, page 515

This slice of eighteenth-century London life seems replete with human failings: Betty (a conventional name for a servant) sleeping with her master and trying to hide the evidence, prisoners released from jail in order to steal. Swift's couplets describe not the highborn but the common people, for whom a hackney coach heralded dawn in place of mythology's grander chariot driven across the sky by Phoebus Apollo. Although Swift crams his lines with images of city dirt and human corruption, the humor of his poem implies considerable affection for London's streets and sinners. If students see no humor in his view, let them compare this poem with another poem about eighteenth-century streets, Blake's angry "London," or a rhapsodic, Romantic description of a London morning, Wordsworth's "Composed upon Westminster Bridge."

Larissa Szporluk, VERTIGO, page 516

In 2001, Larissa Szporluk told an interviewer: "I want readers to feel I am opening something from the unknown. I want my poems to show the uncertainty that lies in where I'm going and what I'm seeing." Her work has been described as "hypnotic" and "incantatory," and reading "Vertigo" aloud will help to demonstrate why. The poem is divided into two sentences: the first one is two words long; the second, twenty-seven lines. From the second line on, we are carried dizzily forward by the swirl of images as our footing is undermined by the systematic denial of certainties—*maybe* in lines 6, 9, and 10; "and the stars that you think / . . . / there should be / aren't even stars / . . . / and don't serve as guides" (lines 13, 15–16, 19); "they don't know who you are" (line 23). The effect is heightened by sound patterns of assonance and internal rime: from the summit of *high*, *tiny*, *mite*, *light*, *find*, and *height* in the first half of the poem, to the swoop of *don't*, *below*, *know*, *droves*, and *fold* as it rushes toward its seemingly inevitable (but still open-ended) conclusion.

Sara Teasdale, THE FLIGHT, page 517

Just as romantic love was Sara Teasdale's great theme, the concept of flight was clearly one of great significance to her in the working out of this theme, since she published no fewer than three poems titled "The Flight." Our text of that title appeared in her 1926 collection, *Dark of the Moon*. In this poem, Teasdale's eagles never seem to be entirely real birds of prey: a metaphor in the first stanza, a simile in the second, they are purely symbolic from the opening lines, representing the adventurous love and passionate union of two people. Their spirits are so closely united that the speaker wishes that when one of them dies, the other will follow, a highly romantic aspiration that strongly contrasts with the behavior of eagles—as well as, for that matter, the behavior of most human beings.

Alfred, Lord Tennyson, DARK HOUSE, BY WHICH ONCE MORE I STAND, page 517

In Memoriam, section 7. "This is great poetry," wrote T. S. Eliot, "economical of words, a universal emotion related to a particular place; and it gives me the shudder that I fail to get from anything in *Maud*" (Introduction to *Poems of Tennyson* [London: Nelson, 1936]). The dark house was indeed a particular place—"67, Wimpole Street," as Tennyson noted—the house of Henry Hallam. The poem contains at least two allusions, whether or not we are expected to pick them up: "And then it started, like a guilty thing" (Horatio describing the ghost in *Hamlet*, I, i, 148); and "He is not here, but is risen" (Luke 24:6). In line 11 of one manuscript version, Tennyson wrote *dripping* instead of *drizzling*. Why is *drizzling* superior? The highest moment in the poem occurs in the last line in the two spondees, at least equal in their effect to Yeats's "And the *white breast* of the *dim sea*" ("Who Goes with Fergus?").

For some of these notes we are indebted to Christopher Ricks's matchless edition of *The Poems of Tennyson* (New York: Norton, 1969).

MyLiteratureLab Resources. Biography, critical overview, and bibliography for Tennyson.

Alfred, Lord Tennyson, ULYSSES, page 518

The following inadequate précis, meant to make lovers of Tennyson's poem irate, might be quoted to students to see whether they agree with it: A hardy old futzer can't stand life in the old folks' home and calls on his cronies to join him in an escape, even though the whole lot of them are going to break their necks.

For criticism, see Paul F. Baum, *Tennyson Sixty Years After* (Chapel Hill: U of North Carolina P, 1948) 92–94; and John Pettigrew, "Tennyson's 'Ulysses': A Reconciliation of Opposites," *Victorian Poetry* 1 (Jan. 1963): 27–45.

MLL *MyLiteratureLab Resources.* Biography, critical overview, and bibliography for Tennyson.

Dylan Thomas, FERN HILL, page 520

Fern Hill is the farm of Thomas's aunt, Ann Jones, with whom he spent boyhood holidays. In line 2 the poet cites a favorite saying of his father's, "Happy as the grass is green." The saying is echoed again in line 38. As students may notice, Thomas likes to play upon familiar phrases and transform them, as in line 7, "once *below* [not *upon*] a time."

It came as a great shock when we first realized that this poem, which XJK had thought a quite spontaneous burst of lyric energy, is shaped into a silhouette, and that the poet contrived its form by counting syllables. Such laborious working methods were customary for Thomas. John Malcolm Brinnin has recalled seeing more than 200 separate and distinct versions of "Fern Hill"—a fact worth conveying to students who think poets simply overflow.

We take the closing line to express Thomas's view of his own poetry, lyrical and rule-bound at the same time: a song uttered in chains. Of course, the last line also means that the boy in the poem was held in chains by Time, the villain, who informs the whole poem (except for stanzas 3 and 4, which see childhood as Eden). Students may be asked to trace all the mentions of Time throughout the poem, then to sum up the poet's theme. William York Tindall, who offers a line-by-line commentary, makes a fine distinction: "Not how it feels to be young, the theme of 'Fern Hill' is how it feels to have been young" (*A Reader's Guide to Dylan Thomas* [New York: Noonday, 1962]). And we'd add, "how it would have felt to grow old, if the boy had realized he wouldn't live forever."

According to Tindall (in a lecture), Thomas used to grow huffy whenever asked if he were an admirer of Gerard Manley Hopkins. Still, to hear aloud both "Fern Hill" and Hopkins's "Pied Beauty" is to notice much similarity of sound and imagery. Hopkins studied Welsh for a time, while Thomas never did learn the language; but both at least knew of ancient Welsh poetry and its ingeniously woven sound patterns.

Thomas's magnificent (or, some would say, magnificently hammy) reading of this poem can be heard on Caedmon recording TC 1002, cassette 51002, compact disk Z1002. The recording, *A Child's Christmas in Wales and Other Poems*, also contains "Do not go gentle into that good night."

John Updike, Ex-Basketball Player, page 521

Updike's ex-basketball player suffers the fate that Housman's athlete escapes by dying young. Flick Webb has to live on, unsung, in "fields where glory does not stay." The man whose "hands were like wild birds" now uses those hands to pump gas, check oil, and change flat tires. "Once in a while, / As a gag, he dribbles an inner tube." In his spare time, he sits in Mae's luncheonette and "just nods / Beyond her face toward bright applauding tiers / Of Necco Wafers, Nibs, and Juju Beads." (Are today's students familiar with those brand names?)

Updike's light tone does not obscure the pathos of Flick's situation. (Students might be asked if they know anyone like Flick Webb.) Though Updike has written notable light verse, he says of this early poem, his second to be accepted by the *New Yorker*, that it "is 'serious' and has enjoyed a healthy anthology life, though its second stanza now reads strangely to students. . . . That is, they have never seen glass-headed pumps, or gas stations with a medley of brands of gasoline, or the word *Esso*" (foreword to a new edition of Updike's first book, *The Carpentered Hen* [New York: Knopf, 1982]).

See how quickly your class can identify the poem's form as blank verse.

MyLiteratureLab Resources. Biography, photos, critical overview, and bibliography for Updike.

Derek Walcott, The Virgins, page 522

Walcott provides an ironic view of the main seaport of the Virgin Islands. The irony begins with the title, in which the islands seem waiting to be raped or seduced by outsiders. The sun is like a drug ("sun-stoned"), and the term *free port* is used sarcastically to underscore how little of any worth freedom has brought this city. The dense images and careful rhetoric of the poem create the impression of a dead place where no genuine life is possible.

Edmund Waller, Go, Lovely Rose, page 523

In some ways quieter than Marvell's "To His Coy Mistress" or Herrick's "To the Virgins, to Make Much of Time," this poem has the same theme: *carpe diem*. "Go, Lovely Rose" merits admiration for its seemingly effortless grace and for the sudden, gently shocking focus on our mortality in the poem's final stanza.

Students may enjoy reading Ezra Pound's imitative tribute to Waller: the "Envoi" to *Hugh Selwyn Mauberley*, beginning "Go, dumb-born book . . . ," in *Personae*, Pound's collected shorter poems (New York: New Directions, 1949).

Walt Whitman, from Song of the Open Road, page 524

This is the fifteenth and concluding section of a poem that first appeared (as "Poem of the Road") in the second edition of *Leaves of Grass*. It was retitled for the 1867 edition and thereafter underwent only slight revision, mainly the elimination of a few lines. Thus it belongs to the early part of Whitman's mature career, and it reflects the themes of universal oneness and transcendental optimism that characterize that phase of his work.

In his freewheeling and quirky but often shrewdly insightful *Studies in Classic American Literature* (1923), the great British novelist D. H. Lawrence observes:

> This is Whitman's message of American democracy.
>
> The true democracy, where soul meets soul, in the open road. Democracy. American democracy where all journey down the open road, and where a soul is known at once in its going. Not by its clothes or appearance. . . . Not by its family name. Not even by its reputation. . . . Not by a progression of piety, or by works of Charity. Not by works at all. Not by anything, but just itself. . . .
>
> The love of man and woman: a recognition of souls, and a communion of worship. The love of comrades: a recognition of souls, and a communion of worship. Democracy: a recognition of souls, all down the open road, and a great soul seen in its greatness, as it travels on foot among the rest, down the common way of the living. A glad recognition of souls, and a gladder worship of great and greater souls, because they are the only riches. . . .
>
> The only riches, the great souls.

MyLiteratureLab Resources. Biography, critical overview, and bibliography for Whitman.

Walt Whitman, I HEAR AMERICA SINGING, page 525

In "I Hear America Singing," the twentieth of twenty-one "Inscriptions" with which he began the third edition of his *Leaves of Grass*, Walt Whitman presents a vision of America in which people of varied trades and walks of life each sing his or her own individual song ("what belongs to him or her and to none else"), and these individual songs somehow blend to form a harmonious whole, reflective of Whitman's vision of, and for, America itself. Whitman biographer David S. Reynolds observes that this "picture . . . was more than just a metaphor. It reflected a pre-mass-media culture in which Americans often entertained themselves and each other" (*Walt Whitman's America: A Cultural Biography*, [New York: Knopf, 1995]).

Even if the image is grounded in fact, we cannot help but wonder how realistic a depiction it was of Whitman's society, as opposed to an idealistic vision of what America could and, Whitman no doubt hoped, would be. "I Hear America Singing" was first published, after all, in 1860, the year before the beginning of the Civil War, hardly the most harmonious moment in American history. And it may also be worth pointing out that it was the title piece of a British selection of Whitman's most idealistic and affirmative verses about American society that was rushed into print in the wake of the terrorist attacks of September 11, 2001 (*I Hear America Singing: Poems of Democracy, Manhattan, and the Future* [London: Anvil, 2001]).

MyLiteratureLab Resources. Biography, critical overview, and bibliography for Whitman.

Richard Wilbur, The Writer, page 525

A searching criticism of Wilbur's work, and this poem, is offered by Andrew Hudgins (*Hudson Review,* Winter 1989). Sometimes Wilbur implies that it is possible to master the world and its complicated problems in much the same way that a poet, in a successful poem, masters the language—but it isn't, of course. Wilbur thus places himself in a dilemma, one he is aware of. Hudgins summarizes "The Writer" and interprets it:

> Hearing his daughter as she types a story in her room, he compares the house to a ship and the sound of the typewriter keys to "a chain hauled over a gunwale," while the "stuff" of his daughter's life is "a great cargo and some of it heavy." Then, rather glibly, he wishes her a "lucky passage." As soon as he's completed the metaphor, however, he rejects the "easy figure" because he remembers how difficult the life of a writer can be. The next metaphor he advances is embedded in the anecdote of a "dazed starling" that once became trapped in the same room his daughter is now working in. . . . Though the poem is touching and even powerful, the implied final metaphor, and the ending of the poem, while infinitely better than the rejected first metaphor of the ship, still have a bit of its premeditated neatness about them.

Whether or not the poem is autobiographical, Wilbur does have a daughter, Ellen Wilbur, a widely published fiction writer and the author of *Wind and Birds and Human Voices,* a collection of short stories (Stuart Wright, 1984: NAL paperback, 1985).

MyLiteratureLab Resources. Critical essay by Wilbur, "Cold War Poetry."

C. K. *Williams,* Elms, page 526

There is perhaps little for the instructor to add for students to achieve an understanding of "Elms." The poem's basic situation is clear, and it is described clearly, in a focused presentation that avoids all distractions. Modifiers constantly supply us with the qualities we are to associate with the various components of the poem: "stricken elms," "pitiless electric chain saws," "diesel choppers . . . shredding . . . feverishly, incessantly," and so on. In line 5 we are told overtly that "it is as though illusions of reality were stripped," and in the last line, in "the unhealing evening" the refrain of "'Insolent, unconscionable, the winds of time. . . .'"

With little or nothing to interpret in the face of such direct communication, you might ask your students how well they relate to the presentation. Does the poem describe something that they themselves have witnessed at one time or another? If so, does the description seem apt? And, ultimately, do they agree that the sentiments with which the author has invested the situation are appropriate and are supported by his description?

William Carlos Williams, SPRING AND ALL, page 527

QUESTIONS FOR DISCUSSION

1. *Why cannot Williams's attitude toward spring be called "poetic" and "conventional"? What is his attitude toward the approaching season? By what means is it indicated? Consider especially lines 14–15 and 24–25, and the suggestion of* contagious *in the opening line*. Spring is stealing over the land as a contagious disease infects a victim. But spring is not a disease: it has a "stark dignity."

2. *An opinion: "This poem clearly draws from the poet's experience as a pediatrician who had attended hundreds of newborns, and whose work was often to describe with clinical exactness the symptoms of his patients." Discuss*. Lines 16–18 especially seem to contain a metaphor of newborn infants. The adjectives *mottled, dried, sluggish* could occur in a physician's report. In lines 9–13 also, the description of bushes, trees, and vines seems painstakingly exact in its detail.

Recalling his life as writer and physician in an article for a popular magazine, Williams once told how poems would come to him while driving on his daily rounds. "When the phrasing of a passage suddenly hits me, knowing how quickly such things are lost, I find myself at the side of the road frantically searching in my medical bag for a prescription blank" ("Seventy Years Deep," *Holiday* [Nov. 1954]: 78). "By the road to the contagious hospital" was one such poem, originally recorded on prescription blanks (Roy Miki, "Driving and Writing," *William Carlos Williams: Man and Poet*, ed. Carroll F. Terrell [Orono: National Poetry Foundation, 1983] 113).

Scholars have speculated that the brief lines of many of Williams's poems may have been decreed by the narrow width of a prescription blank, but we don't buy that guess. Had he wanted longer lines Williams would have turned the blanks sideways or composed in smaller handwriting.

MyLiteratureLab Resources. Biography, critical overview, and bibliography for Williams.

William Carlos Williams, TO WAKEN AN OLD LADY, page 528

QUESTIONS FOR DISCUSSION

1. *By which words or phrases does Williams suggest the physical ravages of old age? What very different connotations do the phrases* broken / seedhusks *and* shrill / piping *carry, as well as the suggestions of feeble and broken senility?* Broken husks suggest a feast, piping suggests merriment.

2. *What is the* dark wind? *Can a wind be literally dark?* No, it can't; Williams means dark in the sense of sinister or menacing. This wind is like the passage of time that buffets or punishes.

3. *What is the dictionary definition of* tempered? *What does the word mean in this poem?*

 *MyLiteratureLab Resources*. Biography, critical overview, and bibliography for Williams.

William Wordsworth, Composed upon Westminster Bridge, page 529

Imaginary conversation:

Instructor: What do you make of the title? Is this a poem composed upon the subject of a bridge, or a poem composed while standing on a bridge's sidewalk?
Student: The latter, obviously.
Instructor: How do you know?
Student: His eye is located up on the bridge. Otherwise he wouldn't see with such a wide-angle lens.
Instructor: You genius! To the head of the class!

Whose is the "mighty heart"? Wordsworth is describing the city as a sleeping beauty about to awaken. Of course, the brightness of the scene is increased by the poet's being out for his stroll before a hundred thousand chimneys have begun to smoke from coal fires preparing kippers for breakfast. Charles Lamb, in a letter to Wordsworth, had chided the poet that the urban emotions must be unknown to him, so perhaps this famous sonnet is an answer to the charge.

Compare "The World Is Too Much with Us" for a different Wordsworth attitude toward commerce; or compare Wordsworth's London of 1807 with Blake's "London" of 1794—practically the same city, but seen from a different perspective. (Wordsworth up on the bridge at dawn, letting distance lend enchantment; Blake down in the city streets by night, with the chimney sweep, the teenage whore, and the maimed veteran.)

 *MyLiteratureLab Resources*. Biography, critical overview, and bibliography for Wordsworth. Audio clip for "Composed upon Westminster Bridge."

James Wright, A Blessing, page 530

At first, students are likely to regard "A Blessing" as "a delicate poem about the kinship between men and horses," as Ralph J. Mills sees it (*Contemporary American Poetry* [New York: Random, 1965]). They will be right, of course; but to take them a step further, they can be asked what *blessing* the poem refers to, and to ponder especially its last three lines. In a sense, the image of stepping over barbed wire into an open pasture (line 7) anticipates the idea of stepping out of one's body into—what? Any paraphrase is going to be clumsy; but Wright hints at nothing less than the loneliness of every creature alive. Although they are together, the two ponies are lonely to an extreme and are apparently overjoyed to see people. By implication, maybe the speaker and his friend are lonely together as well. In lines 15–21 the speaker, to his astonishment, finds himself falling in love with one of the ponies; he sees her beauty as that of a girl. At this point, we might expect him to recoil and cry, "Good grief! what's the matter with me?"—but he persists and becomes enlightened, at least for a moment. Only his physical body, he realizes, keeps him alone and separated. What if he were to shed it? He'd bloom.

A master of open form, Wright knows how to break off a line at a moment when a pause will throw weight upon sense: "Suddenly I realize / That if I stepped out of my body I would break / Into blossom."

Maybe the best way to teach "A Blessing" is just to read it aloud and then say nothing at all.

James Wright, AUTUMN BEGINS IN MARTINS FERRY, OHIO, page 530

Martins Ferry was Wright's home town. The speaker of the poem describes the men of Martins Ferry sitting in the high school stadium, the only place in the vicinity where heroes are likely to appear. Certainly these working-class men have given up dreams of heroism in their own lives. Grey-faced, ruptured, worn out by their jobs in heavy industry, they sit in taverns over their beer, "ashamed to go home" to their wives. Unable even to satisfy the romantic or sexual longings of their wives, who are "dying for love," these men turn to their sons for inspiration. In October, as the year begins to die, they watch the heroic spectacle of their sons' football games. While there is something gloriously primal about Wright's scene, there is also something darkly ironic. Will the sons of Martins Ferry achieve true heroism on the gridiron? Or will they just bang up their knees and dislocate their shoulders for a season or two before they go on to equally unheroic adult lives? The poem masterfully has it both ways—both heroic and doomed.

Perhaps the fathers were once football heroes themselves, as George S. Lensing and Ronald Moran point out in *Four Poets and the Emotive Imagination* (Baton Rouge: Louisiana State UP, 1976), a study that discusses nearly the whole of Wright's work. "From this there is the suggestion that the futures of the current community heroes may be as bleak as the present time assuredly is for the fathers."

Did Wright mean to protest the violence of football—at least, football of the Martins Ferry kind? Not according to the poet himself, who once played on an Ohio River Valley semipro team. Although the high school games were "ritualized, formalized violence," they had positive qualities: "the expression of physical grace," "terrific aesthetic appeal." Wright's own high school produced not just lads doomed to frustration (like their fathers), but at least one football hero—Lou Groza, placekicker for the Cleveland Browns. (Wright made his remarks in an interview reprinted in *The Pure Clear Word: Essays on the Poetry of James Wright*, ed. Dave Smith [Urbana: U of Illinois P, 1982] 3–4.)

In the same critical anthology, Robert Hass sees football in the poem as a harvest ritual, which, like all good harvest rituals, celebrates sexual potency and the fruitfulness of the earth (two positive qualities apparently not conspicuous in Martins Ferry). "Even the stanzaic structure of the poem participates in the ritual. The first two stanzas separate the bodies of the men from the bodies of the women, and the third stanza gives us the boys pounding against each other, as if they could, out of their wills, effect a merging" (210).

Jan Hodge, of Morningside College in Sioux City, Iowa, wrote us a long letter full of insights about this poem. (We have incorporated a few of his remarks into our comments above.) He ends his reading of the poem with some especially interesting observations:

> Isn't the third stanza (introduced by that powerful placement of "Therefore" on a line by itself) the logical culmination of the first *two* stanzas—the point being that it is because of *both* the larger community's need for heroes *and* their fathers' need to find (vicarious) pride in them that the sons give themselves so suicidally (and so beautifully?) to football? The speaker understands the harshness of the lives around him and why therefore football becomes so important. He is also I think compassionate, but refuses to sentimentalize either the game or the failures he sees so accurately. I find Wright's use of the two oxymorons—"suicidally beautiful" and "gallop terribly"—particularly effective to express his ambiguous attitude toward football, the sons, the fathers, and the workers. If there is violence, there is also a kind of grace in their sacrifice—all the more poignant because (as you and others have pointed out) it is almost certainly futile.
>
> "Does Wright mean to protest the violence of football?" you ask. A majority of my students argue so—but less I think because of the poem than because they think (wrongly) I am opposed to football and assign the poem for that reason. I end up in discussion defending the poem against their second-guessing of it. I had assumed for years that such a protest was not Wright's intent; your notes confirm my view.

Finally, some comments by poet William Virgil Davis of Baylor University, who considers "Autumn Begins in Martins Ferry" to be the key poem in Wright's work. In an article on "James Wright's *Cogito*" in *Notes on Contemporary Literature* (Jan. 1993), Davis describes the structure of the poem:

> The poem follows the pattern of a logical argument, the three stanzas paralleling the arrangement of a syllogism. Indeed, the first stanza asserts, "I think it" (l. 2), and the third begins, "Therefore" (l. 9). The two "terms" of the argument are defined at the conclusions of stanzas one and two in the parallel phrases, "Dreaming of heroes" (l. 5) and "Dying for love" (l. 8). These are respectively associated with men (fathers) and women (mothers), and the results of these kinds of "deaths" create situations in which the "sons" of such parents "grow suicidally beautiful / At the beginning of October, / And gallop terribly against each other's bodies" (ll. 10–12). This conclusion, following the "Therefore" of line 9, is more than the "*sum*" of Descartes's principle, but, like it, it defines a being born of the realization of a logical argument: what one is is what he believes and feels, based upon his past experiences and his personal history. Still, the "essence," although born of "existence," exceeds it. This is, then, beauty born out of the death of self for the sake of self-realization.
>
> Therefore, what the poem "means" is what the speaker reads or feels at the end of it; and, even if the argument is invalid, it is true.

Mary Sidney Wroth, IN THIS STRANGE LABYRINTH, page 531

Feminist scholarship has uncovered many unjustly neglected works by women, but surely Mary Sidney Wroth must rank among the most interesting—and most overdue—additions to the canon. The niece of Sir Philip Sidney and Lady Mary Herbert, the Countess of Pembroke, Mary Sidney grew up in a talented and cultivated family. An arranged marriage to Sir Robert Wroth, however, proved unhappy during his lifetime and financially precarious after his death.

Wroth's sonnets were added to her prose romance *Urania* (1621), which she boldly published under her own name. Titled *Pamphilia to Amphilanthus*, the poems (which constitute the first sonnet sequence by an Englishwoman) speak in the voices of the prose romance's two main characters, but the poems also reflect her personal experience after her husband's death, especially her romantic liaison with her married cousin, the Earl of Pembroke, by whom she had two children.

"In this strange labyrinth" employs the image of the labyrinth as a symbol for erotic confusion. Each direction the speaker contemplates taking poses some danger or disappointment. This conceit is developed for thirteen lines until a detail from the myth—Ariadne's thread—is introduced in the final line. As Ariadne's thread guided her lover through the dangers of the labyrinth, so will "the thread of love" guide the speaker.

Sir Thomas Wyatt, THEY FLEE FROM ME THAT SOMETIME DID ME SEKË, page 532

Surely Wyatt knew what he was about. Sounding the final *e*'s helps to fulfill the expectations of iambic pentameter in lines 2, 12, 15, 17, 20, and 21, lines that otherwise would seem to fall short. In other lines, however, Wyatt appears to make the rhythm deliberately swift or hesitant in order to fit the sense. Line 7 ("Busily seeking with a continual change") seems busy with extra syllables and has to be read quickly to fit the time allotted it. Such a metrical feast seems worthy of Yeats, as does line 11, in which two spondees ("loose gown," "did fall") cast great stress upon that suddenly falling garment.

What line in English love poetry, by the way, is more engaging than "Dear heart, how like you this?" And when have a lover's extended arms ever been more nicely depicted? (This line may be thrown into the teeth of anyone who thinks that, in descriptive writing, adjectives are bad things.)

William Butler Yeats, CRAZY JANE TALKS WITH THE BISHOP, page 533

Piecing together a history from this Crazy Jane poem and others, John Unterecker has identified the Bishop as a divinity student who had courted Jane in his youth. She rejected him in favor of a wild, disreputable lover: Jack the journeyman. As soon as he got enough authority, the Bishop-to-be had Jack banished, but Jane has remained faithful to her lover (at least in spirit). (See *A Reader's Guide to William Butler Yeats* [New York: Noonday, 1959].) In this poem, the Bishop's former interest in Jane has dwindled to a concern for her soul alone.

Or has it? Perhaps the Bishop, no doubt a handsome figure in his surplice, may be demonstrating Yeats's contention that fair needs foul. Jane is living in lonely squalor. The grave, she says, can affirm the truth that her friends are gone, for it holds many of them; and her own empty bed can affirm that Jack is gone, too. Still, she firmly renounces the Bishop and his advice.

Each word of the poem is exact. Love has *pitched* his mansion as one would pitch a tent. The next-to-last line ends in two immense puns: *sole or whole*. The Bishop thinks that soul is all that counts, but Jane knows that both soul and hole are needed. Such puns may be why Yeats declared (in a letter) that he wanted to stop writing the Crazy Jane series: "I want to exorcise that slut, Crazy Jane, whose language has become unendurable."

What does Yeats mean by the paradoxical statement in the last two lines? Perhaps (1) that a woman cannot be fulfilled and remain a virgin—that, since fair and foul are near of kin, one cannot know Love, the platonic ideal, without going through the door of the physical body; and (2) that the universe is by nature a yin/yang combination of fair and foul (or, as Yeats would have it in *A Vision*, a pair of intertwining gyres). Crazy Jane may be crazy, but in Yeats's view she is a soothsayer.

MyLiteratureLab Resources. Biography, critical overview, and bibliography for Yeats.

William Butler Yeats, THE MAGI, page 534

After writing a lesser poem than this—"The Dolls," in which dolls hurl resentment at a "noisy and filthy thing," a human baby—Yeats had a better idea. "I looked up one day into the blue of the sky, and suddenly imagined, as if lost in the blue of the sky, stiff figures in procession" (Yeats's note at the back of his *Collected Poems*). Like dolls, the Magi seem frozen, somewhat inhuman ("rain-beaten stones"), unfulfilled. They are apparently troubled that Christ, whose birth was a miracle, died as a man. In hopes of regaining the peace of the Nativity, they pursue a second journey.

Bestial will seem to students an odd word to apply to a stable floor, unless they catch its literal sense: "belonging to beasts." But they will also need to see that its connotations of brutality fit the poem and interact with *Calvary's turbulence*. Compare "The Magi" with the rough beast in "The Second Coming," a poem written after Yeats had more fully worked out his notion that historical events move in a cycle of endless return. ("Leda and the Swan" can be brought in, too, if there is time for it.)

If comparing Yeats's unsatisfied wise men to Eliot's in "Journey of the Magi," good questions to ask include, Which poet writes as a Christian? How can you tell?

MyLiteratureLab Resources. Biography, critical overview, and bibliography for Yeats.

William Butler Yeats, WHEN YOU ARE OLD, page 534

Yeats wrote this poem to the actress Maud Gonne in October 1891. It is based very loosely on Ronsard's sonnet "Quand Vous Serez Bien Vielle," but it is not a translation. Yeats merely took Ronsard's premise (an old woman rereading the verses a poet wrote to her in their youth) and developed it in his own way.

In this gentlest of love poems, the speaker is resigned to not winning the woman he loves. He is merely one of many men who love her. His claim, however, is that his love was not for the surface charms of her grace or beauty; he alone loved her for her searching soul. And he has the satisfaction of being able to preserve the unique quality of his devotion in words. Yeats's lyric, therefore, celebrates the ennobling power of both love and poetry.

To be candidly emotional risks seeming sentimental, but as we approach the end of the notes to the "Poems for Further Reading," we hope that many years from now a few of our students will take down this book to reread a few of the poems we taught them and realize that we spoke to "the pilgrim soul" in them.

MLL *MyLiteratureLab Resources.* Biography, critical overview, and bibliography for Yeats.

Bernice Zamora, PENITENTS, page 535

Bernice Zamora was born and raised in Colorado. Though she came from a Spanish-speaking family, she was given an education that stressed assimilation into the mainstream American culture—a process which, as an adult, she came to resent. *Restless Serpents* (1976), her first—and for a long time, only—volume of poetry, has had a great deal of influence, especially in the Chicano community, and has been praised for the power and fierceness of its writing and for its uncompromising confrontation of the world's injustices.

"Penitents" describes a secret ritual that seeks to replicate the passion and suffering of Christ, in order that its enacters may mortify their flesh, achieve humility of spirit, and come to a deeper understanding of the magnitude of Christ's sacrifice on behalf of their souls. Class discussion of this poem might provoke a lively response: it should prove interesting to sample the students' reactions to the values and the behavior of the *penitentes*, and interesting as well to gauge their sense of Zamora's own attitude toward the material. Despite the seemingly clear statements of the poem's last five lines, critic Juan Bruce-Novoa has written of Zamora's "alienation from the male rituals in 'Penitents.'" Is this, do you think, a view imposed on the text from his wider reading in Zamora's work, or can it be discovered and defended through a careful, objective reading of the poem itself?

22
Lives of the Poets

Instead of being strewn throughout the poetry section, biographical notes on the poets are collected in this chapter. The intent is to make them easy to find and to keep them from interrupting the poetry. Biographies are supplied for poets represented by two or more poems.

Envoi

Let us end this section with another poem about teaching poetry—one by Paul Lake, a professor at Arkansas Technical University in Russellville. Lake's "Introduction to Poetry" appears in his collection *Another Kind of Travel* (Chicago: U of Chicago P, 1988).

Introduction to Poetry

She comes in late, then settles like a sigh
On the first day, returning every week
Promptly at ten, each Monday Wednesday Friday,
To study Shakespeare, Jonson, Donne, and Blake;

Enters the room to an approving murmur,
Straightens her dress, then, brushing back her hair,
Arches her body with the slightest tremor,
And sits, while the room grows breathless, in her chair;

Sits for an hour, while busy sophomores worry
Each turgid line, a Botticellian smile
On her rapt face, who's learned how little study
Love involves; who, walking down the aisle,

Knows in her bones how little poetry
Words breathe, and how—on turning to go home—
All eyes will watch her rise above her "C"
And walk off, like a goddess on the foam.

WRITING

23
Writing About Literature

This chapter is a brief guide to informal and formal writing about literature, with emphasis on writing short critical essays. As succinctly as we can, we escort the student through the various procedures of reading and thinking about a poem; doing some pre-writing exercises to discover writing ideas; finding a topic, developing a literary argument; and organizing, drafting, revising, correctly formatting, and finishing a paper. (In the chapter "Writing a Research Paper," we present material appropriate to gathering information and writing and documenting a long, well-researched critical essay.)

If these writing chapters fulfill their purpose, they will save you some breath and spare you from reading many innocent (and perhaps not-so-innocent) plagiarisms, floating unidentified quotations (of the kind that suddenly interrupt the student's prose with Harold Bloom's prose in quotation marks), and displays of ill-fitting critical terminology.

Preparing to Write: Discovering Ideas

The section "Preparing to Write" quickly covers a number of tried-and-true pre-writing exercises and provides a student example of each, using Frost's "Nothing Gold Can Stay" as a text. You may also wish to dedicate some class time to invention exercises that help students generate topics. Asking and answering questions is always an excellent way to generate material for an essay. Questions and answers can help students clarify their views on a subject, identify patterns, and make connections. You might develop some questions on different elements of a text: plot, theme, point of view, style, setting, character. Students can work in small groups on one element and then come together as a whole class to discuss their "findings" and brainstorm to generate specific topics. Individually, students can then generate a working thesis.

Anonymous, A Little Poem Regarding Computer Spell Checkers, page 587

This poem, which was first shown to us by Cara Nusinov, of Miami, Florida, is a poem that has long circulated on the Internet. The poem reprinted in our book seems to be based on a longer piece of light verse by Jerrold H. Zar, who is the Associate Provost for Graduate Studies of Northern Illinois University. His original poem was titled "Candidate for a Pullet Surprise" (note the pun) and was first published in the *Journal of Irreproducible Results* (39.1, Jan./Feb. 1994). The Internet seems to have worked rather like the old oral tradition in compressing and modifying his text into a new collective and anonymous version, but Professor Zar deserves proper credit for its early version.

Once—at the end of a class in which argument had waxed over the question "Is 'Naming of Parts' an antiwar poem or isn't it?"—XJK made the mistake of cutting off the discussion and telling students to go home and write their opinions down on paper. The result was to cool future class discussions: students were afraid that if they talked animatedly, they would be told to write. A different approach is that of an instructor who would halt a class discussion that had grown driveling, or bad-tempered, or without heart, and cry, "For God's sake, let's all stop talking! Now get out your pencils and write me a paragraph. . . . " He claimed that in the next class the discussion improved markedly.

24
Writing About a Poem

Here are notes on the two poems contained in "Writing About a Poem."

Robert Frost, DESIGN, page 590

If you wish to deal with this section in class, you might have students read "Design," the two student papers that follow the poem, and Randall Jarrell's explication. What did these writers notice about the poem that you didn't notice? What did you notice about it that they left out?

Besides Jarrell's classic explication, many other good discussions of the poem can be consulted. Elizabeth Drew has a succinct explication in *Poetry: A Modern Guide to Its Understanding and Enjoyment* (New York: Norton, 1959), and there is a more detailed reading by Richard Ohmann in *College English* 28 (Feb. 1967): 359–67.

Also of interest is Frost's early draft of this poem, titled "In White," and found on page 612 of the text. What is the theme of each version? Is it more difficult to tell from the vaguer, more general draft? In rewriting, Frost seems to have made his details more specific and also to have defined the central idea.

My *Literature Lab Resources*. Biography, critical overview, critical articles, and bibliography for Frost.

Abbie Huston Evans, WING-SPREAD, page 606

The student's evaluation seems just to us. While "Wing-Spread" is not so vivid a cameo as "Design," nor so troubling in its theme, and while it contains trite rimes (except for *beryl/peril*), we think it a decent poem and admirably terse. Insufficiently recognized (like most poets), Evans (1881–1979) had a long, productive life. Her *Collected Poems* was published in 1970 by the University of Pittsburgh Press. There are dozens of poems better than "Wing-Spread" in it.

SUGGESTIONS FOR WRITING

Here are a few more topics for paper assignments to supplement the list at the end of the chapter.

Topics for Brief Papers (250–500 words)

1. A *précis* (French, from Latin: "to cut short") is a short abstract or condensation of a literary work that tries to sum up the work's most essential elements. Although a précis, like a paraphrase, states the poet's thought in the writer's own words, a paraphrase is sometimes as long as the original poem, if not longer. A précis, while it tends to be much briefer than a poem, also takes in essentials: theme, subject, tone, character, events (in a narrative poem), and anything else that strikes the writer as important. A précis might range in length from one ample sentence to a few hundred words (if, say, it were condensing a long play or novel, or a complex longer poem). Here, for instance, is an acceptable précis of Robert Browning's "Soliloquy of the Spanish Cloister":

   > The speaker, a monk in a religious community, voices to himself while gardening the bitter grudge he has against Brother Lawrence, one of his fellow monks. He charges Lawrence with boring him with dull talk at mealtime, sporting monogrammed tableware, ogling women, drinking greedily, ignoring rituals (unlike the speaker, who after a meal lays knife and fork in a cross—which seems overly scrupulous). Having vented his grudge by slyly scissoring Lawrence's favorite flowering shrubs, the speaker is now determined to go further, and plots to work Lawrence's damnation. Perhaps he will lure Lawrence into misinterpreting a text in Scripture, or plant a pornographic volume on him. So far gone is the speaker in his hatred that he is even willing to sell his soul to the devil if the devil will carry off Lawrence's; and so proud is the speaker in his own wiles that he thinks he can cheat the devil in the bargain. Vespers ring, ending the meditation, but his terrible grudge seems sure to go on.

   As the detailed précis makes clear, Browning's poem contains a chronicle of events and a study in character. The précis also indicates the tone of the poem and (another essential) its point of view.

   Students might be supplied with a copy of the above material to guide them and be asked to write précis of four or five poems, chosen from a list the instructor compiles of six or eight poems in the "Poems for Further Reading."

2. Find a poem that you like, one not in this book so it may be unfamiliar to other members of the class. Insert into it a passage of five or six lines that you yourself write in imitation of it. Your object is to lengthen the poem by a bit of forgery that will go undetected. Type out the whole poem afresh, inserted lines and all, and have copies duplicated for the others in the class. Then let them try to tell your forged lines from those of the original. A successful forgery will be hard to detect, since you will have imitated the poet's language, handling of form, and imagery—indeed, the poet's voice.

Topics for More Extensive Papers (600–1,000 words)

1. Relate a personal experience of poetry: a brief history of your attempts to read it or to write it; a memoir of your experience in reading poetry aloud; a report of a poetry reading you attended; an account of how reading a poem

brought a realization that affected you personally (no instructor-pleasing pieties!); or an account of an effort to foist a favorite poem upon your friends, or to introduce young children to poetry. Don't make up any fabulous experiences or lay claim to profound emotions you haven't had; the result could be blatantly artificial ("How I Read Housman's 'Loveliest of trees' and Found the Meaning of Life"). But if you honestly can sum up what you learned from your experience, then do so, by all means.

2. Write an imitation or a parody of any poem in the book. This and the following topic may result in a paper of fewer words than the essay topics, but the amount of work required is likely to be slightly more.

   (Note: This assignment will be too much of a challenge for some students and not all ought to be required to do it. But those who possess the necessary skills may find themselves viewing the poet's work as if they were insiders.) The instructor has to insist that the student observe the minimal formal requirements of a good imitation. A convincing imitation of, say, Thomas Hardy can hardly be written in Whitmanic free verse. Students may be urged to read whole collections of work in order to soak up a better sense of the poet. This assignment asks much but the quality of the results is often surprising. Honestly attempted, such an exercise requires far more effort from students than the writing of most critical essays, and probably teaches them more.

3. After you have read several ballads (both folk ballads and literary ballads), write a ballad of your own, at least twenty lines long. If you need a subject, consider some event recently in the news: an act of bravery, a wedding that took place despite obstacles, a murder or a catastrophe, a report of spooky or mysterious happenings. Then in a prose paragraph, state what you learned from your reading of traditional or literary ballads that proved useful to you as a ballad composer yourself.

Topics for Longer Papers (1,500 words or more)

1. Leslie Fiedler, the critic and novelist, once wrote an essay in which he pretended to be a critic of the last century ("A Review of *Leaves of Grass* and *Hiawatha* as of 1855," *American Poetry Review* 2 [Mar.–Apr. 1973]). Writing as if he subscribed to the tastes of that age, Fiedler declared Whitman's book shaggy and shocking, and awarded Professor Longfellow all the praise. If you can steep yourself in the literature of a former age (or recent past year) deeply enough to feel confident, such an essay might be fun to write (and to read). Write about some poem once fashionable, now forgotten; or about some poem once spurned, now esteemed. Your instructor might have some suggestions.

2. For a month (or some other assigned period of time), keep a personal journal of your reading of poetry and your thinking about it. To give direction to your journal, you might confine it to the work of, say, half a dozen poets who interest you; or you might concentrate on a theme common to a few poems by various poets.

25
Writing a Research Paper

This chapter builds on the information presented in Chapter 23, "Writing About Literature." (As students prepare to embark on a research essay, you might encourage them to review those sections in Chapter 23 that talk about discovering writing ideas, developing a literary argument, defining a thesis, and outlining.) This chapter focuses on the essential aspects of a research paper:

- **Doing Research for an Essay: Using Print, Electronic, and Web Resources**—finding research resources, recording information, analyzing research material.
- **Evaluating and Using Internet Sources**—conducting worthwhile Internet searches, determining reliable resources.
- **Guarding Academic Integrity**—covering both intentional and unintentional plagiarism. Includes the disconcerting issue of plagiarized term papers (note that in the short section "A Warning Against Internet Plagiarism," we detail how professors can now use software and services to identify plagiarized work—our token contribution to your ongoing battle).
- **Acknowledging and Documenting Sources**—acknowledging others' ideas and words, using citations within an essay, preparing a Works Cited list based on MLA standards.
- **Using Visual Images**—finding, integrating, and documenting visual images into a research paper.

For many students the Internet is their primary research tool, and too often there is only cursory evaluation of the source of the accessed material. We have given specific examples of reliable Web sites and explained why these sites can be regarded as reliable. We have also provided a checklist for judging the reliability of both Print and Web resources. Some instructors report they like to spend a class session in the school's computer lab exploring both reliable and unreliable sites. They identify topics pertaining to a story or poem from the syllabus, and they search out a number of sites for students to consider in advance of the class session. This hands-on exercise can help students learn to differentiate between reliable sites and questionable sites as they do their own research.

When developing your research paper assignment, determine the number and type of Internet sources that you will allow students to use. Students should understand they need to use both printed resources as well as electronic. Obviously, search engines such as *Google* have transformed the landscape of research and the Internet should never be banned out of hand as a place to find research material, but much valuable scholarship is still not available online. To reduce the chance of plagiarism (unintended or blatant) from the World Wide Web, and to ensure that Internet referenced material is from a reliable source, you might require students to turn in a printed copy of the Internet source material with their final papers.

If you want to encourage students to begin their research in their own college library, you might consider having the Reference Librarian conduct a class session devoted to doing literary research. Many students do not know how to use all the resources available in their college library. An introduction tailored to their needs for your specific assignment may help make them efficient academic researchers.

Documenting sources, especially Internet sources, is challenging for most students and many professors as well. We have provided detailed information for citing print and Internet sources, a sample Works Cited list, and a comprehensive guide to the types of citations that students will likely use in their papers. Encourage students to allow sufficient time to prepare their Works Cited page and review their papers for scrupulous documentation.

Because students are human and we humans procrastinate, it is advisable to break the task of generating a research essay into dated steps. Establish a calendar of due dates when you issue your assignment: topic with working thesis statement; working list of reference material; outline; first draft; revised draft; peer review session; final draft. Our goal should be to have students engage in the real writing process—that process by which writing, thinking, rewriting, and rethinking, leads to real re-vision. We want our students to realize the depths of meaning present in the literature that they read and the depths of their own responses and ideas through continued exploration.

26
Critical Approaches to Literature

Purpose of Critical Approaches

This chapter is designed to introduce students to the variety of possible approaches they can take in analyzing literature. Theory and criticism have become such important aspects of undergraduate literary study that many instructors have asked for an informed beginner's guide to the subject. Our objective has been to cover the area intelligently without overwhelming or confusing the beginning student.

This section presents overviews of ten critical approaches. While these ten methods do not exhaust the total possibilities of literary criticism, they represent the most influential and widely used contemporary approaches. Each approach is introduced with an overview designed to explain to beginning students the central ideas of the critical method. The general note does not try to explain every aspect of a critical school or summarize its history; instead, it focuses on explaining the fundamental insights that motivate each approach. While many contemporary critics combine methodologies, it seemed wisest to keep the categories as simple and separate as possible, since students may be wrestling with these ideas for the first time.

Critical Selections

After the introductory note each critical school is illustrated by two critical excerpts. The first excerpt is usually a theoretical statement explaining the general principles of the approach. In each case, we have selected a passage from one of the methodology's leading practitioners that summarizes its central ideas in an accessible way. There is, for example, Cleanth Brooks listing the principles of Formalist Criticism, Elaine Showalter outlining the issues of Feminist Poetics, Northrop Frye explaining the concept of Mythic Archetypes, and Stanley Fish presenting the parameters of the Reader-Response method. These selections reinforce and broaden the ideas found earlier in the introductory notes. They also familiarize the student with a major figure in each school.

This general statement is then followed by a critical excerpt that discusses actual works in the book. These critical analyses have been selected with great care to provide illuminating but accessible examples of each school. These excerpts are not only well argued and informed analyses, but they are also clearly written with a minimum of theoretical jargon. Footnotes have also been added to explain any references that might be unfamiliar to students.

It was not always possible to find critical excerpts that could do the double duty of illustrating a school of thought while analyzing a text at hand. Sometimes, as in Harold Bloom's discussing of poetic influence or Roland Barthes's announcement of "the death of the author," we chose the clearest exposition available of an influential critical concept. (We also felt that students would profit by seeing where these influential ideas originated.) Some of these critical texts are challenging because the ideas are subtle and complex, but—once again—we have always tried to find the most accessible excerpt possible.

Poems Discussed

Critical methods are always easier to understand when they discuss a poem you know. Consequently, we have tried to find noteworthy excerpts that illustrate a particular critical approach and *that also focus on a literary text found in the book.* This feature allows the instructor the possibility of assigning many of these critical texts as ancillary readings.

Robert Langbaum's formalist analysis of **"My Last Duchess"** makes a good supplementary assignment to reading Browning's poem. Brett Millier's biographical comment on Elizabeth Bishop's **"One Art"** might broaden a discussion of the villanelle into other issues. Hugh Kenner recreates the heady atmosphere of Modernist London in a way that places Ezra Pound's **"In a Station of the Metro"** in a historical context. Joseph Moldenhauer provides students with an informed but accessible historical account of how Andrew Marvell used elements of the Renaissance tradition in **"To His Coy Mistress,"** while Geoffrey Hartman deconstructs Wordsworth's **"A Slumber Did My Spirit Seal."** Alfred Kazin explains that Walt Whitman was the only writer to describe Lincoln "with love" during his lifetime in a piece which provides invaluable sociological background for reading **"O Captain! My Captain!"** Camille Paglia uses the perspectives of Cultural Studies to provide a reading of William Blake's **"The Chimney Sweeper."**

Using the Chapter

Some instructors may want to use "Critical Approaches to Literature" as a formal part of the course, but more, we suspect, will prefer to use it in a less systematic way as a resource that can be tailored to whatever occasion seems suitable. An excellent way to introduce students to the section is to assign a short paper analyzing a single poem according to the critical approach of their choice. This method allows them to explore the introductory material for each critical school and then learn one approach in depth by trying it on a specific text.

Many poems in the book lend themselves to this assignment. Some likely choices (from the first few chapters) would include: D. H. Lawrence's "Piano," Robert Browning's "My Last Duchess," Theodore Roethke's "My Papa's Waltz," Anne Bradstreet's "The Author to Her Book," Anne Sexton's "Her Kind," Wilfred Owen's "Dulce et Decorum Est," Langston Hughes's "Theme for English B," and Alfred Tennyson's "Tears, Idle Tears." All of these poems invite multiple readings from a variety of perspectives.

Other Resources

If any of your brighter students should start writing papers following any of these critical approaches, and you should wish to provide them with models longer than the brief illustrative samples we supply, a new series of paperbacks may be helpful to them. It will be still more helpful if they are familiar with a classic such as *Frankenstein*, *The Scarlet Letter*, *Wuthering Heights*, *Heart of Darkness*, *Hamlet*, *Portrait of the Artist as a Young Man*, *Gulliver's Travels*, *The Awakening*, or *The House of Mirth*. Titles dealing with each of these classics and others have appeared, or will appear shortly, in the series "Case Studies in Contemporary Criticism," whose general editor is Ross C. Murfin of the University of Miami (Bedford Books and St. Martin's Press). Each book contains five essays on its novel, illustrating five different approaches: psychoanalytic criticism, reader-response criticism, feminist criticism, deconstruction, and the new historicism. There are also readable essays that explain each critical school, and bibliographies of critical books representing each of them.

Appendix 1
Teaching Creative Writing

WRITING A POEM *(Some notes by XJK)*

These notes are provided mainly for the instructor who employs this anthology in a creative writing course. Some may be of interest, however, to anyone who in teaching composition includes a unit on writing poems. Such an instructor will probably have firm persuasions about poetry and about the teaching of poets. Instead of trying to trumpet any persuasions of my own, let me just set down some hunches that, from teaching poetry workshops, I have come to feel are mostly true.

In reading a student's poem, you have to look at it with your mind a blank, reserving judgment for as long as possible. Try to see what the student is doing, being slow to compare a fledgling effort to the classics. There's no use in merely reading the poem and spotting any influences you find in it—"Ha, I see you've been reading Williams!" You can, however, praise any virtues you discover and you can tell the student firmly, kindly, and honestly any adverse reactions you feel. Point to anything in the poem that causes you to respond toward it, or against it. Instead of coldly damning the poem's faults, you can inquire why the writer said something in such-and-such a way, rather than in some other. You can ask to have anything you don't understand explained. If a line or a passage doesn't tell you anything, you can ask the student to suggest a fresh way of wording it. Perhaps the most valuable service you can perform for a student poet is to be hard to please. Suggest that the student not settle for the first words that flash to mind, but reach deeper, go after the word or phrase or line that will be not merely adequate, but memorable.

The greatest method of teaching poetry writing I have ever heard of was that of the late John Holmes. Former students at Tufts remember that Holmes seldom made comments on a poem, but often would just lay a finger next to a suspect passage and fix the student with a look of expectancy until the silence became unendurable, and the student began explaining what the passage meant and how it could be put better. (I have never made the Holmes method succeed for me. I can't keep from talking too much.)

Most workshop courses in poetry fall into a classic ritual. Students make copies of their poems, bring them in, and show them around to the class. This method of procedure is hard to improve upon. Some instructors find that the effort of screening the work themselves first and deciding what to spend time on in class makes for more cogent class sessions, with less time squandered on boring or inferior material. In general, class sessions won't be any more lively and valuable than the poems that are on hand. (An exception was a workshop I once visited years ago at MIT. The poems were literal, boring stuff, but the quality of the students' impromptu critical analyses was sensational.) Often a great class discussion will revolve around a fine poem with deep faults in it.

The severest challenge for the instructor, incidentally, isn't a *bad* poem. A bad poem is easy to deal with; it always gives you plenty of work to do—passages to delete, purple adjectives to question. The challenge comes in dealing with a truly surprising, original, and competent poem. This is risky and sensitive work because genuine poets usually know what they are doing to a greater degree than you or any other outsider does; and you don't want to confuse them with reactions you don't trust. For such rare students, all a poetry workshop probably does is supply an audience, a little encouragement, and sometimes even an insight.

There are natural temptations, of course, to which teachers of poets fall prey. Like coin collectors, they keep wanting to overvalue the talents they have on hand, to convince themselves that a student is a Gem Mint State poet, when a less personal opinion might find the student just an average specimen, although uncirculated. It's better to be too slow than too quick to encourage a student to seek nationwide publication. It is another temptation, if you have a class with a competent poet in it, to devote most of each session to that poet's latest works, causing grumblings of discontent (sometimes) among the other paying customers. I believe that a more competent poet deserves more time, but you have to conduct a class and not a tutorial.

Poetry workshops can become hideously intimate. They are bound to produce confessional or diary poems that, sometimes behind the thinnest of fictive screens, confide in painful detail the writer's sexual, psychic, and religious hang-ups. I have known poetry workshops where, by semester's end, the participants feel toward one another like the members of a hostile therapy group. That is why I believe in stressing that a poem is not merely the poet's self-revelation. It usually helps to insist at the start of the course that poems aren't necessarily to be taken personally. (See "Poetry and Personal Identity," if you want any ammunition.) Everybody will know, of course, that some poets in the class aren't capable of detached art and that a poem about a seduction may well be blatant autobiography; but believe me, you and your students will be happier if you can blow the trumpet in favor of the Imagination. There is no use in circulating poems in class anonymously, pretending that nobody knows who wrote them. Somebody will know and I think that the sooner the members of the class freely admit their identities, the more easy and relaxed and open the situation will be. To know each one personally, as soon as you can, is essential.

As the workshop goes on, I don't always stick to a faithful conference schedule. Some will need (and wish for) more of your time than others, but I like to schedule at least one conference right away, at the beginning of the course. This is a chance to meet with students in private and get a sense of their needs. I tell them to bring in a few poems they've already written, if they've written any. But I make it clear that class sessions will deal only with brand-new poems. At the end of the course, I program another such conference (instead of a final exam), sit down with each student, and ask, "Well, where are you now?"

Some students will lean on you for guidance ("What shall I write about?"); others will spurn all your brilliant suggestions and want to roar away in their own directions. Fine. I believe in offering the widest possible latitude in making assignments—but in having some assignments. Even the most inner-directed poet can learn something from being expected to move in a new direction. Having a few assignments will discourage the customers who think they can get through any number of creative writing courses by using the same old yellowed sheaf of poems. Encourage revision. Now and then, suggest a revision as an assignment instead of a new poem.

In "Writing a Poem" I offer a radical suggestion: that the students memorize excellent poems. Feeling like a curmudgeon for making this recommendation, I was happy to find some support for it in the view of Robert Bly, who remarked in *Coda* (June/July 1981):

> I won't even read a single manuscript now, when I visit a university workshop, unless the poet in advance agrees to memorize fifty lines of Yeats. At the first workshop I visited last fall it cut the number of graduate-student writers who wanted to see me from 15 to 2. Next year I'm changing that to fifty lines of *Beowulf*.

Bly may seem unreasonably stern, but he and I agree on the value of memorization. I believe it helps coax the writing of poetry down out of the forebrain, helps it unite with the pulse.

Bly has sane things to say, in this same article, about the folly of thirsting for publication too early. And incidentally, here's one of his unorthodox exercises for a writing workshop (imparted in an interview in the *Boston Globe Magazine* for April 10, 1988):

> One workshop, I brought in an onion for each of the students. I asked everybody to spend 10 to 15 minutes describing the exterior of the onion, using all of their senses. That requires every bit of observation you have, to remain looking at the onion. Then, in the second part of the exercise, I said, "Now I want you to compare the onion to your mother."

That must have rocked 'em! I wonder if it produced any good results.

For a textbook wholly devoted to the writing of poetry, quite the best thing of its kind, see Robert Wallace's *Writing Poems*, Third Edition (New York: HarperCollins, 1991).

Another book crammed with teaching hints and lively writing exercises for student poets is *The Teachers & Writers Handbook of Poetic Forms*, edited by Ron Padgett (1987) and sold by Teachers & Writers Collaborative, 5 Union Square West, New York, NY 10003. Besides supplying unstuffy definitions and examples of many expected forms, the handbook deals with blues poems, collaborations, ghazals, insult poems, light verse, pantoums, performance poems, raps, renga, and more.

Creative Writing Resources in *An Introduction to Poetry*

Although knowing something about any element of poetry may benefit a poet-in-training, here is a list, chapter by chapter, of material in *An Introduction to Poetry* that may be particularly useful in a creative writing class.

Chapter 2, THE PERSON IN THE POEM, page 24

Novice poets often think of their poems as faithful diary accounts of actual experiences. This section may be useful to suggest to them that, in the process of becoming art, the raw material of a poem may be expected to undergo change.

Chapter 5, ABOUT HAIKU, page 94

Assignment: Write some haiku, either original or in imitation of classic Japanese haiku.

Chapter 5, EXPERIMENT: *Writing with Images*, page 98

A poetry writing assignment with possible examples.

Chapter 6, *Howard Moss*, SHALL I COMPARE THEE TO A SUMMER'S DAY?, page 112

Assignment: Choosing a different famous poem, write a Mosslike version of it. Then try to indicate what, in making your takeoff, was most painful to leave out.

Chapter 6, *Jane Kenyon*, THE SUITOR, page 125

Assignment: Write a poem similarly constructed of similes, or metaphors.

Chapter 7, *Paul Simon*, RICHARD CORY, page 136

Assignment: In somewhat the fashion of Simon's treatment of Robinson, take a well-known poem and rewrite it as a song lyric. Try singing the result to a tune.

Chapter 8, EXERCISE: *Listening* to *Meaning*, page 155

Assignment: After reading these examples, write a brief poem of your own, heavy with sound effects.

Chapter 8, READING AND HEARING POEMS ALOUD, page 167

Assignment: Ponder this section before reading your own poems aloud in class.

Chapter 9, METER, page 180

Assignment: After working through this section on your own, write a poem in meter.

Chapter 10, CLOSED FORM, page 194

This chapter may be of particular value to a poetry writing class. Not only does it analyze some traditional forms, it also suggests a rationale for formally open verse.

Assignment: After considering the definition of *syllabic verse* given in this chapter, carefully read Dylan Thomas's "Fern Hill." Work out the form of the Thomas poem with pencil and paper, then try writing a syllabic poem of your own.

Chapter 11, OPEN FORM, page 217

This chapter is important for students to read and consider because it tries to suggest why competent verse is seldom entirely "free." It also helps students who are enamored with traditional, formal notions of poetry to open themselves up to new possibilities.

Assignment: Ponder, not too seriously, Wallace Stevens's "Thirteen Ways of Looking at a Blackbird." Then, as the spirit moves you, write a unified series of small poems. Or, on a more modest scale, write a fourteenth way of looking at these poetic fowls.

Chapter 13, MYTH AND NARRATIVE, page 253

Assignment: Read the final section of the chapter, "Myth and Popular Culture." Retell a popular story (from the Bible, folklore, or the movies) in the form of a poem, but give the story some new twist that allows the reader to see the familiar tale in a novel way.

Chapter 15, TRANSLATION, page 297

Assignment: Consider the translations in this section and decide what you admire or dislike in each of them. Translate a poem of your choice, from any language with which you are familiar or can follow in a bilingual edition.

Chapter 15, PARODY, page 304

Assignment: Read these parodists, comparing their work with the originals. Then, choosing some poet whose work you know thoroughly, write a parody yourself.

Appendix 2
Notes on Teaching Poetry
by XJK

These notes are offered in response to the wishes of several instructors for additional practical suggestions for teaching poetry. They are, however, mere descriptions of a few strategies that have proved useful in my own teaching. For others, I can neither prescribe nor proscribe.

1. To a greater extent than in teaching prose, the instructor may find it necessary to have poems read aloud. It is best if students do this reading. Since to read a poem aloud effectively requires that the reader understand what is said in it, students will need advance warning so that they can prepare their spoken interpretations. Sometimes I assign particular poems to certain people, or ask each person to take his or her choice. Some advice on how to read poetry aloud is given in the chapter "Sound." I usually suggest only that students beware of waxing overemotional or rhetorical, and I urge them to read aloud outside of class as often as possible. If the student or the instructor has access to a tape recorder, it may be especially helpful.

2. It is good to recall occasionally that poems may be put back together as well as taken apart. Sometimes I call on a student to read a previously prepared poem, just before opening a discussion of the poem. Then, the discussion over and the poem lying all around in intelligible shreds, I ask the same student to read it over again. It is often startling how the reading improves from the student's realizing more clearly what the poet is saying.

3. I believe in asking students to do a certain amount of memorization. Many groan that such rote learning is mindless and grade-schoolish, but it seems to me one way to defeat the intellectualizations that students (and the rest of us) tend to make of poetry. It is also a way to suggest that we do not read a poem primarily for its ideas: to learn a poem by heart is one way to engrave oneself with the sound and weight of it. I ask for twenty or thirty lines at a time, of the student's choice, then have them write the lines out in class. Some students have reported unexpected illuminations. Some people, of course, can't memorize a poem to save their souls, and I try to encourage but not to pressure them. These written memorizations take very little of the instructor's time to check and need not be returned to the students unless there are flagrant lacunae in them.

4. The instructor has to sense when a discussion has gone on long enough. It is a matter of watching each student's face for the first sign of that fixed set of the mouth. Elizabeth Bishop once wisely declared that, while she was not opposed to all close analysis and criticism, she was against "making poetry monstrous and boring and proceeding to talk the very life out of it." I used to be afraid of classroom silences. Now, I find it helps sometimes to stop a discussion that is getting lost, and say, "Let's all take three minutes and read this poem again and think about it silently." When the discussion resumes, it is usually improved.

Some of the finest, most provocative essays on teaching poetry in college I have seen are these:

Alice Bloom, "On the Experience of Unteaching Poetry," *Hudson Review* (Spring 1979): 7–30. Bloom: "I am interested in the conditions of education that would lead a student to remark, early in a term, as one of mine did, that 'I wish we didn't know these were poems. Then it seems like it would be a lot easier.'"

Clara Clairborne Park, "Rejoicing to Concur with the Common Reader" in her volume *Rejoining the Common Reader: Essays, 1962–1990* (Evanston: Northwestern, 1991). Park is now a professor at Williams College, but for many years she taught in a community college. This essay recounts the joys and disappointments of working with students who were just discovering literature. Park is most concerned by how to relate literature to the lives of her students without condescending to them. She praises a kind of simplicity in approaching literature that "need not mean narrowness." Discussing the teacher's realization that he or she participates "in a process that changes lives," Park writes an essay that proves both moving and enlightening.

Appendix 3
Integrating Poetry and Composition

How do you teach students to read poetry and, at the same time, to write good prose? Instructors who face this task may find some useful advice in the following article, first published in The English Record, bulletin of the New York State English Council. It is reprinted here by the kind permission of the author, Irwin Weiser, director of developmental writing, Purdue University.

THE PROSE PARAPHRASE
INTEGRATING POETRY AND COMPOSITION

Irwin Weiser

Many of us teach composition courses which demand that we not only instruct our students in writing but that we also present literature to them as well. Such courses often frustrate us, since a quarter or a semester seems too brief to allow us to teach fundamentals of composition alone. How are we to integrate the teaching of literature with the teaching of writing? What are we to do with a fat anthology of essays, fiction, poetry, or drama and a rhetoric text and, in some cases, a separate handbook of grammar and usage?

Recently, I tried an approach which seemed to provide more integration of reading and writing than I previously had felt I attained in similar courses. The course was the third quarter of a required freshman composition sequence; the departmental course description specifies the teaching of poetry and drama, but also states "English 103 is, however, primarily a composition, not a literature, course. Major emphasis of the course should be on writing." The approach I will describe concerns the study of poetry.

Because this is a writing course, I explained to my students that we would approach poetry primarily as a study of the way writers can use language, and thus our work on denotation and connotation, tone, irony, image, and symbol should help them learn to make conscious language choices when they write. Chapters in Kennedy/Gioia's *An Introduction to Poetry* entitled "Words," "Saying and Suggesting," and "Listening to a Voice" fit nicely with this approach. Further, because this is a writing course, I wanted my students to have frequent opportunities to write without burying myself under an even greater number of formal, longish papers than I already required. An appropriate solution seemed to be to have my students write prose paraphrases of one or two poems from those assigned for each discussion class.

During the first week of the course, we discussed and practiced the paraphrase technique, looking first at Kennedy's explanation of paraphrasing and then at his paraphrase of Housman's "Loveliest of trees, the cherry now." By reading my own paraphrase, not among the ablest in the class, I was able to place myself in the position of coinquirer into these poems, most of which I had not previously taught. This helped establish a classroom atmosphere similar to that of a creative writing workshop, one conducive to the discussion of both the poetry in the text and the writing of the students. In fact, while the primary purpose of assigning the paraphrases was to give my students extra writing practice, an important additional result was that throughout the quarter their paraphrases, not the teacher's opinions and interpretations, formed the basis for class discussion. There was rarely a need for the teacher to *explain* a poem or a passage: someone, and frequently several people, had an interpretation which satisfied most questions and resolved most difficulties.

At the end of this essay are examples of the prose paraphrases students wrote of Emily Dickinson's "I heard a Fly buzz—when I died." Two of the paraphrases, at 90 and 112 words, are approximately as long as Dickinson's 92-word poem; the 160-word third paraphrase is over 75% longer because this student interpreted as she paraphrased, explaining, for example, that the narrator willed her earthly possessions in a futile attempt to hasten death. Such interpretation, while welcome, is not at all necessary, as the two shorter, yet also successful, paraphrases indicate. In fact I had to remind students that paraphrases are not the same as analyses, and that while they might have to interpret a symbol—as these students variously explained what the fly or the King meant—or unweave a metaphor, their major task was to rewrite the poem as clear prose.

The first paraphrase is perhaps the most straightforward of this group. The author's voice is nearly inaudible. He has stripped the poem of its literary qualities—no "Heaves of Storm," only "the air before a storm"; no personification; the author is only present in the choice of the word "sad" to describe the final buzz of the fly. His paraphrase is a prose rendering of the poem with no obvious attempt to interpret it.

Paraphrase II seems to ignore the symbolic importance of the fly, and perhaps in the very casualness of the phrase "and the last thing I was aware of was this fly and its buzz" suggests the same insignificance of death from the perspective of the hereafter that Dickinson does. More interesting is this student's treatment of the willing of the keepsakes: the formal diction of "proper recipients," "standard fashion," and "officially ready to die" suggests death as a ritual. Unexpected interpretations like this appear frequently in the paraphrases, demonstrating the flexibility and richness of language, emphasizing the error in assuming that there is one right way to interpret a poem, and sometimes, when the interpretations are less plausible, leading to discussions of what constitutes valid interpretation and how one finds support for interpretations of what one reads.

The third paraphrase, as I suggested before, offers more interpretation as well as a stronger authorial voice than the previous two. The author adds a simile of her own, "as if the winds had ceased temporarily to catch their breaths," and more obviously than the other students uses the fly as a metaphor for death in her final sentence.

I will not take the space for a thorough analysis of these paraphrases, but I think that they suggest what a teacher might expect from this kind of assignment. Clearly, these three students have read this poem carefully and understand what it says, the first step towards understanding what it means. Small group and classroom discussions would allow us to consider these paraphrases individually and comparatively, to point out their merits and weaknesses, and then to return to the original verse with new perspectives.

Most heartening were the comments of several students during the quarter who told me that they felt more confident about reading poetry than they previously had. Though I doubt that my students are any more ardently devoted to poetry now than they were before the course began, they are not intimidated by verse on the page. They have an approach, a simple heuristic, for dealing with any unfamiliar writing. Ideally, my students will remember and use their ability to paraphrase and their ability to use their paraphrases to understand and evaluate what they read when they come upon a particularly difficult passage in their chemistry or history texts during the next three years or in the quarterly reports or technical manuals or journals they will read when they leave the university and begin their careers.

Appendix: Sample Paraphrases

Paraphrase I

I heard death coming on. The stillness in the room was like the stillness in the air before a storm. The people around me had wiped their eyes dry, and they held their breaths waiting for that moment when death could be witnessed in the room. I wrote a will which gave away my possessions—that being the only part of me I could give away. A fly then flew between the light and me making a sad, uncertain buzz. My eyesight faded and I could not see to see.

Paraphrase II

I heard a fly buzz as I was about to die. The sound of the fly broke the quietness in the room which was like the calm before a storm. The people sitting around waiting for me to die cried until they could not cry anymore. They began to breathe uneasily in anticipation of my death when God would come down to the room to take me away. I had willed all of my valuables to the proper recipients in the standard fashion. I was officially ready to die, going through the final dramatic moments of my life, and the last thing I was aware of was this fly and its buzz.

Paraphrase III

I could feel the approach of death just as I could hear the buzz of an approaching fly. I knew death was buzzing around, but I did not know when and where it would land. The stillness of death was like the calmness that exists between storms, as if the winds had ceased temporarily to catch their breaths.

I was aware of the sorrow in the room. There were those who had cried because death was near, and they waited for death to stalk into the room like a king and claim its subject.

I willed all of my earthly possessions, all that could legally be assigned to a new owner, in an attempt to hasten death. But there was no way to control death; I was at the mercy of its timing. And then like the fly that finally lands on its choice place, death fell upon me, and shut my eyes, and I could no longer see.

* * *

Mr. Weiser reported in a letter that, once again, he had used the method of poetry paraphrase in his writing course, and remained pleased with it. "My students," he remarked, "no longer treat poems as holy scripts written in some mystical code, but attack them fearlessly." The course had proved fun both for them and for him, and he felt he was paying his dues to both writing and literature.

Index of Authors with Titles